Twentieth-
Century
Literary
Movements
INDEX

Twentieth-Century Literary Movements INDEX

A Guide to 500 Literary Movements, Groups, Schools, Tendencies, and Trends of the Twentieth Century, Covering More than 3,000 Novelists, Poets, Dramatists, Essayists, Artists, and Other Seminal Thinkers from 80 Countries as Found in Standard Literary Reference Works

Laurie Lanzen Harris
Editor

Helene Henderson
Associate Editor

Omnigraphics, Inc.

Penobscot Building • Detroit, Michigan 48226

LITERARY MOVEMENTS REFERENCE SERIES

Essays
Indexes
Documents

Laurie Lanzen Harris, Editor
Helene Henderson, Associate Editor

Library of Congress Cataloging-in-Publication Data

Twentieth-century literary movements index : a guide to 500 literary movements, groups, schools, tendencies, and trends of the twentieth century, covering more than 3,000 novelists, poets, dramatists, essayists, artists, and other seminal thinkers from 80 countries as found in standard literary reference works / Laurie Lanzen Harris, editor, Helene Henderson, associate editor.
    p.   cm. — (Literary movements reference series)
Includes bibliographical references.
ISBN 1-55888-306-1 (lib. bdg. : acid-free paper)
    1. Literary movements—Indexes. 2. Literature, Modern—20th century—Indexes. 3. Literature, Modern—20th century—Societies, etc.—Indexes. I. Harris, Laurie Lanzen. II. Henderson, Helene, 1963-   . III. Title: 20th-century literary movements index. IV. Series.
Z6514.L57T9 1991
[PN597]
016.809'91'0904—dc20
                                        90-20189
                                            CIP

Omnigraphics, Inc.

* * *

Laurie Lanzen Harris, *Editorial Director*
Frank R. Abate, *Vice President – Dictionaries*
Annie M. Brewer, *Vice President – Research*
Peter E. Ruffner, *Vice President – Administration*
James A. Sellgren, *Vice President – Operations & Finance*
Eric F. Berger, *Production Manager*

* * *

Frederick G. Ruffner, Jr., *Publisher*

Copyright © 1991
Omnigraphics, Inc.

ISBN 1-55888-306-1

Printed in the United States of America

CONTENTS

PREFACE

The twentieth century has been a time of extraordinary growth and change in literature and the arts. No other era in literary history has witnessed such a proliferation of literary movements whose adherents, in an effort to define themselves, their art, and their relationship to their age, created a myriad of literary associations.

The Objective of the Work

Twentieth-Century Literary Movements Index provides a guide to the student in search of information on over 500 major and minor literary movements, trends, and ideologies in twentieth-century world literature; over 3,000 writers from over seventy-five nations associated with those literary schools; and the key era and area of each movement's influence. Both movements and individuals are indexed, with references leading the reader to more than twenty-five of the best-known and respected literary dictionaries, encyclopedias, and handbooks. *Twentieth-Century Literary Movements Index* is part of the Literary Movements Reference Series published by Omnigraphics, Inc. So that students and librarians can appreciate the scope of this series, a description appears below.

In compiling the volume, the editors reviewed the twenty-eight sources indexed here, and all major and minor literary movements of the twentieth century were included. The sources often offer contradictory information in defining a literary movement, some referring to a particular group as a "school," while others label it a "tendency" or a "type." We have therefore scrutinized all movements, groups, schools, tendencies, "isms," etc., listed by the sources. When, after research, the editors discovered that certain possible entries, such as "postmodernism" or "regionalism," had never been clearly defined or delineated in the literary reference books indexed here, we decided not to include them.

Those movements that are clearly and solely of the nineteenth century will be treated in a later volume in the series. However, we have chosen to include such major nineteenth-century movements as Symbolism, Naturalism, and Realism, which, although they began in nineteenth-century Europe, exerted a great influence on twentieth-century letters and gave rise to similar movements throughout the world in the early decades of our century. For example, American Realism and Naturalism continued well into the twentieth century, whereas their European counterparts had run their course by 1900. The original movements have also been included to allow the student to understand the scope and precepts of the original school, which is so important to understanding its dissemination to other lands.

Literary criticism, which has had an extraordinary effect on literature in the twentieth century, is also represented in the inclusion of the most significant schools, i.e., New Criticism, Structuralism, and Feminist Criticism. A number of individuals whose disciplines fall outside of the study of literature but whose influence on twentieth-century literature has been enormous, notably Freud, Marx, and Jung, have also been included in the Index. However, with the exception of Marx, including the schools of criticism associated with these individuals—Freudian and Myth or Archetypal Criticism—proved more difficult. The theories of these seminal thinkers have been so widely accepted and applied to the study of literature that it is difficult to find any consensus among the sources as to who is a member of the group and who has been simply influenced by it.

Major theater groups of the twentieth century associated with a particular school or movement, such as the Freie Bühne and the Théatre Libre, both associated with furthering the aims and influence of such Naturalists as Gerhart Hauptmann and Emile Zola are included, as is the Abbey Theater, which produced the works of such noted members of the Irish Literary Renaissance as William Butler Yeats and Sean O'Casey.

It has been our intent to list under the movement headings those individuals involved with the movement itself, not those who were precursors of it. Thus, such individuals as Alfred Jarry, whose dramatic theories influenced both Surrealism and the Theater of the Absurd, but whose works predate those movements by several decades, are not included.

The listing of an author or artist under a movement does not indicate a life-long adherence to that group's precepts or methodology. Some writers were part of a movement for a brief period in their creative lives, and later repudiated their affiliation. Their listing here reflects their appearance under a particular heading in the reference works indexed for this volume.

The Plan of the Work

The Index is divided into two sections: Part I is an index to movements and Part II is an index to authors. Part I provides an alphabetical listing of the movements, and for each movement heading, a list of the reference sources in which the movement appears, followed by the authors, artists, philosophers, and critics affiliated with it. The reference sources are given in an abbreviated code form (explained below), followed by the date of publication.

As an additional aid to the user, the entry includes the national origin and dates of greatest influence for each movement. The dates for movements are often given as decades; if the sources acknowledged specific dates, particularly for short-lived movements, those are given. For groups associated with a particular periodical, the inclusive dates of publication are given, if offered in the sources consulted. For the ease of the user, we have divided the largest movements into national sections. If the reference sources give an English translation of a foreign language movement or group, we have listed the movement under the English form followed by the original language. Individual names are followed by birth and death dates. In the cases where no dates were offered in the sources, the name is followed by the designation "n.d."

Part II provides an alphabetically arranged index to individuals. Each author heading gives the name, birth and death dates, and nationality of the individual, followed by a listing of the sources in which he or she appears (with publication dates) and the movement(s) with which each is associated. Since variations in the form of the name occur among the sources, the form of the name used here is derived from that used in the majority of the works consulted. Determining the nationality for each author sometimes proved difficult, so, relying on the sources, we have endeavored to denote the national origin and any variances in citizenship or language in the author heading.

Audience

The Literary Movements Reference Series is directed to students in late high school and early college who are examining literature from the perspective of the literary movements which chart the development of the literary history of the modern era. Thus the student beginning preliminary research on a literary topic such as the Beat Generation can use the *Twentieth-Century Literary Movements Index* in one of two ways: through the author index, he or she could obtain references for further research on Allen Ginsberg, Lawrence Ferlinghetti, Gregory Corso or other Beat poets, or, in using the Movement portion of the Index, could find a list of references and also see at a glance the major and minor figures associated with the movement, the era of its greatest influence, and its country of origin.

The reader should note that each source handles movements and authors differently: some contain separate entries for movements and for individuals, while others include information on movements within essays on national literatures. Please be aware that you might need to scan the sections on national literatures to find commentary on a particular movement.

Acknowledgments

The editors wish to thank our Advisory Board, including Arthur Woodford, Michael Deller, Holde Borchert, James Ruffner, Brenda Burrell Evans, Robert Reimer, and Donald Worrell, who evaluated the Literary Movements Reference Series in its early stages. We hope their comments and suggestions have helped us to provide a comprehensive and useful guide to the user. We also wish to acknowledge the contribution of the Grosse Pointe Public Libraries for their generosity in making their resources available to us.

Suggestions

The editors welcome the commentary and recommendations of readers to enhance the value of the series.

Laurie Lanzen Harris

TITLE CODES FOR SOURCES

BenReEncy-1987   *Benet's Reader's Encyclopedia.* 3rd Edition. New York: Harper & Row, 1987.

CamGLE-1988   *Cambridge Guide to Literature in English.* Edited by Ian Ousby. Cambridge: Cambridge University Press, 1988.

CaribWr-1979   *Caribbean Writers: A Bio-Bibliographical-Critical Encyclopedia.* Edited by Donald E. Herdeck. Washington, D.C.: Three Continents Press, 1979.

CasWL-1973   *Cassell's Encyclopedia of World Literature.* Edited by J. Buchanan-Brown. London: Cassell, 1973.

CEnMWL-1963   *Concise Encyclopedia of Modern World Literature.* 2nd Edition. Edited by Geoffrey Grigson. New York: Hawthorne Books, 1963.

ClDMEuL-1980   *Columbia Dictionary of Modern European Literature.* 2nd Edition. Edited by Jean-Albert Bédé and William B. Edgerton. New York: Columbia University Press, 1980.

DCLT-1979   *Dictionary of Literary Terms.* Revised edition. By J.A. Cuddon. London: Andre Deutsch Ltd., 1979.

DOrLit-1974   *Dictionary of Oriental Literatures.* Edited by Jaroslav Prusek. New York: Basic Books, 1974.

EncWL-1981   *Encyclopedia of World Literature in the Twentieth Century.* 2nd. Edition. Edited by Leonard S. Klein. New York: Continuum, 1981.

GdMWL-1985   *Guide to Modern World Literature*. 3rd Edition. By Martin Seymour-Smith. London: Macmillan Press, 1985.

HandLit-1986   *Handbook to Literature*. 5th Edition. Edited by C. Hugh Holman and William Harmon. New York: Macmillan Publishing, 1986.

HarDMT-1988   *Harper Dictionary of Modern Thought*. Revised Edition. Edited by Alan Bullock and Stephen Trombley. New York: Harper & Row, 1988.

LongCTCL-1975   *Longman Companion to Twentieth-Century Literature*. 2nd Edition. By A.C. Ward. London: Longman, 1975.

McGWD-1984   *McGraw-Hill Encyclopedia of World Drama*. 2nd Edition. Edited by Stanley Hochman. New York: McGraw-Hill, 1984.

OxAm-1983   *Oxford Companion to American Literature*. 5th Edition. Edited by James D. Hart. Oxford: Oxford University Press, 1983.

OxAmThe-1984   *Oxford Companion to American Theatre*. Edited by Gerald Bordman. Oxford: Oxford University Press, 1984.

OxCan-1983   *Oxford Companion to Canadian Literature*. Edited by William Toye. Oxford: Oxford University Press, 1983.

OxEng-1985   *Oxford Companion to English Literature*. 5th Edition. Edited by Margaret Drabble. Oxford: Oxford University Press, 1985.

OxFr-1959   *Oxford Companion to French Literature*. Edited by Sir Paul Harvey and J.E. Heseltine. Oxford: Oxford University Press, 1959.

OxGer-1986   *Oxford Companion to German Literature*. 2nd Edition. Edited by Henry Garland and Mary Garland. Oxford: Oxford University Press, 1986.

OxSpan-1978   *Oxford Companion to Spanish Literature.* Edited by Philip Ward. Oxford: Oxford University Press, 1978.

OxThe-1983   *Oxford Companion to the Theatre.* 4th Edition. Edited by Phyllis Hartnoll. Oxford: Oxford University Press, 1983.

PengAm-1971   *Penguin Companion to American Literature.* Edited by Malcolm Bradbury, Eric Mottram, and Jean Franco. New York: McGraw-Hill, 1971.

PengCOAL-1969   *Penguin Companion to Classical, Oriental, and African Literature.* Edited by D.M. Lang and D.R. Dudley. New York: McGraw-Hill, 1969.

PengEng-1971   *Penguin Companion to English Literature.* Edited by David Daiches. New York: McGraw-Hill, 1971.

PengEur-1969   *Penguin Companion to European Literature.* Edited by Anthony Thorlby. New York: McGraw-Hill, 1971.

PrEncyPP-1974   *Princeton Encyclopedia of Poetry and Poetics.* Revised Edition. Edited by Alex Preminger. Princeton: Princeton University Press, 1974.

RCom-1973   *Reader's Companion to World Literature.* 2nd Edition. Edited by Lillian Herlands Hornstein, Leon Edel, and Horst Frenz. New York: New American Library, 1973.

THE LITERARY MOVEMENTS REFERENCE SERIES

The Literary Movements Reference Series is a set of publications designed to offer a comprehensive introduction to the study of literary movements of all eras and countries. The series is designed to provide a starting point for the student requiring introductory **essays** on the major and minor movements and periods of literature and literary history, **indexes** to biographical and critical information contained in literary reference works, and **documents** relating to literary movements. The series will cover the literary history of one era at a time and will begin with the literary movements of the twentieth century. Divided into three categories, the set offers a variety of reference tools:

LITERARY MOVEMENTS: ESSAYS. These volumes contain entries on the movements, schools, genres, techniques, and terms associated with a specific era of literature, as well as the novelists, poets, dramatists, short story writers, and essayists identified with those movements. In addition, entries on the most important and representative works of literature associated with the literary schools are included. International in scope, the Essays volumes will cover major and minor literary movements, trends, and ideologies that originated in over seventy-five nations.

The essay covering each movement will detail its philosophical and artistic tenets, the historical and cultural settings out of which it grew, the writers and works of literature with which it is associated, the key era and area of the movement's influence, the way in which it influenced later movements and works of literature, and the literary techniques associated with it. Each entry is followed by a bibliography of suggested further reading. Illustrations depicting authors, artists, and works provide an additional perspective for the student.

The first volume—*Twentieth-Century Literary Movements: Essays*—will be published in 1991.

LITERARY MOVEMENTS: INDEXES. This group of volumes indexes information found in the best-known and most respected literary dictionaries, encyclopedias, and handbooks. Divided by century, these guides provide a useful source for students needing information on literary movements and the individuals associated with them.

These volumes are divided into two sections: Part I, an index to movements, provides an alphabetical listing of the movements. The heading for each movement includes the national origin and dates of greatest influence for the movement, followed by an alphabetical listing of the reference sources in which it appears and the authors, artists, philosophers, and critics affiliated with it. Part II, an index to authors, is arranged alphabetically and gives birth and death dates and nationality for each author, followed by a listing of the sources in which he or she appears and the movements with which each is associated.

LITERARY MOVEMENTS: DOCUMENTS. This group of volumes is a collection of original materials, including manifestos, declarations of intent, statements of poetics, philosophical tracts, and other documents that outline the goals and methods of the various schools of literature appearing in the Essays and Indexes volumes, as well as annotated examples of poetry, prose, and art drawn from the anthologies, periodicals, and other publications of the movements. They are reprinted in the Documents volumes with commentary on their influence and importance as well as a full bibliographical citation noting original publication information. These documents have never before been gathered together in a similar arrangement, and most have only been available in the original language. This series will offer English translations of these important texts of literary history for research and review. Cross references to the entries on each movement in the Essays and Indexes volumes make this a helpful companion to students needing primary research materials for their studies.

The first volume—*Twentieth-Century Literary Movements: Documents*—will be available in 1992.

Frederick G. Ruffner, Jr.
Publisher

Index to Movements

**Abbaye Group/Groupe de l'Abbaye
(France, 1906-1908)**
BenReEncy-1987
EncWL-1981
GdMWL-1985
OxFr-1959

Arcos, René 1881-1948
Barzun, Henri-Martin 1881-(?)
Divoire, Fernand 1883-1951
Duhamel, Georges 1884-1966
Durtain, Luc 1881-1959
Gleizes, Albert 1881-1953
Jouve, Pierre-Jean 1887-1976
Rolland, Romain 1866-1944
Romains, Jules 1885-1972
Vildrac, Charles 1882-1971

**Abbey Theater (Ireland, 1904-
1930s)**
BenReEncy-1987
CamGLE-1988
CEnMWL-1963
EncWL-1981
GdMWL-1985
HandLit-1986
HarDMT-1988
McGWD-1984
LongCTCL-1975
OxAmThe-1984
OxEng-1985
OxThe-1983
RCom-1973

Æ (pseud. of George William
Russell) 1867-1935

Allgood, Sarah 1883-1950
Behan, Brendan 1923-1964
Blythe, Ernest 1889-1975
Boyle, William 1853-1923
Colum, Padriac 1881-1972
Dunsany, Edward John
Moreton Drax Plunkett 1878-
1957
Ervine, St. John Greer 1883-
1971
Fay, Frank J. 1870-1931
Fay, William 1872-1947
Gregory, Lady Isabella Augusta
1852-1932
Horniman, Annie E. 1860-1937
Hunt, Hugh 1911-
MacNamara, Brinsley 1890-1963
Martyn, Edward 1859-1923
Mooney, Ria 1903-1973
Murray, Thomas Cornelius
1873-1959
O'Casey, Sean 1880-1964
O'Connor, Frank 1903-1966
Robinson, Lennox 1886-1958
Shaw, George Bernard 1856-1950
Shiels, George 1881-1949
Sinclair, Arthur n.d.
Synge, John Millington 1871-
1909
Yeats, William Butler 1865-1939

See also **Irish Literary Theater, Irish
Renaissance**

Abstract Movement (Turkey, 1950s)
PrEncyPP-1974

1

Berk, Ilhan 1916-
Cansever, Edip 1928-
Ilhan, Attilâ 1925-
Süreya, Cemal 1931-
Uyar, Turgut 1926-

Acmeism (Russia, 1910-1917)
BenReEncy-1987
ClDMEuL-1980
DCLT-1979
EncWL-1981
GdMWL-1985
HarDMT-1988
OxEng-1985
PengEur-1969
PrEncyPP-1974

Adamovich, Georgy Viktorovich
    1894-1972
Akhmatova, Anna 1888-1966
Annensky, Innokenti
    Fedorovich 1856-1909
Bagritsky, Edvard 1895-1934
Gorodetsky, Sergei
    Mitrofanovich 1884-1967
Gumilyov, Nikolai Stepanovich
    1886-1921
Ivanov, Georgy Vladimirovich
    1894-1958
Kuzmin, Mikhail Alekseyevich
    1875-1935
Lozinsky, Mikhail 1886-1955
Mandels(h)tam, Osip 1891(?)-
    1938(?)

**Afro-Cubanism (Caribbean
Islands, 1926-1938)**
CaribWr-1979
EncWL-1981
OxSpan-1978
PengAm-1971

Ballagas, Emilio 1910-1954
Cabrera, Lydia 1900-
Carpentier, Alejo 1904-1980

Castro, José Antonio Fernández
    de 1897-1951
Guillén, Nicolás 1902-(?)
Guirao, Ramón 1908-1949
Marinello, Juan 1898-(?)
Ortiz, Fernando 1881-1969
Palés Matos, Luis 1899-1959
Pedroso, Reginio 1896-
Tallet, José Zacarías 1893-(?)
Valdés, Ildefonso Pereda 1899-
    (?)

**Agitprop Theater (United States,
1930s)**
McGWD-1984

Meyerhold, Vsevolod
    Emilyevich 1874-1940
Odets, Clifford 1906-1963

Agrarians

See **The Fugitives**

**Andalusian League (Lebanese exiles
in Brazil, 1930s)**
EncWL-1981

Farhat, Ilyas 1893-(?)
al-Ma'luf, Fawzi 1889-1930
al-Ma'luf, Shafiq 1905-

Angry Penguins (Australia, 1940s)
PrEncyPP-1974

McAuley, James P. 1917-1976
Stewart, Harold 1916-

**Angry Young Men (England, 1950s-
1960s)**
BenReEncy-1987
CamGLE-1988
DCLT-1979
EncWL-1981
HandLit-1986

HarDMT-1988
LongCTCL-1975
OxEng-1985
RCom-1973

Amis, Kingsley 1922-
Braine, John 1922-1986
Osborne, John 1929-
Paul, Leslie 1905-1985
Sillitoe, Alan 1928-
Wain, John 1925-
Wesker, Arnold 1932-
Wilson, Colin 1931-

**Antievasion Group/Anti-Evasao
(Cape Verde, 1960s)**
EncWL-1981

Mariano, Gabriel 1928-
Martins, Ovídio 1928-
Silveira, Onésimo 1937-

Antropofagia Group (Brazil, 1930s)
EncWL-1981
PrEncyPP-1974

Andrade, Oswald de 1890-1954
Bopp, Raul 1898-

**Apollo School of Poets (Egypt,
1930s)**
EncWL-1981

Abu Shadi, Admad Zaki 1892-
1955
Naji, Ibrahim 1893-1953
Taha, 'Ali Mahmud 1902-1949

Aprismo (Latin America, 1930s)
OxSpan-1978

Haya de la Torre, Victor Raúl
1895-1979

Arpas Cubanas Group (Cuba, 1900s)
CaribWr-1979

Borrero, Dulce María 1883-1945
Carbonell, José Manuel 1880-(?)
Díaz Silveira, Francisco 1871-
1924
Hernández Miyares, Enrique
1859-1915

**Ascent Group/Hsin-yüeh she
(China, 1920s)**
DOrLit-1974

Wen I-to 1889-1946

**Assembly of the Men of Good
Taste (Pakistan, 1940s)**
EncWL-1981

Miraji 1913-1950
Shah, Sayyid Nasir Ahmad n.d.

**Association of Angola's Native Sons
(Angola, 1950s)**
EncWL-1981

Cruz, Viriato da 1928-1973
Jacinto, António 1924-
Neto, António Agostinho 1922-
1979

**Atheneum of Youth (Mexico, 1910s-
1920s)**
EncWL-1981

Caso, Antonio 1883-1946
González Martínez, Enrique
1871-1952
Reyes, Alfonso 1889-1959
Vasconcelos, José 1882-1959

Authenticism (Poland, 1930s)
ClDMEuL-1980

Czernik, Stanislaw 1899-1969
Ozóg, Jan Boleslaw 1913-

B

Beat Generation (United States, 1950s-1960s)
BenReEncy-1987
CamGLE-1988
DCLT-1979
EncWL-1981
GdMWL-1985
HandLit-1986
HarDMT-1988
LongCTCL-1975
OxAm-1983
OxEng-1985
PengAm-1971
PrEncyPP-1974

Burroughs, William S. 1914-
Cassady, Neal 1926-1968
Corso, Gregory 1930-
Ferlinghetti, Lawrence 1919-
Ginsberg, Allen 1926-
Holmes, John Clellon 1926-
Kerouac, Jack 1922-1969
Lamantia, Philip 1927-
Loewinsohn, Ron 1937-
McClure, Michael 1932-
Meltzer, David 1937-
Miller, Henry 1891-1980
Rexroth, Kenneth 1905-1982
Rumaker, Michael 1932-
Snyder, Gary 1930-
Watts, Alan 1915-1973
Whalen, Philip 1923-

Bergson, Henri 1859-1941 (French)
BenReEncy-1987
CasWL-1973

OxEng-1985
OxFr-1959
PengEur-1969
RCom-1973

Berlin Ensemble/Berliner Ensemble (Germany, 1950s)
BenReEncy-1987
EncWL-1981
HarDMT-1988
McGWD-1984
OxAmThe-1984
OxGer-1986
OxThe-1983
RCom-1973

Besson, Benno 1922-
Brecht, Bertolt 1898-1956
Dessau, Paul 1894-1979
Eisler, Hanns 1898-1962
Engel, Erich 1891-1966
Hacks, Peter 1928-
Neher, Caspar 1897-1962
Palitzsch, Peter 1918-
Piscator, Erwin 1893-1966
Weigel, Helene 1900-1971
Wekwerth, Manfred 1929-

Bitterfeld Movement/Bitterfelder Weg (Germany, 1960s)
EncWL-1981
OxGer-1986

Strittmatter, Erwin 1912-
Wolf, Christa 1929-

Black Consciousness Movement (South Africa, 1970s)
EncWL-1981

Gwala, Mafika Pascal 1946-
Mtshali, Oswald Mbuyiseni 1940-
Sepamla, Sydney Sipho 1932-
Serote, Mongane Wally 1944-

Black Mountain Poets (United States, 1950s-1960s)
BenReEncy-1987
CamGLE-1988
DCLT-1979
EncWL-1981
GdMWL-1985
HandLit-1986
HarDMT-1988
OxAm-1983
OxEng-1985
PengAm-1971
PrEncyPP-1974

Albers, Josef 1888-1976
Baraka, Imamu Amiri 1934-
Blackburn, Paul 1926-1971
Creeley, Robert 1926-
Dawson, Fielding 1930-
Dorn, Ed 1929-
Duncan, Robert 1919-1988
Levertov, Denise 1923-
Olson, Charles 1910-1970
Oppenheimer, Joel 1930-1988
Wieners, John 1934-
Williams, Jonathan 1929-

Bloomsbury Group (England, 1910s-1940s)
BenReEncy-1987
CamGLE-1988
CEnMWL-1963
DCLT-1979
EncWL-1981
HandLit-1986

HarDMT-1988
LongCTCL-1975
OxEng-1985
PengEng-1971
RCom-1973

Bell, Clive 1881-1964
Bell, Vanessa 1879-1961
Birrell, Francis 1889-1935
Brooke, Rupert 1887-1915
Forster, E(dward) M(organ) 1879-1970
Fry, Roger 1866-1934
Garnett, David 1892-1981
Grant, Duncan 1885-1978
H.D. 1886-1961
Keynes, John Maynard 1883-1946
MacCarthy, Desmond 1878-1952
Moore, G(eorge) E(dward) 1873-1958
Morrell, Ottoline 1873-1938
Russell, Bertrand 1872-1970
Shove, Gerald 1887-1947
Strachey, James 1887-1967
Strachey, (Giles) Lytton 1880-1932
Strachey, Marjorie 1882-1964
Sydney-Turner, Saxon 1880-1962
Woolf, Leonard 1880-1969
Woolf, Virginia 1882-1941

Blue Horns Group/Tsispheri q'antsebi (Georgia, 1910s)
EncWL-1981
PrEncyPP-1974

Apchaidse, S. n.d.
Gaprindashvili, Valerian 1889-1941
Iashvili, Paolo 1895-1937
Leonidze, Giorgi 1899-1966
Nadiradse, K. n.d.

Robakidse, Grigol 1884-1962
Tabidze, Galaktion 1892-1959
Tabidze, Titsian 1895-1937
Tsirekidse, C. n.d.

Blue Stars Society (China, 1950s)
EncWL-1981

Yü Kuang-chung 1928-

Boedo Group (Argentina, 1920s)
EncWL-1981
GdMWL-1985
OxSpan-1978

Amorim, Enrique 1900-1960
Arlt, Roberto 1900-1942
Barletta, Leónidas 1902-
Castelnuovo, Elías 1893-
González Tuñón, Raul n.d.

Tiempo, César 1906-
Yunque, Álvaro 1889-(?)

Breton Movement (France, 1900s-1940s)
EncWL-1981
PrEncyPP-1974

Hémon, Roparz 1900-1978
Malmanche, Tanguy 1875-1953
Riou, Jakez 1899-1937

Bucharest Group (Romania, 1940s)
EncWL-1981

Caraion, Ion 1923-
Dumitrescu, Geo 1920-
Stelaru, Dimitrie 1917-1971
Tonegaru, Constant 1919-1952

C

Cambridge Group (England, 1930s)
EncWL-1981

    Empson, William 1906-1984
    Madge, Charles 1912-
    Raine, Kathleen 1908-

Carolina Playmakers (United States, 1920s-1960s)
OxAm-1983
OxAmThe-1984

    Green, Paul Eliot 1894-1981
    Koch, Frederick Henry 1877-1944
    Wolfe, Thomas 1900-1938

Celtic Renaissance, Celtic Revival, Celtic Twilight

    See **Irish Renaissance**

Cenáculo Group (Cuba, 1900s)
CaribWr-1979

    Gay Calbó, Enrique 1889-(?)
    Torralva Navarro, Fernándo 1885-1913

Centrifuge (Russia, 1910s)
ClDMEuL-1980
EncWL-1981

    Aseyev, Nikolay Nikolayevich 1889-1963
    Pasternak, Boris 1890-1960

    See also **Cubo-Futurism, Ego-Futurism, Mezzanine of Poetry**

Chicago Critics (United States, 1950s)
DCLT-1979
EncWL-1981
PengAm-1971
PrEncyPP-1974

    Booth, Wayne C. 1921-
    Crane, R.S. 1886-1967
    Friedman, Norman 1925-
    Hipple, Walter J., Jr. 1921-
    Keast, William R. 1914-
    McKeon, Richard 1900-1985
    McLaughlin, C.A. n.d.
    Maclean, Norman 1902-
    Marsh, Robert H. 1926-
    Olson, Elder 1909-
    Weinberg, Bernard 1909-1973
    Wright, Austin McGiffert 1922-

Chicago Group/Renaissance (United States, 1910s-1920s)
BenReEncy-1987
EncWL-1981

    Anderson, Margaret C. 1886-1973
    Anderson, Sherwood 1876-1941
    Dell, Floyd 1887-1969
    Dreiser, Theodore 1871-1945
    Fuller, Henry Blake 1857-1929
    Hecht, Ben 1894-1964
    Lindsay, Vachel 1879-1931

Masters, Edgar Lee 1869(?)-1950
Monroe, Harriet 1860-1936
Sandburg, Carl 1878-1967

Claridade Movement (Cape Verde, 1930s-1950s)
EncWL-1981

Alcântara, Oswaldo 1907-
Barbosa, Jorge 1901-1971
Ferreira, Manuel 1917-
Gonçalves, António Aurélio 1901-
Lopes, Manuel 1907-

Clarté Group (Sweden, 1930s)
EncWL-1981

Boye, Karin 1900-1941

Cobra (Belgium, Denmark, Holland, 1948-1951)
EncWL-1981
HarDMT-1988

Alechinsky, Pierre 1927-
Appel, Karel 1921-
Claus, Hugo 1929-
Jorn, Asger 1914-1973
Nieuwenhuys, Constant 1920-

Cologne School of New Realism/ Kölner Schule des neuen Realismus (Germany, 1960s)
EncWL-1981
OxGer-1986

Born, Nicolas 1937-1979
Brinkmann, Rolf Dieter 1940-1975
Brunk, Sigrid n.d.
Fischer, U.Chr. n.d.
Harig, Ludwig n.d.
Herburger, Günter 1932-

Pörtner, Paul n.d.
Rasp, Renate n.d.
Schnell, Robert Wolfgang n.d.
Seuren, Günter n.d.
Steffen, Günter n.d.
Wellershoff, Dieter 1925-

Comedy of Menace (England, 1950s)
EncWL-1981
HarDMT-1988

Campton, David 1924-
Pinter, Harold 1930-

Concrete Poetry (Austria, 1950s-1960s)
DCLT-1979

Achleitner, Friedrich 1930-
Artmann, Hans Carl 1921-
Jandl, Ernst 1925-
Rühm, Gerhard 1930-

Concrete Poetry (Belgium, 1950s-1960s)
DCLT-1979
EncWL-1981

Insingel, Mark 1935-
Vree, Paul de 1909-

Concrete Poetry (Brazil, 1950s-1960s)
CamGLE-1988
ClDMEuL-1980
DCLT-1979
EncWL-1981
GdMWL-1985
HarDMT-1988
OxEng-1985
OxGer-1986
PengAm-1971
PrEncyPP-1974

Campos, Augusto de 1931-

Campos, Haroldo de 1929-
Pignatari, Décio 1927-
Xisto, Pedro n.d.

**Concrete Poetry (England, 1950s-
1960s)**
CamGLE-1988
DCLT-1979
OxEng-1985

Cutts, Simon 1944-
Finlay, Ian Hamilton 1925-
Houedard, Dom Sylvester 1924-
Morgan, Edwin 1920-

**Concrete Poetry (Germany, 1950s-
1960s)**
EncWL-1981
OxGer-1986

Bense, Max 1910-
Heissenbüttel, Helmut 1921-
Mon, Franz 1926-

**Concrete Poetry (Norway, 1950s-
1960s)**
EncWL-1981

Vold, Jan Erik 1939-

**Concrete Poetry (Sweden, 1950s-
1960s)**
ClDMEul-1980

Fahlström, Öjvind 1928-1976
Johnson, Bengt Emil 1936-
Reuterswärd, Carl Fredrik 1934-

**Concrete Poetry (Switzerland,
1950s-1960s)**
EncWL-1981

Bill, Max 1908-
Gomringer, Eugen 1925-

**Concrete Poetry (United States,
1950s-1960s)**
OxEng-1985

Solt, Mary Ellen 1920-
Williams, Emmett 1925-

**Condemned Generation Poets
(Poland, 1940s)**
EncWL-1981

Baczynski, Krzysztof K. 1921-
1944
Borowski, Tadeusz 1922-1951
Gajcy, Tadeusz 1922-1944
Stroinski, Zdzisslaw 1920-1943
Trzebinski, Andrzej 1922-1943

**Confederation Poets (Canada, 1850s-
1920s)**
OxCan-1983

Cameron, George Frederick
1854-1885
Campbell, (William) Wilfred
1858-1918
Carman, Bliss 1861-1929
Crawford, Isabella Valancy
1850-1887
Lampman, Archibald 1861-1899
Roberts, Charles G.D. 1860-
1943
Scott, Duncan Campbell 1862-
1947

**Confessional Poetry (United States,
1950s-1960s)**
BenReEncy-1987
CamGLE-1988
DCLT-1979
EncWL-1981
GdMWL-1985
HandLit-1986
PrEncyPP-1974
RCom-1973

Berryman, John 1914-1972
Ginsberg, Allen 1926-
Lowell, Robert 1917-1977
Plath, Sylvia 1932-1963
Rich, Adrienne 1929-
Roethke, Theodore 1908-1963
Sexton, Anne 1928-1974
Snodgrass, W(illiam) D(ewitt)
1926-

Constructivism (Russia, 1920s)
BenReEncy-1987
ClDMEuL-1980
DCLT-1979
EncWL-1981
HarDMT-1988
PengEur-1969
PrEncyPP-1974

Bagritsky, Edvard 1895-1934
Gabo, Naum 1890-1977
Gan, Alexei n.d.
Inber, Vera Mikhaylovna 1893-1972
Meyerhold, Vsevolod
Emilyevich 1874-1940
Pevsner, Anton 1886-1962
Rodchenko, Alexander 1891-1956
Selvinsky, Ilya Lvovich 1899-1968
Stepanova, Varvara 1894-1958
Tatlin, Vladimir 1885-1953
Zelinski, Korneliy L. 1896-

Contemporaries/*Contemporáneos*
(Mexico, 1928-1931)
EncWL-1981
OxSpan-1978

Barreda, Octavio G. n.d.
Cuesta, Jorge n.d.
Gastelúm, Bernardo J. n.d.
González Martínez, Enrique
1871-1952

González Rojo, Enrique n.d.
Gorostiza, José 1901-1973
Nandino, Elías n.d.
Novo Lopez, Salvador 1904-1974
Ortiz de Montellano, Bernardo
1899-1949
Owen, Gilberto 1905-1952
Pellicer, Carlos 1899-1977
Torres Bodet, Jaime 1902-1974
Villaurrutia, Xavier 1903-1950

Council of Brilliant Knowledge
(Uruguay, 1900s)
EncWL-1981

Quiroga, Horacio 1878-1937

Cracow Avant-Garde (Poland,
1920s-1930s)
ClDMEuL-1980
EncWL-1981
PrEncyPP-1974

Brzekowski, Jan 1903-
Czechowicz, Józef 1903-1939
Czuchnowski, Marian 1909-
Galczynski, Konstanty Ildefons
1905-1953
Kurek, Jalu 1904-
Milosz, Czeslaw 1911-
Peiper, Tadeusz 1891-1969
Przybos, Julian 1901-1970
Wazyk, Adam 1905-1982
Zagórski, Jerzy 1907-

Creation Society/Ch'uang-tsao she
(China, 1920s)
EncWL-1981
GdMWL-1985
DOrLit-1974

Chang Tzu-p'ing n.d.
Ch'eng Fang-wu n.d.
Kuo Mo-jo 1892-1978

T'ien Han 1898-1968
Yü Ta-Fu 1896-1945

**Creationism/Creacionismo
(Argentina, Chile, Spain, 1916-
1918)**
DCLT-1979
GdMWL-1985
OxSpan-1978
PrEncyPP-1974

Díaz Casanueva, Humberto
    1905-
Diego, Gerardo 1896-1987
Huidobro, Vincente 1893-1948
Larrea, Juan 1895-1982
Reverdy, Jacques 1889-1960
Valle, Juvencio n.d.
Valle, Rosamel del n.d.

Crepuscolarismo (Italy, 1900s)
BenReEncy-1987
ClDMEuL-1980
EncWL-1981
GdMWL-1985
OxThe-1983
PengEur-1969
PrEncyPP-1974

Benelli, Sem 1875-1949
Borgese, Guiseppe Antonio
    1882-1952
Campana, Dino 1885-1932
Chiaves, Carlo 1883-1919
Corazzini, Sergio 1887-1907
Govoni, Corrado 1884-1965
Gozzano, Guido 1883-1916
Lodovici, Cesare Vico 1885-1968
Martini, Fausto Maria 1886-1931
Montale, Eugenio 1896-1981
Moretti, Marino 1885-1979
Morselli, Ercole Luigi 1882-1921
Palazzeschi, Aldo 1885-1974
Pascoli, Giovanni 1855-1912
Rebora, Clemente 1885-1957

Saba, Umberto 1883-1957
Sbarbaro, Camillo 1888-1967

Crescent Society (China, 1930s)
EncWL-1981
GdMWL-1985

Hsü Chih-mo 1897-1931
Wen I-to 1899-1946

**Criollismo (Argentina, Chile,
Columbia, Venezuela, 1890s-
1900s)**
EncWL-1981
GdMWL-1985
OxSpan-1978

Barrios, Eduardo 1884-1963
Blanco-Fombona, Rufino 1874-
    1944
Borges, Jorge Luis 1899-1986
Carpentier, Alejo 1904-1980
Diego, Eliseo 1920-
Durand, Luis 1895-1954
Edwards Bello, Joaquín 1887-
    1968
Erro, Carlos Alberto 1899-
Güiraldes, Ricardo 1886-1927
Latorre, Mariano 1886-1955
Lezama Lima, José 1910-1976
Romero García, Vicente 1865-
    1917

***Critica, La* (Italy, 1903-1944)**
ClDMEuL-1980

Croce, Benedetto 1866-1952
Gentile, Giovanni 1875-1944

Cubism (France, 1910s)
BenReEncy-1987
EncWL-1981
HandLit-1986
HarDMT-1988
LongCTCL-1975

OxFr-1959
PrEncyPP-1974
RCom-1973

Apollinaire, Guillaume 1880-
1918
Archipenko, Alexander 1881-
1964
Braque, Georges 1882-1963
Cendrars, Blaise 1887-1961
Cézanne, Paul 1839-1906
Cocteau, Jean 1889-1963
Delaunay, Sonia 1885-1979
Fargue, Léon-Paul 1876(?)-1947
Gleizes, Albert 1881-1953
Gris, Juan 1887-1927
Jacob, Max 1876-1944
Laurens, Henri 1885-1954
Léger, Fernand 1881-1955
Lipchitz, Jacques 1891-1973
Metzinger, Jean 1883-1956
Paulhan, Jean 1884-1968
Picasso, Pablo 1881-1973
Reverdy, Jacques 1889-1960
Salmon, André 1881-1969
Stein, Gertrude 1874-1946

**Cubo-Futurism/Hylaea (Russia,
1912-1918)**
BenReEncy-1987
ClDMEuL-1980
DCLT-1979
EncWL-1981
GdMWL-1985

HarDMT-1988
McGWD-1984
PengEur-1969
PrEncyPP-1974

Bagritsky, Edvard 1895-1934
Burlyuk, David 1882-1967
Guro, Yelena Genrikhovna
1877-1913
Kamensky, Vasily 1884-1961
Khlebnikov, Velemir
Vladimirovich 1885-1922
Kruchyonykh, Alexey
Eliseyevich 1886-1968
Larionov, Mikhail 1881-1964
Livshits, Benedikt 1887-1939
Malevich, Kazimir Severinovich
1878-1935
Mayakovsky, Vladimir 1893-
1930
Meyerhold, Vsevolod 1874-1940
Pasternak, Boris 1890-1960
Popova, Liubov 1889-1924
Pougny, Jean 1894-1956
Udaltsova, Nadezhda 1885-1961

See also **Centrifuge, Ego-Futurism,
Futurism, Mezzanine of Poetry**

Czartak Group (Poland, 1922-1928)
ClDMEuL-1980

Zegadlowicz, Emil 1888-1941

D

Dadaism (France 1916-1923)
BenReEncy-1987
ClDMEuL-1980
DCLT-1979
EncWL-1981
GdMWL-1985
HandLit-1986
HarDMT-1988
LongCTCL-1975
OxEng-1985
OxFr-1959
OxGer-1986
OxThe-1983
PengEur-1969
PrEncyPP-1974
RCom-1973

Apollinaire, Guillaume 1880-1918
Aragon, Louis 1897-1982
Arp, Jean (Hans) 1887-1966
Baader, Johannes 1875-1955
Baargeld, Johannes (?)-1927
Ball, Hugo 1886-1927
Bonset, I.K. 1883-1931
Breton, André 1896-1966
Duchamp, Marcel 1887-1968
Éluard, Paul 1895-1952
Ernst, Max 1891-1976
Grosz, George 1893-1959
Hausmann, Raoul 1886-1971
Heartfield, John 1891-1968
Huelsenbeck, Richard 1892-1974
Mehring, Walter 1896-1981
Neuhuys, Paul 1897-

Pansaers, Clément 1885-1922
Picabia, Francis 1879-1953
Ray, Man 1890-1948
Ribemont-Dessaignes, Georges 1884-(?)
Schwitters, Kurt 1887-1948
Soupault, Philippe 1897-
Tzara, Tristan 1896-1963
Vaché, Jacques 1895-1919

DAV Group (Czechoslovakia, 1924-1937)
ClDMEuL-1980
EncWL-1981
GdMWL-1985

Jilemnicky, Peter 1901-1949
Novomesky, Ladislav (Laco) 1904-1976
Ponican, Ján 1902-

Dawn Group/Grupo Saker Ti (Guatemala, 1940s)
OxSpan-1978

Alvarado, Huberto 1925-
Barahona, Melvin René n.d.
Martínez Torres, Olga n.d.
Ovalle López, Werner n.d.
Palencia, Oscar Arturo n.d.
Palma, Oscar Edmundo n.d.
Sosa, Rafael n.d.

Dawn of the Future/Fecr-i Ati (Turkey, 1910s)
ClDMEuL-1980

GdMWL-1985

Hasim, Ahmet 1884-1933
Karaosmanoglu, Yakup Kadri
  1889-1974
Köprülü, Mehmed Fuad 1890-
  1966

Decadents/Burai-ha (Japan, 1940s)
  DOrLit-1974

Dazai Osamu 1909-1948
Sakaguchi Ango 1906-1955

**Deconstructionism (France and
  United States, 1960s)**
  CamGLE-1988
  EncWL-1981
  GdMWL-1985
  HandLit-1986
  HarDMT-1988
  OxEng-1985

Bate, Walter Jackson 1918-
Bloom, Harold 1930-
De Man, Paul 1919-1983
Derrida, Jacques 1930-
Hartman, Geoffrey 1929-
Johnson, Barbara n.d.
Lacan, Jacques 1901-1981
Miller, J. Hillis 1928-

**Democratic Poets (Georgia, 1900-
  1914)**
  EncWL-1981

Evdoshvili, Irodion 1873-1916

Dertigers, The (South Africa, 1930s)
  EncWL-1981
  GdMWL-1985
  PrEncyPP-1974

Eybers, Elisabeth 1915-
Heerden, Ernst van 1916-

Krige, Uys 1910-
Louw, Nicholaas Petrus Van
  Wyck 1906-1970
Louw, W.E.G. 1913-
Opperman, D.J. 1914-

**Deutsches Theater (Germany, 1880s-
  1960s)**
  EncWL-1981
  HarDMT-1988
  McGWD-1984
  OxThe-1983

Bahr, Hermann 1863-1934
Besson, Benno 1922-
Bahr, Hermann 1863-1934
Brahm, Otto 1856-1912
Brecht, Bertolt 1898-1956
Hacks, Peter 1928-
Hauptmann, Gerhart 1862-1946
Hilpert, Heinz 1890-1967
Kainz, Josef 1858-1910
Langhoff, Wolfgang 1901-1966
L'Arronge, Adolf 1838-1908
Reinhardt, Max 1873-1943
Schnitzler, Arthur 1862-1931
Sorma, Agnes 1865-1927
Sudermann, Hermann 1857-
  1928
Zuckmayer, Carl 1896-1977

Diepalismo (Puerto Rico, 1920s)
  CaribWr-1979

Diego Padró, José I. de 1899-
Palés Matos, Luis 1899-1959

**Diwan School of Poets (Egypt,
  1920s)**
  EncWL-1981

al-'Aqqad, 'Abbas Mahmud
  1889-1964
al-Mazini, Ibrahim 1890-1949

Shukri, 'Abd al-Rahman 1886-1958

Dông-kinh School of the Just Cause (Vietnam, 1910s)
EncWL-1981

Phan Bôi Châu 1867-1940

Phan Châu Trinh 1872-1926

Dzvony **(Ukraine, 1930-1939)**
ClDMEuL-1980

Antonych, Bohdan Ihor 1909-1937

E

Earth Movement (Lithuania, 1950s)
ClDMEuL-1980
EncWL-1981

Bradunas, Kazys 1917-
Landsbergis, Algirdas 1924-
Nagys, Henrikas 1920-
Nyka-Niliunas, Alfonsas 1920-
Skema, Antanas 1911-1961

École Romane (France, 1890s-1910s)
ClDMEuL-1980
EncWL-1981
GdMWL-1985
OxFr-1959

Du Plessys, Maurice 1864-1924
La Tailhède, Raymond de 1867-1938
Maurras, Charles 1868-1952
Moréas, Jean 1856-1910
Raynaud, Ernest 1864-1936

Edwardian Literature (England and Ireland, 1900s)
BenReEncy-1987
DCLT-1979
HandLit-1986
OxEng-1985

Barrie, James M. 1860-1937
Bennett, (Enoch) Arnold 1867-1931
Butler, Samuel 1835-1902
Conrad, Joseph 1857-1924
Dunsany, Lord Edward John

Moreton Drax Plunkett 1878-1957
Ford, Ford Madox 1873-1939
Forster, E(dward) M(organ) 1879-1970
Galsworthy, John 1867-1933
Granville-Barker, Harley 1877-1946
Gregory, Lady Isabella Augusta 1852-1932
Hardy, Thomas 1840-1928
Hudson, W(illiam) H(enry) 1841-1922
Hyde, Douglas 1911-
James, Henry 1843-1916
Joyce, James 1882-1941
Kipling, (Joseph) Rudyard 1865-1936
Masefield, John 1878-1967
Robinson, Lennox 1886-1958
Sackville-West, Victoria 1892-1962
Shaw, George Bernard 1856-1950
Stephens, James 1882(?)-1950
Synge, John Millington 1871-1909
Wells, H(erbert) G(eorge) 1866-1946
Yeats, William Butler 1865-1939

Ego-Futurism (Russia, 1910s)
ClDMEuL-1980
DCLT-1979
EncWL-1981
GdMWL-1985

PrEncyPP-1974

Severyanin, Igor 1887-1942

See also **Centrifuge, Cubo-Futurism, Futurism, Mezzanine of Poetry**

Ensueñismo Group (Puerto Rico, 1950s)
CaribWr-1979

Franco Oppenheimer, Félix 1912-
Martin Montes, José Luis 1921-
Rentas Lucas, Eugenio 1910-
Rosa-Nieves, Cesáreo 1901-

Epic Theater/Episches Theater (Germany, 1920s-1950s)
BenReEncy-1987
ClDMEuL-1980
DCLT-1979
EncWL-1981
GdMWL-1985
HarDMT-1988
McGWD-1984
OxGer-1986
OxThe-1983
PengEur-1969
RCom-1973

Brecht, Bertolt 1898-1956
Bronnen, Arnolt 1895-1959
Dorst, Tankred 1925-
Dürrenmatt, Friedrich 1921-
Frisch, Max 1911-
Hacks, Peter 1928-
Hildesheimer, Wolfgang 1916-
Paquet, Alfons 1881-1944
Piscator, Erwin 1893-1966
Walser, Martin 1927-
Weiss, Peter 1916-1982

Estos 13/*Hora Cero* (Peru, 1970s)
OxSpan-1978

Burgos, Elqui n.d.
Cerna, José n.d.
Cilloniz, Antonio 1944-
Málaga, Oscar n.d.
Mejía, Feliciano n.d.
Mora, Tulio n.d.
Nájar, Jorge n.d.
Ribeiro, José Rosas n.d.
Ruiz, Juan Ramírez n.d.
Sánchez León, Abelardo n.d.
Verástegui, Enrique 1950-
Watanabe, José n.d.

Estridentismo (Mexico, 1922-1927)
EncWL-1981
OxSpan-1978
PrEncyPP-1974

Arzubide, Germán List n.d.
Gallardo, Salvador n.d.
Maples Arce, Manuel 1898-
Quintanilla, Luis n.d.
Vela, Arqueles n.d.

Excelsior Group/*Uzvyssa* (Byelorussia, 1920s)
ClDMEuL-1980
EncWL-1981

Babareka, Adam 1899-1937
Chorny, Kuzma 1900-1944
Dubowka, Uladzimier 1900-1975
Krapiva, Kandrat 1896-
Pushcha, Yazep 1902-1964
Zaretski, Michás 1901-1941

Existentialism (France, 1940s-1960s)
BenReEncy-1987
CEnMWL-1963
ClDMEuL-1980

DCLT-1979
EncWL-1981
GdMWL-1985
HandLit-1986
HarDMT-1988
LongCTCL-1975
McGWD-1984
OxAm-1983
OxEng-1985
OxFr-1959
OxGer-1986
PrEncyPP-1974
RCom-1973

Beauvoir, Simone de 1908-1986
Camus, Albert 1913-1960
Malraux, André 1901-1976
Marcel, Gabriel 1889-1973
Merleau-Ponty, Maurice 1908-1961
Sartre, Jean-Paul 1905-1980

Existentialism (Germany, 1940s-1960s)
BenReEncy-1987
DCLT-1979
EncWL-1981
HandLit-1986
HarDMT-1988
OxEng-1985
OxGer-1986
RCom-1973

Buber, Martin 1878-1965
Heidegger, Martin 1889-1976
Husserl, Edmund 1859-1938
Jaspers, Karl 1883-1969

Existentialism (Spain, 1940s-1960s)
BenReEncy-1987
DCLT-1979
EncWL-1981
RCom-1973

Ortega y Gasset, José 1883-1955

Unamuno y Jugo, Miguel de 1864-1936

Experimentalists/Experimentelen (Netherlands, 1950s)
DCLT-1979

Jorn, Asgar 1914-1973
Lodeizen, Hans 1924-1950

Expressionism (Czechoslovakia, 1920s)
ClDMEuL-1980
HandLit-1986

Capek, Karel 1890-1938
Deml, Jakub 1878-1961
Weiner, Richard 1884-1937

Expressionism (Germany and Austria, 1910s-1920s)
BenReEncy-1987
CamGLE-1988
CEnMWL-1963
ClDMEuL-1980
DCLT-1979
EncWL-1981
GdMWL-1985
HandLit-1986
HarDMT-1988
LongCTCL-1975
McGWD-1984
OxAm-1983
OxAmThe-1984
OxEng-1985
OxGer-1986
OxThe-1983
PengEur-1969
PrEncyPP-1974
RCom-1973

Ball, Hugo 1886-1927
Barlach, Ernst 1870-1938
Becher, Johannes R. 1891-1958
Beckmann, Max 1884-1950
Benn, Gottfried 1886-1956

Berg, Alban 1885-1935
Blei, Franz 1871-1942
Bonnelycke, Emil 1893-1953
Brecht, Bertolt 1898-1956
Bronnen, Arnold 1895-1959
Döblin, Alfred 1878-1957
Edschmid, Kasimir 1890-1966
Ehrenstein, Albert 1886-1950
Einstein, Carl 1885-1940
Ermanis, Peteris 1893-1969
Ernst, Paul 1866-1933
Frank, Leonhard 1882-1961
Goering, Reinhard 1887-1936
Goll, Yvan 1891-1950
Hasenclever, Walter 1890-1940
Heckel, Erich 1883-1970
Heym, Georg 1887-1912
Hiller, Kurt 1885-1972
Hoddis, Jakob van 1887-1942
Hoel, Sigurd 1890-1960
Johst, Hanns 1890-1978
Kafka, Franz 1883-1924
Kaiser, Georg 1878-1945
Kandinsky, Wassily 1866-1944
Kerr, Alfred 1867-1948
Kirchner, Ernst Ludwig 1880-1938
Klee, Paul 1879-1940
Kokoschka, Oskar 1886-1980
Kraus, Karl 1874-1936
Kubin, Alfred 1877-1959
Lang, Fritz 1890-1976
Lasker-Schüler, Else 1869-1945
Leonhard, Rudolf 1889-1953
Lichtenstein, Alfred 1889-1914
Loerke, Oskar 1884-1941
Lotz, Ernst Wilhelm 1890-1914
Marc, Franz 1880-1916
Marsman, Hendrik 1889-1940
Mendelsohn, Erich 1887-1953
Modersohn-Becker, Paula 1876-1907
Munch, Edvard 1863-1944
Nolde, Emil 1867-1956
Ostaijen, Paul van 1896-1928

Otten, Karl 1889-1963
Pfemfert, Franz 1879-1954
Pinthus, Kurt 1886-1975
Sack, Gustav 1885-1916
Schickele, René 1883-1940
Schmidt-Rottluff, Karl 1884-1976
Schnack, Friedrich 1888-1977
Sorge, Reinhard 1892-1916
Stadler, Ernst 1883-1914
Sternheim, Carl 1878-1942
Stramm, August 1874-1915
Strindberg, Johan August 1849-1912
Taut, Bruno 1880-1938
Toller, Ernst 1893-1939
Trakl, Georg 1887-1914
Unruh, Fritz von 1885-1970
Walden, Herwarth 1878-1941
Wedekind, Frank 1864-1918
Wegener, Paul 1874-1948
Werfel, Franz 1890-1945
Wiene, Robert 1881-1938
Worringer, Wilhelm 1881-1965
Zech, Paul 1881-1946
Zuckmayer, Carl 1896-1977

Expressionism (United States, 1920s-1930s)
    CamGLE-1988
    DCLT-1979
    HandLit-1986
    OxAm-1983
    OxAmThe-1984
    OxThe-1983
    PrEncyPP-1974

Connelly, Marc 1890-1980
O'Neill, Eugene 1888-1953
Rice, Elmer 1892-1967
Wilder, Thornton 1897-1975

Expressionism (Yugoslavia, 1920s-1930s)
    EncWL-1981

Podbevsek, Anton 1898-
Simic, Antun Branko 1898-1925
Ujevic, Augustin 1891-1955
Vodnik, Anton 1901-1965

Exteriorismo (Nicaragua, 1960s)
EncWL-1981

Cardenal, Ernesto 1925-
Coronel Urtecho, José 1906-

F

Fantaisistes Group (France, 1910s)
ClDMEuL-1980
EncWL-1981
OxFr-1959

Bernard, Jean-Marc 1881-1915
Carco, Francis 1886-1958
Cendrars, Blaise 1887-1961
Derème, Tristan 1889-1942
Fagus 1872-1933
Klingsor, Tristan 1874-1966
Larbaud, Valéry Nicholas 1881-1957
Toulet, Paul Jean 1867-1920

Félibrige Movement (France, 1860s-1920s)
ClDMEuL-1980
EncWL-1981
GdMWL-1985
PengEur-1969
PrEncyPP-1974

Arbaud, Joseph d' 1872-1950
Aubanel, Théodore 1829-1886
Brunet, Jean 1823-1894
Camélat, Michel 1871-1962
Giera, Paul 1816-1861
Gras, Felix 1884-1901
Marcellin, Remy 1832-1908
Mathieu, Anselme 1828-1925
Mistral, Frédéric 1830-1914
Perbosc, Antonin 1861-1944
Roumanille, Joseph 1818-1891

Feminist Criticism (England, France, United States, 1960s-present)
CamGLE-1988
HandLit-1986
HarDMT-1988
OxEng-1985

Beauvior, Simone de 1908-1986
Cixous, Hélène 1937-
Figes, Eva 1932-
Gilbert, Sandra M. 1936-
Gornick, Vivian 1935-
Greer, Germaine 1939-
Gubar, Susan 1944-
Hardwick, Elizabeth 1916-
Irigaray, Luce n.d.
Kristeva, Julia 1941-
Millett, Kate 1934-
Moers, Ellen 1928-1979
Morgan, Robin 1941-
Schneir, Miriam 1933-
Showalter, Elaine 1941-

Festa Group (Brazil, 1920s)
EncWL-1981
PrEncyPP-1974

Bandeira, Manuel 1886-1968
Meireles, Cecília 1901-1964
Silveira, Tasso da 1895-1968

Fifties Poets/Vijftigers (Belgium, 1950s)
ClDMEuL-1980
EncWL-1981

Bontridder, Albert 1921-
Brouwers, Jaak n.d.
Claus, Hugo 1929-
Durant, Rudo n.d.
Gils, Gust 1924-
Peel, Adriaan n.d.
Pernath, Hugues C. 1931-1975
Roover, Adriaan de n.d.
Snoek, Paul 1933-
Speliers, Hedwig n.d.
Van der Hoeven, Jan n.d.
Vree, Paul de 1909-

**Fifties Poets/Vijftigers
(Netherlands, 1950s)**
EncWL-1981

Campert, Remco 1929-
Elburg, Jan 1919-
Kouwenaar, Gerrit 1923-
Lucebert 1924-
Schierbeek, Bert 1918-

**Fifty-Five Poets/Vijfenvijftigers
(Belgium, 1955-1960s)**
EncWL-1981

Gils, Gust, 1924-
Pernath, Hugues C. 1931-1975
Snoek, Paul 1933-

***First Statement* Group (Canada,
1942-1945)**
OxCan-1983

Aikman, Audrey n.d.
Anderson, Patrick 1915-1979
Ashe, Geoffrey 1923-
Dudek, Louis 1918-
Layton, Irving 1912-
MacLellan, Keith n.d.
Simpson, Robert n.d.
Sutherland, Betty n.d.
Sutherland, John 1919-1956
Waddington, Miriam 1917-

**Five Young Men/Fem Unga
(Sweden, 1930s)**
ClDMEuL-1980
EncWL-1981
PrEncyPP-1974

Lundkvist, Artur 1906-
Martinson, Harry (Edmund)
1904-1978

**Flame Bearers Group/Tulenkantajat
(Finland, 1920s)**
ClDMEuL-1980
EncWL-1981
GdMWL-1985
PengEur-1969
PrEncyPP-1974

Hellaakoski, Aaro 1893-1952
Jylhä, Yrjö 1903-1956
Kailas, Uuno 1901-1933
Kivimaa, Arvi 1904-
Mustapää, P. 1899-(?)
Paavolainen, Olavi 1903-1964
Sarkia, Kaarlo 1902-1945
Seppänen, Unto 1904-1955
Vaara, Elina 1903-
Vala, Katri 1901-1944
Viljanen, Lauri 1900-
Waltari, Mika 1908-1979

Flame Group (Byelorussia, 1920s)
EncWL-1981

Kolas, Yakub 1882-1956
Kupala, Yanka 1881-1942

Florida Group (Argentina, 1920s)
EncWL-1981
GdMWL-1985
OxSpan-1978

Bernárdez, Francisco Luis 1900-
Borges, Jorge Luis 1899-1986

González Lanuza, Eduardo
1900-
Lange, Norah 1906-
Marechal, Leopoldo 1900-1970
Molinari, Ricardo E. 1898-

Form Revolution (Iceland, 1940s)
ClDMEuL-1980

Bödvarsson, Gudmundur 1904-
1974
Bragi, Einar 1921-
Kötlum, Jóhannes úr 1899-1972
Sigússon, Hannes 1922-
Steinarr, Steinn 1908-1958
Vör, Jón úr n.d.

47 Workshop (United States, 1905-1920)
LongCTCL-1975
OxThe-1983

Baker, George Pierce 1866-1935
O'Neill, Eugene 1888-1953

***Forum* Group (Netherlands, 1930s)**
EncWL-1981
GdMWL-1985
PrEncyPP-1974

Braak, Menno ter 1902-1940
Perron, Edgar du 1899-1940
Roelants, Maurice 1895-1966
Slauerhoff, Jan Jacob 1898-1936
Vestdijk, Simon 1898-1971

Four Horsemen (Canada, 1970s)
OxCan-1983

Barreto-Rivera, Rafael n.d.
Dutton, Paul 1934-
McCaffery, Steven n.d.
Nichol, B(arrie) P(hillip) 1944-

Four Winds Movement/Keturi Vejai (Lithuania, 1920s)
ClDMEuL-1980
EncWL-1981
GdMWL-1985
PrEncyPP-1974

Binkis, Kazys 1893-1942
Petrenas-Tarulis, Juozas 1896-1980
Tilvytis, Teofilis 1904-1969

Free Academy of Proletarian Literature/VAPLITE (Ukraine, 1925-1928)
ClDMEuL-1980

Dosvitny, Oles 1891-1934
Khvylovy, Mykola 1893-1933
Kulish, Mykola 1892-1937
Slisarenko, Oleska 1891-1937
Smolych, Yury 1900-1976
Yanovsky, Yuriy 1902-1954
Yohansen, Mayk 1895-1937

Freie Bühne (Germany, 1890s-1900s)
HandLit-1986
HarDMT-1988
McGWD-1984
OxGer-1986
OxThe-1983

Anzengruber, Ludwig 1839-
1889
Bie, O. 1864-1938
Bierbaum, Otto Julius 1865-1910
Björnson, Björn 1832-1910
Bölsche, Wilhelm 1861-1939
Brahm, Otto 1856-1912
Harden, Maximilian 1861-1927
Hart, Julius 1859-1930
Hauptmann, Gerhart 1862-1946
Holz, Arno 1863-1929
Schlaf, Johannes 1862-1941

Schlenther, P. 1854-1916
Sorma, Agnes 1865-1927
Strindberg, August 1849-1912
Wolff, Th. 1868-1916
Zola, Émile 1840-1902

See also **Naturalism**

**Freud, Sigmund 1856-1939
(Austrian)**
BenReEncy-1987
CasWL-1973
OxEng-1985
OxGer-1986
PengEur-1969
RCom-1973

**Friends of the Inkstone/Ken'yusha
(Japan, 1885-1900s)**
DOrLit-1974
GdMWL-1985

Ozaki Koyo 1868-1903
Yamada Bimyo 1868-(?)

**Fugitives/Agrarians (United States
1920s-1930s)**
BenReEncy-1987
DCLT-1979
EncWL-1981
GdMWL-1985
HandLit-1986
OxAm-1983
PengAm-1971
PrEncyPP-1974

Anderson, Sherwood 1876-1941
Davidson, Donald 1893-1968
Fletcher, John Gould 1886-1950
Jackson, Laura (Riding) 1901-
Lytle, Andrew 1902-
Moore, Merrill 1903-1957
Ransom, John Crowe 1888-1974
Tate, Allen 1899-1979
Warren, Robert Penn 1905-1989

Futurism (France, 1910s)
HarDMT-1988
OxFr-1959

Apollinaire, Guillaume 1880-
1918
Delaunay, Sonia 1885-1979
Léger, Fernand 1881-1955

Futurism (Georgia, 1920s)
EncWL-1981

Chikovani, Simone 1903-1966
Shengelaia, Demna 1896-

Futurism (Italy, 1910s-1920s)
BenReEncy-1987
ClDMEuL-1980
DCLT-1979
EncWL-1981
GdMWL-1985
HarDMT-1988
LongCTCL-1975
McGWD-1984
OxEng-1985
OxFr-1959
OxThe-1983
PengEur-1969
PrEncyPP-1974

Balla, Giacomo 1871-1958
Boccioni, Umberto 1882-1916
Bontempelli, Massimo 1878-1960
Carrà, Carlo 1881-1966
Govoni, Corrado 1884-1965
Marinetti, Filippo Tommaso
1876-1944
Palazzeschi, Aldo 1885-1974
Papini, Giovanni 1881-1956
Pratella, Francesco 1880-1955
Prezzolini, Giuseppi 1882-1982
Russolo, Luigi 1885-1947
Sant'Elia, Antonio 1888-1916
Severini, Gino 1883-1966
Soffici, Ardengo 1879-1964

See also **Cubo-Futurism, Ego-Futurism, Mezzanine of Poetry**

Futurism (Poland, 1920s)
ClDMEuL-1980
EncWL-1981

Czyzewski, Tytus 1885-1945
Jasienski, Bruno 1901-1939
Mlodozeniec, Stanislaw 1895-1959
Stern, Anatol 1899-1968
Wat, Aleksander 1900-1967

Futurism (Ukraine, 1910s-1920s)
ClDMEuL-1980
EncWL-1981

Semenko, Mykhaylo 1892-1939
Shkurupy, Geo 1903-1934

***Füyüzat* Movement (Azerbaijan, 1906-1907)**
EncWL-1981

Khadi, Mukhamedi 1879-1920
Sikhat, Abbas 1874-1918

G

Gang Group/Khalyastre (Poland, 1922-1925)
ClDMEuL-1980
EncWL-1981
GdMWL-1985

Greenberg, Uri Zvi 1894-1981
Markish, Peretz 1895-1952
Ravitch, Meilech 1893-1976

Garip Movement (Turkey, 1940s-1950s)
EncWL-1981
PrEncyPP-1974

Anday, Melih Cevdet 1915-
Eyüboglu, Bedri Rahmi 1913-
Kanik, Orhan Veli 1914-1950
Külebi, Cahit 1917-
Rifat, Oktay 1914-

Gate Theater (England, 1925-1940)
HarDMT-1988
LongCTCL-1975

Godfrey, Peter 1917-
Marshall, Norman 1901-1980

Gaucho Literature (Argentina and Uruguay, 1870s-1920s)
BenReEncy-1987
EncWL-1981
OxSpan-1978
PengAm-1971
PrEncyPP-1974

Acevedo Díaz, Eduardo 1851-1921
Ascásubi, Hilario 1807-1875
Campo, Estanislao del 1834-1880
Godoy, Juan G. 1793-1864
Güiraldes, Ricardo 1886-1927
Gutiérrez, Eduardo 1853-1890
Hernández, José 1834-1886
Hidalgo, Bartolomé 1788-1822
Lynch, Benito 1885-1951
Sarmiento, Domingo Faustino 1811-1888
Viana, Javier de 1868-1926
Zavala Muñiz, Justino 1897-

Genç Kalemlev (Turkey, 1910s)
ClDMEuL-1980
GdMWL-1985

Ömer Seyfettin 1884-1920

Generation of 1898/Generación del 1898 (Spain, 1900-1910s)
BenReEncy-1987
DCLT-1979
EncWL-1981
GdMWL-1985
McGWD-1984
OxSpan-1978

Azorín 1873-1969
Baroja y Nessi, Ricardo (Pío) 1872-1956
Benavente, Jacinto 1866-1954

Costa y Martínez, Joaquín 1846-1911
Ganivet, Angel 1865-1898
Gómez de la Serna, Ramón 1888-1963
Machado, Antonio 1875-1939
Maeztu y Whitney, Ramiro de 1874-1936
Onís y Sánchez, Federico de 1886-?
Ortega Munilla, José 1856-1922
Ortega y Gasset, José 1883-1955
Pérez de Ayala, Ramón 1881-1962
Unamuno y Jugo, Miguel de 1864-1936
Valle-Inclán, Ramón 1866-1936

Generation of 1900/Generación del 1900 (Paraguay, 1900s)
EncWL-1981

Báez, Cecilio 1862-1941
Domínguez, Manuel 1869-1935
Garay, Blas 1873-1899
Gondra, Manuel 1871-1927
Guanes, Alejandro 1872-1925
Moreno, Fulgencio R. 1872-1935
O'Leary, Juan E. 1879-1969

Generation of 1900/Generación del 1900 (Uruguay, 1900s)
EncWL-1981

Acevedo Díaz, Eduardo 1851-1921
Quiroga, Horacio 1878-1937
Reyles, Carlos 1868-1838
Viana, Javier de 1868-1926
Zavala Muñiz, Justino 1897-

Generation of 1905 (Norway, 1905-1920)
EncWL-1981

Aukrust, Olav 1883-1929
Bull, Olav 1883-1933
Larsen, Alf 1885-1967
Nygard, Olav 1884-1924
Orjasæter, Tore 1886-1968
Wildenvey, Herman 1886-1959

Generation of 1918/Generación del 1918 (Venezuela, 1920s)
EncWL-1981

Arraiz, Antonio 1903-1963
Castro, Luis 1909-1933
Eloy Blanco, Andrés 1897-1955
Fernández Alvarez, Luis 1902-1952
Otero Silva, Miguel 1908-
Rodríguez Cárdenas, Manuel 1912-

Generation of 1927 (also 1925)/Generación del 1927 (Spain, 1920s)
BenReEncy-1987
CIDMEuL-1980
EncWL-1981
GdMWL-1985
OxSpan-1978

Alberti, Rafael 1902-
Aleixandre, Vicente 1898-1984
Alonso, Dámaso 1898-
Altolaguirre, Manuel 1906-1959
Cernuda, Luis 1902-1963
Cossío, José María de 1893-
Diego, Gerardo 1896-1987
Domenchina, Juan José 1898-1959
Espina, Antonio 1894-
García Lorca, Federico 1898-1936
Guillén, Jorge 1893-1984
Jarnés Millán, Benjamín 1888-1949
Miró, Gabriel 1879-1930

Ortega y Gasset, José 1883-1955
Prados, Emilio 1899-1962
Salinas, Pedro 1891(?)-1951

Generation of 1930 (Greece, 1930s)
ClDMEuL-1980
EncWL-1981

Antoniou, Dimitrios I. 1906-
Baras, Alexandros 1906-
Boumi-Pappa, Rita 1907-
Elytis, Odysseus 1911-
Embirikos, Andreas 1901-1975
Engonopoulos, Nikos 1910-
Gatsos, Nikos 1915-
Matsas, Alexandros 1911-1969
Panagiotopoulos, Ioannis M.
  1901-
Pappas, Nikos 1906-
Politis, Kosmas 1888-1974
Ritsos, Yannis 1909-
Sarandaris, Giorgos 1908-1941
Seferis, George 1900-1971
Theotakas, Yorghos 1905-1966
Vrettakos, Nikiforos 1911-

**Generation of 1936/Generación del
1936 (Spain, 1930s)**
BenReEncy-1987
EncWL-1981

Bousoño, Carlos 1923-
Cela, Camilo José 1916-
Celaya, Gabriel 1911-
Gaos, Vicente 1919-
Hernández, Miguel 1910-1942
Hierro, José 1922-
Otero, Blas de 1916-
Panero Torbado, Leopoldo 1909-
  1962
Ridruejo, Dionisio 1912-1975
Rosales, Luis 1910-

**Generation of 1938/Generación del
1938 (Chile, 1930s)**
EncWL-1981

Alegría, Fernando 1918-
Atías, Guillermo 1917-
Droguett, Carlos 1915-
Godoy, Juan 1911-
Guzmán, Nicomedes 1914-1964

**Generation of 1940/Generación del
1940 (Paraguay, 1940s)**
EncWL-1981

Campos Cervera, Hérib 1908-
  1953
Casaccia, Gabriel 1907-
Plá, Josefina 1909-
Roa Bastos, Augusto 1917-
Romero, Elvio 1926-

**Generation of 1940/Generación del
1940 (Puerto Rico, 1940s)**
EncWL-1981

Díaz Valcárcel, Emilio 1929-
Soto, Pedro Juan 1928-

Generation of 1945 (Brazil, 1940s)
EncWL-1981
PrEncyPP-1974

Alceu Amoroso, Lima 1893-(?)
Campos, Geir 1924-
Ivo, Lêdo 1924-
Mota, Mauro 1912-
Neto, Joao Cabral de Melo 1920-

Reis, Marcos Konder 1922-
Silva, Domingos Carvalho da
  1915-

**Generation of 1945 (Indonesia,
1940s)**
DOrLit-1974

EncWL-1981
GdMWL-1985
PrEncyPP-1974

Chairil Anwar 1922-1949

Generation of 1945/Generación del 1945 (Uruguay, 1940s)
EncWL-1981

Benedetti, Mario 1920-
Hernández, Felisberto 1902-
1964
Martínez Moreno, Carlos 1917-
Onetti, Juan Carlos 1909-
Rama, Angel 1926-

Generation of 1950/Generación del 1950 (Chile, 1950s)
EncWL-1981

Donoso, José 1924-
Edwards, Jorge 1931-
Heiremans, Luis Alberto 1928-
1964
Lafourcade, Enrique 1927-
Laso, Jaime 1926-

Generation of 1950 (Indonesia, 1950s)
EncWL-1981
PrEncyPP-1974

Asrul Sani n.d.
Nugroho Notosutanto n.d.
Rivai Apin n.d.
Sitor Situmorang 1923-
Rendra, W.S. 1935-

Generation of 1954 (Algeria, 1950s)
EncWL-1981

Dib, Mohammed 1920-
Mammeri, Mouloud 1917-

Generation of 1955 (Hungary, 1950s)
ClDMEuL-1980

Csurka, István n.d.
Kamondy, László n.d.
Moldova, György 1934-
Sánta, Ferenc 1927-
Szábo, István n.d.

Generation of the 1950s/Asas '50 (Malaysia, 1950s)
EncWL-1981

Asmal 1924-
Awam-il-Sarkam 1918-
Hamzah Hussein 1927-
Keris Mas 1922-
Mahsuri Salikon 1927-
Suratman Markasan 1930-
Usman Awang 1929-
Wijaya Mala 1923-

Generation of the 1960s/ Shestydesyatnyky (Ukraine, 1960s)
ClDMEuL-1980
EncWL-1981
GdMWL-1985

Drach, Ivan 1936-
Korotych, Vitaly 1936-
Kostenko, Lina 1930-
Rylsky, Maxym 1895-1964
Symonenko, Vasyl 1935-1963
Vinhranovsky, Mykola 1936-

Geneva School of Critics (Switzerland, 1950s-1970s)
EncWL-1981
PrEncyPP-1974

Béguin, Albert 1898-1957
Miller, J. Hillis 1928-
Poulet, Georges 1902-
Raymond, Marcel 1897-1957

Richard, Jean-Pierre 1922-
Rousse, Jean 1910-
Starobinski, Jean 1920-

Genteel Tradition (United States, 1880s-1900s)
HandLit-1986

Aldrich, Thomas Bailey 1836-1907
Sill, Edward Roland 1841-1887
Stedman, Edmund Clarence 1833-1908
Stoddard, Richard Henry 1825-1903
Taylor, Bayard 1825-1878

Georgian Literature (England and Ireland, 1910s-1930s)
BenReEncy-1987
CamGLE-1988
DCLT-1979
EncWL-1981
GdMWL-1985
HandLit-1986
LongCTCL-1975
OxEng-1985
PengEng-1971
PrEncyPP-1974

Abercrombie, Lascelles 1881-1938
Baring, Maurice 1874-1945
Bennett, (Enoch) Arnold 1867-1931
Blunden, Edmund 1896-1974
Bottomley, Gordon 1874-1948
Brooke, Rupert 1887-1915
Conrad, Joseph 1857-1924
Coward, Noel 1899-1973
Davies, W(illiam) H(enry) 1871-1940
De la Mare, Walter 1873-1956

Drinkwater, John 1882-1937
Eliot, T(homas) S(tearns) 1888-1965
Empson, William 1906-1984
Flecker, (Herman) James Elroy 1884-1915
Galsworthy, John 1867-1933
Gibson, Wilfred Wilson 1878-1962
Graves, Robert 1895-1985
Greene, (Henry) Graham 1904-
Hodgson, Ralph 1871-1962
Housman, A(lfred) E(dward) 1859-1936
Hulme, T(homas) E(rnest) 1883-1917
Huxley, Aldous 1894-1963
Jones, Henry Arthur 1851-1929
Joyce, James 1882-1941
Lawrence, D(avid) H(erbert) 1885-1930
Lewis, Percy Wyndham 1884(?)-1957
Marsh, Edward 1872-1953
Masefield, John 1878-1967
Maugham, W(illiam) Somerset 1874-1965
Monro, Harold 1879-1932
Owen, Wilfred 1893-1918
Pinero, Arthur Wing 1855-1934
Read, Herbert 1893-1968
Richards, I(vor) A(rmstrong) 1893-1979
Richardson, Dorothy 1873-1957
Rosenberg, Isaac 1890-1918
Sassoon, Siegfried 1886-1967
Shaw, George Bernard 1856-1950
Squire, J(ohn) C(ollings) 1884-1958
Stephens, James 1882(?)-1950
Thomas, Edward 1878-1917
Turner, Walter James Redfern 1889-1946
Waugh, Evelyn 1903-1966

Wells, H(erbert) G(eorge) 1866-
    1946
Woolf, Virginia 1882-1941
Yeats, William Butler 1865-1939
Young, Andrew 1885-1971

**Gîndirea (also Gândirea) (Romania,
1920s)**
    ClDMEuL-1980
    EncWL-1981
    GdMWL-1985

    Arghezi, Tudor 1880-1967
    Blaga, Lucian 1895-1961
    Petrescu, Cezar 1892-1961
    Philippide, Alexandru 1900-
        1979
    Pillat, Ion 1891-1945
    Stancu, Zaharia 1902-1974
    Voiculescu, Vasile 1884-1963

**Golden Horn/*Zlatorog* Group
(Bulgaria, 1920s-1944)**
    ClDMEuL-1980
    EncWL-1981

    Bagryana, Elisaveta 1893-
    Raychev, Georgi 1882-1947
    Vasilev, Vladimir 1883-1963
    Yovkov, Yordan 1880-1937

**Great Game Group/*Le Grand Jeu*
(France, 1930s)**
    EncWL-1981

    Daumal, René 1908-1944
    Gilbert-Lecomte, Roger 1907-
        1943
    Roland de Renéville, André
        1903-1962
    Sima, Joseph 1891-1971
    Vailland, Roger 1907-1965

Group, The (England, 1955-1965)
    CamGLE-1988

HarDMT-1988
OxEng-1985

Adcock, Fleur 1934-
Brownjohn, Alan 1931-
Hobsbaum, Philip 1932-
Hughes, Ted 1930-
Johnson, B.S. 1933-1973
Lucie-Smith, Edward 1933-
MacBeth, George 1932-
Porter, Peter 1929-
Redgrove, Peter 1932-

Group 42 (Czechoslovakia, 1940s)
    ClDMEuL-1980

    Hauková, Jirina 1919-
    Kainer, Josef 1917-1972
    Mikulásek, Oldrich 1910-

**Group 47/Gruppe 47 (Germany,
1947-1967)**
    BenReEncy-1987
    ClDMEuL-1980
    EncWL-1981
    GdMWL-1985
    HarDMT-1988
    McGWD-1984
    OxGer-1986
    PengEur-1969

    Aichinger, Ilse 1921-
    Andersch, Alfred 1914-1980
    Bachmann, Ingeborg 1926-1973
    Bobrowski, Johannes 1917-1956
    Böll, Heinrich 1917-1985
    Celan, Paul 1920-1970
    Eich, Günter 1907-1972
    Enzenberger, Hans Magnus
        1929-
    Fried, Erich 1921-1988
    Grass, Günter 1927-
    Hildesheimer, Wolfgang 1916-
    Höllerer, Walter 1922-
    Jens, Walter 1923-

Johnson, Uwe 1934-1984
Kolbenhoff, Walter 1908-
Lenz, Siegfried 1926-
Mayer, Hans 1907-
Richter, Hans Werner 1908-
Schallück, Paul 1922-1976
Schnurre, Wolfdietrich 1920-
Walser, Martin 1927-
Weyrauch, Wolfgang 1907-1980
Wohmann, Gabriele 1932-

Group 61/Gruppe 61 (Germany, 1960s)
CIDMEuL-1980
OxGer-1986

Grün, Max von der 1926-
Hüser, Fritz 1908-1979
Körner, Wolfgang n.d.
Reding, Josef 1929-
Wallraff, Günter 1942-

Group 63/Gruppo 63 (Italy, 1960s)
CIDMEuL-1980
EncWL-1981
GdMWL-1985

Anceschi, Luciano 1911-
Arbasino, Alberto 1930-
Balestrini, Nanni 1935-
Barilli, Renato 1935-
Buttitta, Piero A. 1931-
Colombo, Furio 1931-
Del Buono, Oreste 1923-
Eco, Umberto 1932-
Giuliani, Alfredo 1924-
Guglielmi, Angelo 1924-
La Capria, Raffaele 1922-
Malerba, Luigi 1927-
Manganelli, Giorgio 1922-
Pagliarini, Elio 1927-
Porta, Antonio 1935-
Sanguineti, Edoardo 1930-

Group of Guayaquil/Grupo de Guayaquil (Ecuador, 1930s)
EncWL-1981
GdMWL-1985
OxSpan-1978

Aguilera Malta, Demetrio 1909-
Cuadra, José de la 1903-1941
Gallegos Lara, Joaquín 1911-1947
Gilbert, Enrique Gil 1912-
Pareja Diezcanseco, Alfredo 1908-

Group Theater (England, 1933-1953)
BenReEncy-1987
HarDMT-1988
OxThe-1983

Auden, W(ystan) H(ugh) 1907-1973
Eliot, T(homas) S(tearns) 1888-1965
Isherwood, Christopher 1904-1986
Spender, Stephen 1909-

Group Theater (United States, 1931-1941)
BenReEncy-1987
CamGLE-1988
HandLit-1986
HarDMT-1988
McGWD-1984
OxAm-1983
OxAmThe-1984
OxThe-1983
PengAm-1971

Anderson, Maxwell 1888-1959
Ardrey, Robert 1908-1980
Blitzstein, Marc 1905-1964
Carnovsky, Morris 1897-
Clurman, Harold 1901-1980

Crawford, Cheryl 1902-1986
Green, Paul Eliot 1894-1981
Kazan, Elia 1909-
Kingsley, Sidney 1906-
Lawson, John Howard 1894-1977
Levy, Melvin n.d.
Odets, Clifford 1906-1963
O'Neill, Eugene 1888-1953
Saroyan, William 1908-1981
Shaw, Irwin 1913-1984
Strasberg, Lee 1901-1982
Weill, Kurt 1900-1950

Grupo Acento (Guatemala, 1940s)
OxSpan-1978

González, Otto-Raúl 1921-
Illescas, Carlos n.d.
Leiva, Raúl 1916-
Toledo, Enrique Juárez

Grupo Elan (Ecuador, 1930s)
OxSpan-1978

Arias, Augusto Sacotto n.d.
Carrión, Alejandro 1915-

Cuesta y Cuesta, Alfonso 1912-
Fernández, Jorge 1912-
Lasso, Ignacio n.d.
Llerena, José Alfredo n.d.
Vacas, Humberto n.d.

Grupo Espadaña (Spain, 1940s)
OxSpan-1978

Crémer, Victoriano 1908-
Lama, Antonio G. de n.d.
Luis, Leopoldo de 1918-
Mügica Celaya, Rafael 1911-
Nora, Eugenio G. de 1923-
Otero, Blas de 1916-
Pérez Valiente, Salvador n.d.

Grupo Tzántzico (Ecuador, 1960s)
OxSpan-1978

Corral, Simón n.d.
Estrella, Ulises 1940-
Larrea, Rafael n.d.
Murriagui, Alfonso 1930-
Ordóñez, Antonio n.d.

H

Harlem Renaissance (United States, 1920s)

BenReEncy-1987
CamGLE-1988
EncWL-1981
HandLit-1986
OxAm-1983
PrEncyPP-1974

Bennett, Gwendolyn B. 1902-1981
Bontemps, Arna 1902-1973
Brown, Sterling A. 1901-1989
Cullen, Countee 1903-1946
Cuney, Waring 1906-1976
DuBois, W.E.B. 1868-1963
Fauset, Jessie Redmon 1884(?)-1961
Fisher, Rudolph 1897-1934
Horne, Frank 1899-1974
Hughes, (James) Langston 1902-1967
Hurston, Zora Neale 1903-1960
Johnson, Georgia Douglas 1886-1966
Johnson, Helene 1907-
Johnson, James Weldon 1871-1938
Larsen, Nella 1891-1964
Locke, Alain 1886-1954
McKay, Claude 1889-1948
Schuyler, George 1895-1977
Spencer, Anne 1882-1975
Thurman, Wallace 1902-1934
Toomer, Jean 1894-1967
Walrond, Eric 1898-1966

White, Walter 1893-1955

Heimatkunst (Germany, 1900s-1930s)

GdMWL-1985
OxGer-1986

Anzengruber, Ludwig 1839-1889
Bartels, Adolf 1862-1945
Bartsch, Rudolf Hans 1873-1952
Blunck, Hans Friedrich 1888-1961
Ernst, Otto 1862-1926
Ertl, Emil 1860-1935
Federer, Heinrich 1866-1928
Frenssen, Gustav 1863-1945
Ganghofer, Ludwig 1855-1920
Griese, Friedrich 1890-1975
Hansjakob, Heinrich 1837-1916
Heer, Jakob Christoph 1859-1925
Holzamer, W. n.d.
Jensen, Wilhelm 1837-1911
Kröger, T. 1844-1918
Lienhard, Friedrich 1865-1929
Lobsien, Wilhelm 1872-1947
Löns, Hermann 1866-1914
Perkonig, Josef Friedrich 1890-1959
Polenz, Wilhelm von 1861-1903
Rosegger, Peter 1843-1918
Schäfer, Wilhelm 1868-1952
Schönherr, Karl 1867-1943
Schroer, G. n.d.
Sohnrey, H. 1859-1948

Stavenhagen, Fritz 1876-1906
Stehr, Hermann 1864-1940
Strauss und Torney, Lulu von
   1873-1956
Viebig, Clara 1860-1952
Voight-Diederichs, Helene
   1875-1961
Zacchi, Ferdinand 1884-1966
Zahn, Ernst 1867-1952

Heretica Poets (Denmark, 1948-1953)

ClDMEuL-1980
EncWL-1981
GdMWL-1985
PrEncyPP-1974

Bjornvig, Thorkild 1918-
Jæger, Frank 1926-1977
Knudsen, Erik 1922-
Sarvig, Ole 1921-1981
Wivel, Ole 1921-

Hermeticism (Italy, 1915-1940s)

BenReEncy-1987
ClDMEuL-1980
DCLT-1979
EncWL-1981
HarDMT-1988
OxEng-1985
PengEur-1969
PrEncyPP-1974

Betocchi, Carlo 1899-
Bigongiari, Piero 1914-
Bo, Carlo 1911-
Campana, Dino 1885-1932
De Robertis, Giuseppe 1888-
   1963
Flora, Francesco 1891-1962
Gatto, Alfonso 1909-1976
Luzi, Mario 1914-
Macrì, Oreste 1913-
Montale, Eugenio 1896-1981
Onofri, Arturo 1885-1928

Parronchi, Alessandro 1914-
Quasímodo, Salvatore 1901-
   1968
Ramat, Silvio 1939-
Sereni, Vittorio 1913-1983
Sinisgalli, Leonardo 1908-1981
Ungaretti, Giuseppe 1888-1970
Zanzotto, Andrea 1921-

Het Fonteintje (Belgium, 1920s)

ClDMEuL-1980

Herreman, Raymond 1896-
Ridder, Alfons de n.d.

Hexagone Group (Canada, 1953-1963)

OxCan-1983

Giguère, Roland 1929-
Hénault, Gilles 1920-
Lapointe, Paul-Marie 1929-
Marchand, Olivier n.d.
Miron, Gaston 1928-
Ouellette, Fernand 1930-
Pilon, Jean-Guy 1930-

Hid Group (Yugoslavia, 1930s)

EncWL-1981

Gál, Laszló 1902-
Laták, István 1910-
Sinkó, Ervin 1898-
Thurzó, Lajos 1915-1950

Hototogisu Poets (Japan, 1900s-1920s)

DOrLit-1974
EncWL-1981

Iida Dakotsu 1885-1962
Ishida Hakyo 1913-1969
Kato Shuson 1905-
Kawahigashi Hekigodo 1873-
   1937

Masaoka Shiki 1867-1902
Mizuhara Shuoshi 1892-1981
Murakami Kijo 1865-1938
Nakamura Kusatao 1901-
Takahama Kyoshi 1874-1959
Yamaguchi Seishi 1901-

Hu-Feng Group (China, 1940s-1950s)
DOrLit-1974

Hu Feng 1903-

Humanisme (France, 1900s)
DCLT-1979
EncWL-1981
OxFr-1959

Gregh, Fernand 1873-1960

I

Imaginists (Russia, 1920s)

BenReEncy-1987
ClDMEuL-1980
EncWL-1981
GdMWL-1985

Esenin, Sergei Aleksandrovich 1895-1925
Klyuev, Nikolai 1887-1937(?)
Shershenevich, Vadim 1893-1942

Imagism (England and United States, 1912-1917)

BenReEncy-1987
CamGLE-1988
DCLT-1979
EncWL-1981
GdMWL-1985
HandLit-1986
HarDMT-1988
LongCTCL-1975
OxAm-1983
OxEng-1985
PengAm-1971
PengEng-1971
PrEncyPP-1974
RCom-1973

Aldington Richard 1892-1962
Cannell, Skipwith 1887-1957
Cournos, John 1881-1966
Fletcher, John Gould 1886-1950
Flint, Frank Stuart 1885-1960
Ford, Ford Madox 1873-1939

H.D. (Hilda Doolittle) 1886-1961
Hulme, T(homas) E(rnest) 1883-1917
Joyce, James 1882-1941
Lawrence, D(avid) H(erbert) 1885-1930
Lowell, Amy 1874-1925
Pound, Ezra 1885-1972
Upward, Allen 1863-1926
Williams, William Carlos 1883-1963
Wylie, Elinor 1885-1928

Impressionism (Germany, 1880s-1920s)

BenReEncy-1987
OxGer-1986
PrEncyPP-1974

Dauthendey, Max 1867-1918
Dehmel, Richard 1863-1920
Falke, Gustav 1853-1916
Fontane, Theodor 1819-1898
Hauptmann, Gerhart 1862-1946
Hofmannsthal, Hugo von 1874-1929
Liliencron, Detlev von 1844-1909
Mann, Thomas 1875-1955
Rilke, Rainer Maria 1875-1926
Schlaf, Johannes 1862-1941
Schnitzler, Arthur 1862-1931
Storm, Theodor 1817-1888

Inklings, The (England, 1940s)
EncWL-1981
OxEng-1985

Lewis, C.S. 1898-1963
Tolkien, J(ohn) R(onald) R(euel)
  1892-1973
Williams, Charles 1886-1945

**I-Novel/Watakushi-shosetsu
(Japan, 1910s-1920s)**
DOrLit-1974
EncWL-1981

Dazai Osamu 1909-1948
Ibuse Masuji 1898-
Kasai Zenzo 1887-1928
Mushanokoji Saneatsu 1885-
  1976
Shiga Naoya 1881-1971
Tayama Katai 1872-1930

Intimismo (Italy, 1900s)
ClDMEuL-1980

Bracco, Roberto 1862-1943
Giacosa, Giuseppe 1847-1906

**Introspectivists Movement/Inzikh
(United States, 1920s-1930s)**
ClDMEuL-1980
EncWL-1981
GdMWL-1985
PrEncyPP-1974

Glanz-Leyeles, Aaron 1889-
  1966
Glatstein, Jacob 1896-1971
Minkoff, Nokhum Borekh 1898-
  1958

**Irish Literary Theater (Ireland, 1899-
1903)**
CEnMWL-1963
HandLit-1986

LongCTCL-1975
McGWD-1984
OxEng-1985
OxThe-1983

Dunsany, Lord Edward John
  Moreton Drax Plunkett 1878-
  1957
Gregory, Lady Isabella Augusta
  1852-1932
Hyde, Douglas 1911-
Martyn, Edward 1859-1923
Milligan, Alice 1866-1953
Moore, George 1852-1933
O'Casey, Sean 1880-1964
Synge, John Millington 1871-
  1909
Yeats, William Butler 1965-1939

See also **Abbey Theater, Irish
Renaissance**

**Irish Renaissance [also known as
Celtic Renaissance, Celtic
Revival, Celtic Twilight, Irish
Literary Movement, Irish Literary
Revival], (Ireland, 1890s-1920s)**
BenReEncy-1987
CamGLE-1988
DCLT-1979
EncWL-1981
GdMWL-1985
HandLit-1986
LongCTCL-1975
OxEng-1985
PrEncyPP-1974
RCom-1973

Æ (pseud. of George William
  Russell) 1867-1935
Allgood, Sarah 1883-1950
Behan, Brendan 1923-1964
Carroll, Paul Vincent 1900-1968
Colum, Padraic 1881-1972

Duffy, Charles Gavan 1816-
  1903
Dunsany, Lord Edward John
  Moreton Drax Plunkett 1878-
  1957
Fay, Frank J. 1870-1931
Fay, William George 1872-1947
Ferguson, Samuel 1810-1886
Gogarty, Oliver St. John 1878-
  1957
Gregory, Isabella Augusta 1852-
  1932
Higgins, Frederick Robert 1896-
  1941
Hyde, Douglas 1911-
Johnston, Denis 1901-1984
Joyce, James 1882-1941

Martyn, Edward 1859-1923
Moore, George 1852-1933
O'Casey, Sean 1880-1964
O'Connor, Frank 1903-1966
O'Faoláin, Sean 1900-
O'Flaherty, Liam 1896-1984
O'Grady, Standish 1846-1928
Robinson, Lennox 1886-1958
Shaw, George Bernard 1856-
  1950
Stephens, James 1882(?)-1950
Synge, John Millington 1871-
  1909
Yeats, William Butler 1865-1939

See also **Abbey Theater, Irish
  Literary Theater**

J

Jazz Age (United States, 1920s)
BenReEncy-1987
EncWL-1981
GdMWL-1985
HarDMT-1988
LongCTCL-1975
OxAm-1983
RCom-1973

Baker, Dorothy 1907-1968
Dos Passos, John 1896-1970
Farrell, James T. 1904-1979
Fitzgerald, F. Scott 1896-1940
Held, John 1889-1958
Lindsay, Vachel 1879-1931
Marks, Percy 1891-1956

Jazz Poetry (England, 1950s-1980s)
DCLT-1979
HarDMT-1988
OxEng-1985

Brown, Pete 1940-
Fisher, Roy 1930-
Hawkins, Spike 1942-
Horovitz, Michael 1935-
Logue, Christopher 1926-

Jazz Poetry (United States, 1920s-1950s)
DCLT-1979
HarDMT-1988
OxEng-1985

Baraka, Imamu Amiri 1934-
Hughes, Langston 1902-1967

Joans, Ted 1928-
Lindsay, Vachel 1879-1931
Patchen, Kenneth 1911-1972
Rexroth, Kenneth 1905-1982

Jindyworobak Movement (Australia, 1938-1950s)
BenReEncy-1987
GdMWL-1985
PrEncyPP-1974

Ingamells, Rex 1913-1955

Journal de Poètes (Belgium, 1920s-1940s)
ClDMEuL-1980

Bourgeois, Pierre n.d.
Carême, Maurice 1899-1978
Haulot, Arthur n.d.
Verhesen, Fernand 1913-

Jugendstil (Germany, 1890s-1900s)
ClDMEuL-1980
DCLT-1979
OxGer-1986
PrEncyPP-1974

Beer-Hofmann, Richard 1866-1945
Dauthendey, Max 1867-1918
Dehmel, Richard 1863-1920
Flaischlen, Cäsar 1864-1920
George, Stefan 1868-1933

Hirth, George n.d.
Hofmannsthal, Hugo von 1874-
    1929
Kokoschka, Oskar 1886-1980
Rilke, Rainer Maria 1875-1926
Schaukal, Richard von 1874-
    1942

Jung, Carl 1875-1961 (Swiss)
    BenReEncy-1987
    CasWL-1973
    EncWL-1981
    OxEng-1985
    OxGer-1986
    RCom-1973

K

Kalangya **Group (Yugoslavia, 1930s)**
EncWL-1981

Csuka, Zoltán 1901-
Debreczeni, József 1905-
Dudás, Kálmán 1912-
Herceg, János 1909-
Szenteleky, Kornél 1893-1933

Kiev Group (Ukraine, 1920s)
ClDMEuL-1980
GdMWL-1985

Bergelson, David 1884-1952
Hofstein, David 1889-1952
Kvitko, Leib 1890-1952
Markish, Peretz 1895-1952
Nister, Der 1884-1950

Kitchen Sink Drama (England, 1950s)
DCLT-1979
HarDMT-1988
LongCTCL-1975
OxEng-1985
OxThe-1983

Delaney, Shelagh 1939-
Osborne, John 1929-
Owen, Alun 1926-
Tynan, Kenneth 1927-1980
Wesker, Arnold 1932-

Komma **Group (Belgium, 1965-1969)**
ClDMEuL-1980

Gysen, Rene n.d.
Roggeman, Willy 1934-
Wevergergh, Julien n.d.
Wispeleare, Paul de 1928-

Kontynenty **Group (Polish exiles in England, 1960s)**
ClDMEuL-1980

Busza, Andrzej 1938-
Czaykowski, Bogdan 1932-
Czerniawski, Adam 1934-
Darowski, Jan 1926-
Lawrynowicz, Zygmunt 1925-
Sito, Jerzy S. n.d.
Smieja, Florian 1925-
Taborski, Boleslaw 1927-

L

League of Left-Wing Writers (China, 1930s)
EncWL-1981

Lu Hsün 1881-1936

LEF (Left Front of Art) (Russia, 1920s)
ClDMEuL-1980

Aseyev, Nikolay 1889-1963
Brik, Osip 1888-1945
Eikhenbaum, Boris 1886-1959
Mayakovsky, Vladimir 1893-1930
Rodchenko, Alexander 1891-1956
Shklovsky, Victor Borisovich 1893-1984
Tretyakov, Sergey Mikhailovich 1892-1939

Lettrism (France, 1940s)
GdMWL-1985
HarDMT-1988
OxFr-1959

Isou, Isidore 1925-
Lemaître, Maurice n.d.

Link/Lanka (Ukraine, 1920s)
ClDMEuL-1980
GdMWL-1985

Kosynka, Hryhoriy 1899-1934

Pidmohylny, Valeriyan 1901-1941
Pluzhnyk, Yevhen 1898-1936

Literary Research Association (China, 1920s)
EncWL-1981

Chou Tso-jen 1885-1966
Mao Tun 1896-1981
Yeh Sheng-t'ao 1894-

Literary School of Montreal/École Littéraire de Montreal (Canada, 1895-1925)
EncWL-1981
OxCan-1983
PrEncyPP-1974

Charbonneau, Jean 1875-1960
Fréchette, Louis 1839-1908
Gill, Charles 1871-1918
Grignon, Claude-Henri 1894-1976
Laberge, Albert 1877-1960
Loranger, Jean-Aubert 1896-1942
Lozeau, Albert 1878-1924
Nelligan, Émile 1879-1941
Panneton, Philippe 1895-1960

Literature and Industry (Italy, 1960s)
EncWL-1981

Ottieri, Ottiero 1924-

Volponi, Paolo 1924-

Little Theater Movement

> *See* **Freie Bühne, Germany; Group Theater, United States; Irish Literary Theater, Ireland; Provincetown Players, Theater Guild, United States; Théâtre Libre, France; Washington Square Players, United States.**

Liverpool Poets (England, 1960s)
> *CamGLE-1988*
> *DCLT-1979*
> *OxEng-1985*

> Henri, Adrian 1932-
> McGough, Roger 1937-
> Patten, Brian 1946-

Living Theater (United States, 1950s-1960s)
> *HarDMT-1988*
> *McGWD-1984*
> *OxAmThe-1984*
> *OxThe-1983*
> *PengAm-1971*

> Beck, Julian 1925-1985
> Brown, Kenneth 1936-
> Chaiken, Joseph 1935-
> Gelber, Jack 1932-
> MacLow, Jackson 1922-
> Malina, Judith 1926-

Loafers/Dagdrivarna (Finland, 1900s)
> *CIDMEuL-1980*

> Hemmer, Jarl 1893-1944
> Schildt, Runar 1888-1925

Local Color School (Canada, 1900s-1920s)
> *OxCan-1983*

> Barr, Robert 1850-1912
> Cody, Hiram 1872-1948
> Duncan, Norman 1871-1916
> Duncan, Sara Jeanette 1861-1922
> Fraser, William Alexander 1857-1933
> Gordon, Charles W. 1860-1937
> Grainger, Martin Allerdale 1874-1941
> Grenfell, Wilfred 1865-1940
> Jones, Alice 1853-1933
> King, Basil 1859-1929
> Knowles, Robert E. 1868-1946
> Leacock, Stephen 1869-1944
> McClung, Nellie 1873-1951
> MacGregor, Mary Esther 1876-1961
> Montgomery, Lucy Maud 1874-1942
> Niven, Frederick 1878-1944
> Parker, Gilbert 1862-1932
> Roberts, Charles G.D. 1860-1943
> Roberts, Theodore Goodridge 1877-1953
> Service, Robert 1874-1958
> Stead, Robert 1880-1959
> Stringer, Arthur 1874-1950

Local Color School (United States, 1870s-1900s)
> *DCLT-1979*
> *EncWL-1981*
> *HandLit-1986*
> *OxAm-1983*

> Bunner, H.C. 1855-1896
> Cable, George Washington 1844-1925

Chopin, Kate 1851-1904
Cooke, Rose Terry 1827-1892
Davis, Richard Harding 1864-1916
Eggleston, Edward 1837-1902
Eggleston, George Cary 1839-1911
Fox, John 1862(?)-1919
Freeman, Mary Wilkins 1852-1930
Gale, Zona 1874-1938
Garland, (Hannibal) Hamlin 1860-1940
Harris, Joel Chandler 1848-1908
Harte, (Francis) Bret 1836(?)-1902
Hay, John 1838-1905
Hearn, Lafcadio 1850-1904
Henry, O. 1862-1910
Howe, E(dgar) W(atson) 1853-1937
Jewett, Sarah Orne 1849-1909
Matthews, Brander 1852-1929
Miller, Joachin 1837-1913
Murfree, Mary Noailles 1850-1922
Page, Thomas Nelson 1853-1922
Riley, James Whitcomb 1849-1916
Smith, Francis Hopkinson 1838-1915

Stowe, Harriet Beecher 1811-1896
Twain, Mark 1835-1910

Logos Group (Ukraine, 1930s)
EncWL-1981

Koroleva, Natalena 1889-1966
Luznytsky, Hryhory 1903-

Lost Generation (American writers in France, 1920s)
BenReEncy-1987
EncWL-1981
HandLit-1986
LongCTCL-1975
OxAm-1983
PengAm-1971
RCom-1973

Anderson, Sherwood 1876-1941
Bromfield, Louis 1896-1956
Cowley, Malcolm 1898-1989
Crane, (Harold) Hart 1899-1932
Cummings, E.E. 1894-1962
Dos Passos, John 1896-1970
Fitzgerald, F. Scott 1896-1940
Hemingway, Ernest 1899-1961
MacLeish, Archibald 1892-1982
Pound, Ezra 1885-1972
Ray, Man 1890-1976
Stein, Gertrude 1874-1946

M

Magic Realism (Latin America, 1950s-present)
BenReEncy-1987
CamGLE-1988
EncWL-1981
GdMWL-1985
HarDMT-1988
OxEng-1985

Aguilera Malta, Demetrio 1909-
Alexis, Jacques-Stéphen 1922-1961
Asturias, Miguel Ángel 1899-1974
Bontempelli, Massimo 1878-1960
Borges, Jorge Luis 1899-1986
Carpentier, Alejo 1904-1980
Carter, Angela 1940-
Cortázar, Julio 1914-1984
Daisne, Johan 1912-1978
Flores, Ángel 1900-
Fuentes, Carlos 1929-
García Márquez, Gabriel 1928-
Kundera, Milan 1929-
Lampo, Hubert 1920-
Rulfo, Juan 1918-1986
Rushdie, Salman 1947-
Tennant, Emma 1937-
Uslar Pietri, Anturo 1905-
Vargas Llosa, Mario 1936-

Manzanillo Group (Cuba, 1920s)
CaribWr-1979

Navarro Luna, Manuel 1894-

Rodríguez, Luis Felipe 1888-1947

Marx, (Heinrich) Karl 1818-1883 (German)
BenReEncy-1987
CasWL-1973
HarDMT-1988
LongCTCL-1975
OxEng-1985
OxFr-1959
OxGer-1986
RCom-1973

Marxist Criticism (Europe, England, United States, 1920s-1970s)
CamGLE-1988
EncWL-1981
OxEng-1985
PengEur-1969

Althusser, Louis 1918-
Benjamin, Walter 1892-1940
Calverton, Victor Francis 1900-1940
Caudwell, Christopher 1907-1937
Eagleton, Terry 1943-
Garaudy, Roger 1913-
Goldmann, Lucien 1913-1970
Gramsci, Antonio 1891-1937
Hicks, Granville 1901-1982
Krleza, Miroslav 1893-
Lukács, Georg 1885-1971
Machery, Pierre n.d.
Markiewicz, Henryk 1922-

Smith, Bernard 1906-
Václavek, Bedrich 1897-1943
Volpe, Galvano della 1895-1968
Williams, Raymond 1921-

Matinée Poétique (Japan, 1940s-1970s)
DOrLit-1974

Fukanga Takehiko 1918-1979
Kato Shuichi 1919-
Nakamura Shin'ichiro 1918-

May Fourth Movement/Wu-ssu yün-tung (China, 1916-1921)
DOrLit-1974
GdMWL-1985

Ch'en Tu-hsiu 1879-1942
Hu Shih 1891-1962
Lu Hsün 1881-1936
Ts'ai Yüan-p'ei n.d.

May Group/Kveten (Czechoslovakia, 1950s-1960s)
CIDMEuL-1980
McGWD-1984

Holub, Miroslav 1923-
Sotola, Jiri 1924-

Mbari Club (Nigeria, 1960s)
EncWL-1981

Achebe, Chinua 1930-
Beier, Ulli 1922-
Lapido, Duro 1931-1978

Mehian **Group (Armenia, 1910s)**
EncWL-1981

Dadourian, Aharon 1877-1965
Oshagan, Hagop 1883-1948
Varoujan, Daniel 1884-1915
Zarian, Gosdan 1885-1969

Merz (Germany, 1920s)
HarDMT-1988

Schwitters, Kurt 1887-1948

Metarealism (Israel, 1960s)
CIDMEuL-1980

Appelfeld, Aharon 1932-
Eliraz, Israel 1936-
Orpaz, Yitzhak 1923-
Shahar, David 1926-
Tammuz, Binyamin 1919-
Yehoshua, Avraham B. 1936-

Mezzanine of Poetry (Russia, 1910s)
CIDMEuL-1980
EncWL-1981

Shershenevich, Vadim 1893-1942

Minsk Group (Russia, 1930s)
CIDMEuL-1980

Axelrod, Selig 1904-1941
Charik, Izzy 1898-1937
Erik, Max 1898-1937
Kulbak, Moshe 1896-1940

Misul **Group (Bulgaria, 1892-1907)**
CIDMEuL-1980
EncWL-1981

Krustev, Krustyo 1866-1919
Slaveykov, Pencho 1866-1912
Todorov, Petko 1879-1916
Yavorov, Peyo 1878-1914

Moderna **(Croatia, Serbia, Slovenia [later Yugoslavia], 1895-1918)**
CIDMEuL-1980
McGWD-1984

Begovic, Milan 1876-1948

Brlic-Mazuranic, Ivana 1874-
1938
Cankar, Ivan 1875-1918
Cankar, Izidor 1889-1957
Cihlar-Nehajev, Milutin 1880-
1931
Domjanic, Dragutin 1875-1933
Ducic, Jovan 1871-1943
Galovic, Fran 1887-1914
Kette, Dragotin 1876-1899
Kosor, Josip 1879-1961
Kranjcevic, Silvije Strahimir
1865-1908
Marjanovic, Milan 1879-1955
Masaryk, Tomás 1850-1937
Matos, Gustav 1873-1914
Murn-Aleksandrov, Josip 1879-
1901
Nazor, Vladimir 1876-1949
Ogrizovic, Milan 1877-1923
Rakic, Milan 1876-1938
Santic, Aleksa 1868-1924
Simunovic, Dinko 1893-1933
Vidric, Vladimir 1875-1909
Vodnik, Branko 1879-1926
Vojnovic, Ivo 1857-1929
Zupancic, Oton 1878-1949

Modernism (Brazil, 1920s-1940s)
EncWL-1981
GdMWL-1985
PengAm-1971
PrEncyPP-1974

Almeida, Guilherme de 1890-
1969
Almeida, José Américo de 1887-
Amado, Jorge 1912-
Andrade, Mário de 1893-1945
Andrade, Oswald de 1890-1954
Aranha, José da Graça 1868-
1931
Bandeira, Manuel 1886-1968
Bopp, Raul 1898-

Buarque de Holanda, Sérgio
1902-1982
Carvalho, Ronald de 1893-1935
Cunha, Euclides da 1866-1909
Drummond de Andrade, Carlos
1902-1987
Freyre, Gilberto 1900-1987
Lima, Jorge de 1895-1953
Lobato, José Monteiro 1882-
1948
Meireles, Cecília 1901-1964
Mendes, Murilo 1902-
Morais, Vinícius de 1913-1980
Neto, Joao Cabral de Melo 1920-

Picchia, Menotti del 1892-
Ramos, Graciliano 1892-1953
Rêgo, José Lins do 1901-1957
Ricardo, Cassiano 1895-1974
Rosa, Joao Guimaraes 1908-
1967
Salgado, Plínio 1901-1975
Schmidt, Augusto Frederico
1906-
Silveira, Tasso da 1895-1968
Torres, Alberto 1865-1917

**Modernism (Czechoslovakia, 1900s-
1910s)**
CIDMEuL-1980
EncWL-1981

Jesensky, Janko 1874-1945
Krasko, Ivan 1876-1958
Rázus, Martin 1888-1937
Roy, Vladimír 1885-1935
Votruba, Frantisek 1880-1953

Modernism (Denmark, 1950s-1960s)
CIDMEuL-1980
EncWL-1981

Ornsbo, Jess 1932-
Rifbjerg, Klaus 1931-
Seeberg, Peter 1925-

Sorensen, Villy 1929-

Modernism (England, 1900s-1930s)
CamGLE-1988
DCLT-1979
EncWL-1981
HandLit-1986
HarDMT-1988
OxEng-1985
RCom-1973

Auden, W(ystan) H(ugh) 1907-
1973
Bennett, (Enoch) Arnold 1867-
1931
Bridges, Robert 1844-1930
Cary, (Arthur) Joyce 1888-1957
Connolly, Cyril 1903-1974
Conrad, Joseph 1857-1924
Coward, Noel 1899-1973
Eliot, T(homas) S(tearns) 1888-
1965
Empson, William 1906-1984
Ford, Ford Madox 1873-1939
Forster, E(dward) M(organ)
1879-1970
Fry, Christopher 1907-
Galsworthy, John 1867-1933
Green, Henry 1905-1974
Greene, Graham 1904-
Hopkins, Gerard Manley 1844-
1889
Hulme, T(homas) E(rnest) 1883-
1917
Huxley, Aldous 1894-1963
Jones, Henry Arthur 1851-1929
Joyce, James 1882-1941
Lawrence, D(avid) H(erbert)
1885-1930
Leavis, F(rank) R(aymond)
1895-1978
Lewis, (Percy) Wyndham
1884(?)-1957
Mansfield, Katherine 1888-1923
Masefield, John 1878-1967

Maugham, W(illiam) Somerset
1874-1965
O'Brien, Flann 1911-1966
O'Casey, Sean 1880-1964
Owen, Wilfred 1893-1918
Pinero, Arthur Wing 1855-1934
Pound, Ezra 1885-1972
Rattigan, Terence 1911-1977
Read, Herbert 1893-1968
Richards, I(vor) A(rmstrong)
1893-1979
Richardson, Dorothy 1873-1957
Shaw, George Bernard 1856-
1950
Sitwell, Edith 1887-1964
Thomas, Dylan 1914-1953
Waugh, Evelyn 1903-1966
Wells, H(erbert) G(eorge) 1866-
1946
Woolf, Virginia 1882-1941
Yeats, William Butler 1865-1939

Modernism (Finland, 1940s-1950s)
ClDMEuL-1980

Anhava, Tuomas 1927-
Haavikko, Paavo 1931-
Heikkilä, Lasse 1925-1961
Holappa, Pentti 1927-
Juvonen, Helvi 1919-1959
Kivikkaho, Eila 1921-
Manner, Liisa 1921-
Meriluoto, Aila 1924-
Nummi, Lassi 1928-

Modernism (Iceland, 1940s-1950s)
EncWL-1981

Bragi, Einar 1921-
Daoason, Sigfús 1928-
Grímsson, Stefán Hördur 1919-
Óskar, Jón 1921-
Sigússon, Hannes 1922-
Steinarr, Stein 1908-1958
Vilhjálmsson, Thor 1925-

Modernism (Latvia, 1950s)
EncWL-1981

Sodums, Dzintars 1922-
Zarins, Guntis 1926-1965
Zeberins, Modris 1923-

Modernism (Russia, 1900s)
EncWL-1981

Babel, Isaak 1894-1941(?)
Fedin, Konstantin 1892-1977
Gladkov, Fyodor 1883-1958
Ivanov, Vsevolod 1895-1963
Lavrenyov, Boris Andreyevich
1894-1959
Olesha, Yury 1899-1960
Pilnyak, Boris 1894-1937(?)
Platonov, Andrey 1899-1951
Shklovsky, Viktor 1893-1984

Modernism (Sweden, 1920s)
EncWL-1981
PrEncyPP-1974

Blomberg, Erik 1894-1965
Ekelöf, Gunnar 1907-1968
Lagerkvist, Pär 1891-1974
Sjöberg, Birger 1885-1929

Modernism (Swedish-Finnish,
1920s)
ClDMEuL-1980
EncWL-1981
PrEncyPP-1974

Björling, Gunnar 1887-1960
Carpelan, Bo 1926-
Diktonius, Elmer 1896-1961
Eklund, R.R. 1894-1946
Enckell, Rabbe 1903-1974
Olsson, Hagar 1893-1978
Parland, Henry 1908-1930
Parland, Ralf 1914-
Schoultz, Solveig von 1907-

Sjöberg, Birger 1885-1929
Södergran, Edith 1892-1923

Modernism (Ukraine, 1905-1920)
EncWL-1981

Cheremshyna, Marko 1874-1927
Chernyavsky, Mykola 1867-
1937
Hrynevych, Katrya 1875-1947
Khotkevych, Hnat 1877-1942
Kotsyubynsky, Mykhaylo 1864-
1913
Martovych, Les (Olexandr)
1871-1916
Osmachka, Todos 1895-1962
Vasylchenko, Stepan 1878-1932
Yanovsky, Yury 1902-1954

Modernism (Yugoslavia, 1895-
1910s)
EncWL-1981
PrEncyPP-1974

Begovic, Milan 1876-1948
Cankar, Ivan 1876-1918
Cihlar-Nehajev, Milutin 1880-
1931
Domjanic, Dragutin 1875-1933
Marjanovic, Milan 1879-1955
Nazor, Vladimir 1876-1949
Vidric, Vladimir 1875-1909
Zupancic, Oton 1878-1949

Modernismo (Central & South
America, Mexico, Spain, 1880s-
1910s)
BenReEncy-1987
ClDMEuL-1980
DCLT-1979
EncWL-1981
GdMWL-1985
McGWD-1984
OxSpan-1978
PengAm-1971

PrEncyPP-1974

Arvelo Larriva, Alfredo 1883-1934
Azorín 1873-1969
Barba Jacob, Porfirio 1883-1942
Blanco-Fombona, Rufino 1874-1944
Casal, Julián del 1863-1893
Castro, Eugénio de 1869-1944
Darío, Rubén 1867-1916
Dávilia, Virgilio 1869-1943
Díaz, Leopoldo 1862-1947
Díaz Mirón, Salvador 1853-1928
Díaz Rodríguez, Manuel 1868-1927
Fierro, Humberto 1890-1929
Gómez Carillo, Enrique 1873-1927
González Martínez, Enrique 1871-1952
González Prada, Manuel 1848-1918
Gutiérrez Nájera, Manuel 1859-1895
Herrera y Reissig, Julio 1875-1910
Jaimes Freye, Ricardo 1868-1933
Jiménez, Juan Ramón 1881-1958
Lloréns Torres, Luis 1878-1944
Lugones, Leopoldo 1873-1938
Machado y Ruiz, Antonio 1875-1939
Machado y Ruiz, Manuel 1874-1947
Magallanes Moure, Manuel 1878-1924
Martí, José 1853-1895
Mesa y Rosales, Enrique de 1878-1929
Nervo, Amado 1870-1919
Palés Matos, Luis 1898-1959
Palma, Clemente 1875-1946
Pezoa Véliz, Carlos 1879-1908

Ribera-Chevremont, Evaristo 1896-
Rodó, José Enrique 1871-1917
Rueda Santos, Salvador 1857-1933
Santos Chocano, José 1875-1934
Silva, José Asunción 1865-1896
Silva, Medardo Angel 1898-1919
Tablada, José Juan 1871-1945
Unamuno y Jugo, Miguel de 1864-1936
Urbina, Luis G. 1868-1934
Valencia, Guillermo 1873-1943
Valle-Inclán, Ramón 1866-1936
Villaespesa, Francisco 1877-1936

Modernist School (China, 1950s)
EncWL-1981

Chi Hsien 1913-

Molla Nasreddin **Movement (Azerbaijan, 1906-1930)**
EncWL-1981

Mamedkulizade, Djalil 1866-1932
Sabir, Mirza Alekper 1862-1911

Montreal Movement (Canada, 1920s)
EncWL-1981
GdMWL-1985
OxCan-1983
PrEncyPP-1974

Finch, Robert 1900-
Kennedy, Leo 1907-
Klein, A(braham) M(oses) 1909-1972
Pratt, E(dwin) J(ohn) 1883-1964
Scott, F(rancis) R(eginald) 1899-1985

Smith, A(rthur) J(ames)
M(arshall) 1902-1980

Moscow Art Theater (Russia, 1898-1930s)
BenReEncy-1987
ClDMEuL-1980
EncWL-1981
GdMWL-1985
McGWD-1984
OxAmThe-1984
OxThe-1983

Afinogenov, Aleksandr
Nikolayevich 1904-1941
Bulgakov, Mikhail Afanaseyev
1891-1940
Chekhov, Anton 1860-1904
Gorky, Maxim 1868-1936
Ivanov, Vsevolod 1895-1963
Kachalov, Vasili Ivanovich 1875-1948
Knipper-Chekhova, Olga
Leonardovna 1870-1959
Lunacharsky, Anatoli 1875-1933
Meyerhold, Vsevolod
Emilyevich 1874-1940
Moskvin, Ivan Mikhailovich
1874-1946
Nemirovich-Danchenko,
Vladimir 1858-1943
Stanislovsky, Konstantin
Sergeivich 1863-1938
Tolstoy, Lev Nikolayevich 1828-1910
Yefremon, Oleg Nikolayevich
1927-

Movement, The (England, 1950s)
CamGLE-1988
DCLT-1979
EncWL-1981
GdMWL-1985
HarDMT-1988
OxEng-1985

Amis, Kingsley 1922-
Conquest, Robert 1917-
Davie, Donald 1922-
Enright, D.J. 1920-
Fuller, Roy 1912-
Gunn, Thom 1929-
Holloway, John 1920-
Jennings, Elizabeth 1926-
Larkin, Philip 1922-1985
Wain, John 1925-

See also **New Lines Poets**

**Movement, The/*De Beweging*
(Netherlands, 1905-1920s)**
ClDMEuL-1980

Bloem, Jakobus Cornelis 1887-1966
Eyck, Pieter Nicolaas van 1887-1954
Gossaert, Geerten n.d.
Haan, Jacob Israël de 1881-1924
Leeuw, Aart van der 1876-1932
Mouw, Johan Andreas dèr n.d.
Nijhoff, Martinus 1894-1953
Prins, Jan n.d.
Van Moerkerken, P.H. n.d.
Verway, Albert 1865-1937

**Movement of the Eighties/
Beweging van Tachtig
(Netherlands, 1880s-1900s)**
ClDMEuL-1980
EncWL-1981
GdMWL-1985
PrEncyPP-1974

Boutens, Pieter Cornelis 1870-1943
Deyssel, Lodewijk van 1864-1952
Eeden, Frederik Willem van
1860-1932
Gorter, Herman 1864-1927

Kloos, Willem 1859-1938
Paap, Willem 1856-1923
Perk, Jacques 1859-1881
Roland Holst van den Schalk,
   Henriette 1869-1952
Van der Goes, Frank n.d.
Verway, Albert 1865-1937

Muckrakers (United States, 1900s)
BenReEncy-1987
EncWL-1981
HandLit-1986
LongCTCL-1975
OxAm-1983

Adams, Samuel Hopkins 1871-
   1958
Baker, Ray Stannard 1870-1946
Churchill, Winston 1871-1947
Lawson, Thomas W. 1857-1925
McClure, Samuel Sidney 1857-
   1949

Phillips, David Graham 1867-
   1911
Sinclair, Upton 1878-1968
Steffens, Lincoln 1866-1936
Sullivan, Mark 1874-1952
Tarbell, Ida M. 1857-1944

My **Group (Ukrainian exiles in
Poland, 1930s)**
ClDMEuL-1980

Olkhivsky, Borys 1908-1944

Myojo **Group (Japan, 1900s)**
DOrLit-1974

Ishikawa Takuboku 1885-1912

N

Nadrealisti Movement (Czechoslovakia, 1930s-1940s)
ClDMEuL-1980
EncWL-1981

Buncak, Pavel 1915-
Fabry, Rudolf 1915-
Reisel, Vladimír 1919-
Záry, Stefan 1918-

National Literature Movement/ Millî Edebiyat (Turkey, 1910s)
ClDMEuL-1980

Müftüoglu, Ahmet Hikmet 1870-1927
Yurdakul, Mehmet Emin 1869-1944

National Neoromanticism (Finland, 1890s-1910s)
ClDMEuL-1980

Aho, Juhani 1861-1921
Kilpi, Volter 1874-1939
Lehtonen, Joel 1881-1934
Leino, Eino 1878-1926

Naturalism (Denmark, 1880s-1900s)
ClDMEuL-1980
EncWL-1981

Brandes, Edvard 1847-1931
Brandes, Georg 1842-1927
Drachmann, Holger 1846-1908
Gjellerup, Karl 1857-1919

Jacobsen, Jens Peter 1847-1885
Jæger, Frank 1926-1977
Wied, Gustav 1858-1914

Naturalism (England, 1880s-1900s)
BenReEncy-1987
CamGLE-1988
DCLT-1979
HandLit-1986
LongCTCL-1975
RCom-1973

Butler, Samuel 1835-1902
Eliot, George 1819-1880
Galsworthy, John 1867-1933
Gissing, George 1857-1903
Hardy, Thomas 1840-1928
Hunter, N.C. 1908-1971
Maugham, W(illiam) Somerset 1874-1965

Naturalism (France, 1880s-1900s)
BenReEncy-1987
CamGLE-1988
ClDMEuL-1980
DCLT-1979
EncWL-1981
HandLit-1986
HarDMT-1988
GdMWL-1985
LongCTCL-1975
McGWD-1984
OxAm-1983
OxAmThe-1984
OxEng-1985

OxFr-1959
OxGer-1986
OxThe-1983
PrEncyPP-1974
RCom-1973

Alexis, Paul 1847-1901
Antoine, André 1858-1934
Becque, Henri 1837-1899
Brieux, Eugène 1858-1932
Céard, Henry 1851-1924
Daudet, Alphonse 1840-1897
Flaubert, Gustave 1821-1880
Goncourt, Edmond de 1822-
   1896
Goncourt, Jules de 1830-1870
Huysmans, Joris Karl 1848-1907
Ibsen, Henrik 1828-1906
Maupassant, Guy de 1850-1893
Moore, George 1852-1933
Strindberg, August 1849-1912
Synge, John Millington 1871-
   1909
Taine, Hippolyte 1828-1893
Zola, Émile 1840-1902

Naturalism (Germany, 1880s-1900s)
BenReEncy-1987
CIDMEuL-1980
DCLT-1979
EncWL-1981
GdMWL-1985
OxEng-1985
OxGer-1986
OxThe-1983
PrEncyPP-1974

Adamus, Franz 1867-1948
Bleibtreu, Karl 1859-1928
Bohlau, Helene 1859-1940
Bölsche, Wilhelm 1861-1939
Brecht, Bertolt 1898-1956
Conrad, Michael Georg 1846-
   1927
Conradi, Hermann 1862-1890

Dehmel, Richard 1863-1920
Halbe, Max 1865-1944
Hart, Heinrich 1855-1906
Hart, Julius 1859-1930
Hartleben, Otto Erich 1864-1905
Hauptmann, Carl 1858-1921
Hauptmann, Gerhart 1862-1946
Hirschfeld, Georg 1873-1942
Holz, Arno 1863-1929
Kretzer, Max 1854-1941
Liliencron, Detlev von 1844-
   1909
Polenz, Wilhelm von 1861-1903
Schlaf, Johannes 1862-1941
Sudermann, Hermann 1857-
   1928
Viebig, Clara 1860-1952

Naturalism (Italy)

See **Verismo**

Naturalism/Shizenshugi (Japan, 1900s-1910s)
DOrLit-1974
EncWL-1981
GdMWL-1985

Iwano Homei 1873-1920
Kunikida Doppo 1871-1908
Masamune Hakucho 1879-1962
Shimazaki Toson 1872-1943
Tayama Katai 1872-1930
Tokuda Shusei 1871-1943

Naturalism (Korea, 1920s)
EncWL-1981

Hyon Chin-gon 1900-1943
Kim Tong-in 1900-1951
Yi Sang 1910-1937
Yom Sang-sop 1897-1963

Naturalism (Norway, 1880s)
CIDMEuL-1980

HarDMT-1988

Garborg, Arne 1851-1924
Ibsen, Henrik 1828-1906
Lie, Jonas 1883-1908
Skram, Amalie 1846-1905

Naturalism (Puerto Rico, 1890s-1900s)
CaribWr-1979

Zeno Gandia, Manuel 1855-1930

Naturalism (Russia, 1880s-1900s)
DCLT-1979

Chekhov, Anton 1860-1904
Gorky, Maxim 1868-1936
Tolstoy, Lev Nikolayevich 1828-1910

Naturalism/Naturalismo (Spain, 1880s-1890s)
ClDMEuL-1980
OxSpan-1978

Benavente, Jacinto 1866-1954
Blasco Ibáñez, Vicente 1867-1928
Clarín 1852-1901
Pardo Bazán, Emilia 1851-1921
Trigo, Felipe 1864-1916
Zamacois, Eduardo 1873-1971

Naturalism (United States, 1880s-1910s)
BenReEncy-1987
CamGLE-1988
DCLT-1979
EncWL-1981
GdMWL-1986
HandLit-1986
HarDMT-1988
OxAm-1983
OxAmThe-1984

PengAm-1971
RCom-1973

Anderson, Maxwell 1888-1959
Crane, Stephen 1871-1900
Dos Passos, John 1896-1970
Dreiser, Theodore 1871-1945
Farrell, James T. 1904-1979
Frederic, Harold 1856-1898
Garland, (Hannibal) Hamlin 1860-1940
Herrick, Robert Welch 1868-1938
Jones, James 1921-1977
London, Jack 1876-1916
Norris, Frank 1870-1902
O'Hara, John 1905-1970
O'Neill, Eugene 1888-1953
Steinbeck, John 1902-1968

Naturism/Naturisme (France, 1895-1900s)
ClDMEuL-1980
EncWL-1981
OxFr-1959

Fort, Paul 1872-1960
Jammes, Francis 1868-1938
Noailles, Comtesse Mathieu du 1876-1933
Saint Georges de Bouhélier 1889-1942

***Nazustrich* (Ukraine, 1934-1939)**
ClDMEuL-1980
EncWL-1981

Hordynsky, Svyatoslav 1909-
Kosach, Yuriy 1909-
Rudnytsky, Mykhaylo 1889-1975

Negrismo (Latin America, 1920s-1940s)
OxSpan-1978

Ballagas, Emilio 1910-1954
Guillén Batista, Nicolás 1902-
Palés Matos, Luis 1898-1959
Pereda Valdés, Ildefonso 1899-

Négritude (French Guiana, Haiti, Martinique, Senegal, 1930s-1960s)
BenReEncy-1987
CaribWr-1979
DCLT-1979
EncWL-1981
GdMWL-1985
HarDMT-1988
OxEng-1985
PrEncyPP-1974

Césaire, Aimé 1913-
Damas, Léon-Gontran 1912-1978
Diakhaté, Lamine 1928-
Diop, Alioune 1910-1980
Diop, Birago 1906-
Diop, David 1927-1960
Diop, Ousmane Socé 1911-
Fanon, Frantz 1925-1961
Maran, René 1887-1960
Niang, Lamine 1928-
Roumain, Jacques 1907-1944
Senghor, Léopold Sédar 1906-

Neoclassic Group (Ukraine, 1920s)
ClDMEuL-1980
EncWL-1981
GdMWL-1985

Burghardt, Osvald 1891-1947
Dray-Khmara, Mykhaylo 1889-1938
Fylypovych, Pavlo 1891-1937
Rylsky, Maksym 1895-1964
Zerov, Mykola 1890-1941

Neoclassicism (Sudan, 1930s)
EncWL-1981

al-Abbassi, Muhammad Sa'id 1880-1963
al-Banna, 'Abdallah 1890-(?)
al-Rahman, 'Abdallah 'abd 1891-1964

Neorealism (Italy, 1930s-1950s)
BenReEncy-1987
ClDMEuL-1980
EncWL-1981
GdMWL-1985
HarDMT-1988
McGWD-1984
OxEng-1985

Alvaro, Corrado 1896-1956
Barbaro, Umberto 1902-1959
Bassani, Giorgio 1916-
Bernari, Carlo 1909-
Berto, Giuseppe 1912-1978
Boccelli, Arnaldo 1900-1976
Borgese, Guiseppe Antonio 1882-1952
Calvino, Italo 1923-1985
Cassola, Carlo 1917-
De Gasperi, Alcide 1881-1954
De Santis, Vincent P. 1918-
De Sica, Vittorio 1901(?)-1974
Del Buono, Oreste 1923-
Fenoglio, Beppe 1922-1963
Gramsci, Antonio 1891-1937
Jovine, Francesco (?)-1950
Lattuada, Alberto 1914-
Levi, Carlo 1902-1975
Levi, Primo 1919-
Micheli, Silvio 1911-
Morante, Elsa 1918-
Moravia, Alberto 1907-
Olmi, Ermanno 1931-
Ortese, Anna Maria 1915-
Pasolini, Pier Paolo 1922-1975
Pavese, Cesare 1908-1950
Piovene, Guido 1907-1974
Pratolini, Vasco 1913-
Prisco, Michele 1920-

Rea, Domenico 1921-
Rimanelli, Giose 1926-
Rosi, Francesco 1922-
Rossellini, Roberto 1906-1977
Sciascia, Leonardo 1921-
Silone, Ignazio 1900-1978
Soldati, Mario 1906-
Stern, Mario Rigoni 1921-
Tobino, Mario 1910-
Tozzi, Federigo 1883-1920
Viganó, Renata 1900-1976
Visconti, Luchino 1906-1976
Vittorini, Elio 1908-1966
Zavattini, Cesare 1902-

Neorealism (Portugal, 1930s)
ClDMEuL-1980
EncWL-1981

Cabral, Alexandre 1917-
Castro, José Maria Ferreira de
1898-1974
Cochofel, Joao José 1919-1982
Correia, Romeu 1917-
Dionísio, Mário 1916-
Ferreira, José Gomes 1900-
Fonseca, Manuel da 1911-
Gomes, Joaquim Soeiro Pereira
1910-1949
Namora, Fernando 1919-1989
Oliveira, Carlos de 1921-1981
Redol, António Alves 1911-1969
Rosa, Faure da 1912-
Santos, Políbio Gomes dos 1911-
1939
Silva, José Marmelo e 1913-

Neoromanticism/Neuromantik (Germany, 1900s)
EncWL-1981
McGWD-1984
OxGer-1986

Beer-Hofmann, Richard 1866-
1945

Hauptmann, Gerhart 1862-1946
Hesse, Hermann 1877-1962
Hofmannsthal, Hugo von 1874-
1929
Huch, Ricarda 1864-1947
Vollmoeller, Karl 1878-1948
Wassermann, Jakob 1873-1934

Neoromanticism (Latvia, 1890s-1900s)
EncWL-1981

Barda, Fricis 1880-1919
Poruks, Janis 1871-1911

Neoromanticism (Norway, 1890s-1900s)
ClDMEuL-1980

Garborg, Arne 1851-1924
Hamsun, Knut 1859-1952
Lie, Jonas 1883-1908
Obstfelder, Sigbjorn 1866-1900
Vogt, Nils Collett 1864-1937

Neoromanticism (Ukraine, 1920s-1930s)
EncWL-1981

Bazhan, Mykola 1904-
Sosyra, Volodymyr 1894-1965
Vylsko, Olexa 1908-1934

New Apocalypse (England, 1940s)
BenReEncy-1987
CamGLE-1988
EncWL-1981
HarDMT-1988
OxEng-1985
PengEng-1971

Barker, George Granville 1913-
Fraser, G.S. 1915-1980
Hendry, James Findlay 1912-
MacCaig, Norman 1910-

Moore, Nicholas 1918-
Read, Herbert 1893-1968
Thomas, Dylan 1914-1953
Treece, Henry 1912-1966
Watkins, Vernon 1906-1967

New Criticism (England and United States, 1930s-1950s)

BenReEncy-1987
CamGLE-1988
DCLT-1979
EncWL-1981
HandLit-1986
HarDMT-1988
LongCTCL-1975
OxAm-1983
OxEng-1985
PengAm-1971
PrEncyPP-1974

Blackmur, R.P. 1904-1965
Bowers, Fredson 1905-
Brooks, Cleanth 1906-
Burke, Kenneth 1897-
Eliot, T(homas) S(tearns) 1888-1965
Empson, William 1906-1984
Jackson, Laura (Riding) 1901-
Krieger, Murray 1923-
Leavis, F(rancis) R(aymond) 1895-1978
Pound, Ezra 1885-1972
Ransom, John Crowe 1888-1974
Richards, I(vor) A(rmstrong) 1893-1979
Spingarn, Joel 1875-1939
Spurgeon, Caroline 1869-1942
Tate, Allen 1899-1979
Warren, Austin 1899-1986
Warren, Robert Penn 1905-1989
Wellek, René 1903-
Wimsatt, W(illiam) K(urtz), Jr. 1907-1975
Winters, (Arthur) Yvor 1900-1968

New Current Movement (Latvia, 1890s-1900s)

EncWL-1981
GdMWL-1985

Rainis, Aspazija 1868-1943
Rainis, Janis 1865-1929

New Humanism (United States, 1910s-1930s)

BenReEncy-1987
DCLT-1979
EncWL-1981
GdMWL-1985
HandLit-1986
OxAm-1983
PengAm-1971
PrEncyPP-1974

Babbitt, Irving 1865-1933
Eliot, T(homas) S(tearns) 1888-1965
Foerster, Norman 1887-1972
More, Paul Elmer 1864-1937
Shafer, Robert 1889-1956
Sherman, Stuart 1881-1926

New Lines Poets (England, 1950s)

EncWL-1981
OxEng-1985

Amis, Kingsley 1922-
Conquest, Robert 1917-
Davie, Donald 1922-
Enright, D.J. 1920-
Gunn, Thom 1929-
Holloway, John 1920-
Jennings, Elizabeth 1926-
Larkin, Philip 1922-1985
McBeth, George 1932-
Scannell, Vernon 1922-
Thwaite, Anthony 1930-
Wain, John 1925-

See also **The Movement**

New Literature Movement (China, 1918-1920s)
EncWL-1981

Lao She 1899-1966

New Novel/Nouveau Roman (France, 1950s-1960s)
BenReEncy-1987
ClDMEuL-1980
DCLT-1979
EncWL-1981
GdMWL-1985
HandLit-1986
HarDMT-1988
OxEng-1985

Beckett, Samuel 1906-1990
Blanchot, Maurice 1907-
Butor, Michel 1926-
Duras, Marguerite 1914-
Heppenstall, Rayner 1911-1981
Mauriac, Claude 1914-
Ollier, Claude 1922-
Pinget, Robert 1919-
Ricardou, Jean 1932-
Robbe-Grillet, Alain 1922-
Sarraute, Nathalie 1900-
Simon, Claude 1913-
Sollers, Philippe 1936-

New Objectivity/Neue Sachlichkeit (Germany, 1920s)
ClDMEuL-1980
EncWL-1981
GdMWL-1985
HarDMT-1988
McGWD-1984
OxGer-1986

Bauer, Walter 1904-1976
Beckmann, Max 1884-1950
Brecht, Bertolt 1898-1956

Bruckner, Ferdinand 1891-1958
Carossa, Hans 1878-1956
Dix, Otto 1891-1969
Döblin, Alfred 1878-1957
Edfelt, Bo Johannes 1904-
Engel, Erich 1891-1966
Fallada, Hans 1893-1947
Fleisser, Marie Luise 1901-1974
Grosz, George 1893-1959
Hartlaub, G.F. 1884-1963
Horváth, Ödön von 1901-1938
Kästner, Erich 1899-1974
Kisch, Egon Erwin 1885-1974
Kramer, Theodor 1897-1958
Renn, Ludwig 1889-1979
Schlichter, Rudolf 1890-1955(?)
Seghers, Anna 1900-1983
Tschichold, Jan 1902(?)-1974
Tucholsky, Kurt 1890-1935
Walschap, Gerard 1898-
Weill, Kurt 1900-1950
Zuckmayer, Carl 1896-1977
Zweig, Arnold 1887-1968

New Poetry Movement/Nayi kavita (India, 1930s-1960s)
DOrLit-1974

Agraval, Bharatbhusan n.d.
Ajñeya, Saccidanada n.d.
Bharti ao, Dharmvir n.d.
Jain, Nemicandra n.d.
Macve, Prabhakar n.d.
Mathur, Girijakumar n.d.
Mehta, Nares n.d.
Muktibodh, Gajanan Madhav n.d.
Sahay, Raghuvir n.d.
Saksena ao, Sarvesvardayal n.d.
Sarma, Ramvilas n.d.
Simh, Kedarnath n.d.
Simh, Samserbahadur n.d.

New Poetry Movement (Korea, 1910s)
EncWL-1981

Ch'oe Nam-son 1890-1957

New Psychological School/ Shinshinrigaku-ha (Japan, 1930s)
DOrLit-1974

Ito Sei 1905-1970

New School of Athens (also known as the Greek Parnassians) (Greece, 1880s-1900s)
ClDMEuL-1980
EncWL-1981
GdMWL-1985
PrEncyPP-1974

Crystallis, Costas n.d.
Dhrossinis, Yorghos 1859-1949
Gryparis, George (Ioannis) 1872-1942
Hatzopoulos, Constantine 1871-1920
Kambas, Nikolaos 1857-1932
Malakasis, Miltiadis 1869-1943
Palamas, Kostes 1859-1943
Polemis, John (Ioannis) 1862-1925
Politis, Nikolaos 1852-1921
Porfyras, Lambros 1879-1932
Psykharis, Ioannis 1854-1929
Sikelianos, Angelos 1884-1951
Straittigis, Yorghos 1860-1938

New Sensationalist School (also translated as New Perceptionists, New Sense-Impressionists)/ Shinkankaku-ha (Japan, 1920s)
EncWL-1981

Kawabata Yasunari 1899-1972
Yokomitsu Riichi 1898-1947

New Sensibility Movement (Germany, 1970s-1980s)
EncWL-1981

Wohmann, Gabriele 1932-

New Short Story Movement/Nayi Kahani (India, 1950s)
DOrLit-1974
EncWL-1981

Bhandari, Mennu n.d.
Kamalesvar 1932-
Priyamvada, Usa n.d.
Rakesh, Mohan 1925-1972
Varma, Nirmal n.d.
Yadav, Rajendra 1929-

New Tendency School (Japan, 1910s)
EncWL-1981
GdMWL-1985

Seisensui Ogiwara 1884-1976
Taneda Santoka 1882-1940

New Wave/Nouvelle Vague (France, 1950s-1960s; also England)
BenReEncy-1987
DCLT-1979
HarDMT-1988

Adamov, Arthur 1908-1970
Beckett, Samuel 1906-1990
Burns, Alan 1929-
Butor, Michel 1926-
Chabrol, Claude 1930-
Genet, Jean 1910-1986
Godard, Jean-Luc 1930-
Ionesco, Eugene 1912-
Johnson, B(ryan) S(tanley) 1933-1973
Malle, Louis 1932-
Marker, Chris 1921-

Pinter, Harold 1930-
Resnais, Alain 1922-
Rivette, Jacques 1928-
Robbe-Grillet, Alain 1922-
Rohmer, Eric 1920-
Sarraute, Nathalie 1900-
Simpson, N.F. 1919-
Truffaut, François 1932-1984
Vadim, Roger 1928-

New Wave Movement (Iran, 1950s)
  EncWL-1981

  Farrokhzad, Forugh 1935-1967

**New Writers' Circle/Pudjangga
Baru (Indonesia, 1930s)**
  EncWL-1981
  PrEncyPP-1974

  Amir Hamzah 1911-1946
  Sanusi Pané 1905-
  Takdir Alisjahbana, Sutan 1908-

**New York Group (Latvian exiles in
the United States, 1950s-1960s)**
  EncWL-1981

  Bicole, Baiba 1931-
  Gale, Rita 1925-
  Kraajiete, Aina 1923-
  Salins, Gunars 1924-
  Tauns, Linards 1922-1963

New York Group (Ukraine, 1960s)
  EncWL-1981

  Andiyevska, Emma 1931-
  Boychuk, Bohdan 1927-
  Rubchak, Bohdan 1935-
  Tarnawsky, Yuriy 1934-

**New York School (United States,
1950s-1960s)**
  BenReEncy-1987

EncWL-1981
GdMWL-1985
HandLit-1986
HarDMT-1988
OxAm-1983
PrEncyPP-1974

Ashbery, John 1927-
Berrigan, Ted 1934-1983
De Kooning, Willem 1904-
Field, Edward 1924-
Gorky, Arshile 1905-1948
Gottlieb, Adolph 1903-1974
Guest, Barbara 1920-
Hofmann, Hans 1923-
Kline, Franz 1910-1962
Koch, Kenneth 1925-
Newman, Barnett 1905-1970
O'Hara, Frank 1926-1966
Pollack, Jackson 1912-1956
Schuyler, James 1923-
Shapiro, David 1947-

Ngày nay **Group (Vietnam, 1930s)**
  EncWL-1981

  Hoàng Dao 1907-1948
  Khái Hung 1896-1947
  Nhat-Linh 1906-1963
  The-Lu 1907-
  Thach Lam 1909-1943
  Tú Mo 1900-1976

**Nine Powers Group/Devetsil
(Czechoslovakia, 1920s)**
  EncWL-1981
  GdMWL-1985

  Nezval, Vítezslav 1900-1958
  Teige, Karel 1900-1951
  Wolker, Jirí 1900-1924

Nittiotalister (Sweden, 1890s-1900s)
  ClDMEuL-1980
  EncWL-1981

PrEncyPP-1974

Fröding, Gustaf 1860-1911
Hallström, Per 1866-1960
Heidenstam, (Carl Gustaf)
    Verner von 1859-1940
Karlfeldt, Erik Axel 1864-1931
Lagerlöf, Selma 1858-1940
Levertin, Oscar 1862-1906

**North Africa Group of Writers
(France, 1950s)**
EncWL-1981

Roblès, Emmanuel 1914-

Noucentismo (Spain, 1906-1930s)
EncWL-1981
GdMWL-1985
McGWD-1984
OxSpan-1978

Agelet, Jaume 1888-1981
Arbó, Sebastià Juan 1902-
Carner, Josep 1884-1971
Gassol, Ventura 1893-1980
Liost, Guerau de 1878-1933
Pons, Josep Sebastià 1886-1962
Ors y Rovira, Eugenio d' 1882-
    1954
Riba, Carles 1893-1959
Riba, Enric Prat de la 1870-1917
Ruyra, Joachim 1858-1939

**Nouvelle Revue Française Group
(France, 1908-1943)**
ClDMEuL-1980
EncWL-1981
OxEng-1985
OxFr-1959

Arland, Marcel 1899-
Claudel, Paul 1868-1955
Copeau, Jacques 1879-1949
Gide, André 1869-1951

Giraudoux, Jean 1882-1944
Martin du Gard, Roger 1881-
    1958
Mauriac, François 1885-1970
Péguy, Charles Pierre 1873-1914
Ponge, Francis 1899-1988
Rivière, Jacques 1886-1925
Romains, Jules 1885-1972
Saint-John Perse 1887-1975
Schlumberger, Jean 1877-1968
Valéry, Paul 1871-1945

Novecentismo (Spain, 1900s)
OxSpan-1978

Linares Rivas, Manuel 1878-
    1938
Martínez Sierra, Gregorio 1881-
    1948
Ortega y Gasset, José 1883-1955
Pérez de Ayala, Ramón 1881-
    1962
Riba Bracóns, Carles 1897-1959
Salinas, Pedro 1891(?)-1951
Valle-Inclán, Ramón 1866-1936

Novísmos Group (Spain, 1970s)
EncWL-1981

Álvarez, José María 1942-
Vázquez Montalbán, Manuel
    1939-

Nuevos, Los (Peru, 1960s)
OxSpan-1978

Cisneros, Antonio 1942-
Hinostroza, Rodolfo 1941-
Lauer, Mirko 1947-
Ortega, Julio 1942-

**Nyugat Group (Hungary, 1908-
1920s)**
ClDMEuL-1980

EncWL-1981
GdMWL-1985
PengEur-1969

Ady, Endre 1877-1919
Babits, Mihály 1883-1941
Bródy, Sándor 1863-1924
Cholnoky, Viktor n.d.
Csáth, Géza n.d.
Dsida, Jeno 1907-1938
Fenyo, Miksa n.d.
Fodor, József n.d.
Füst, Milán 1888-1967
Gellért, Oszkár 1882-1967
Gyergyai, Albert 1893-
Halász, Gábor n.d.
Hatvany, Lajos 1880-1961
Ignotus, Paul 1869-1949
Jékely, Zoltán n.d.
Juhász, Gyula 1883-1937
Kaffka, Margit 1880-1918
Kálnoky, László n.d.
Karinthy, Frigyes 1887-1938

Kemény, Simon 1883-1945
Kosztolányi, Deszo 1885-1936
Krúdy, Gyula 1878-1933
Lesznai, Anna 1885-1966
Márai, Sándor 1900-
Móricz, Zsigmond 1879-1942
Osvát, Erno 1877-1929
Radnóti, Miklós 1904-1944
Rónay, György n.d.
Sárközi, György n.d.
Schöpflin, Aladár 1872-1950
Szabó, László n.d.
Szabó, Lorinc 1900-1957
Szép, Erno 1884-1953
Szerb, Antal 1901-1945
Szomory, Dezso 1869-1944
Tersánszky, Jeno J. n.d.
Török, Gyula n.d.
Tóth, Arpád 1886-1928
Vas, István 1910-
Viegelsberg, Hugo (Ignotus
　Osvát) 1869-1950
Weöres, Sándor 1913-

O

OBEIRIU (Obyedineniye realnogo iskusstva/Association for Real Art) (Russia, 1920s)
ClDMEuL-1980
EncWL-1981
GdMWL-1985

Kharms, Daniil Ivanovich 1905-1942
Vaginov, Konstantin Konstantinovich 1899-1934
Vvedensky, Alexandr 1904-1941
Zabolotsky, Nikolay 1903-1958

Objectivism (Spain, 1950s)
EncWL-1981

Aldecoa, Ignacio 1925-1969
Sánchez Ferlosio, Rafael 1927-

Objectivism (United States, 1930s)
BenReEncy-1987
CamGLE-1988
EncWL-1981
GdMWL-1985
HandLit-1986
OxAm-1983
PrEncyPP-1974

Bunting, Basil 1900-1985
Niedecker, Lorine 1903-1970
Oppen, George 1908-1984
Reznikoff, Charles 1894-1976
Williams, William Carlos 1883-1963
Zukofsky, Louis 1904-1978

Oneiric Movement (Romania, 1960s)
EncWL-1981

Dimov, Leonid 1926-
Tanase, Virgil 1940-
Tepeneag, Dumitru 1936-

Onitsha Novels, or Chapbooks (Nigeria, 1950s)
EncWL-1981

Bell-Gam, Leopold n.d.
Ekwenski, Cyprian 1921-
Nwana, Peter n.d.

Oriente Group (Cuba, 1910s)
CaribWr-1979

Boti, Regino 1878-1958
Nolasco, Sócrates 1884-(?)

***Orígenes* Group (Cuba, 1940s-1950s)**
CaribWr-1979
EncWL-1981

Baquero Diego, Gastón 1916-
García Marruz, Fina 1923-
Lezama Lima, José 1910-1976
Rodríguez Feo, José 1920-
Vitier, Cintio 1921-

***Orpheu* Group (Portugal, 1910s)**
ClDMEuL-1980
GdMWL-1985

Almada-Negreiros, José de
1893-1970
Carvalho, Ronald de 1893-1935
Pessoa, Fernando 1888-1953
Sá-Carneiro, Mário de 1890-
1916

**Our Own Things Group/Wie Eegie
Sanie (Surinam, 1950s)**
CaribWr-1979
EncWL-1981

Bruma, Eddy 1925-
Trefossa (Henri Frans de Ziel)
1916-

**Our Soil Group/Nasaniustva
(Byelorussia, 1910s-1920)**
ClDMEuL-1980

EncWL-1981
GdMWL-1985
PrEncyPP-1974

Bahdanovich, Maksim 1891-
1917
Biadula, Zmitrok 1886-1941
Haertski, Maksim 1893-1939
Harun, Ales 1887-1920
Kolas, Yakub 1882-1956
Kupala, Yanka 1882-1942

Oxford Group (Norway, 1930s)
EncWL-1981
LongCTCL-1975

Buchman, Frank 1878-1961
Fangen, Ronald 1895-1946

P

Parnassian-Symbolist School (Lebanon, 1930s)
EncWL-1981

'Aql, Sa'id 1912-

Pass/Pereval (Russia, 1920s)
ClDMEuL-1980

Voronsky, Alexandr 1884-1943

Pau Brasil Group (Brazil, 1920s)
EncWL-1981
McGWD-1984

Andrade, Oswald de 1890-1954

Pléiade du Congo Group (Zaire, 1964-1966)
EncWL-1981

Nzuji, Clémentine 1944-

Plough/Pluh (Ukraine, 1920s)
ClDMEuL-1980

Pylypenko, Serhiy 1891-1943

Pluralist Movement (Dominican Republic, 1960s)
CaribWr-1979
EncWL-1981

Rueda, Manuel 1921-

Poetic Realism (Turkey, 1940s)
ClDMEuL-1980

Anday, Melih Cevdet 1915-
Kanik, Orhan Veli 1914-1950
Rifat, Oktay 1914-

Poeticism (Czechoslovakia, 1920s-1930s)
ClDMEuL-1980
EncWL-1981
GdMWL-1985
PrEncyPP-1974

Halas, Frantisek 1901-1949
Holan, Vladimir 1905-
Hora, Josef 1891-1945
Nezval, Vítêzslav 1900-1958
Seifert, Jaroslav 1901-1986
Teige, Karel 1900-1951
Vancura, Vladislav 1891-1942

***Poetry* (United States, 1912-)**
BenReEncy-1987
CamGLE-1988
HarDMT-1988
OxAm-1983
OxEng-1985

Carruth, Hayden 1921-
Crane, (Harold) Hart 1899-1932
DeVries, Peter 1910-
Eliot, T(homas) S(tearns) 1888-1965
Ford, Ford Madox 1873-1939
Frost, Robert 1874-1963

H.D. 1886-1961
Lowell, Amy 1875-1925
Monroe, Harriet 1860-1936
Moore, Marianne 1887-1972
Pound, Ezra 1885-1972
Sandburg, Carl 1878-1967
Shapiro, Karl 1913-
Stevens, Wallace 1879-1955
Williams, William Carlos 1883-1963
Winters, (Arthur) Yvor 1900-1968

Poetry 61 Movement (Portugal, 1960s)
EncWL-1981

Brandao, Fiama Hasse Pais 1938-
Horta, Maria Teresa 1937-
Melo e Castro, E.M. de 1932-

Poets' Cloister/Skit Poetov (Russian emigres in Czechoslovakia, 1920s-1930s)
ClDMEuL-1980

Bem, Alfred 1886-1945

Poets of the Forties/Fyrtiotalisterna (Sweden, 1940s)
ClDMEuL-1980
DCLT-1979
EncWL-1981
PrEncyPP-1974

Ahlin, Lars Gustaf 1915-
Alfons, Sven 1918-
Arnér, Sivar 1909-
Aspenström, Karl Werner 1918-
Carlson, Stig 1920-
Dagerman, Stig 1923-1954
Erikson, Bernt 1918-
Grave, Elsa 1918-
Isaksson, Ulla 1916-

Lindegren, Erik 1910-1968
Oswald, Gösta 1926-1950
Sjödin, Stig 1917-
Thoursie, Ragnar 1919-
Vennberg, Karl 1910-

Poporanism (Romania, 1910s)
ClDMEuL-1980
GdMWL-1985

Agârbiceanu, Ion 1882-1963
Galaction, Gala 1879-1961
Ibraileanu, Garabet 1871-1936
Topîrceanu, George 1886-1937

Popular National School (Hungary, 1890s-1900s)
ClDMEuL-1980

Arany, János 1817-1882
Gyulai, Pal 1826-1909
Jókai, Mór 1825-1904

Populisme (France, 1929-1930)
BenReEncy-1987
ClDMEuL-1980
EncWL-1981
GdMWL-1985
OxFr-1959

Dabit, Eugène 1898-1936
Guilloux, Louis 1899-1980
Lemonnier, Léon 1892-1953
Poulaille, Henri 1896-
Thérive, André 1891-1967

Populist Literature Movement (Romania, 1910s)
EncWL-1981

Ibraileanu, Garabet 1871-1936
Iorga, Nicolae 1871-1940
Stere, Constantin 1865-1936

Populist Movement (Hungary, 1930s)
CIDMEuL-1980

Darvas, József 1912-
Erdei, Ferenc n.d.
Erdélyi, József 1896-1978
Féjadarvas, Géza n.d.
Illyés, Gyula 1902-
Kodolányi, János 1899-1969
Kovács, Imre n.d.
Németh, László 1901-1975
Pap, Károly n.d.
Sinka, István n.d.
Szabó, Dezso 1879-1945
Szabó, Pál 1893-1970
Szabó, Zoltán n.d.
Tamási, Áron 1897-1966
Veres, Péter n.d.

Porch Group/De Stoep (Dutch Antilles, 1940s)
CaribWr-1979

Corsen, Charles 1927-
Corsen, Yolanda 1918-1969
Marugg, Tip 1923-
Tournier, Luc 1907-
Van Nuland, Wim 1920-
Wit, Hendrik de n.d.

Portuguese Renascence (Portugal, 1910s-1920s)
CIDMEuL-1980
EncWL-1981
PrEncyPP-1974

Braga, Teófilo 1834-1924
Coimbra, Leonardo 1883-1936
Cortesao, Jaime 1884-1960
Machado, Bernardino 1851-1944
Pascoaes, Joaquim Teixeira de 1877-1952
Pessoa, Fernando 1888-1935

Sousa, António Sérgio 1883-1969
Teixeira-Gomes, Manuel 1860-1941
Vieira, Afonso Lopes 1878-1946

Posthumanismo (Dominican Republic, 1920s-1930s)
CaribWr-1979

Moreno Jiménes, Domingo 1894-

Postvanguardist Poetry (Mexico, 1930s)
EncWL-1981

Paz, Octavio 1914-

Prague Linguistic Circle (Czechoslovakia, 1920s-1930s)
CIDMEuL-1980

Jakobson, Roman 1896-1982
Mukarovsky, Jan 1891-1975

***Presencistas* Group (Portugal, 1920s-1940)**
CIDMEuL-1980
EncWL-1981
GdMWL-1985
McGWD-1984
PrEncyPP-1974

Almada-Negreiros, José de 1893-1970
Bettencourt, Edmundo de 1899-1973
Botto, António 1897-1959
Fonseca, António José Branquinho 1905-
Lisboa, Irene 1892-1958
Monteiro, Adolfo Casais 1908-1972
Nemésio, Vitorino 1901-1978

Pessoa, Fernando 1888-1935
Régio, José 1901-1969
Sá-Carneiro, Mário de 1890-
1916
Serpa, Alberto de 1906-
Simoes, Joao Gaspar 1903-
Torga, Miguel 1907-

Profil Group (Norway, 1960s)
ClDMEuL-1980

Haavardsholm, Espen 1945-
Haugen, Paal-Helge 1945-
Obrestad, Tor 1938-
Okland, Einar 1940-
Solstad, Dag 1943-
Vold, Jan Erik 1939-

Progressive Romanticism (Iceland, 1910s)
EncWL-1981

Benediktsson, Einar 1864-1940
Sigurjónsson, Jóhann 1880-1919

Progressive Writers' Movement (Pakistan, 1930s-1950s)
EncWL-1981

Ali, Ahmed 1910-
Ayaz, Skeikh 1923-
Faiz, Faiz Ahmad 1912(?)-1984
Premchand 1880-1936
Qasmi, Ahmad Nadim 1916-
Zaheer, Sajjad 1905-1973

Projective Verse

See **Black Mountain School**

Proletarian Literature (England, 1930s)
BenReEncy-1987
DCLT-1979
EncWL-1981

OxAm-1983
PrEncyPP-1974

Bates, Ralph 1899-
Greenwood, Walter 1903-1974

Proletarian Literature (Czechoslovakia, 1920s-1930s)
GdMWL-1985

Hora, Josef 1891-1945
Horejsí, Jindrich 1886-1941
Seifert, Jaroslav 1901-
Wolker, Jirí 1900-1924

Proletarian Literature (United States, 1930s)
BenReEncy-1987
OxAm-1985

Calverton, Victor Francis 1900-
1940
Cantwell, Robert 1908-1978
Conroy, Jack 1899-
Dahlberg, Edward 1900-1977
Dos Passos, John 1896-1970
Farrell, James T. 1904-1979
Frank, Waldo 1889-1967
Freeman, Joseph 1897-1965
Gold, Michael 1894-1967
Halper, Albert 1904-1984
Herbst, Josephine 1897-1969
Hicks, Granville 1901-1982
Lawson, John Howard 1894-
1977
Lumpkin, Grace n.d.
Odets, Clifford 1906-1963
Shaw, Irwin 1913-1984
Steinbeck, John 1902-1968
Wright, Richard 1908-1960

Proletarian Writers/Arbetardiktare (Sweden, 1930s)
ClDMEuL-1980
EncWL-1981

GdMWL-1985

Andersson, Dan 1888-1920
Fridegård, Jan 1897-1968
Hedenvind-Eriksson, Gustav
1880-1967
Johnson, Eyvind 1900-1976
Koch, Martin 1882-1940
Lo-Johansson, Ivar 1901-
Martinson, Moa 1890-1964
Moberg, Vilhelm 1898-1973

**Proletkult (Proletarian Cultural and
Educational Organization)
(Russia, 1920s)**
ClDMEuL-1980
DCLT-1979
EncWL-1981
GdMWL-1985

Bogdanov, Aleksandr
Aleksandrovich 1873-1928
Gorky, Maxim 1868-1928

See also **Smithy Poets**

**Promotion of 1948 (Dominican
Republic, 1948-1950s)**
CaribWr-1979

Blonda Acosta, Máximo Avilés
1931-
Francisco, Ramón 1929-
Vicioso, Abelardo 1929-

**Provincetown Players (United
States, 1915-1929)**
BenReEncy-1987
HandLit-1986
HarDMT-1988
McGWD-1984

OxAm-1983
OxAmThe-1984
OxThe-1983
PengAm-1971
RCom-1973

Anderson, Sherwood 1876-1941
Barnes, Djuna 1892-1982
Beach, Lewis 1891-1947
Cook, George Cram 1873-1924
Cummings, E.E. 1894-1962
Dell, Floyd 1887-1969
Ferber, Edna 1887-1968
Glaspell, Susan 1882-1948
Green, Paul Eliot 1894-1981
Jones, Robert Edmund 1887-
1954
Langner, Lawrence 1890-1962
Macgowan, Kenneth 1888-1963
Millay, Edna St. Vincent 1892-
1950
O'Neill, Eugene 1888-1953
Reed, John 1887-1920
Wilson, Edmund 1895-1972

Przedmiescie Group (Poland, 1930s)
ClDMEuL-1980

Boguszewska, Helena 1886-
1978
Kornacki, Jerzy 1908-

Pylon School (England, 1930s)
OxEng-1985

Auden, W(ystan) H(ugh) 1907-
1973
Day-Lewis, C(ecil) 1904-1972
MacNeice, Louis 1907-1963
Spender, Stephen 1909-

Q

Quadriga (Poland, 1920s-1930s)
ClDMEuL-1980
EncWL-1981

Galcznski, Konstanty Ildefons
1905-1953

Maliszewski, Aleksander 1901-
1978
Piechal, Marian 1905-
Sebyla, Wladyslaw 1902-1941
Slobodnik, Wlodzimierz 1900-
Unilowski, Zbigniew 1909-1937

R

Rab'e Group (Iran, 1930s)
DOrLit-1974

'Alavi, Aqa Buzurg 1907-
Farzad, Mas'ud 1906-
Hedayat, Sadeq 1903-1951
Minovi, M. n.d.

Realism (Cuba, 1910s-1920s)
CaribWr-1979

Brull, Mariano 1891-1956
Castellanos, Jésus 1879-1912
Hernández Catá, Alfonso 1885-1940
Loveira, Carlos 1882-1928
Marcos Suárez, Miguel de 1894-1954
Ramos, José Antonio 1885-1946

Realism (Denmark, 1880s-1900s)
EncWL-1981

Larsen, Karl 1860-1927

Realism (England, 1850s-1890s)
CamGLE-1988
DCLT-1979
EncWL-1981
HandLit-1986
HarDMT-1988
OxEng-1985
PrEncyPP-1974
RCom-1973

Bennett, (Enoch) Arnold 1867-1931
Browning, Robert 1812-1889
Dickens, Charles 1812-1870
Eliot, George 1819-1880
Galsworthy, John 1867-1933
Gaskell, Elizabeth 1810-1865
Gissing, George 1857-1903
Hardy, Thomas 1840-1928
Kipling, (Joseph) Rudyard 1865-1936
Maugham, W(illiam) Somerset 1874-1965
Morrison, Arthur 1863-1945
O'Casey, Sean 1880-1964
Sassoon, Siegfried 1886-1967
Wells, H(erbert) G(eorge) 1866-1946

Realism (France, 1850s-1870s)
BenReEncy-1987
CamGLE-1988
DCLT-1979
EncWL-1981
GdMWL-1985
HandLit-1986
HarDMT-1988
OxAm-1983
OxEng-1985
OxFr-1959
OxGer-1986
OxThe-1983
PrEncyPP-1974
RCom-1973

Balzac, Honoré de 1799-1850

Béranger, Pierre-Jean 1780-
1857
Champfleury (Jules Husson)
1821-1889
Coppée, François 1842-1907
Daudet, Alphonse 1840-1897
Duranty, Louis 1833-1880
Feydeau, Ernest 1821-1873
Flaubert, Gustave 1821-1880
Goncourt, Edmond de 1822-
1896
Goncourt, Jules de 1830-1870
Maupassant, Guy de 1850-1893
Taine, Hippolyte 1828-1893
Zola, Émile 1840-1902

Realism (Germany, 1840s-1880s)
HarDMT-1988
OxGer-1986
PrEncyPP-1974

Beck, Karl 1817-1879
Fontane, Theodor 1819-1898
Freiligrath, Ferdinand 1810-
1876
Herwegh, Georg 1817-1875
Keller, Gottfried 1819-1890
Mann, Thomas 1875-1955
Mörike, Eduard 1804-1875
Raabe, Wilhelm 1831-1910
Stifter, Adalbert 1805-1868

Realism (Iceland, 1880s-1890s)
ClDMEuL-1980

Drachmann, Holger 1848-1908
Erlingsson, Thorsteinn 1858-
1914
Hafstein, Hannes 1861-1922
Kvaran, Einar H. 1859-1938
Pálsson, Gestur 1852-1891
Stephansson, Stephan
Gudmundsson 1853-1927
Trausti, Jón 1873-1918

Realism/Pragati-vada (India, 1930s)
DOrLit-1974
EncWL-1981
PrEncyPP-1974

Nagarjun 1911-
Nirala, S.T. 1898-1961
Pant, Sumitranandan 1900-
Premchand (Dhanpat Rai
Srivastav) 1880-1936
Raghav, Rangey 1923-1962
Ray, Amrt 1921-
Sankrtyayan, Rahul n.d.
Sarma, N. n.d.
Shukla, Rameshawar 1915-
Suman, S. n.d.
Tripathi, Suryakant 1896-1961
Yashpal 1904-

Realism (Ireland, 1850s-1890s)
OxEng-1985

Moore, George 1852-1933
Synge, John Millington 1871-
1909

Realism (Italy)

See **Verismo**

Realism (Latin America, 1880s-1910s)
OxSpan-1978

Alegría, Ciro 1909-1966
Arguedas, José María 1911-1969
Azuela, Mariano 1873-1952
Blest Gana, Alberto 1830-1920
Cambaceres, Eugenio 1843-1888
Gallegos, Rómulo 1884-1968
Gálvez, Manuel 1882-1962
Güiraldes, Ricardo 1886-1927
Guzmán, Martín Luis 1887-1976
Icaza, Jorge 1906-
Quiroga, Horacio 1878-1937
Rivera, José Eustasio 1889-1928

Rojas Sepúlveda, Manuel 1896-
1973
Romero, José Rubén 1890-1952

Realism (Latvia, 1880s-1900s)
EncWL-1981

Deglavs, Augusts 1862-1922
Dzilums, Alfreds 1907-1966
Jansevskis, Jekabs 1865-1931
Jaunsudrabins, Janis 1877-1962
Klidzejs, Janis 1914-
Niedra, Aida 1898-1972

Realism (Norway, 1870s)
ClDMEuL-1980
DCLT-1979
OxThe-1983

Bjornson, Bjornstjerne 1832-
1910
Elster, Kristian 1841-1881
Ibsen, Henrik 1828-1906
Kielland, Alexander 1849-1906
Lie, Jonas 1883-1908

Realism (Poland, 1870s-1880s)
EncWL-1981

Orzeszkowa, Eliza 1841-1910
Prus, Boleslaw 1845-1912
Sienkiewicz, Henryk 1846-1916

Realism (Russia, 1840s-1880s)
CamGLE-1988
DCLT-1979
HarDMT-1988
OxThe-1983
RCom-1973

Chekhov, Anton 1860-1904
Dostoevski, Fedor 1821-1881
Gogol, Nikolay Vasilyevich
1809-1852

Goncharov, Ivan Alexandrovich
1812-1891
Gorky, Maxim 1868-1936
Stanislovsky, Konstantin
Sergeivich 1863-1938
Tolstoy, Lev Nikolayevich 1828-
1910
Turgenev, Ivan Segeyevich
1818-1883

Realism (Spain, 1870s-1890s)
ClDMEuL-1980
OxSpan-1978

Alarcón, Pedro Antonio 1833-
1891
Clarín 1852-1901
Coloma, Luis 1851-1915
Pardo Bazán, Emilia 1851-1921
Pereda, José María 1833-1906
Pérez Galdós, Benito 1943-1920
Valera, Juan 1824-1905

Realism (Spain—Catalan, 1900s)
ClDMEuL-1980

Bertrana, Prudenci 1867-1942
Català, Victor 1873-1966
Oller i Moragues, Narcis 1846-
1930
Pin i Soler, Josep 1842-1927
Ruyra i Oms, Joaquim 1858-
1939

Realism (Sudan, 1950s-1960s)
EncWL-1981

Hasan, Isma'il (?)-1982
al-Majdhub, Muhammad al-
Mahdi 1919-

**Realism (United States, 1880s-
1910s)**
BenReEncy-1987

CamGLE-1988
DCLT-1979
EncWL-1981
HandLit-1986
HarDMT-1988
OxAm-1983
PengAm-1971
PrEncyPP-1974
RCom-1973

Cable, George Washington
  1844-1925
Cather, Willa 1873-1947
Davis, Rebecca H. 1831-1910
De Forest, John William 1826-
  1906
Eggleston, Edward 1837-1902
Fuller, Henry Blake 1857-1929
Garland, Hamlin 1860-1940
Glasgow, Ellen 1873(?)-1945
Harte, Bret 1836(?)-1902
Howe, E(dgar) W(atson) 1853-
  1937
Howells, William Dean 1837-
  1920
James, Henry 1843-1916
Jewett, Sarah Orne 1849-1909
Kirkland, Joseph 1830-1893
Lewis, Sinclair 1885-1951
Marquand, John P. 1893-
  1960
Masters, Edgar Lee 1869(?)-
  1950
O'Neill, Eugene 1888-1953
Poole, Ernest 1880-1950
Robinson, Edwin Arlington
  1869-1935
Sandburg, Carl 1878-1967
Sinclair, Upton 1878-1968
Smith, Francis Hopkinson 1838-
  1915
Stowe, Harriet Beecher 1811-
  1896
Twain, Mark 1835-1910
Wharton, Edith 1862-1937

**Region-Tradition Movement
(Brazil, 1920s-1930s)**
  EncWL-1981

  Freyre, Gilberto 1900-1987
  Rego, José Lins do 1901-1957

**Renaissance Group/Adradzenstva
(Byelorussia, 1910s-1920s)**
  ClDMEuL-1980

  Bahdanovic, Maksm 1891-1917
  Harecki, Maksim 1893-1939
  Harun, Ales 1887-1920
  Kolas, Yakub 1882-1956
  Kupala, Yanka 1882-1942

***Revue Indigène* Group (Haiti,
1920s)**
  CaribWr-1979
  EncWL-1981

  Price-Mars, Jean 1876-1969
  Roumain, Jacques 1907-1944
  Thoby-Marcelin, Philippe 1904-
  1975

**Romantic Movement/Bungakkai
(Japan, 1890s-1900s)**
  DOrLit-1974
  GdMWL-1985

  Mori Ogai 1862-1922
  Shimazaki Toson 1872-1943
  Tokoku Kitamura 1868-1894

**Romantic Poets (Sudan, 1930s-
1940s)**
  EncWL-1981

  Bashir, Tijani Yusuf 1910-1936
  Jamma', Idris 1922-1980
  Mahjub, Muhammad Ahmad
  1910-1976

Tambal, Hamza 1893-1960

Romanticism/Chhaya-vada (India, 1920s-1930s)
DOrLit-1974
EncWL-1981
PrEncyPP-1974

Nirala, S.T. 1898-1961
Pant, Sumitranand 1900-
Prasad, Jaysankar 1889-1937
Tagore, Rabindranath 1861-1941
Tripathi, Suryakant 1896-1961
Varma, Mahadevi 1907-
Varma, Ramkumar 1905-

Rondismo (Italy, 1920s)
CIDMEuL-1980

Bacchelli, Riccardo 1891-
Cardarelli, Vincenzo 1887-1959
Cecchi, Emilio 1884-1966

***Ruimte* Group (Belgium, 1917-1920s)**
CIDMEuL-1980
EncWL-1981

Brunclair, Victor J. 1899-1944
Burssens, Gaston 1896-1965
Gijsen, Marnix 1899-
Moens, Wies 1898-
Mussche, Achilles 1896-
Ostaijen, Paul van 1896-1928

Russian Formalism (Russia, 1920s)
BenReEncy-1987
CamGLE-1988
DCLT-1979
EncWL-1981
PrEncyPP-1974

Eikhenbaum, Boris 1886-1959
Jakobson, Roman 1896-1982
Shklovsky, Viktor Borisovich 1893-1984
Tomashevsky, Boris Viktorovich 1890-
Tynyanov, Yury Nikolayevich 1894-1943
Zamyatin, Evgeny Ivanovich 1884-1937
Zhirmunsky, Viktor 1891-1971

S

Samanatorism (Romania, 1900s)
ClDMEuL-1980

Cosbuc, George 1866-1918
Iorga, Nicolae 1871-1940
Vlahuta, Alexandru 1858-1919

San Francisco School (United States, 1960s)
EncWL-1981
PrEncyPP-1974

Corso, Gregory 1930-
Duncan, Robert 1919-1988
Everson, William 1912-
Ferlinghetti, Lawrence, 1919(?)-
Ginsberg, Allen 1926-
Lamantia, Philip 1927-
Rexroth, Kenneth 1905-1982

Sardio Group (Venezuela, 1955)
EncWL-1981

Garmendia, Salvador 1928-

***Sburatorul* Group (Romania, 1920s)**
ClDMEuL-1980

Lovinescu, Eugen 1881-1943
Rebreanu, Liviu 1885-1944

Scottish Renaissance (Scotland, 1920s-1940s)
BenReEncy-1987
CamGLE-1988
EncWL-1981

GdMWL-1985
PrEncyPP-1974

Angus, Marion 1866-1946
Daiches, David 1912-
Garioch, Robert 1909-1981
Gibbon, Lewis Grassic 1901-1935
Gray, Alexander 1882-1968
Hay, George Campbell 1915-
Jacob, Violet 1863-1946
Lindsay, J(ohn) Maurice 1918-
MacDiarmid, Hugh 1892-1978
MacLean, Sorley 1911-
Mitchell, James Leslie 1901-1935
Scott, Tom 1918-
Smith, Sydney Goodsir 1915-1975
Soutar, William 1898-1943
Spence, Lewis 1874-1955
Young, Douglas 1913-1973

***Scrutiny* Group (England, 1932-1953)**
BenReEncy-1987
CamGLE-1988
EncWL-1981
HarDMT-1988
LongCTCL-1975
OxEng-1985
PengEng-1971

Enright, D(ennis) J(oseph) 1920-
Harding, D(enys) W(yatt) 1906-

Knights, L(ionel) C(harles) 1906-
Leavis, F(rank) R(aymond) 1895-
1978
Leavis, Q(ueenie) D. 1906-1981
Rickword, Edgell 1898-1982
Traversi, Derek A. 1912-

Seara Nova Group (Portugal, 1921-1974)
EncWL-1981

Brandao, Raúl 1867-1930
Castro, José Maria Ferreira de
1898-1974
Cortesao, Jaime 1884-1960
Miguéis, José Rodrigues 1901-
Ribeiro, Aquilino 1885-1963
Sousa, António Sérgio de 1883-
1968

Second New, The (Turkey, 1950s)
ClDMEuL-1980

Berk, Ilhan 1916-
Cansever, Edip 1928-
Eloglu, Metin 1927-
Rifat, Oktay 1914-
Süreya, Cemal 1931-

Self-Reliant Group (Vietnam, 1930s)
EncWL-1981

Hàn Mac Tu 1913-1940
Nhat-Linh 1906-1963
The Lu 1907-
Xuân Diêu 1917-

Semiotics (France, 1960s-1980s)
CamGLE-1988
DCLT-1979
EncWL-1981
HandLit-1986
HarDMT-1988

OxEng-1985
PrEncyPP-1974

Barthes, Roland 1915-1980
Greimas, A.J. 1917-
Kristeva, Julia 1941-
Lévi-Strauss, Claude 1908-
Lotman, Yury 1922-
Pierce, C.S. 1839-1914
Sarduy, Severo 1937-
Saussure, Ferdinand de 1857-
1913

Serapion Brotherhood (Russia, 1920s)
BenReEncy-1987
ClDMEuL-1980
DCLT-1979
EncWL-1981
GdMWL-1985
HarDMT-1988
PengEur-1969

Fedin, Konstantin 1892-1977
Gruzdev, Ilya n.d.
Ivanov, Vsevolod 1895-1963
Kaverin, Veniamin
Aleksandrovich 1902-
Lunts, Lev Natanovich 1901-
1924
Nikitin, Nikolay Nikolayevich
1895-1963
Polonskaya, Elizaveta n.d.
Shklovsky, Viktor 1893-1984
Slonimsky, Mikhail Leonidovich
1897-1972
Tikhonov, Nikolay 1896-
Zamyatin, Evgeny 1884-1937
Zoshchenko, Mikhail 1895-1958

Servet-i Fünun/Edebiyat-i Cedide (Turkey, 1890s-1910s)
ClDMEuL-1980
EncWL-1981
GdMWL-1985

PrEncyPP-1974

Fikret, Tevfik 1867-1915
Sehabettin, Cenap 1870-1934

Sestigers, The (South Africa, 1960s)
EncWL-1981
GdMWL-1985

Aucamp, Hennie 1934-
Barnard, Chris 1939-
Blum, Peter 1925-
Breytenbach, Breyten 1939(?)-
Brink, André P. 1935-
Haasbroek, P.J. 1943-
Jonker, Ingrid 1933-1965
Leroux, Étienne 1922-
Miles, John 1938-
Rabie, Jan 1920-
Small, Adam 1936-
Smit, Bartho 1924-
Vries, Abraham H. de 1937-

Seven Torches/Yedi Mes'ale (Turkey, 1920s)
ClDMEuL-1980

Çamlibel, Faruk Nafiz 1898-1973
Nayir, Yasar Nabi 1908-
Siyavusgil, Sabri Esat (?)-1968

Al-Shihab (Algeria, 1920s)
EncWL-1981

al-'Id Al Khalifa, Muhammad 1904-1979

Sibiu Group (Romania, 1940s)
EncWL-1981

Doinas, Stefan Augustin 1922-
Negoitescu, Ion 1921-
Regman, Cornel 1919-
Stanca, Radu 1920-1962

Simultanéisme (France, 1910s)
EncWL-1981
OxFr-1959

Barzun, Henri-Martin 1881-(?)
Cendrars, Blaise 1887-1961
Divoire, Fernand 1883-1951

Siuru Group (Estonia, 1917-1920s)
ClDMEuL-1980
EncWL-1981
GdMWL-1985
PrEncyPP-1974

Adson, Artur 1889-1977
Gailit, August 1891-1960
Semper, Johannes 1892-1970
Under, Marie 1883-1980
Visnapuu, Henrik 1890-1951

Skamander **Group (Poland, 1920s-1930s)**
ClDMEuL-1980
EncWL-1981
GdMWL-1985
PrEncyPP-1974

Balinski, Stanislaw 1899-
Broniewski, Wladyslaw 1898(?)-1962
Grydzewski, Mieczyslaw 1894-1970
Illakowicz, Jaroslaw 1894-
Illakowiczówna, Kazimiera 1892-
Iwaszkiewicz, Jaroslaw 1894-1980
Lechón, Jan 1899-1956
Lesmian, Boleslaw 1878-1937
Napierski, Stefan 1899-1940
Pawlikowska-Jasnorzewska, Maria 1891-1945
Slonimski, Antoni 1895-1976
Staff, Leopold 1878-1957
Tuwim, Julian 1894-1953

Wierzynski, Kazimierz 1894-1969
Wittlin, Józef 1896-1976
Zawodzinsik, Karol Wiktor 1980-1949

Smithy Poets/Kuznitsa (Russia, 1920s)
CIDMEuL-1980
DCLT-1979
EncWL-1981
PengEur-1969
PrEncyPP-1974

Gastev, Alexei 1882-1941
Gerasimov, Mikhail 1889-1939
Kazin, Vasili 1898-
Kirillov, Vladimir 1890-1943

See also **Proletcult**

Socialist Realism (Azerbaijan, 1930s-1950s)
EncWL-1981

Abulhasan, Alekperzade 1906-
Djabarly, Djafar 1899-1934
Efendiev, Ilyas 1914-
Gusein, Mehti 1909-1965
Ibrahimov, Mirza 1911-
Ordubady, Mamed Said 1872-1950
Ragimov, Suleiman 1900-
Veliev, Ali 1901-
Vurgun, Samed 1906-1956

Socialist Realism (Bulgaria, 1930s-1950s)
EncWL-1981

Dimov, Dimitur 1909-1966
Georgiev, V. n.d.
Isayev, Mladen n.d.
Karaslavov, Georgi 1904-
Radevski, Hristo 1903-

Stoyanov, Lyudmil 1888-(?)

Socialist Realism (Byelorussia, 1930s-1950s)
PrEncyPP-1974

Browka, P n.d.
Chorny, Kuzma 1900-1944
Hlebka, P n.d.
Kalachynski, M n.d.
Krapiva, K n.d.
Lyn'kow, M n.d.
Makayanka, A n.d.
Panchenko, P n.d.
Trus, R n.d.
Zvonak, A n.d.

Socialist Realism (Chuvashia, 1930s-1950s)
EncWL-1981

Elger, Semyon V. 1894-1966
Ivnik, Ivan 1914-1942
Osipov, Petr N. 1900-
Tuktash, Ilya 1907-

Socialist Realism (Czechoslovakia, 1940s-1950s)
EncWL-1981

Majerová, Marie 1882-1967
Olbracht, Ivan 1882-1952
Ptácník, Karel 1921-
Pujmanová, Marie 1893-1958

Socialist Realism (England, 1930s-1950s)
EncWL-1981

Fox, Ralph 1900-1937

Socialist Realism (France, 1930s-1950s)
EncWL-1981

Aragon, Louis 1897-1982
Stil, André 1921-

Socialist Realism (Germany, 1940s-1950s)
EncWL-1981
OxEng-1985
OxGer-1986

Becher, Johannes R. 1891-1958
Brecht, Bertolt 1898-1956
Nexo, Martin Andersen 1869-1954

Socialist Realism (Hungary, 1940s-1950s)
EncWL-1981

Lukács, Gyorgy 1885-1971

Socialist Realism (Kazakhstan, 1930s-1950s)
EncWL-1981

Müsrepov, Ghabit Makhmudulï 1902-

Socialist Realism (Kirgizia, 1930s-1950s)
EncWL-1981

Bokombaev, Joomart 1910-1944
Osmonov, Alïkul 1915-1950
Sïdïkbekov, Tügelbay 1912-
Tokombaev, Aalï n.d.
Turusbekov, Joomart 1910-1943

Socialist Realism (Latvia, 1940s-1950s)
EncWL-1981

Lams-Eglons, Visvaldis 1923-
Skujins, Zigmunds 1926-

Socialist Realism (Lithuania, 1940s-1950s)
EncWL-1981

Baltakis, Algimantas 1930-
Gira, Liudas 1884-1946
Marcinkevicius, Justinas 1930-
Miezelaitis, Eduardas 1919-
Miskinis, Antanas 1905-
Putinas 1893-1967
Neris, Salomeja 1904-1945
Tilvytis, Teofilis 1904-

Socialist Realism (Poland, 1940s-1950s)
EncWL-1981

Bratny, Roman 1921-
Putrament, Jerzy 1910-

Socialist Realism (Russia, 1930s-1950s)
BenReEncy-1987
ClDMEuL-1980
DCLT-1979
EncWL-1981
HarDMT-1988
McGWD-1984
OxEng-1985
OxGer-1986
OxThe-1983
PrEncyPP-1974

Bukharin, Nicolai 1888-1938
Chapygin, Alexey 1870-1937
Fadeyev, Alexander 1901-1956
Gladkov, Fyodor 1883-1958
Gorky, Maxim 1868-1936
Kataev, Valentin 1897-1986
Leonov, Leonid 1899-
Lunacharsky, Anatoli 1875-1933
Mayakovsky, Vladimir 1893-1930
Nusinov, Isak 1889-1950

Ostrovsky, Nikolay Alexeyevich
1904-1936
Panova, Vera Fyodorovna 1905-
1973
Pavlenko, Pyotr 1899-1951
Pilnyak, Boris 1894-1937(?)
Pogodin, Nikolay Fyodorovich
1900-1962
Polevoy, Boris 1908-1981
Radek, Karl 1885-1939
Rozhkov, P. n.d.
Sholokov, Mikail
Aleksandrovich 1905-1984
Simonov, Konstantin 1915-
Tolstoy, Alexey 1882-1945
Zhdanov, Andrei A. 1896-1948

**Socialist Realism (Slovenia, 1930s-
1950s)**
ClDMEuL-1980

Jiribine, Kün 1903-1970
Kosmac, Ciril 1910-
Kranjec, Misko 1908-
Prezihov, Voranc 1893-1950

**Socialist Realism (Turkey, 1930s-
1950s)**
ClDMEuL-1980

Ali, Sabahattin 1906-1948

**Socialist Realism (Ukraine, 1930s-
1950s)**
EncWL-1981

Ostrovsky, Nikolay 1904-1936

**Socialist Realism (United States,
1930s-1950s)**
EncWL-1981

Fast, Howard 1914-

**Socialist Realism (Yakut, 1930s-
1950s)**
EncWL-1981

Eristin, Erilik 1892-1942
Künde 1898-1934
Ölöksüöyebis, Bylatan 1893-
1939

**Society of the Pen (Lebanonese
exiles in the United States, 1920s)**
EncWL-1981

Gibran, Khalil 1883-1931
Na'ima, Mikha'il 1889-(?)
al-Rihani, Amin 1876-1940

***Solaria* Group (Italy, 1926-1934)**
ClDMEuL-1980

Commisso, Giovanni 1895-1969
Contini, Gianfranco 1902-
Debenedetti, Giacomo 1901-
1967
Gadda, Carlo Emilio 1893-1973
Manzini, Gianna 1896-
Montale, Eugenio 1896-1981
Pavese, Cesare 1908-1950
Quasímodo, Salvatore 1901-
1968
Raimondi, Giuseppe 1898-
Saba, Umberto 1883-1957
Svevo, Italo 1861-1928
Tozzi, Federigo 1883-1920
Vittorini, Elio 1908-1966

**Soothsayers Movement/*Arbujad*
(Estonia, 1930s)**
ClDMEuL-1980
EncWL-1981
GdMWL-1985
PrEncyPP-1974

Alver, Betti 1906-
Asi, Harri 1922-

Grünthal, Ivar 1924-
Kaalep, Ain 1926-
Kangro, Bernard 1910-
Kaplinski, Jaan 1941-
Laaban, Ilmar 1921-
Masing, Uku 1909-
Oras, Ants 1900-
Sand, August 1914-1969
Talvik, Heiti 1904-1947

South China Society (China, 1920s)
EncWL-1981

T'ien Han 1898-1968

Southern Society/Nan-shê Group (China, 1900s-1920s)
DOrLit-1974
EncWL-1981

Liu Ya-tzu 1887-1958
Su Man-shu 1884-1918

Spectra **(United States, 1916-1918)**
OxAm-1983

Bynner, Witter 1881-1968
Ficke, Arthur Davison 1883-1945
Seiffert, Marjorie Allen 1885-(?)

Stone and Sky Movement (Columbia, 1930s)
EncWL-1981

Carranza, Eduardo 1913-
Rojas, Jorge 1911-

Storm Circle/*Der Sturm* (Germany, 1910s)
EncWL-1981
HarDMT-1988
OxGer-1986

Döblin, Alfred 1878-1957

Kokoschka, Oskar 1886-1980
Lasker-Schüler, Else 1869-1945
Marc, Franz 1880-1916
Stramm, August 1874-1915
Walden, Herwarth 1878-1941

Structuralism (France, 1950s-1970s; also United States)
BenReEncy-1987
CamGLE-1988
ClDMEuL-1980
EncWL-1981
GdMWL-1985
HandLit-1986
HarDMT-1988
OxEng-1985
PrEncyPP-1974

Althusser, Louis 1918-
Bachelard, Gaston 1884-1962
Barthes, Roland 1915-1980
Blanchot, Maurice 1907-
Chomsky, Noam 1928-
Culler, Jonathan 1944-
De Man, Paul 1919-1983
Derrida, Jacques 1930-
Foucault, Michel 1926-1984
Genette, Gérard 1930-
Girard, René 1923-
Goldmann, Lucien 1913-1970
Greimas, A.J. 1917-
Jakobson, Roman 1896-1982
Kristeva, Julia 1941-
Lacan, Jacques 1901-1981
Lévi-Strauss, Claude 1908-
Lodge, David 1935-
Ricardou, Jean 1932-
Saussure, Ferdinand de 1857-1913
Sollers, Philippe 1936-
Todorov, Tzvetan 1939-

Surprised Poetry Movement (Dominican Republic, 1940s)
CaribWr-1979

EncWL-1981

Hernández Rueda, Lupo 1930-
Mieses Burgos, Franklin 1907-
Rueda, Manuel 1921-

Surrealism (Belgium, 1920s-1930s)
ClDMEuL-1980
EncWL-1981

Chavée, Achille 1906-1969
Colinet, Paul 1898-1957
Goemans, Camille 1900-1960
Lecomte, Marcel 1900-1966
Magritte, René 1898-1967
Marien, Marcel n.d.
Mesens, E.L.T. 1903-1970
Neuhuys, Paul 1897-
Nougé, Paul 1895-1967
Scutenaire, Louis 1905-
Souris, André 1899-1970

Surrealism (Czechoslovakia, 1930s)
EncWL-1981
GdMWL-1985
HarDMT-1988

Biebl, Konstantín 1898-1951
Nezval, Vítezslav 1900-1958

Surrealism (England, 1920s-1930s)
BenReEncy-1987
EncWL-1981
HarDMT-1988
OxEng-1985

Davies, Hugh Sykes 1909-
    1984(?)
Gascoyne, David 1916-
Penrose, Roland 1900-1984
Read, Herbert 1893-1968
Thomas, Dylan 1914-1953
Todd, Ruthven 1914-

Surrealism (France, 1920s-1930s)
BenReEncy-1987
CEnMWL-1963
ClDMEuL-1980
DCLT-1979
EncWL-1981
GdMWL-1985
HandLit-1986
HarDMT-1988
McGWD-1984
OxEng-1985
OxFr-1959
OxGer-1986
PengEur-1969
PrEncyPP-1974
RCom-1973

Apollinaire, Guillaume 1880-
    1918
Aragon, Louis 1897-1982
Arp, Hans 1887-1966
Artaud, Antonin 1896-1948
Breton, André 1896-1966
Césaire, Aimé 1913-
Char, René 1907-
Chirico, Giorgio di 1888-1978
Cocteau, Jean 1889-1963
Crevel, René 1900-1935
Dalí, Salvadore 1904-1989
Desnos, Robert 1900-1945
Duchamp, Marcel 1887-1968
Éluard, Paul 1895-1952
Ernst, Max 1891-1976
Giacometti, Alberto 1901-1966
Goemans, Camille 1900-1960
Gracq, Julien 1910-
Hugo, Valentine 1890-1968
Jacob, Max 1876-1944
Klee, Paul 1879-1940
Léger, Fernand 1881-1955
Leiris, Michel 1901-
Masson, André 1897-1987
Michaux, Henri 1899-1984
Miró, Joan 1893-1983
Paulhan, Jean 1884-1968

Péret, Benjamin 1899-1959
Picabia, Francis 1879-1953
Picasso, Pablo 1881-1973
Ponge, Francis 1899-1988
Prévert, Jacques 1900-1977
Queneau, Raymond 1903-1976
Ray, Man 1890-1976
Rigaut, Jacques 1899-1929
Roussel, Raymond 1877-1933
Saint-John Perse 1887-1975
Soupault, Philippe 1897-
Tanguy, Yves 1900-1955
Tchelichev, Pavel 1898-1957
Tzara, Tristan 1896-1963

Surrealism (Germany, 1920s-1930s)
OxGer-1986

Benn, Gottfried 1886-1956
Döblin, Alfred 1878-1957
Kasack, Hermann 1896-1966
Nossack, Hans Erich 1901-1977
Stramm, August 1874-1915

Surrealism (Latin America, 1920s-1930s)
EncWL-1981

Moro, César 1903-1956
Neruda, Pablo 1904-1973
Paz, Octavio 1914-
Vallejo, César 1892-1938

Surrealism (Portugal, 1940s-1960s)
EncWL-1981

Lisboa, António Maria 1928-1953
O'Neill, Alexandre 1924-
Ruben, A(dresen) 1920-1975
Vasconcelos, Mário Cesariny de 1924-

Surrealism (Spain, 1920s-1930s)
EncWL-1981

OxSpan-1978
PrEncyPP-1974

Alberti, Rafael 1902-
Aleixandre, Vicente 1898-1984
Azorín 1873-1969
Buñuel, Luis 1900-1983
Cernuda, Luis 1902-1963
Dalí, Salvadore 1904-1989
Espina García, Antonio 1894-
Foix, J(osep) V(icenç) 1893-
García Lorca, Federico 1898-1936
Gómez de la Serna, Ramón 1888-1963
Jarnés, Benjamín 1888-1949
Larrea, Juan 1895-1982
Moreno Villa, José 1887-1955
Prados, Emilio 1899-1962

Surrealism (Sweden, 1930s)
ClDMEuL-1980

Ekelöf, Gunnar 1907-1968
Lundkvist, Artur 1906-

Syllabists/Hececiler (Turkey, 1920s)
ClDMEuL-1980

Koryurek, Enis Behiç 1891-1949
Orhon, Orhan Seyfi 1890-1972
Ortaç, Yusuf Ziya 1895-1967
Ozansoy, Halit Fahri 1891-1971

Symbolic Modernism (Norway, 1950s)
EncWL-1981

Holm, Peter R. 1931-
Mehren, Stein 1935-
Vesaas, Tarjei 1897-1970

Symbolism (Belgium, 1890s-1900s)
ClDMEuL-1980
EncWL-1981

HandLit-1986
OxThe-1983
PrEncyPP-1974

Elskamp, Max 1862-1931
Lerberghe, Charles Van 1861-
1907
Maeterlinck, Maurice 1862-1949
Mockel, Albert 1866-1945
Rodenbach, Georges 1855-1898
Verhaeren, Émile 1855-1916

Symbolism (Brazil and Portugal, 1890s-1900s)
EncWL-1981

Castro, Eugénio de 1869-1944
Cruz e Sousa, Joao da 1861-
1898
Patricio, Antonio 1878-1930
Pessanha, Camilo 1867-1926
Sá-Carneiro, Mario de 1890-
1916

Symbolism (Bulgaria, 1905-1910s)
ClDMEuL-1980
EncWL-1981
PrEncyPP-1974

Debelyanov, Dimcho 1887-1916
Liliev, Nikolay 1885-1960
Milev, Geo 1895-1925
Trayanov, Teodor 1882-1945
Yasenov, Khristo 1889-1925

Symbolism (Czechoslovakia, 1890s)
ClDMEuL-1980
EncWL-1981
PrEncyPP-1974

Brezina, Otokar 1868-1929
Hlavácek, Karel 1874-1898
Sova, Antonín 1864-1928
Theer, Otakar 1880-1917

Symbolism (Denmark, 1890s)
ClDMEuL-1980

Claussen, Sophus 1865-1931
Jorgensen, Johannes 1886-1956
Rode, Helge 1870-1937
Stuckenberg, Viggo 1863-1905

Symbolism (England and Ireland, 1890s-1900s)
BenReEncy-1987
DCLT-1979
EncWL-1981
HarDMT-1988
OxThe-1983

Eliot, T(homas) S(tearns) 1888-
1965
Hulme, T(homas) E(rnest) 1883-
1917
O'Casey, Sean 1880-1964
Symons, Arthur 1865-1945
Synge, John Millington 1871-
1909
Wilde, Oscar 1854(?)-1900
Yeats, William Butler 1865-1939

Symbolism (France, 1870s-1890s)
BenReEncy-1987
CamGLE-1988
CEnMWL-1963
ClDMEuL-1980
DCLT-1979
EncWL-1981
GdMWL-1985
HandLit-1986
HarDMT-1988
McGWD-1984
OxEng-1985
OxFr-1959
OxGer-1986
OxThe-1983
PengEur-1969
PrEncyPP-1974
RCom-1973

Baudelaire, Charles 1821-1867
Beauclair, Henri 1860-1919
Claudel, Paul 1868-1955
Corbiére, Edouard Joachim
     1845-1875
Dujardin, Édouard 1861-1949
Ghil, René 1862-1925
Gourmont, Remy de 1858-1915
Huysmans, Joris Karl 1848-1907
Kahn, Gustave 1859-1936
Laforgue, Jules 1860-1887
Mallarmé, Stéphane 1842-1898
Merrill, Stuart 1863-1915
Moréas, Jean 1856-1910
Nerval, Gérard de 1808-1855
Régnier, Henri de 1864-1936
Rimbaud, Arthur 1854-1891
Schwob, Marcel 1867-1905
Valéry, Paul 1871-1945
Verlaine, Paul 1844-1896
Viélé-Griffin, Francis 1864-1937
Vicaire, Gabriel 1848-1900
Villiers de l'Isle-Adam, Philippe
     Auguste Mathias de 1838-
     1889

Symbolism (Germany, 1880s-1900s)
DCLT-1979
HandLit-1986
HarDMT-1988
OxGer-1986
OxThe-1983

George, Stefan 1868-1933
Hauptmann, Gerhart 1862-1946
Hofmannsthal, Hugo von 1874-
     1929
Rilke, Rainer Maria 1875-1926

Symbolism (Lithuania, 1930s)
EncWL-1981
PrEncyPP-1974

Baltrusaitis, Jurgis 1873-1944
Kirsa, Faustas 1891-1964

Putinas, Vincas Mykolaitis 1893-
     1967
Sruoga, Balys 1896-1947

Symbolism (Romania, 1900s-1910s)
ClDMEuL-1980
EncWL-1981

Anghel, Dimitrie 1872-1914
Bacovia, George 1884-1957
Densusianu, Ovid 1873-1937
Macedonski, Alexandru 1854-
     1920
Minulescu, Ion 1881-1944

Symbolism (Russia, 1890s-1900s)
ClDMEuL-1980
DCLT-1979
EncWL-1981
GdMWL-1985
HarDMT-1988
OxThe-1983
PrEncyPP-1974

Andreyev, Leonid Nikolaivich
     1871-1919
Annensky, Innokenti
     Fedorovich 1856-1909
Balmont, Konstantin 1867-1943
Bely, Andrey 1880-1934
Blok, Alexandr 1880-1921
Bryusov, Valery Yakovlevich
     1873-1924
Evreinov, Nikolai Nikolaivich
     1879-1953
Hippius, Zinaida 1869-1945
Ivanov, Vyacheslav Ivanovich
     1866-1949
Klyuev, Nikolay Alexeevich
     1887-1937(?)
Merezhkovsky, Dmitry 1865-
     1941
Shaginyan, Marietta 1888-1982
Sologub, Fyodor 1863-1927
Solovyov, Vladimir 1853-1900

Voloshin, Maximilian 1877-1932
Volynsky, A. 1863-1926

Symbolism (Ukraine, 1910s-1920s)
CIDMEuL-1980
EncWL-1981

Filyansky, Mykola 1873-1937

Kobylyansky, Volodymyr 1895-1919
Savchencko, Yakiv 1890-1937
Svidzinsky, Volodymyr 1885-1941
Tychyna, Pavlo 1891-1967
Zahul, Dmytro 1890-1938

T

Taller Group (Mexico, 1939-1941)
OxSpan-1978

Álvarez Quintero, Alberto n.d.
Beltrán, Neftalí n.d.
Huerta, Efraín 1914-1982
Paz, Octavio 1914-

Tank Group (Ukrainian exiles in Poland, 1930s)
EncWL-1981

Livytska-Kholodna, Natalia 1902-
Lypa, Yury 1900-1944

Tel Quel Group (France, 1960s-1980s)
BenReEncy-1987
EncWL-1981

Barthes, Roland 1915-1980
Derrida, Jacques 1930-
Kristeva, Julia 1941-
Ricardou, Jean 1932-
Sarduy, Severo 1937-
Sollers, Philippe 1936-
Todorov, Tzvétan 1939-

Teraz Group (Poland, 1960s-1970s)
ClDMEuL-1980

Balcerzan, Edward 1937-
Baranczak, Stanislaw 1946-
Kornhauser, Julian 1946-
Krynicki, Ryszard 1943-

Zagajewski, Adam 1945-

Terroir School (Canada, 1900-1930s)
PrEncyPP-1974

Lamontagne, Blanche 1889-1958

Testing of the Age/Khit-sam Group (Burma, 1930s)
DOrLit-1974

Zodji 1907-

Theater Guild (United States, 1920s-1930s)
EncWL-1981
GdMWL-1985
HandLit-1986
McGWD-1984
OxAm-1983
OxAmThe-1984
OxThe-1983
PengAm-1971

Anderson, Maxwell 1888-1959
Clurman, Harold 1901-1980
Copeau, Jacques 1879-1949
Crawford, Cheryl 1902-
Digges, Dudley 1879-1947
Helburn, Theresa 1887-1959
Langner, Lawrence 1890-1962
Moeller, Philip 1880-1958
O'Neill, Eugene 1888-1953
Odets, Clifford 1906-1963
Peters, Rollo 1892-1967
Rice, Elmer 1892-1967

Shaw, George Bernard 1856-
1950
Sherwood, Robert E. 1896-1955
Simonson, Lee 1888-1967
Strasberg, Lee 1901-1982
Werfel, Franz 1890-1945
Westley, Helen 1879-1942

Theater Laboratory (Poland, 1959-
1969)
HarDMT-1988

Grotowsky, Jerzy 1933-

Theater of Cruelty/Théâtre de la
Cruauté (France, 1930s-1960s; also
Germany, Poland, United States)
BenReEncy-1987
DCLT-1979
EncWL-1981
GdMWL-1985
HandLit-1986
HarDMT-1988
LongCTCL-1975
McGWD-1984
OxThe-1983

Adamov, Arthur 1908-1970
Albee, Edward 1928-
Arrabal, Fernando 1932-
Artaud, Antonin 1896-1948
Audiberti, Jacques 1900-1965
Barrault, Jean-Louis 1910-
Blin, Roger 1907-1984
Brook, Peter 1925-
Genet, Jean 1910-1986
Grotowski, Jerzy 1933-
Orton, Joe 1933-1967
Pinter, Harold 1930-
Vauthier, Jean 1910-
Vilar, Jean 1912-1971
Weiss, Peter 1916-1982

Theater of Fact (England, 1950s)
OxThe-1983

Brook, Peter 1925-
Kipphardt, Heinar 1922-1982
Littlewood, Joan 1914-
Weiss, Peter 1916-1982

Theater of Panic/Théâtre Panique
(France, 1960s)
DCLT-1979
EncWL-1981
HarDMT-1988

Arrabal, Fernando 1932-

Theater of Silence/Théâtre de
l'Inexprimé (France, 1920s)
CIDMEuL-1980
DCLT-1979
GdMWL-1985
McGWD-1984
OxThe-1983

Bernard, Jean-Jacques 1888-
1972
Maeterlinck, Maurice 1862-1949

Theater of the Absurd (France,
1950s-1960s; also Czechoslovakia,
England, Germany, Poland,
Switzerland, United States)
BenReEncy-1987
CamGLE-1988
CIDMEuL-1980
DCLT-1979
EncWL-1981
GdMWL-1985
HandLit-1986
HarDMT-1988
LongCTCL-1975
McGWD-1984
OxEng-1985
OxThe-1983
RCom-1973

Adamov, Arthur 1908-1970
Albee, Edward 1928-

Arrabal, Fernando 1932-
Artaud, Antonin 1896-1948
Beckett, Samuel 1906-1990
Bialoszewski, Miron 1922-
Campton, David 1924-
Esslin, Martin 1918-
Frisch, Max 1911-
Gelber, Jack 1932-
Genet, Jean 1910-1986
Grass, Günter 1927-
Grochowiak, Stanislaw 1934-
  1976
Havel, Václav 1936-
Herbert, Zbigniew 1924-
Hildesheimer, Wolfgang 1916-
Ionesco, Eugène 1912-
Karpowicz, Tymoteusz 1921-
Kopit, Arthur 1937-
Mrozek, Slawomir 1930-
Pinget, Robert 1919-
Pinter, Harold 1930-
Robbe-Grillet, Alain 1922-
Rózewicz, Tadeusz 1921-
Rymkiewicz, Jaroslaw Marek
  1934-
Simpson, N.F. 1919-
Stoppard, Tom 1937-
Tarn, Adam 1902-1972
Van Itallie, Jean-Claude 1936-
Vian, Boris 1920-1959
Vitrac, Roger 1899-1952

**Theater of the Grotesque/Teatro
del grottescco (Italy, 1910s)**
  ClDMEuL-1980
  GdMWL-1985
  McGWD-1984
  OxThe-1983

Antonelli, Luigi 1882-1942
Cavacchioli, Enrico 1885-1954
Chiarelli, Luigi 1880-1947
Pirandello, Luigi 1867-1936
San Secondo, Rosso di 1887-
  1956

**Theater Workshop (England, 1940s-
1970s)**
  HarDMT-1988
  OxThe-1983

Bart, Lionel 1930-
Behan, Brendan 1923-1964
Delaney, Shelagh 1939-
Lewis, Stephen n.d.
Littlewood, Joan 1914-
McColl, Ewan 1915-
Norman, Frank 1930-1980
Raffles, Gerald n.d.

**Théâtre du Vieux-Colombier
(France, 1910s-1920s)**
  ClDMEuL-1980
  McGWD-1984
  OxFr-1959
  OxThe-1983

Copeau, Jacques 1877-1949
Dullin, Charles 1885-1949
Jouvet, Louis 1887-1951

Théâtre Libre (France, 1887-1896)
  HandLit-1986
  McGWD-1984
  OxFr-1959
  OxGer-1986
  OxThe-1983

Alexis, Paul 1847-1901
Antoine, André 1858-1934
Becque, Henri 1837-1899
Brieux, Eugène 1858-1932
Byl, Arthur n.d.
Curel, François de 1854-1928
Duranty, Louis 1833-1880
Hauptmann, Gerhart 1862-1946
Hennique, Léon 1851-1935
Ibsen, Henrik 1828-1906
Strindberg, August 1849-1912
Vidal, Jules n.d.

See also **Naturalism**

**Theatrical Arts Research Society/
Kuk yesel yon'guhoe (Korea,
1931-1938)**
EncWL-1981

Yu Ch'i-jin 1905-

**Third Front Movement/Trecias
Frontas (Lithuania, 1920s-1930s)**
ClDMEuL-1980
EncWL-1981
GdMWL-1985
PrEncyPP-1974

Cvirka, Petras 1909-1947
Korsakas, Kostas 1909-
Neris, Salomeja 1904-1945
Venclova, Antanas 1906-

**Tide/*Het Getij* (Netherlands, 1920s-
1930s)**
ClDMEuL-1980

Bergh, Herman van den 1897-
1967
Nijhoff, Martinus 1894-1953
Slauerhoff, Jan Jacob 1898-1936

Tiotalister (Sweden, 1910s)
ClDMEuL-1980
EncWL-1981

Bergman, Hjalmar 1883-1931
Hellström, Gustaf 1882-1953
Lidman, Sven 1882-1960
Nordström, Ludvig 1882-1942
Siwertz, Sigfrid 1882-1970
Wägner, Elin 1882-1949

***Tish* Group (Canada, 1960s)**
OxCan-1983

Bowering, George 1935-

Davey, Frank 1940-
Kroetsch, Robert 1927-
Marlatt, Daphne 1942-
Musgrave, Susan 1951-

**Today Group/*Ma* Group (Hungary,
1920s)**
ClDMEuL-1980

Déry, Tibor 1894-1977
Illyés, Gyula 1902-
Kassák, Lajos 1887-1967
Komját, Aladár n.d.
Lengyel, József 1896-
Németh, Andor n.d.
Petlyura, Symon 1879-1926
Révai, József n.d.

**Total Theater (England, France,
Germany, Italy, 1940s-1970s)**
DCLT-1979
HarDMT-1988
OxThe-1983

Barrault, Jean-Louis 1910-
Claudel, Paul 1868-1955
Gide, André 1869-1951
Gropius, Walter 1883-1969
Littlewood, Joan 1914-
Piscator, Erwin 1893-1966
Ronconi, Luca 1913-

**Transcendentalist Group (Cuba,
1937-1940s)**
CaribWr-1979
EncWL-1981

Franco Oppenheimer, Félix
1912-
Lezama Lima, José 1910-1976
Lluch Mora, Francisco 1924-
Matos Paoli, Francisco 1915-
Rentas Lucas, Eugenio 1910-

**Transylvanian Helicon Group
(Romania, 1926)**
ClDMEuL-1980
EncWL-1981

Áprily, Lajos 1887-1967
Bartalis, János 1893-1976
Dsida, Jeno 1907-1938
Reményik, Sándor 1890-1941

Tremendismo (Spain, 1940s)
BenReEncy-1987
EncWL-1981

GdMWL-1985
HarDMT-1988
OxSpan-1978

Cela, Camilio José 1916-
Laforet, Carmen 1921-
Romero, Luis 1916-

Turia Group (Spain, 1950s)
EncWL-1981

Goytisolo, Juan 1931-
Matute, Ana María 1925-

U

Ujhold Group (Hungary, 1950s-1960s)
ClDMEuL-1980

Kálnoky, László n.d.
Mándy, Iván 1918-
Nagy, Ágnes Nemes n.d.
Ottlik, Géza n.d.
Pilinszky, János 1921-
Rába, György n.d.
Rákos, Sándor n.d.
Szábo, Magda 1917-

Ukrainian Home Group (Ukraine, 1920s)
ClDMEuL-1980

Chuprynka, Hryhoriy 1879-1921
Oles, Oleksander 1878-1944
Vorony, Mykola 1871-1942

Ultraism/Ultraismo (Spain and Latin America, 1920s)
ClDMEuL-1980
DCLT-1979
EncWL-1981
GdMWL-1985
HarDMT-1988
OxSpan-1978
PrEncyPP-1974

Aroca, J. de n.d.
Borges, Jorge Luis 1899-1986
Bóveda, Xavier n.d.
Caballero, Fernando Iglesias n.d.
Cansinos Asséns, Rafael 1883-1964
Cernuda, Luis 1902-1963
Comet, César A. n.d.
Diego, Gerardo 1896-1987
Fernández, Macedonio 1874-1952
García Lorca, Federico 1898-1936
Garfias, Pedro n.d.
Güiraldes, Ricardo 1886-1927
Huidobro, Vincente 1893-1948
Larrea, Juan 1895-1982
Marechal, Leopoldo 1900-1970
Martínez Estrada, Ezequiel 1895-1964
Panedas, J. Rivas n.d.
Salinas, Pedro 1891(?)-1951
Torre, Guillermo de 1900-
Vallejo, César 1892-1938

Unanimism/Unamisme (France, 1908-1920)
BenReEncy-1987
ClDMEuL-1980
DCLT-1979
EncWL-1981
GdMWL-1985
HandLit-1986
OxFr-1959
PrEncyPP-1974

Arcos, René 1881-1948

Chennevière, Georges 1884-
1929
Duhamel, Georges 1884-1966
Durtain, Luc 1881-1959
Romains, Jules 1885-1972
Vildrac, Charles 1882-1971

**Under the Ramparts/Taht al-Sur
Group (Tunisia, 1940s)**
EncWL-1981

Du'aji, 'Ali 1909-1949

**Underground Poetry (England,
1950s-1970s)**
OxEng-1985

Mitchell, Adrian 1932-
Nuttall, Jeff 1933-
Pickard, Tom 1946-
Trocchi, Alexander 1925-1984
Williams, Heathcote 1941-

**Unity Theater (England, 1930s-
1940s)**
HarDMT-1988
OxThe-1983

Gyseghem, André van n.d.
Marshall, Herbert 1906-

V

Van nu en straks Group (Belgium, 1890s)
ClDMEuL-1980
EncWL-1981

Buysse, Cyriel 1859-1932
Langendonck, Prosper van 1862-1920
Streuvels, Stijn 1871-1969
Teirlinck, Herman 1879-1967
Vermeylen, August 1872-1945
Woestijne, Karel van de 1878-1929

Verde-Amarelismo (Brazil, 1920s)
EncWL-1981
PrEncyPP-1974

Cunha, Euclides da 1866-1909
Picchia, Menotti del 1892-
Ricardo, Cassiano 1895-1974
Salgado, Plínio 1901-1975
Torres, Alberto 1865-1917

Verismo (Italy, 1860s-1910s)
ClDMEuL-1980
EncWL-1981
GdMWL-1985
HarDMT-1988
OxThe-1983
RCom-1973

Aleramo, Sibilla 1876-1960
Alvaro, Corrado 1896-1956
Capuana, Luigi 1839-1915
DeAmicis, Edmondo 1846-1908

Deledda, Grazia 1871-1936
De Marchi, Emilio 1851-1901
De Roberto, Federico 1861-1927
Di Giacomo, Salvatore 1860-1934
Fogazzaro, Antonio 1842-1911
Fucini, Renato 1843-1921
Giacosa, Giuseppe 1847-1906
Jovine, Francesco 1902-1950
Mascagni, Pietro 1863-1945
Negri, Ada 1870-1945
Nieri, Ildefonso 1853-1920
Pirandello, Luigi 1867-1936
Pratesi, Mario 1842-1921
Puccini, Giacomo 1858-1924
Serao, Matilde 1850-1927
Silone, Ignazio 1900-1978
Verga, Giovanni 1840-1922
Zena, Remigio 1850-1917

Vernacular Movement/Pai-hua (China, 1920s)
DOrLit-1974
EncWL-1981
GdMWL-1985

Hu Shih 1891-1962

Vero Ani Group (Iceland, 1880s-1900s)
ClDMEuL-1980

Drachmann, Holger 1848-1908
Hafstein, Hannes 1861-1922
Kvaran, Einar H. 1859-1938
Pálsson, Gestur 1852-1891

**Vienna Group/Wiener Gruppe
(Austria, 1952-1964)**
ClDMEuL-1980
EncWL-1981
GdMWL-1985
McGWD-1984
OxGer-1986

Achleitner, Friedrich 1930-
Artmann, Hans Carl 1921-
Bayer, Konrad 1932-1964
Jandl, Ernst 1925-
Mayröcker, Friederike 1924-
Rühm, Gerhard 1930-
Wiener, Oswald 1935-

Viernes **Group (Venezuela, 1940s)**
EncWL-1981

D'Sola, Otto 1912-
Gerbasi, Vicente 1912-
Olivares Figueroa, Rafael 1893-
1972
Venegas Filardo, Pascual 1911-

Village Fiction (Turkey, 1950s)
ClDMEuL-1980

Apaydin, Talip 1926-
Basaran, Mehmet 1926-
Baykurt, Fakir 1929-
Bilbasar, Kemal 1910-
Kemal, Yashar 1922-
Kocagöz, Samim 1916-
Makal, Mahmut 1930-

Village Prose (Russia, 1950s-1960s)
ClDMEuL-1980
EncWL-1981

Abramov, Fyodor
Alexandrovich 1920-1983
Amalrik, Andrey Alekseyevich
1938-1981
Belov, Vasily Ivanovich 1932-

Dorosh, Yefim Yakovlevich
1908-1972
Kazakov, Yury 1927-
Mozhayev, Boris Andreyevich
1923-
Ovechkin, Valentin
Vladimirovich 1904-1968
Rasputin, Valentin Grigoryevich
1937-
Shukshin, Vasily 1929-1974
Soloukhin, Vladimir Alexeevich
1924-
Tendryakov, Vladimir
Fyodorovich 1923-
Yashin, Alexandr Yakovlevich
1913-1968
Zalygin, Sergey Pavlovich 1913-

Visnyk **(Ukraine, 1933-1939)**
ClDMEuL-1980

Dontsov, Dmytro 1883-1973
Kravtsiv, Bohdan 1904-1975
Lyaturynska, Oksana 1902-1970
Lypa, Yuriy 1900-1944
Malanyuk, Yevhen 1897-1968
Mosendz, Leonid 1897-1948
Olzhych, Oleh (Oleh Kandyba)
1909-1944
Stefanovych, Oleksa 1900-1970
Teliha, Olena 1907-1942

Vorticism (England, 1914-1915)
BenReEncy-1987
CamGLE-1988
DCLT-1979
EncWL-1981
GdMWL-1985
HandLit-1986
HarDMT-1988
OxEng-1985
PrEncyPP-1974

Bomberg, David 1890-1957
Epstein, Jacob 1880-1959

Etchells, Frederick 1886-1973
Ford, Ford Madox 1873-1939
Gaudier-Brzeska, Henri 1891-
1915
Hamilton, Cuthbert 1884-1959
Hulme, T(homas) E(rnest) 1883-
1917

Lewis, (Percy) Wyndham
1884(?)-1957
Nevinson, Christopher 1889-
1946
Pound, Ezra 1885-1972
Roberts, William 1895-1980
Wadsworth, Edward 1889-1949

W

Washington Square Players (United States, 1910s)
GdMWL-1985
HandLit-1986
McGWD-1984
OxAm-1983
OxAmThe-1984
OxThe-1983

Akins, Zoë 1886-1958
Gale, Zona 1874-1938
Goodman, Edward n.d.
Jones, Robert Edmond 1887-1954
Langner, Lawrence 1890-1962
Moeller, Philip 1880-1958
Peters, Rollo 1892-1967
Simonson, Lee 1888-1967
Westley, Helen 1879-1942

Wave Movement/Onda (Mexico, 1960s)
EncWL-1981

Agustín, José 1944-
Sainz, Gustavo 1940-

Wedge Group/Kiila (Finland, 1930s)
ClDMEuL-1980
EncWL-1981
PengEur-1969
PrEncyPP-1974

Kajava, Viljo 1909-
Pennanen, Jarno 1906-1969
Sinervo, Elvi 1912-
Turtiainen, Arvo 1904-1980

White Birch School/Shirakaba-ha (Japan, 1910-1923)
DOrLit-1974
EncWL-1981

Arishima Takeo 1878-1923
Mushanokoji Saneatsu 1885-1976
Satomi Ton 1888-(?)
Shiga Naoya 1883-1971

Wspólczesnosc Generation (Poland, 1950s)
ClDMEuL-1980

Bialoszewski, Miron 1922-
Bursa, Andrzej 1932-1957
Czachorowski, Stanislaw Swen 1920-
Grochowiak, Stanislaw 1934-1976
Harasymowicz, Jerzy 1933-
Herbert, Zbigniew 1924-
Karpowicz, Tymoteusz 1921-
Koziol, Urszula 1931-
Nowak, Tadeusz 1930-
Rymkiewicz, Jaroslaw Marek 1934-
Szymborska, Wislawa 1923-

Y

Yale School of Critics (United States, 1970s)
EncWL-1981
HarDMT-1988

Bate, Walter Jackson 1918-
Bloom, Harold 1930-
De Man, Paul 1919-1983
Derrida, Jacques 1930-
Hartman, Geoffrey 1929-
Miller, J. Hillis 1928-

Yoruba Opera (Nigeria, 1940s)
EncWL-1981
McGWD-1984

Lapido, Duro 1931-1978
Ogunde, Hubert 1916-
Ogunmola, E. Kola 1925-1973

Young Estonia Group (Estonia, 1905-1910s)
ClDMEuL-1980
EncWL-1981
GdMWL-1985
PrEncyPP-1974

Aavik, Johannes 1880-1973
Enno, Ernst 1875-1934
Kallas, Aino 1878-1956
Oks, Jaan 1884-1918
Ridala, Villem 1885-1942
Suits, Gustav 1883-1956
Tuglas, Friedebert 1886-1971

Young Frisian Movement (Netherlands, 1915-1935)
EncWL-1981
PrEncyPP-1974

Brouwer, Jelle Hindriks 1900-1981
Kalma, Douwe 1896-1953
Kiestra, Douwe Hermans 1899-1970
Schurer, Fedde 1898-1968
Sybesma, Rintsje Piter 1894-1975

Young Israel (Israel, 1950s)
ClDMEuL-1980
EncWL-1981

Pinski, David 1872-1959
Yungman, Moyshe 1922-1983

Young Kashubian Movement (Poland, 1910s)
EncWL-1981

Heyke, Leon 1885-1939
Karnowski, Jan 1886-1939
Majowski, Alexander 1876-1938
Patock, Jan 1886-1940
Sedzicki, Franciszek 1882-1957

Young Muse Group/Moloda Muza (Ukraine, 1920s)
ClDMEuL-1980
EncWL-1981

Charnetsky, Stepan 1881-1945
Karmansky, Petro 1878-1956
Lustky, Ostap n.d.
Pachovsky, Vasyl 1878-1942
Shchurat, Vasyl 1872-1948
Turyansky, Osyp 1890-1933
Yatskiv, Mykhaylo 1873-1961

Young Ones/Die Yunge (United States, 1920s)
ClDMEuL-1980
EncWL-1981
GdMWL-1985
PrEncyPP-1974

Boraisho, Menachem 1888-1949
Halpern, Moyshe Leyb 1886-1932
Iceland, Reuben 1884-1955
Ignatov, David 1885-1953
Landau, Zishe 1889-1937
Leyb, Mani 1883-1953
Nadir, Moyshe 1885-1943
Naydus, Leyb 1890-1918
Opatoshu, Joseph 1886-1954
Raboy, Isaac 1882-1944
Schwartz, I. Jacob 1885-1971

Young Poland/Mloda Polska (Poland, 1890-1920)
ClDMEuL-1980
EncWL-1981
GdMWL-1985
PrEncyPP-1974

Berent, Waclaw 1873-1940
Brzozowski, Stanislaw 1878-1911
Górski, Artur 1870-1959
Irzykowski, Karol 1873-1944
Kasprowicz, Jan 1860-1926
Lange, Antoni 1861-1929
Lesmian, Boleslaw 1877-1937
Matuszewski, Ignacy 1858-1919
Micinski, Tadeusz 1873-1918

Nalkowska, Zofia 1884-1954
Nowaczynski, Adolf 1876-1944
Orkan, Wladyslaw 1875-1930
Przesmycki, Zenon 1861-1944
Przybyszewski, Stanislaw 1868-1927
Reymont, Wladyslaw Stanislaw 1867-1925
Rolicz-Lieder, Waclaw 1866-1912
Sieroszweski, Waclaw 1858-1945
Staff, Leopold 1878-1957
Strug, Andrzej 1871-1937
Tetmajer, Kazimierz 1865-1940
Wyspianski, Stanislaw 1869-1907
Zelinski, Tadeusz 1874-1941
Zeromski, Stefan 1864-1925

Young Vienna Group/Jungwien (Austria, 1890s-1900)
ClDMEuL-1980
EncWL-1981
GdMWL-1985
McGWD-1984
PrEncyPP-1974

Altenberg, Peter 1859-1919
Bahr, Hermann 1863-1934
Beer-Hofmann, Richard 1866-1945
Hofmannsthal, Hugo von 1874-1929
Salten, Felix 1869-1945
Schnitzler, Arthur 1862-1931
Zweig, Stefan 1881-1942

Young Vilna (Lithuania, 1930s)
ClDMEuL-1980
EncWL-1981
PrEncyPP-1974

Glik, Hirsh 1922-1944
Grade, Chaim 1910-1982
Kaczerginski, Schmerke 1908-
  1954
Sutzkever, Abraham 1913-
Vogler, Elkhanon 1907-1969

**Young Yiddish Group (Poland,
1920s)**
  EncWL-1981

Adler, Yankev 1895-1949
Broderzon, Moyshe 1890-1956

Z

Zagary **Group (Lithuania, 1930s)**
ClDMEuL-1980

Milosz, Czeslaw 1911-
Putrament, Jerzy 1910-
Rymkiewicz, Aleksander 1913-
Zagórski, Jerzy 1907-

Zavety (Behests) School (Russia, 1910s)
EncWL-1981

Prishvin, Mikhail 1873-1954
Remizov, Alexey 1877-1957
Zamyatin, Evgeny Ivanovich
1884-1937

Zdroj **Group (Poland, 1917-1922)**
ClDMEuL-1980

Berent, Waclaw 1873-1940
Hulewicz, Jerzy 1886-1941
Kasprowicz, Jan 1860-1926
Orkan, Wladyslaw 1875-1930

Przybyszewski, Stanislaw 1868-
1927
Wittlin, Józef 1896-1976
Zegadlowicz, Emil 1888-1941

Znanie Group (Russia, 1890s-1900s)
ClDMEuL-1980
EncWL-1981
GdMWL-1985

Andreyev, Leonid Nikolayevich
1871-1919
Bunin, Ivan 1870-1953
Gorky, Maxim 1868-1936
Kuprin, Alexandr 1870-1938
Prishvin, Mikhail 1873-1954
Serafimovich, Aleksandr 1863-
1949
Shmelyov, Ivan Sergeyevich
1873-1950
Veresayev, Vikenty 1867-1945
Zaytsev, Boris Konstantinovich
1881-1972

Index to Authors

Aavik, Johannes 1880-1973
(Estonian)
ClDMEuL-1980
EncWL-1981

Young Estonia Group

al-Abbassi, Muhammad Sa'id 1880-
1963 (Sudanese)
EncWL-1981

Neoclassicism

Abercrombie, Lascelles 1881-1938
(English)
BenReEncy-1987
CamGLE-1988
GdMWL-1985
LongCTCL-1975
OxEng-1985
PengEng-1971
PrEncyPP-1974

Georgian Literature

Abramov, Fyodor Alexandrovich
1920-1983 (Russian)
ClDMEuL-1980
EncWL-1981
GdMWL-1985

Village Prose

Abulhasan, Alekperzade 1906-
(Azerbaijani)
EncWL-1981

Socialist Realism

Abu Shadi, Admad Zaki 1892-1955
(Egyptian)
CasWL-1973
DOrLit-1974
EncWL-1981

Apollo School of Poets

Acevedo Díaz, Eduardo 1851-1921
(Uruguayan)
BenReEncy-1987
CasWL-1973
EncWL-1981
GdMWL-1985
OxSpan-1978
PengAm-1971

Gaucho Literature
Generation of 1900

Achebe, Chinua 1930-   (Nigerian)
BenReEncy-1987
CamGLE-1988
CasWL-1973
EncWL-1981
GdMWL-1985
LongCTCL-1975
OxEng-1985
PengEng-1971

PengCOAL-1969

Mbari Club

**Achleitner, Friedrich 1930-
(Austrian)**
ClDMEuL-1980
EncWL-1981
McGWD-1984
OxGer-1986

Concrete Poetry
Vienna Group/Wiener Gruppe

**Adamov, Arthur 1908-1970
(Russian-born French)**
CasWL-1973
ClDMEuL-1980
EncWL-1981
GdMWL-1985
McGWD-1984
OxEng-1985
OxThe-1983
PengEur-1969

New Wave/Nouvelle Vague
Theater of Cruelty/Théâtre de
la Cruauté
Theater of the Absurd

**Adamovich, Georgy Viktorovich
1894-1972 (Russian)**
ClDMEuL-1980
EncWL-1981
GdMWL-1985

Acmeism

**Adams, Samuel Hopkins 1871-1958
(American)**
BenReEncy-1987
OxAm-1983

Muckrakers

**Adamus, Franz 1867-1948 (Polish-
born German)**
OxGer-1986

Naturalism

**Adcock, Fleur 1934- (New Zealand-
born English)**
CamGLE-1988
GdMWL-1985
OxEng-1985

The Group

**Adler, Yankev 1895-1949 (Yiddish-
speaking Polish)**
EncWL-1981

Young Yiddish Group

Adson, Artur 1889-1977 (Estonian)
EncWL-1981
PrEncyPP-1974

Siuru Group

Ady, Endre 1877-1919 (Hungarian)
CasWL-1973
ClDMEuL-1980
EncWL-1981
GdMWL-1985
PengEur-1969

Nyugat Group

**Æ (pseud. of George William
Russell) 1867-1935 (Irish)**
BenReEncy-1987
CamGLE-1988
CasWL-1973
EncWL-1981
GdMWL-1985
LongCTCL-1975
McGWD-1984
OxEng-1985

OxThe-1983
PengEng-1971
PrEncyPP-1974

Abbey Theater
Irish Renaissance

Afinogenov, Aleksandr
Nikolayevich 1904-1941
(Russian)
  ClDMEuL-1980
  EncWL-1981
  McGWD-1984
  OxThe-1983
  PengEur-1969

Moscow Art Theater

Agârbiceanu, Ion 1882-1963
(Romanian)
  CasWL-1973
  ClDMEuL-1980
  EncWL-1981

Poporanism

Agelet, Jaume 1888-1981 (Spanish)
  EncWL-1981

Noucentismo

Agraval, Bharatbhusan n.d. (Indian)
  DOrLit-1974

New Poetry Movement/Nayi
  Kavita

Aguilera Malta, Demetrio 1909-
(Ecuadorian)
  EncWL-1981
  McGWD-1984
  OxSpan-1978
  PengAm-1971

Group of Guayaquil/Grupo de
  Guayaquil
Magic Realism

Agustín, José 1944-   (Mexican)
  EncWL-1981

Wave Movement/Onda

Ahlin, Lars Gustaf 1915-
(Swedish)
  CasWL-1973
  ClDMEuL-1980
  EncWL-1981
  GdMWL-1985
  PengEur-1969

Poets of the Forties/
  Fyrtiotalisterna

Aho, Juhani 1861-1921 (Finnish)
  CasWL-1973
  ClDMEuL-1980
  EncWL-1981
  GdMWL-1985
  PengEur-1969

National Neoromanticism

Aichinger, Ilse 1921-   (Austrian)
  BenReEncy-1987
  CasWL-1973
  ClDMEuL-1980
  EncWL-1981
  GdMWL-1985
  OxGer-1986
  PengEur-1969

Group 47/Gruppe 47

Aikman, Audrey n.d. (Canadian)
  OxCan-1983

First Statement Group

Ajñeya, Saccidanada 1911-
(Indian)
   DOrLit-1974

   New Poetry Movement/Nayi
     Kavita

Akhmatova, Anna (pseud. of Anna
Andreevna Gorenko) 1888-1966
(Russian)
   BenReEncy-1987
   CasWL-1973
   ClDMEuL-1980
   EncWL-1981
   GdMWL-1985
   LongCTCL-1975
   OxEng-1985
   PengEur-1969
   PrEncyPP-1974

   Acmeism

Akins, Zoë 1886-1958 (American)
   OxAm-1983
   OxAmThe-1984

   Washington Square Players

Alarcón, Pedro Antonio 1833-1891
(Spanish)
   OxSpan-1978

   Realism

'Alavi, Aqa Buzurg 1907-
(Iranian)
   CasWL-1973
   DOrLit-1974
   EncWL-1981

   Rab'e Group

Albee, Edward 1928- (American)
   BenReEncy-1987
   CamGLE-1988

   CasWL-1973
   EncWL-1981
   GdMWL-1985
   LongCTCL-1975
   McGWD-1984
   OxAm-1983
   OxAmThe-1984
   OxEng-1985
   OxThe-1983
   PengAm-1971
   RCom-1973

   Theater of Cruelty/Théâter de
    la Cruauté
   Theater of the Absurd

Albers, Josef 1888-1976 (German-
born American)
   OxAm-1983

   Black Mountain Poets

Alberti, Rafael 1902- (Spanish)
   BenReEncy-1987
   CasWL-1973
   CEnMWL-1963
   ClDMEuL-1980
   EncWL-1981
   GdMWL-1985
   McGWD-1984
   OxSpan-1978
   OxThe-1983
   PengEur-1969

   Generation of 1927/Generación
    del 1927
   Surrealism

Alcántara, Oswaldo (pseud. of
Baltasar Lopes da Silva) 1907-
(Cape Verdean)
   ClDMEuL-1980
   EncWL-1981

PengCOAL-1969

Claridade Movement

Aldecoa, Ignacio 1925-1969 (Spanish)
ClDMEuL-1980
EncWL-1981
OxSpan-1978

Objectivism

Aldington, Richard 1892-1962 (English)
BenReEncy-1987
CamGLE-1988
CasWL-1973
EncWL-1981
GdMWL-1985
LongCTCL-1975
OxAm-1983
OxEng-1985
PengEng-1971
RCom-1973

Imagism

Aldrich, Thomas Bailey 1836-1907 (American)
BenReEncy-1987
CamGLE-1988
CasWL-1973
GdMWL-1985
OxAm-1983
OxEng-1985
PengAm-1971

Genteel Tradition

Alechinsky, Pierre 1927- (Belgian)
HarDMT-1988

Cobra

Alegría, Ciro 1909-1966 (Peruvian)
BenReEncy-1987
CasWL-1973
EncWL-1981
GdMWL-1985
OxSpan-1978
PengAm-1971

Realism

Alegría, Fernando 1918- (Chilean)
EncWL-1981
OxSpan-1978

Generation of 1938/Generación del 1938

Aleixandre, Vicente 1898-1984 (Spanish)
BenReEncy-1987
CasWL-1973
ClDMEuL-1980
EncWL-1981
OxSpan-1978
PengEur-1969
PrEncyPP-1974

Generation of 1927/Generación del 1927
Surrealism

Aleramo, Sibilla 1876-1960 (Italian)
CasWL-1973
ClDMEuL-1980
EncWL-1981
GdMWL-1985

Verismo

Alexis, Jacques-Stéphen 1922-1961 (Haitian)
CaribWr-1979
CasWL-1973
EncWL-1981

GdMWL-1985

Magic Realism

Alexis, Paul 1847-1901 (French)
GdMWL-1985
OxFr-1959

Naturalism
Théâtre Libre

Alfons, Sven 1918- (Swedish)
ClDMEuL-1980
EncWL-1981
PrEncyPP-1974

Poets of the Forties/
    Fyrtiotalisterna

Ali, Ahmed 1910-   (Pakistani)
CamGLE-1988
CasWL-1973
DOrLit-1974
EncWL-1981
GdMWL-1985
PengCOAL-1969

Progressive Writers' Movement

**Ali, Sabahattin, 1906-1948
(Turkish)**
ClDMEuL-1980
DOrLit-1974
EncWL-1981

Socialist Realism

Allgood, Sarah 1883-1950 (Irish)
OxAmThe-1984
OxEng-1985
OxThe-1983

Abbey Theater
Irish Renaissance

**Almada-Negreiros, José de 1893-
1970 (Portuguese)**
ClDMEuL-1980
EncWL-1981
McGWD-1984

Orpheu Group
Presencistas Group

**Almeida, Guilherme de 1890-1969
(Brazilian)**
GdMWL-1985
PrEncyPP-1974

Modernism

Alonso, Dámaso 1898-   (Spanish)
CasWL-1973
ClDMEuL-1980
EncWL-1981
GdMWL-1985
OxSpan-1978
PengEur-1969

Generation of 1927/Generación
    del 1927

**Altenberg, Peter 1859-1919
(Austrian)**
EncWL-1981
GdMWL-1985
OxGer-1986
PrEncyPP-1974

Young Vienna Group/Jungwien

Althusser, Louis 1918-   (French)
ClDMEuL-1980
EncWL-1981
OxEng-1985
PrEncyPP-1974

Marxist Criticism
Structuralism

Altolaguirre, Manuel 1906-1959 (Spanish)
BenReEncy-1987
CasWL-1973
ClDMEuL-1980
GdMWL-1985
OxSpan-1978
PengEur-1969

Generation of 1927/Generación del 1927

Alvarado, Huberto 1925- (Guatemalan)
OxSpan-1978

Dawn Group/Grupo Saker Ti

Álvarez, José María 1942- (Spanish)
EncWL-1981

Novísmos Group

Álvarez Quintero, Alberto n.d. (Mexican)
EncWL-1981
OxSpan-1978

Taller Group

Alvaro, Corrado 1895-1956 (Italian)
CasWL-1973
ClDMEuL-1980
EncWL-1981
GdMWL-1985
PengEur-1969

Neorealism
Verismo

Alver, Betti 1906-   (Estonian)
ClDMEuL-1980
EncWL-1981
GdMWL-1985

PrEncyPP-1974

Soothsayers Movement/ Arbujad

Amado, Jorge 1912-   (Brazilian)
BenReEncy-1987
CasWL-1973
EncWL-1981
GdMWL-1985
PengAm-1971

Modernism

Amalrik, Andrey Alekseyevich 1938-1981 (Russian)
BenReEncy-1987
ClDMEuL-1980
EncWL-1981

Village Prose

Amir Hamzah 1911-1946 (Indonesian)
EncWL-1981
PengCOAL-1969
PrEncyPP-1974

New Writers' Circle/Pudjangga Baru

Amis, Kingsley 1922- (English)
BenReEncy-1987
CamGLE-1988
CasWL-1973
CEnMWL-1963
EncWL-1981
GdMWL-1985
LongCTCL-1975
OxEng-1985
PengEng-1971

Angry Young Men
The Movement
New Lines Poets

Amorim, Enrique 1900-1960
(Uruguayan)
CasWL-1973
EncWL-1981
OxSpan-1978
PengAm-1971

Boedo Group

Amoroso Lima, Alceu 1893-
(Brazilian)
PengAm-1971
PrEncyPP-1974

Generation of 1945

Anceschi, Luciano 1911-   (Italian)
ClDMEuL-1980
EncWL-1981

Group 63/Gruppo 63

Anday, Melih Cevdet 1915-
(Turkish)
ClDMEuL-1980
DOrLit-1974
EncWL-1981
GdMWL-1985
McGWD-1984
PrEncyPP-1974

Garip Movement
Poetic Realism

Andersch, Alfred 1914-1980
(German)
BenReEncy-1987
CasWL-1973
ClDMEuL-1980
EncWL-1981
GdMWL-1985
OxGer-1986
PengEur-1969

Group 47/Gruppe 47

Anderson, Margaret C. 1886-1973
(American)
BenReEncy-1987

Chicago Group/Renaissance

Anderson, Maxwell 1888-1959
(American)
BenReEncy-1987
CamGLE-1988
CasWL-1973
EncWL-1981
GdMWL-1985
LongCTCL-1975
OxAm-1983
OxAmThe-1984
OxThe-1983
PengAm-1971

Group Theater
Naturalism
Theater Guild

Anderson, Patrick 1915-1979
(English-born Canadian)
OxCan-1983

First Statement Group

Anderson, Sherwood 1876-1941
(American)
BenReEncy-1987
CamGLE-1988
CasWL-1973
CEnMWL-1963
EncWL-1981
GdMWL-1985
LongCTCL-1975
OxAm-1983
OxEng-1985
PengAm-1971

Chicago Group/Renaissance
The Fugitives/Agrarians
Lost Generation

Provincetown Players

Andersson, Dan 1888-1920
(Swedish)
  CasWL-1973
  ClDMEuL-1980
  EncWL-1981
  GdMWL-1985
  PengEur-1969

Proletarian Writers/
  Arbetardiktare

Andiyevska, Emma 1931-
(Ukrainian)
  EncWL-1981

New York Group

Andrade, Mário de 1893-1945
(Brazilian)
  BenReEncy-1987
  CasWL-1973
  EncWL-1981
  GdMWL-1985
  McGWD-1984
  PengAm-1971
  PrEncyPP-1974

Modernism

Andrade, Oswald de 1890-1954
(Brazilian)
  CasWL-1973
  EncWL-1981
  GdMWL-1985
  McGWD-1984
  PengAm-1971
  PrEncyPP-1974

Antropofagia Group
Modernism
Pau Brasil Group

Andreyev, Leonid Nikolayevich
1871-1919 (Russian)
  BenReEncy-1987
  CasWL-1973
  ClDMEuL-1980
  EncWL-1981
  GdMWL-1985
  McGWD-1984
  OxEng-1985
  OxThe-1983
  PengEur-1969

Symbolism
Znanie Group

Anghel, Dimitrie 1872-1914
(Romanian)
  CasWL-1973
  ClDMEuL-1980

Symbolism

Angus, Marion 1866-1946 (Scottish)
  CamGLE-1988
  EncWL-1981
  PengEng-1971

Scottish Renaissance

Anhava, Tuomas 1927-   (Finnish)
  ClDMEuL-1980
  EncWL-1981
  GdMWL-1985
  PengEur-1969

Modernism

Annensky, Innokenti Fëdorovich
1856-1909 (Russian)
  CasWL-1973
  ClDMEuL-1980
  EncWL-1981
  GdMWL-1985
  McGWD-1984
  PengEur-1969

Acmeism
Symbolism

Antoine, André 1858-1934 (French)
CamGLE-1988
ClDMEuL-1980
LongCTCL-1975
McGWD-1984
OxFr-1959
OxThe-1983

Naturalism
Théâtre Libre

Antonelli, Luigi 1882-1942 (Italian)
ClDMEuL-1980
OxThe-1983

Theater of the Grotesque/Teatro
del grottescco

**Antoniou, Dimitrios I. 1906-
(Greek)**
ClDMEuL-1980
GdMWL-1985

Generation of 1930

**Antonych, Bohdan Ihor 1909-1937
(Ukrainian)**
ClDMEuL-1980
EncWL-1981
GdMWL-1985

Dzvony

**Anzengruber, Ludwig 1839-1889
(Austrian)**
CasWL-1973
OxGer-1986
OxThe-1983
PengEur-1969

Freie Bühne
Heimatkunst

Apaydin, Talip 1926-   (Turkish)
ClDMEuL-1980

Village Fiction

Apchaidse, S. n.d. (Georgian)
PrEncyPP-1974

Blue Horns Group/Tsispheri
q'antesbi

**Apollinaire, Guillaume (pseud. of
Wilhelm Apollinaris de
Kostrowitzky) 1880-1918 (Italian-
born French)**
BenReEncy-1987
CasWL-1973
CEnMWL-1963
ClDMEuL-1980
EncWL-1981
GdMWL-1985
LongCTCL-1975
McGWD-1984
OxEng-1985
OxFr-1959
PengEur-1969
PrEncyPP-1974
RCom-1973

Cubism
Dadaism
Futurism

Appel, Karel 1921-   (Dutch)
HarDMT-1988

Cobra

Appelfeld, Aharon 1932-   (Israeli)
CasWL-1973
ClDMEuL-1980
EncWL-1981
GdMWL-1985

Metarealism

Áprily, Lajos 1887-1967 (Hungarian-speaking Romanian)
EncWL-1981
PengEur-1969

Transylvanian Helicon Group

'Aql, Sa'id 1912-   (Lebanese)
DOrLit-1974
EncWL-1981

Parnassian-Symbolist School

al-'Aqqad, 'Abbas Mahmud 1889-1964 (Egyptian)
CasWL-1973
DOrLit-1974
EncWL-1981

Diwan School of Poets

Aragon, Louis 1897-1982 (French)
BenReEncy-1987
CasWL-1973
ClDMEuL-1980
EncWL-1981
GdMWL-1985
LongCTCL-1975
McGWD-1984
OxEng-1985
OxFr-1959
PengEur-1969
PrEncyPP-1974

Dadaism
Socialist Realism
Surrealism

Aranha, José Pereira da Graça 1868-1931 (Brazilian)
EncWL-1981
PengAm-1971

Modernism

Arany, János 1817-1882 (Hungarian)
ClDMEuL-1980
EncWL-1981
PengEur-1969

Popular National School

Arbasino, Alberto 1930-   (Italian)
ClDMEuL-1980
EncWL-1981

Group 63/Gruppo 63

Arbaud, Joseph d' 1872-1950 (Provençal-speaking French)
ClDMEuL-1980
EncWL-1981
GdMWL-1985

Félibrige Movement

Arbó, Sebastià Juan 1902- (Spanish)
ClDMEuL-1980
EncWL-1981
GdMWL-1985
OxSpan-1978

Noucentismo

Archipenko, Alexander 1887-1964 (Russian)
HarDMT-1988

Cubism

Arcos, René 1881-1948 (French)
OxFr-1959

Abbaye Group
Unanimism/Unanisme

Ardrey, Robert 1908-1980 (American)
BenReEncy-1987

McGWD-1984
OxThe-1983

Group Theater

**Arghezi, Tudor (pseud. of Ion
    Theodorescu) 1880-1967
    (Romanian)**
CasWL-1973
ClDMEuL-1980
EncWL-1981
GdMWL-1985
PengEur-1969

Gîndirea

**Arguedas, José María 1911-1969
    (Peruvian)**
BenReEncy-1987
CasWL-1973
EncWL-1981
GdMWL-1985
OxSpan-1978
PengAm-1971

Realism

**Argüedes, Alcides 1879-1946
    (Bolivian)**
BenReEncy-1987
CasWL-1973
EncWL-1981
GdMWL-1985
OxSpan-1978
PengAm-1971

Realism

**Arias, Augusto Sacotto n.d.
    (Ecuadorian)**
OxSpan-1978

Grupo Elan

**Arishima Takeo 1878-1923
    (Japanese)**
CasWL-1973
DOrLit-1974
EncWL-1981

White Birch School/Shirakaba-
    ha

Arland, Marcel 1899-   (French)
CasWL-1973
ClDMEuL-1980
EncWL-1981
PengEur-1969

Nouvelle Revue Française

Arlt, Roberto 1900-1942 (Argentine)
EncWL-1981
GdMWL-1985
OxSpan-1978
PengAm-1971

Boedo Group

**Arnér, Ernst Nils Sivar Erik 1909-
    (Swedish)**
CasWL-1973
EncWL-1981
PengEur-1969

Poets of the Forties/
    Fyrtiotalisterna

Aroca, J. de n.d. (Spanish)
OxSpan-1978

Ultraism/Ultraismo

**Arp, Jean (Hans) 1887-1966
    (German-born French)**
BenReEncy-1987
CasWL-1973
EncWL-1981
GdMWL-1985

OxEng-1985
OxFr-1959
OxGer-1986
PengEur-1969
PrEncyPP-1974

Dadaism
Surrealism

Arrabal, Fernando 1932-
(Moroccan-born Spanish)
BenReEncy-1987
CasWL-1973
ClDMEuL-1980
EncWL-1981
GdMWL-1985
McGWD-1984
OxSpan-1978
OxThe-1983
PengEur-1969

Theater of Cruelty/Théâtre de
la Cruauté
Theater of Panic/Théâtre
Panique
Theater of the Absurd

Arraiz, Antonio 1903-1963
(Venezuelan)
EncWL-1981
OxSpan-1978

Generation of 1918

Artaud, Antonin 1896-1948 (French)
BenReEncy-1987
CamGLE-1988
CasWL-1973
ClDMEuL-1980
EncWL-1981
GdMWL-1985
LongCTCL-1975
McGWD-1984
OxEng-1985
OxThe-1983

PengEur-1969
PrEncyPP-1974

Surrealism
Theater of Cruelty/Théâtre de
la Cruauté
Theater of the Absurd

Artmann, Hans Carl 1921-
(Austrian)
CasWL-1973
ClDMEuL-1980
EncWL-1981
GdMWL-1985
McGWD-1984
OxGer-1986

Concrete Poetry
Vienna Group/Wiener Gruppe

Arvelo Larriva, Alfredo 1883-1934
(Venezuelan)
EncWL-1981

Modernismo

Arzubide, Germán List n.d.
(Spanish)
OxSpan-1978

Estridentismo

Ascásubi, Hilario 1807-1875
(Spanish-born Argentine)
BenReEncy-1987
CasWL-1973
OxSpan-1978
PengAm-1971
PrEncyPP-1974

Gaucho Literature

Aseyev, Nikolay Nikolayevich 1889-
1963 (Russian)
CasWL-1973

ClDMEuL-1980
EncWL-1981
GdMWL-1985
PengEur-1969

Centrifuge
LEF

Ashbery, John 1927- (American)
   BenReEncy-1987
   CamGLE-1988
   EncWL-1981
   GdMWL-1985
   OxAm-1983
   PengAm-1971
   PrEncyPP-1974

New York School

Ashe, Geoffrey 1923-   (English)
   OxCan-1983

First Statement Group

Asi, Harri 1922-   (Estonian)
   EncWL-1981

Soothsayers Movement/
   Arbujad

Asmal (pseud. of Abdul Samad bin Asmail) 1924-   (Malaysian)
   EncWL-1981

Generation of the 1950s/Asas
   '50

Aspenström, Karl Werner 1918- (Swedish)
   CasWL-1973
   ClDMEuL-1980
   EncWL-1981
   GdMWL-1985
   McGWD-1984
   PrEncyPP-1974

Poets of the Forties/
Fyrtiotalisterna

Asrul Sani n.d. (Indonesian)
   PrEncyPP-1974

Generation of 1950

Asturias, Miguel Ángel 1899-1974 (Guatemalan)
   BenReEncy-1987
   CamGLE-1988
   CasWL-1973
   EncWL-1981
   GdMWL-1985
   McGWD-1984
   OxSpan-1978
   PengAm-1971

Magic Realism

Atías, Guillermo 1917-   (Chilean)
   EncWL-1981

Generation of 1938/Generación
del 1938

Aubanel, Théodore 1829-1886 (French)
   CasWL-1973
   ClDMEuL-1980
   EncWL-1981
   OxFr-1959
   PengEur-1969
   PrEncyPP-1974

Félibrige Movement

Aucamp, Hennie 1934-   (South African)
   EncWL-1981

The Sestigers

**Auden, W(ystan) H(ugh) 1907-1973
(English-born American)**
BenReEncy-1987
CamGLE-1988
CasWL-1973
CEnMWL-1963
EncWL-1981
GdMWL-1985
LongCTCL-1975
McGWD-1984
OxAm-1983
OxEng-1985
PengEng-1971
RCom-1973

Group Theater
Modernism
Pylon School

**Audiberti, Jacques 1900-1965
(French)**
CasWL-1973
ClDMEuL-1980
EncWL-1981
GdMWL-1985
McGWD-1984
OxFr-1959
OxThe-1983
PengEur-1969

Theater of Cruelty/Théâtre de
la Cruauté

**Aukrust, Olav 1883-1929
(Norwegian)**
CasWL-1973
ClDMEuL-1980
EncWL-1981
GdMWL-1985
PengEur-1969

Generation of 1905

**Averbakh, Leopold Leonidovich
1903-   (Russian)**
CasWL-1973

RAPP

**Awam-il-Sarkam 1918-
(Malaysian)**
EncWL-1981

Generation of the 1950s/Asas
'50

**Axelrod, Selig 1904-1941 (Yiddish-
speaking Byelorussian)**
ClDMEuL-1980
EncWL-1981

Minsk Group

**Ayaz, Skeikh Mubarak 1923-
(Pakistani)**
DOrLit-1974
EncWL-1981

Progressive Writers' Movement

**Azorín (pseud. of José Martínez
Ruiz) 1873-1969 (Spanish)**
BenReEncy-1987
CasWL-1973
ClDMEuL-1980
EncWL-1981
GdMWL-1985
McGWD-1984
OxSpan-1978
PengEur-1969

Generation of 1898/Generación
del 1898
Modernismo
Surrealism

Azuela, Mariano 1873-1952
  (Mexican)
    BenReEncy-1987
    CasWL-1973
    EncWL-1981

GdMWL-1985
OxSpan-1978
PengAm-1971

Realism

B

Baader, Johannes 1875-1955 (Swiss)
EncWL-1981

Dadaism

Baargeld, Johannes (?)-1927 (Swiss)
EncWL-1981

Dadaism

**Babareka, Adam 1899-1937
(Byelorussian)**
ClDMEuL-1980

Uzvyssa Group

**Babayevsky, Semën Petrovich 1909-
(Russian)**
CasWL-1973

Socialist Realism

**Babbitt, Irving 1865-1933
(American)**
CamGLE-1988
CasWL-1973
EncWL-1981
LongCTCL-1975
OxAm-1983
OxEng-1985
PengAm-1971
PrEncyPP-1974

New Humanism

**Babel, Isaak Emmanuilovich 1894-
1941(?) (Russian)**
BenReEncy-1987
CasWL-1973
CEnMWL-1963
ClDMEuL-1980
EncWL-1981
GdMWL-1985
LongCTCL-1975
OxEng-1985
PengEur-1969

Modernism

**Babits, Mihály 1883-1941
(Hungarian)**
CasWL-1973
ClDMEuL-1980
EncWL-1981
GdMWL-1985
PengEur-1969

Nyugat Group

**Bacchelli, Riccardo 1891-1985
(Italian)**
BenReEncy-1987
CasWL-1973
ClDMEuL-1980
EncWL-1981
GdMWL-1985
PengEur-1969

Rondismo

**Bachelard, Gaston 1884-1962
(French)**
  BenReEncy-1987
  CasWL-1973
  ClDMEuL-1980
  EncWL-1981
  GdMWL-1985
  PengEur-1969

  Structuralism

**Bachmann, Ingeborg 1926-1973
(Austrian)**
  CasWL-1973
  ClDMEuL-1980
  EncWL-1981
  GdMWL-1985
  OxGer-1986
  PengEur-1969

  Group 47/Gruppe 47

**Bacovia, George 1884-1957
(Romanian)**
  CasWL-1973
  ClDMEuL-1980
  EncWL-1981
  PengEur-1969

  Symbolism

**Baczynski, Krzysztof Kamil 1921-
1944 (Polish)**
  CasWL-1973
  ClDMEuL-1980
  EncWL-1981

  Condemned Generation Poets

**Báez, Cecilio 1862-1941
(Paraguayan)**
  EncWL-1981
  OxSpan-1978

  Generation of 1900

**Bagritsky, Edvard 1895-1934
(Russian)**
  CasWL-1973
  ClDMEuL-1980
  EncWL-1981
  GdMWL-1985
  PengEur-1969

  Acmeism
  Constructivism
  Cubo-Futurism

**Bagryana, Elisaveta 1893-
(Bulgarian)**
  CasWL-1973
  ClDMEuL-1980
  EncWL-1981
  GdMWL-1985
  PengEur-1969

  Golden Horn Movement/
    Zlatorog

**Bahdanovich, Maksim 1891-1917
(Byelorussian)**
  ClDMEuL-1980
  EncWL-1981
  GdMWL-1985
  PrEncyPP-1974

  Our Soil Group/Nasaniustva
  Renaissance Group/
    Adradzenstva

**Bahr, Hermann 1863-1934
(Austrian)**
  CasWL-1973
  ClDMEuL-1980
  EncWL-1981
  GdMWL-1985
  McGWD-1984
  OxGer-1986
  OxThe-1983
  PengEur-1969
  PrEncyPP-1974

Deutsches Theater
Young Vienna Group/Jungwien

Baker, Dorothy 1907-1968
(American)
  OxAm-1983
  PengAm-1971

Jazz Age

Baker, George Pierce 1866-1935
(American)
  OxThe-1983

47 Workshop

Baker, Ray Stannard 1870-1946
(American)
  BenReEncy-1987
  LongCTCL-1975
  OxAm-1983

Muckrakers

Balcerzan, Edward 1937-   (Polish)
  ClDMEuL-1980

Teraz Group

Balestrini, Nanni 1935-   (Italian)
  ClDMEuL-1980
  EncWL-1981

Group 63/Gruppo 63

Balinski, Stanislaw 1899-   (Polish)
  ClDMEuL-1980
  GdMWL-1985
  PrEncyPP-1974

Skamander Group

Ball, Hugo 1886-1927 (German)
  CasWL-1973
  ClDMEuL-1980

EncWL-1981
GdMWL-1985
OxFr-1959
OxGer-1986
PengEur-1969
PrEncyPP-1974

Dadaism
Expressionism

Balla, Giacomo 1871-1958 (Italian)
  BenReEncy-1987
  EncWL-1981
  OxEng-1985

Futurism

Ballagas, Emilio 1910-1954 (Cuban)
  CaribWr-1979
  EncWL-1981
  OxSpan-1978
  PengAm-1971

Afro-Cubanism
Negrismo

Balmont, Konstantin Dimitrievich
1867-1943 (Russian)
  BenReEncy-1987
  CasWL-1973
  ClDMEuL-1980
  EncWL-1981
  GdMWL-1985
  PengEur-1969
  PrEncyPP-1974

Symbolism

Baltakis, Algimantas 1930-
(Lithuanian)
  PrEncyPP-1974

Socialist Realism

**Bal'trushaitis, Jurgis 1873-1944
(Lithuanian)**
CasWL-1973
EncWL-1981
GdMWL-1985
PrEncyPP-1974

Symbolism

**Balzac, Honoré de 1799-1850
(French)**
BenReEncy-1987
CamGLE-1988
CasWL-1973
EncWL-1981
McGWD-1984
OxEng-1985
OxFr-1959
OxThe-1983
PengEur-1969
RCom-1973

Realism

**Bandeira Filho, Manuel Carneiro de
Sousa 1886-1968 (Brazilian)**
BenReEncy-1987
CasWL-1973
EncWL-1981
GdMWL-1985
McGWD-1984
PengAm-1971
PrEncyPP-1974

Festa Group
Modernism

**al-Banna, 'Abdallah 1890-
(Sudanese)**
EncWL-1981

Neoclassicism

**Baquero Diego, Gastón 1916-
(Cuban)**
CaribWr-1979
EncWL-1981

Orígenes Group

**Barahona, Melvin René n.d.
(Guatemalan)**
OxSpan-1978

The Dawn Group/Grupo Saker
Ti

**Baraka, Imamu Amiri (born LeRoi
Jones) 1934- (American)**
BenReEncy-1987
CamGLE-1988
CasWL-1973
EncWL-1981
McGWD-1984
OxAm-1983
PengAm-1971
RCom-1973

Black Mountain Poets
Jazz Poetry

**Baranczak, Stanislaw 1946-
(Polish)**
ClDMEuL-1980
EncWL-1981

Teraz Group

Baras, Alexandros 1906-   (Greek)
ClDMEuL-1980

Generation of 1930

**Barba Jacob, Porfirio 1883-1924
(Columbian)**
CasWL-1973
EncWL-1981
OxSpan-1978

PengAm-1971

Modernismo

Barbaro, Umberto 1902-1959 (Italian)
HarDMT-1988

Neorealism

Barbosa, Jorge 1901-1971 (Cape Verdean)
ClDMEuL-1980
EncWL-1981

Claridade Movement

Barda, Fricis 1880-1919 (Latvian)
EncWL-1981

Neoromanticism

Barilli, Renato 1935-   (Italian)
ClDMEuL-1980

Group 63/Gruppo 63

Baring, Maurice 1874-1945 (English)
BenReEncy-1987
CamGLE-1988
CasWL-1973
LongCTCL-1975
OxEng-1985

Georgian Literature

Barker, George Granville 1913- (English)
BenReEncy-1987
CamGLE-1988
CasWL-1973
CEnMWL-1963
EncWL-1981
GdMWL-1985

LongCTCL-1975
OxEng-1985
PengEng-1971

New Apocalypse

Barlach, Ernst 1870-1938 (German)
BenReEncy-1987
CasWL-1973
ClDMEuL-1980
EncWL-1981
GdMWL-1985
McGWD-1984
OxGer-1986
OxThe-1983
PengEur-1969
PrEncyPP-1974

Expressionism

Barletta, Leónides 1902- (Argentine)
OxSpan-1978

Boedo Group

Barnard, Chris 1939-   (South African)
EncWL-1981

The Sestigers

Barnes, Djuna 1892-1982 (American)
BenReEncy-1987
CamGLE-1988
CasWL-1973
EncWL-1981
GdMWL-1985
LongCTCL-1975
OxEng-1985
PengAm-1971

Provincetown Players

127

Baroja y Nessi, Ricardo (Pío) 1872-1956 (Spanish)
BenReEncy-1987
CasWL-1973
CEnMWL-1963
ClDMEuL-1980
EncWL-1981
GdMWL-1985
OxSpan-1978
PengEur-1969

Generation of 1898/Generación del 1898

Barr, Robert 1850-1912 (Scottish-born Canadian)
OxCan-1983

Local Color School

Barrault, Jean-Louis 1910- (French)
ClDMEuL-1980
EncWL-1981
GdMWL-1985
McGWD-1984
OxFr-1959
OxThe-1983

Theater of Cruelty/Théâtre de la Cruauté
Total Theater

Barreda, Octavio G. n.d. (Mexican)
OxSpan-1978

Contemporaries/
Contemporáneos

Barreto-Rivera, Rafael n.d. (Canadian)
OxCan-1983

Four Horsemen

Barrie, James M(atthew) 1860-1937 (Scottish)
BenReEncy-1987
CamGLE-1988
CasWL-1973
EncWL-1981
GdMWL-1985
LongCTCL-1975
McGWD-1984
OxAmThe-1984
OxEng-1985
OxThe-1983
PengEng-1971

Edwardian Literature

Barrios Hudtwalcker, Eduardo 1884-1963 (Chilean)
BenReEncy-1987
CasWL-1973
EncWL-1981
GdMWL-1985
OxSpan-1978
PengAm-1971

Criollismo

Bart, Lionel 1930- (English)
HarDMT-1988

Theater Workshop

Bartalis, János 1893-1976 (Hungarian-speaking Romanian)
EncWL-1981

Transylvanian Helicon Group

Bartels, Adolf 1862-1945 (German)
EncWL-1981
OxGer-1986

Heimatkunst

Barthes, Roland 1915-1980 (French)
BenReEncy-1987
CamGLE-1988
CasWL-1973
ClDMEuL-1980
EncWL-1981
OxEng-1985
PengEur-1969
PrEncyPP-1974

Semiotics
Structuralism
Tel Quel Group

Bartsch, Rudolf Hans 1873-1952
(Austrian)
OxGer-1986

Heimatkunst

Barzun, Henri-Martin 1881-(?)
(French)
OxFr-1959

Abbaye Group/Groupe de
l'Abbaye
Simultanéisme

Basaran, Mehmet 1926-   (Turkish)
ClDMEuL-1980

Village Fiction

Bashir, Tijani Yusuf 1910-1936
(Sudanese)
EncWL-1981

Romantic Poets

Bassani, Giorgio 1916-   (Italian)
BenReEncy-1987
CasWL-1973
ClDMEuL-1980
EncWL-1981
GdMWL-1985

OxEng-1985
PengEur-1969

Neorealism

Bate, Walter Jackson 1918-
(American)
BenReEncy-1987
EncWL-1981
OxAm-1983

Deconstructionism
Yale School of Critics

Bates, Ralph 1899-   (English)
BenReEncy-1987
LongCTCL-1975
PengEng-1971

Proletarian Literature

Baudelaire, Charles 1821-1867
(French)
BenReEncy-1987
CasWL-1973
ClDMEuL-1980
EncWL-1981
OxEng-1985
OxFr-1959
PengEur-1969
PrEncyPP-1974
RCom-1973

Symbolism

Bauer, Walter 1904-1976 (German)
EncWL-1981
OxCan-1983
OxGer-1986

New Objectivity/Neue
Sachlichkeit

Bayer, Konrad 1932-1964 (Austrian)
ClDMEuL-1980

EncWL-1981
McGWD-1984
OxGer-1986

Vienna Group/Wiener Gruppe

Baykurt, Fakir 1929-   (Turkish)
CasWL-1973
ClDMEuL-1980
EncWL-1981

Village Fiction

**Bazhan, Mykola 1904-
(Ukrainian)**
EncWL-1981

Neoromanticism

Beach, Lewis 1891-1947 (American)
OxAm-1983
OxAmThe-1984

Provincetown Players

Beauclair, Henri 1860-1919 (French)
OxFr-1959

Symbolism

**Beauvior, Simone de 1908-1986
(French)**
BenReEncy-1987
CasWL-1973
CEnMWL-1963
ClDMEuL-1980
EncWL-1981
GdMWL-1985
LongCTCL-1975
OxEng-1985
OxFr-1959
PengEur-1969
RCom-1973

Existentialism

Feminist Criticism

**Becher, Johannes R(obert) 1891-
1958 (German)**
CasWL-1973
ClDMEuL-1980
EncWL-1981
GdMWL-1985
OxGer-1986
PengEur-1969
PrEncyPP-1974

Expressionism
Socialist Realism

Beck, Julian 1925-1985 (American)
OxAmThe-1984

Living Theater

**Beck, Karl 1817-1879 (Hungarian-
born German)**
OxGer-1986
PrEncyPP-1974

Realism

Beckett, Samuel 1906-1989 (Irish)
BenReEncy-1987
CamGLE-1988
CasWL-1973
CEnMWL-1963
ClDMEuL-1980
EncWL-1981
GdMWL-1985
LongCTCL-1975
McGWD-1984
OxAmThe-1984
OxEng-1985
OxThe-1983
PengEng-1971
PengEur-1969
RCom-1973

New Novel/Nouveau Roman

New Wave/Nouvelle Vague
Theater of the Absurd

**Beckmann, Max 1884-1950
(German)**
  OxGer-1986

  Expressionism
  New Objectivity/Neue
    Sachlichkeit

Becque, Henri 1837-1899 (French)
  CasWL-1973
  McGWD-1984
  OxFr-1959
  PengEur-1969

  Naturalism
  Théâtre Libre

**Beer-Hofmann, Richard 1866-1945
(Austrian)**
  CasWL-1973
  ClDMEuL-1980
  EncWL-1981
  GdMWL-1985
  McGWD-1984
  OxGer-1986
  PengEur-1969
  PrEncyPP-1974

  Jugendstil
  Neoromanticism/Neuromantik
  Young Vienna Group/Jungwien

**Begovic, Milan 1876-1948
(Croatian-speaking Yugoslavian)**
  CasWL-1973
  ClDMEuL-1980
  EncWL-1981
  McGWD-1984
  PrEncyPP-1974

  Moderna

Béguin, Albert 1898-1957 (French)
  ClDMEuL-1980
  EncWL-1981
  PrEncyPP-1974

  Geneva School of Critics

Behan, Brendan 1923-1964 (Irish)
  BenReEncy-1987
  CamGLE-1988
  CasWL-1973
  EncWL-1981
  GdMWL-1985
  LongCTCL-1975
  McGWD-1984
  OxEng-1985
  OxThe-1983
  PengEng-1971

  Abbey Theater
  Irish Renaissance
  Theater Workshop

Beier, Ulli 1922-   **(German)**
  EncWL-1981

  Mbari Club

Bell, Clive 1881-1964 (English)
  BenReEncy-1987
  CamGLE-1988
  EncWL-1981
  LongCTCL-1975
  OxEng-1985
  PengEng-1971

  Bloomsbury Group

Bell, Vanessa 1879-1961 (English)
  CamGLE-1988
  EncWL-1981
  LongCTCL-1975
  OxEng-1985

  Bloomsbury Group

Bell-Gam, Leopold n.d. (Nigerian)
EncWL-1981

Onitsha Novels/Chapbooks

Belloli, Carlo n.d. (Italian)
PrEncyPP-1974

Concrete Poetry

**Belov, Vasily Ivanovich 1932-
(Russian)**
ClDMEuL-1980
EncWL-1981
GdMWL-1985

Village Prose

Beltrán, Neftalí n.d. (Mexican)
OxSpan-1978

Taller Group

Bely, Andrey 1880-1934 (Russian)
BenReEncy-1987
CasWL-1973
CEnMWL-1963
ClDMEuL-1980
EncWL-1981
McGWD-1984
OxEng-1985
PengEur-1969
PrEncyPP-1974

Symbolism

Bem, Alfred 1886-1945 (Russian)
ClDMEuL-1980

Poets' Cloister/Skit Poetov

**Benavente y Martínez, Jacinto 1866-
1954 (Spanish)**
BenReEncy-1987
CasWL-1973

ClDMEuL-1980
EncWL-1981
GdMWL-1985
LongCTCL-1975
McGWD-1984
OxEng-1985
OxSpan-1978
PengEur-1969

Generation of 1898/Generación
del 1898
Naturalism

**Benedetti, Mario 1920-
(Uruguayan)**
CasWL-1973
EncWL-1981
GdMWL-1985
OxSpan-1978
PengAm-1971

Generation of 1945

**Benedicktsson, Einar 1864-1940
(Icelandic)**
CasWL-1973
ClDMEuL-1980
EncWL-1981
GdMWL-1985

Progressive Romanticism

Benelli, Sem 1875-1949 (Italian)
CasWL-1973
ClDMEuL-1980
OxThe-1983

Crepuscolarismo

**Benjamin, Walter 1892-1940
(German)**
CasWL-1973
ClDMEuL-1980
EncWL-1981
OxEng-1985

OxGer-1986
PengEur-1969

Marxist Criticism

**Benn, Gottfried 1886-1956
(German)**
CasWL-1973
CEnMWL-1963
ClDMEuL-1980
EncWL-1981
GdMWL-1985
OxGer-1986
PengEur-1969
PrEncyPP-1974

Expressionism
Surrealism

**Bennett, (Enoch) Arnold 1867-1931
(English)**
BenReEncy-1987
CamGLE-1988
CasWL-1973
CEnMWL-1963
EncWL-1981
GdMWL-1985
LongCTCL-1975
McGWD-1984
OxEng-1985
OxThe-1983
PengEng-1971

Edwardian Literature
Georgian Literature
Modernism
Realism

**Bennett, Gwendolyn B. 1902-1981
(American)**
CamGLE-1988
PrEncyPP-1974

Harlem Renaissance

Bense, Max 1910-   (German)
EncWL-1981

Concrete Poetry

**Béranger, Pierre-Jean 1780-1857
(French)**
EncWL-1981
OxEng-1985
OxFr-1959
PengEur-1969
PrEncyPP-1974

Realism

**Berdyayev, Nikolai Aleksandrovich
1874-1948 (Russian)**
BenReEncy-1987
CasWL-1973
ClDMEuL-1980
EncWL-1981
LongCTCL-1975

Existentialism

Berent, Waclaw 1873-1940 (Polish)
ClDMEuL-1980
EncWL-1981
GdMWL-1985
PengEur-1969

Young Poland/Mloda Polska
Zdroj Group

**Bergelson, David 1884-1952
(Yiddish-speaking Russian)**
CasWL-1973
ClDMEuL-1980
EncWL-1981
GdMWL-1985
PengEur-1969

Kiev Group

Bergh, Herman van den 1897-1967 (Dutch)
ClDMEuL-1980

Het Getij

Bergman, Hjalmar Fredrik Elgerus 1883-1931 (Swedish)
BenReEncy-1987
CasWL-1973
ClDMEuL-1980
EncWL-1981
GdMWL-1985
McGWD-1984
OxThe-1983
PengEur-1969

Tiotalister

Bergson, Henri 1859-1941 (French)
BenReEncy-1987
CasWL-1973
ClDMEuL-1980
EncWL-1981
GdMWL-1985
LongCTCL-1975
OxEng-1985
OxFr-1959
PengEur-1969
RCom-1973

Berk, Ilhan 1916-   (Turkish)
ClDMEuL-1980
DOrLit-1974
EncWL-1981
PrEncyPP-1974

Abstract Movement
The Second New

Bernard, Jean-Jacques 1888-1972 (French)
CasWL-1973
ClDMEuL-1980
EncWL-1981

GdMWL-1985
LongCTCL-1975
McGWD-1984
OxFr-1959
OxThe-1983
PengEur-1969

Theater of Silence/Théâtre de l'Inexprimé

Bernard, Jean-Marc 1881-1915 (French)
ClDMEuL-1980
OxFr-1959

Fantaisistes Group

Bernárdez, Francisco Luis 1900- (Argentine)
OxSpan-1978
PengAm-1971

Florida Group

Bernari, Carlo (pseud. of Carlo Bernard) 1909-   (Italian)
ClDMEuL-1980
EncWL-1981
GdMWL-1985

Neorealism

Berrigan, Ted 1934-1983 (American)
BenReEncy-1987
EncWL-1981
GdMWL-1985
OxAm-1983
PengAm-1971

New York School

Berryman, John 1914-1972 (American)
BenReEncy-1987
CamGLE-1988

CasWL-1973
EncWL-1981
GdMWL-1985
OxAm-1983
OxEng-1985
PengAm-1971
PrEncyPP-1974

Confessional Poetry

Berto, Giuseppe 1912-1978 (Italian)
CasWL-1973
ClDMEuL-1980
EncWL-1981
GdMWL-1985

Neorealism

Bertrana, Prudenci 1867-1942 (Catalan-speaking Spanish)
ClDMEuL-1980
EncWL-1981
GdMWL-1985

Realism

Besson, Benno 1922- (Swiss)
OxThe-1983

Berlin Ensemble/Berliner Ensemble
Deutsches Theater

Betocchi, Carlo 1899- (Italian)
CasWL-1973
ClDMEuL-1980
EncWL-1981
GdMWL-1985

Hermeticism/Poesia Ermetica

Bettencourt, Edmundo de 1899-1973 (Portuguese)
ClDMEuL-1980

Presencistas Group

Bhandari, Mennu n.d. (Indian)
DOrLit-1974

New Short Story Movement/ Nayi Kahani

Bharti ao, Dharmvir n.d. (Indian)
DOrLit-1974

New Poetry Movement/Nayi Kavita

Biadula, Zmitrok 1886-1941 (Byelorussian)
EncWL-1981

Our Soil Group/Nasaniustva

Bialoszewski, Miron 1922- (Polish)
CasWL-1973
ClDMEuL-1980
EncWL-1981
GdMWL-1985

Theater of the Absurd
Wspólczesnosc Generation

Bicole, Baiba 1931- (Latvian)
EncWL-1981

New York Group

Bie, O. 1864-1938 (German)
OxGer-1986

Freie Bühne

**Biebl, Konstantín 1898-1951
(Czech)**
CasWL-1973
EncWL-1981

Surrealism

**Bierbaum, Otto Julius 1865-1910
(German)**
CasWL-1973
GdMWL-1985
OxGer-1986
PengEur-1969

Freie Bühne

Bigongiari, Piero 1914-   (Italian)
ClDMEuL-1980
EncWL-1981

Hermeticism/Poesia Ermetica

Bilbasar, Kemal 1910-   (Turkish)
ClDMEuL-1980
DOrLit-1974

Village Fiction

Bill, Max 1908- (Swiss)
HarDMT-1988

Concrete Poetry

**Binkis, Kazys 1893-1942
(Lithuanian)**
ClDMEuL-1980
EncWL-1981
GdMWL-1985
PrEncyPP-1974

Four Winds Movement/Keturi
    Vejai

Birrell, Francis 1889-1935 (English)
HarDMT-1988

Bloomsbury Group

**Björling, Gunnar 1887-1960
(Swedish-speaking Finnish)**
ClDMEuL-1980
EncWL-1981
GdMWL-1985
PengEur-1969
PrEncyPP-1974

Swedish-Finnish Modernists

**Björnson, Björn 1832-1910
(Norwegian)**
BenReEncy-1987
CasWL-1973
ClDMEuL-1980
EncWL-1981
LongCTCL-1975
OxThe-1983
PengEur-1969

Freie Bühne
Realism

**Bjornvig, Thorkild Strange 1918-
(Danish)**
CasWL-1973
ClDMEuL-1980
EncWL-1981
GdMWL-1985
PengEur-1969
PrEncyPP-1974

Heretica Poets

**Blackburn, Paul 1926-1971
(American)**
BenReEncy-1987
CamGLE-1988
EncWL-1981
OxAm-1983
PengAm-1971

PrEncyPP-1974

Black Mountain Poets

Blackmur, R(ichard) P(almer) 1904-1965 (American)
BenReEncy-1987
CasWL-1973
EncWL-1981
LongCTCL-1975
OxAm-1983
OxEng-1985
PengAm-1971
PrEncyPP-1974

New Criticism

Blaga, Lucian 1895-1961 (Romanian)
CasWL-1973
ClDMEuL-1980
EncWL-1981
GdMWL-1985
PengEur-1969

Gîndirea

Blanchot, Maurice 1907- (French)
BenReEncy-1987
CasWL-1973
ClDMEuL-1980
EncWL-1981
GdMWL-1985
PengEur-1969

New Novel/Nouveau Roman
Structuralism

Blanco-Fombona, Rufino 1874-1944 (Venezuelan)
BenReEncy-1987
CasWL-1973
EncWL-1981
OxSpan-1978
PengAm-1971

PrEncyPP-1974

Criollismo
Modernismo

Blasco Ibáñez, Vicente 1867-1928 (Spanish)
BenReEncy-1987
CasWL-1973
ClDMEuL-1980
EncWL-1981
OxSpan-1978
PengEur-1969

Naturalism

Blei, Franz 1871-1942 (Austrian)
EncWL-1981
OxGer-1986

Expressionism

Bleibtreu, Karl 1859-1928 (German)
BenReEncy-1987
OxGer-1986

Naturalism

Blest Gana, Alberto 1830-1920 (Chilean)
BenReEncy-1987
EncWL-1981
OxSpan-1978
PengAm-1971

Realism

Blin, Roger 1907-1984 (French)
EncWL-1981
McGWD-1984
OxThe-1983

Theater of Cruelty/Théâtre de
la Cruauté

**Blitzstein, Marc 1905-1964
(American)**
  CamGLE-1988
  OxAm-1983
  OxAmThe-1984

  Group Theater

**Bloem, Jakobus Cornelis 1887-1966
(Dutch)**
  CasWL-1973
  ClDMEuL-1980
  EncWL-1981
  PengEur-1969

  De Beweging

**Blok, Aleksandr Aleksandrovich
1880-1921 (Russian)**
  BenReEncy-1987
  CasWL-1973
  CEnMWL-1963
  ClDMEuL-1980
  EncWL-1981
  GdMWL-1985
  LongCTCL-1975
  McGWD-1984
  OxEng-1985
  OxThe-1983
  PengEur-1969
  PrEncyPP-1974

  Symbolism

**Blomberg, Erik Axel 1894-1965
(Swedish)**
  CasWL-1973
  EncWL-1981
  PrEncyPP-1974

  Modernism

**Blonda Acosta, Máximo Avilés
1931-   (Dominican Republican)**
  CaribWr-1979

  Promotion of 1948

Bloom, Harold 1930- (American)
  EncWL-1981

  Deconstructionism
  Yale School of Critics

**Blum, Peter 1925-   (South
African)**
  EncWL-1981

  The Sestigers

**Blunck, Hans Friedrich 1888-1961
(German)**
  EncWL-1981
  OxGer-1986

  Heimatkunst

**Blunden, Edmund 1896-1974
(English)**
  BenReEncy-1987
  CamGLE-1988
  CasWL-1973
  EncWL-1981
  GdMWL-1985
  LongCTCL-1975
  OxEng-1985
  PengEng-1971

  Georgian Literature

Blythe, Ernest 1889-1975 (Irish)
  OxThe-1983

  Abbey Theater

Bo, Carlo 1911-   (Italian)
ClDMEuL-1980

Hermeticism/Poesia Ermetica

**Bobrowski, Johannes 1917-1965
(German)**
CasWL-1973
ClDMEuL-1980
EncWL-1981
GdMWL-1985
OxGer-1986
PengEur-1969

Group 47/Gruppe 47

**Boccelli, Arnaldo 1900-1976
(Italian)**
ClDMEuL-1980
EncWL-1981

Neorealism

**Boccioni, Umberto 1882-1916
(Italian)**
BenReEncy-1987
OxEng-1985

Futurism

**Bödvarsson, Guomundur 1904-1974
(Icelandic)**
ClDMEuL-1980
EncWL-1981

Form Revolution

**Bogdanov, Aleksandr
Aleksandrovich 1873-1928
(Russian)**
CasWL-1973
ClDMEuL-1980

Proletkult

**Boguszewska, Helena 1886-1978
(Polish)**
ClDMEuL-1980

Przedmiescie Group

Bohlau, Helene 1859-1940 (German)
OxGer-1986

Naturalism

**Bokombaev, Joomart 1910-1944
(Kirgiz)**
EncWL-1981

Socialist Realism

Böll, Heinrich 1917-1985 (German)
BenReEncy-1987
CasWL-1973
ClDMEuL-1980   *ı*
EncWL-1981
GdMWL-1985
OxEng-1985
OxGer-1986
PengEur-1969

Group 47/Gruppe 47

**Bölsche, Wilhelm 1861-1939
(German)**
GdMWL-1985
OxGer-1986

Freie Bühne
Naturalism

**Bomberg, David 1890-1957
(English)**
HarDMT-1988

Vorticism

**Bonnelycke, Emil 1893-1953
(Danish)**
  CasWL-1973
  EncWL-1981

  Expressionism

Bonset, I.K. 1883-1931 (Dutch)
  EncWL-1981

  Dadaism

**Bontempelli, Massimo 1878-1960
(Italian)**
  CasWL-1973
  ClDMEuL-1980
  EncWL-1981
  GdMWL-1985
  McGWD-1984
  OxThe-1983
  PengEur-1969

  Futurism
  Magic Realism

**Bontemps, Arna 1902-1973
(American)**
  CamGLE-1988
  EncWL-1981
  OxAm-1983
  PrEncyPP-1974

  Harlem Renaissance

**Bontridder, Albert 1921-
(Belgian)**
  ClDMEuL-1980
  EncWL-1981

  Fifties Poets/Vijftigers

**Booth, Wayne C. 1921-
(American)**
  EncWL-1981
  PengAm-1971

PrEncyPP-1974

Chicago Critics

Bopp, Raul 1898-   (Brazilian)
  EncWL-1981
  GdMWL-1985
  PengAm-1971

  Antropofagia Group
  Modernism

**Boraisho, Menachem 1888-1949
(Yiddish-speaking American)**
  EncWL-1981
  GdMWL-1985

  Young Ones/Die Yunge

**Borges, Jorge Luis 1899-1986
(Argentine)**
  BenReEncy-1987
  CasWL-1973
  ClDMEuL-1980
  EncWL-1981
  GdMWL-1985
  OxEng-1985
  OxSpan-1978
  PengAm-1971
  PrEncyPP-1974

  Criollismo
  Florida Group
  Magic Realism
  Ultraism/Ultraismo

**Borgese, Guiseppe Antonio 1882-
1952 (Italian)**
  BenReEncy-1987
  CasWL-1973
  ClDMEuL-1980
  EncWL-1981
  GdMWL-1985
  PengEur-1969

Crepuscolarismo
Neorealism

Born, Nicolas 1937-1979 (German)
ClDMEuL-1980
EncWL-1981
OxGer-1986

Cologne School of New
  Realism/Kölner Schule des
  neuen Realismus

**Borowski, Tadeusz 1922-1951
(Polish)**
CasWL-1973
ClDMEuL-1980
EncWL-1981
GdMWL-1985

Condemned Generation Poets

**Borrero, Dulce María 1883-1945
(Cuban)**
CaribWr-1979

Arpas Cubanas Group

Boti, Regino 1878-1958 (Cuban)
CaribWr-1979

Oriente Group

**Botto, António 1897-1959
(Portuguese)**
ClDMEuL-1980
EncWL-1981
McGWD-1984

Presencistas Group

**Bottomley, Gordon 1874-1948
(English)**
CamGLE-1988
CasWL-1973
EncWL-1981

GdMWL-1985
LongCTCL-1975
OxEng-1985
OxThe-1983
PengEng-1971

Georgian Literature

Boumi-Pappa, Rita 1907-   (Greek)
ClDMEuL-1980

Generation of 1930

Bourgeois, Pierre n.d. (Belgian)
ClDMEuL-1980

Journal de Poètes

Bousoño, Carlos 1923-   (Spanish)
BenReEncy-1987
CasWL-1973
ClDMEuL-1980
EncWL-1981
GdMWL-1985
OxSpan-1978
PengEur-1969

Generation of 1936/Generación
  del 1936

**Boutens, Pieter Cornelis 1870-1943
(Dutch)**
CasWL-1973
ClDMEuL-1980
EncWL-1981

Movement of the Eighties/
  Beweging van Tachtig

Bóveda, Xavier n.d. (Spanish)
OxSpan-1978

Ultraism/Ultraismo

Bowering, George 1935-
(Canadian)
  BenReEncy-1987
  CamGLE-1988
  OxCan-1983

  Tish Group

Bowers, Fredson 1905- (American)
  OxEng-1985

  New Criticism

Boychuk, Bohdan 1927-
(Ukrainian)
  EncWL-1981

  New York Group

Boye, Karin Maria 1900-1941
(Swedish)
  CasWL-1973
  ClDMEuL-1980
  EncWL-1981
  GdMWL-1985
  PengEur-1969

  Clarté Group

Boyle, William 1853-1923 (Irish)
  McGWD-1984
  OxThe-1983

  Abbey Theater

Braak, Menno Ter 1902-1940
(Dutch)
  CasWL-1973
  ClDMEuL-1980
  EncWL-1981
  GdMWL-1985
  PengEur-1969
  PrEncyPP-1974

  Forum Group

Bracco, Roberto 1862-1943 (Italian)
  CasWL-1973
  ClDMEuL-1980
  GdMWL-1985
  OxThe-1983

  Intimismo

Bradunas, Kazys 1917-
(Lithuanian)
  ClDMEuL-1980
  EncWL-1981

  Earth Movement

Braga, Teófilo 1843-1924
(Portuguese)
  CasWL-1973
  ClDMEuL-1980
  GdMWL-1985

  Portuguese Renascence
  Movement

Bragi, Einar 1921-   (Icelandic)
  EncWL-1981

  Form Revolution
  Modernism

Brahm, Otto 1856-1912 (German)
  EncWL-1981
  OxGer-1986

  Deutsches Theater
  Freie Bühne

Braine, John 1922-1986 (English)
  BenReEncy-1987
  CamGLE-1988
  CasWL-1973
  EncWL-1981
  LongCTCL-1975
  OxEng-1985

PengEng-1971

Angry Young Men

**Brandao, Fiama Hasse Pais 1938-
(Portuguese)**
EncWL-1981

Poetry 61 Movement

**Brandao, Raúl 1867-1930
(Portuguese)**
ClDMEuL-1980
EncWL-1981
GdMWL-1985
OxThe-1983
PengEur-1969

Seara Nova Group

**Brandes, Edvard 1847-1931
(Danish)**
ClDMEuL-1980
GdMWL-1985
McGWD-1984
PengEur-1969

Naturalism

Brandes, Georg 1842-1927 (Danish)
BenReEncy-1987
CasWL-1973
ClDMEuL-1980
EncWL-1981
GdMWL-1985
LongCTCL-1975
McGWD-1984
OxGer-1986
OxThe-1983
PengEur-1969
PrEncyPP-1974

Naturalism

Braque, Georges 1882-1963 (French)
BenReEncy-1987
EncWL-1981
OxEng-1985
PrEncyPP-1974

Cubism

Bratny, Roman 1921-   (Polish)
ClDMEuL-1980
EncWL-1981

Socialist Realism

Brecht, Bertolt 1898-1956 (German)
BenReEncy-1987
CasWL-1973
CEnMWL-1963
ClDMEuL-1980
EncWL-1981
GdMWL-1985
LongCTCL-1975
McGWD-1984
OxAmThe-1984
OxEng-1985
OxGer-1986
OxThe-1983
PengEur-1969
PrEncyPP-1974
RCom-1973

Berlin Ensemble/Berliner
    Ensemble
Deutsches Theater
Epic Theater/Episches Theater
Expressionism
New Objectivity/Neue
    Sachlichkeit
Socialist Realism

Breton, André 1896-1966 (French)
BenReEncy-1987
CasWL-1973
ClDMEuL-1980
EncWL-1981

GdMWL-1985
LongCTCL-1975
McGWD-1984
OxEng-1985
OxFr-1959
PengEur-1969
PrEncyPP-1974
RCom-1973

Dadaism
Surrealism

**Breytenbach, Breyten 1939-
(South African)**
CasWL-1973
EncWL-1981
GdMWL-1985

The Sestigers

**Brezina, Otokar (pseud. of V.I.
Jebavy) 1868-1929 (Czech)**
CasWL-1973
ClDMEuL-1980
EncWL-1981
GdMWL-1985
PengEur-1969
PrEncyPP-1974

Symbolism

Bridges, Robert 1844-1930 (English)
BenReEncy-1987
CamGLE-1988
CasWL-1973
EncWL-1981
GdMWL-1985
LongCTCL-1975
OxEng-1985
PengEng-1971

Modernism

Brieux, Eugène 1858-1932 (French)
CasWL-1973

ClDMEuL-1980
EncWL-1981
GdMWL-1985
LongCTCL-1975
OxEng-1985
OxFr-1959
OxThe-1983
PengEur-1969

Théâtre Libre

**Brik, Osip Maximovich 1888-1945
(Russian)**
CasWL-1973
EncWL-1981

LEF

**Brink, André P(hilippus) 1935-
(South African)**
CamGLE-1988
CasWL-1973
EncWL-1981
GdMWL-1985
OxEng-1985
PengCOAL-1969

The Sestigers

**Brinkmann, Rolf Dieter 1940-1975
(German)**
ClDMEuL-1980
EncWL-1981
OxGer-1986

Cologne School of New
Realism/Kölner Schule des
neuen Realismus

**Brlic-Mazuranic, Ivana 1874-1938
(Croatian)**
ClDMEuL-1980

Moderna

Broderzon, Moyshe 1890-1956
(Yiddish-speaking Polish)
  EncWL-1981

  Young Yiddish Group

Bródy, Sándor 1863-1924
(Hungarian)
  ClDMEuL-1980
  EncWL-1981
  McGWD-1984
  PengEur-1969

  Nyugat Group

Bromfield, Louis 1896-1956
(American)
  BenReEncy-1987
  CamGLE-1988
  LongCTCL-1975
  McGWD-1984
  OxAm-1983
  PengAm-1971

  Lost Generation

Broniewski, Wladyslaw 1898-1962
(Polish)
  CasWL-1973
  ClDMEuL-1980
  EncWL-1981
  GdMWL-1985
  PrEncyPP-1974

  Skamander Group

Bronnen, Arnolt 1895-1959
(Austrian)
  ClDMEuL-1980
  GdMWL-1985
  OxGer-1986
  OxThe-1983

  Epic Theater/Episches Theater
  Expressionism

Brook, Peter 1925- (English)
  McGWD-1984
  OxAmThe-1984
  OxThe-1983

  Theater of Cruelty/Théâtre de
    la Cruauté
  Theater of Fact

Brooke, Rupert 1887-1915 (English)
  BenReEncy-1987
  CamGLE-1988
  CasWL-1973
  CEnMWL-1963
  GdMWL-1985
  LongCTCL-1975
  OxEng-1985
  PengEng-1971
  PrEncyPP-1974

  Bloomsbury Group
  Georgian Literature

Brooks, Cleanth 1906- (American)
  BenReEncy-1987
  CamGLE-1988
  CasWL-1973
  EncWL-1981
  LongCTCL-1975
  OxAm-1983
  OxEng-1985
  PengAm-1971

  New Criticism

Brouwer, Jelle Hindriks 1900-1981
(Dutch)
  EncWL-1981
  PrEncyPP-1974

  Young Frisian Movement

145

Brouwers, Jaak n.d. (Belgian)
ClDMEuL-1980

Fifties Poets/Vijftigers

Browka, P. n.d. (Byelorussian)
PrEncyPP-1974

Socialist Realism

Brown, Kenneth 1936- (American)
McGWD-1984

Living Theater

Brown, Pete 1940-   (English)
OxEng-1985

Jazz Poetry

**Brown, Sterling A. 1901-1989
(American)**
CamGLE-1988
OxAm-1983
PrEncyPP-1974

Harlem Renaissance

**Browning, Robert 1812-1889
(English)**
BenReEncy-1987
CamGLE-1988
EncWL-1981
OxEng-1985
OxThe-1983
PengEng-1971
PrEncyPP-1974

Realism

**Brownjohn, Alan Charles 1931-
(English)**
CamGLE-1988

OxEng-1985

The Group

**Bruckner, Ferdinand (pseud. of
Theodor Tagger) 1891-1958
(Austrian)**
BenReEncy-1987
EncWL-1981
GdMWL-1985
OxGer-1986
OxThe-1983

New Objectivity/Neue
Sachlichkeit

Brull, Mariano 1891-1956 (Cuban)
CaribWr-1979

Realism

Bruma, Eddy 1925-   (Surinamese)
CaribWr-1979

Our Own Things Group/Wie
Eegie Sanie

**Brunclair, Victor J. 1899-1944
(Belgian)**
ClDMEuL-1980
EncWL-1981

Ruimte Group

Brunk, Sigrid n.d. (German)
OxGer-1986

Cologne School of New
Realism/Kölner Schule des
neuen Realismus

**Bryusov, Valery Yakovlevich 1873-
1924 (Russian)**
BenReEncy-1987
ClDMEuL-1980

146

EncWL-1981
GdMWL-1985
McGWD-1984
PengEur-1969
PrEncyPP-1974

Symbolism

Brzekowski, Jan 1903-　(Polish)
CasWL-1973
ClDMEuL-1980
EncWL-1981
GdMWL-1985

Cracow Avant-Garde

Brzozowski, Stanislaw 1878-1911 (Polish)
ClDMEuL-1980
GdMWL-1985

Young Poland/Mloda Polska

Buarque de Holanda, Sérgio 1902-1982 (Brazilian)
PengAm-1971
PrEncyPP-1974

Modernism

Buber, Martin 1878-1965 (Austrian-born German)
BenReEncy-1987
EncWL-1981
GdMWL-1985
OxGer-1986

Existentialism

Buchman, Frank 1878-1961 (American)
LongCTCL-1975

Oxford Group

Bukharin, Nicolai Ivanovich 1888-1938 (Russian)
BenReEncy-1987
EncWL-1981
OxEng-1985

Socialist Realism

Bulgakov, Mikhail Afanasyevich 1891-1940 (Russian)
BenReEncy-1987
CasWL-1973
ClDMEuL-1980
EncWL-1981
GdMWL-1985
OxEng-1985
OxThe-1983
PengEur-1969

Moscow Art Theater

Bull, Olaf Jacob Martin Luther 1883-1933 (Norwegian)
CasWL-1973
EncWL-1981
GdMWL-1985
PengEur-1969

Generation of 1905

Buncak, Pavel 1915-　(Czech)
ClDMEuL-1980

Nadrealisti Movement

Bunin, Ivan Alexeyevich 1870-1953 (Russian)
BenReEncy-1987
CasWL-1973
CEnMWL-1963
ClDMEuL-1980
EncWL-1981
GdMWL-1985
LongCTCL-1975
OxEng-1985

PengEur-1969

Znanie Group

Bunner, H(enry) C(uyler) 1855-1896 (American)
OxAm-1983

Local Color School

Bunting, Basil 1900-1985 (English)
BenReEncy-1987
CamGLE-1988
EncWL-1981
OxEng-1985

Objectivism

Buñuel, Luis 1900-1983 (Spanish)
BenReEncy-1987
EncWL-1981
OxSpan-1978

Surrealism

Burgos, Elqui n.d. (Spanish)
OxSpan-1978

Estos 13/Hora Cero

Burke, Kenneth 1897- (American)
BenReEncy-1987
CamGLE-1988
CasWL-1973
EncWL-1981
OxAm-1983
PengAm-1971
PrEncyPP-1974

New Criticism

Burghardt, Osvald 1891-1947 (Ukrainian)
ClDMEuL-1980

EncWL-1981

Neoclassic Group

Burlyuk, David 1882-1967 (Russian)
ClDMEuL-1980
EncWL-1981
GdMWL-1985
PrEncyPP-1974

Cubo-Futurism

Burns, Alan 1929- (English)
DCLT-1979

New Wave/Nouvelle Vague

Burroughs, William S(eward) 1914- (American)
BenReEncy-1987
CamGLE-1988
CasWL-1973
EncWL-1981
GdMWL-1985
OxAm-1983
OxEng-1985
PengAm-1971

Beat Generation

Bursa, Andrzej 1932-1957 (Polish)
ClDMEuL-1980

Wspólczesnosc Generation

Burssens, Gaston 1896-1965 (Belgian)
CasWL-1973
ClDMEuL-1980
EncWL-1981

Ruimte Group

Busza, Andrzej 1938- (Polish)
  ClDMEuL-1980

  Kontynenty Group

Butler, Samuel 1835-1902 (English)
  BenReEncy-1987
  CamGLE-1988
  CasWL-1973
  CEnMWL-1963
  EncWL-1981
  LongCTCL-1975
  OxEng-1985
  PengEng-1971

  Edwardian Literature
  Naturalism

Butor, Michel 1926- (French)
  BenReEncy-1987
  CasWL-1973
  ClDMEuL-1980
  EncWL-1981
  GdMWL-1985
  OxEng-1985
  PengEur-1969

  New Novel/Nouveau Roman
  New Wave/Nouvelle Vague

Buttitta, Piero A. 1931- (Italian)
  ClDMEuL-1980

  Group 63/Gruppo 63

Buysse, Cyriel 1859-1932 (Belgian)
  ClDMEuL-1980
  EncWL-1981
  GdMWL-1985

  Van nu en straks Group

Byl, Arthur n.d. (French)
  OxThe-1983

  Théâtre Libre

Bynner, Witter 1881-1968 (American)
  CasWL-1973
  OxAm-1983
  PengAm-1971

  Spectra

C

Caballero, Fernando Iglesias n.d.
(Spanish)
OxSpan-1978

Ultraism/Ultraismo

Cable, George Washington 1844-
1925 (American)
BenReEncy-1987
CamGLE-1988
CasWL-1973
OxAm-1983
OxEng-1985
PengAm-1971

Local Color School
Realism

Cabral, Alexandre 1917-
(Portuguese)
ClDMEuL-1980

Neorealism

Cabral de Melo Neto, Joao 1920-
(Brazilian)
CasWL-1973
EncWL-1981
GdMWL-1985
OxSpan-1978
PengAm-1971
PrEncyPP-1974

Generation of 1945
Modernism

Cabrera, Lydia 1900-   (Cuban)
CaribWr-1979
EncWL-1981

Afro-Cubanism

Calverton, Victor Francis 1900-1940
(American)
EncWL-1981
OxAm-1983
PengAm-1971

Proletarian Literature
Marxist Criticism

Calvino, Italo 1923-1985 (Cuban-
born Italian)
BenReEncy-1987
CamGLE-1988
CasWL-1973
ClDMEuL-1980
EncWL-1981
GdMWL-1985
OxEng-1985
PengEur-1969

Neorealism

Cambaceres, Eugenio de 1843-1888
(Argentine)
CasWL-1973
OxSpan-1978
PengAm-1971

Realism

**Camélat, Michel 1871-1962
(Provençal-speaking French)**
EncWL-1981

Félibrige Movement

**Cameron, George Frederick 1854-
1885 (Canadian)**
OxCan-1983

Confederation Poets

**Çamlibel, Faruk Nafiz 1898-1973
(Turkish)**
ClDMEuL-1980
EncWL-1981

Seven Torches/Yedi Mes'ale

Campana, Dino 1885-1932 (Italian)
CasWL-1973
CEnMWL-1963
ClDMEuL-1980
EncWL-1981
GdMWL-1985
PengEur-1969

Crepuscolarismo
Hermeticism/Poesia Ermetica

**Campbell, (William) Wilfred 1858-
1918 (Canadian)**
CamGLE-1988
EncWL-1981
McGWD-1984
OxCan-1983

Confederation Poets

**Campert, Remco Wouter 1929-
(Dutch)**
CasWL-1973
EncWL-1981

Fifties Poets/Vijftigers

**Campo, Estanislao del 1834-1880
(Argentine)**
BenReEncy-1987
CasWL-1973
OxSpan-1978
PengAm-1971

Gaucho Literature

**Campos, Augusto de 1931-
(Brazilian)**
EncWL-1981
PrEncyPP-1974

Concrete Poetry

Campos, Geir 1924-　(Brazilian)
PrEncyPP-1974

Generation of 1945

**Campos, Haroldo de 1929-
(Brazilian)**
EncWL-1981

Concrete Poetry

**Campos Cervera, Hérib 1908-1953
(Paraguayan)**
EncWL-1981
OxSpan-1978

Generation of 1940

Campton, David 1924-　(English)
EncWL-1981
McGWD-1984

Comedy of Menace
Theater of the Absurd

**Camus, Albert 1913-1960 (Algerian-
born French)**
BenReEncy-1987
CasWL-1973

CEnMWL-1963
ClDMEuL-1980
EncWL-1981
GdMWL-1985
LongCTCL-1975
McGWD-1984
OxAm-1983
OxEng-1985
OxFr-1959
OxThe-1983
PengEur-1969
RCom-1973

Existentialism

Cankar, Ivan 1876-1918 (Slovene-speaking Yugoslavian)
CasWL-1973
ClDMEuL-1980
EncWL-1981
GdMWL-1985
McGWD-1984

Moderna

Cankar, Izidor 1886-1958 (Slovene-speaking Yugoslavian)
CasWL-1973

Moderna

Cannell, Skipwith 1887-1957 (American)
OxEng-1985

Imagism

Cansever, Edip 1928-   (Turkish)
ClDMEuL-1980
DOrLit-1974
EncWL-1981
PrEncyPP-1974

Abstract Movement
The Second New

Cansinos Asséns, Rafael 1883-1964 (Spanish)
ClDMEuL-1980

Ultraism/Ultraismo

Cantwell, Robert 1908-1978 (American)
CamGLE-1988
GdMWL-1985
OxAm-1983

Proletarian Literature

Capek, Karel 1890-1938 (Czech)
BenReEncy-1987
CasWL-1973
ClDMEuL-1980
EncWL-1981
GdMWL-1985
LongCTCL-1975
McGWD-1984
OxAmThe-1984
OxEng-1985
OxThe-1983
PengEur-1969

Expressionism

Capuana, Luigi 1839-1915 (Italian)
BenReEncy-1987
CasWL-1973
EncWL-1981
GdMWL-1985
McGWD-1984
OxThe-1983
PengEur-1969

Naturalism
Verismo

Caraion, Ion 1923-   (Romanian)
EncWL-1981

Bucharest Group

**Carbonell, José Manuel 1880-(?)
(Cuban)**
CaribWr-1979

Arpas Cubanas Group

Carco, Francis 1886-1958 (French)
CasWL-1973
ClDMEuL-1980
EncWL-1981
LongCTCL-1975
McGWD-1984
OxFr-1959
PengEur-1969

Fantaisistes Group

**Cardarelli, Vincenzo (pseud. of
Nazzareno Caldarelli) 1887-1959
(Italian)**
CasWL-1973
ClDMEuL-1980
EncWL-1981
PengEur-1969

Rondismo

**Cardenal, Ernesto 1925-
(Nicaraguan)**
CasWL-1973
EncWL-1981
GdMWL-1985
OxSpan-1978
PengAm-1971

Exteriorismo

Carême, Maurice 1899-   (Belgian)
CasWL-1973
ClDMEuL-1980
EncWL-1981
GdMWL-1985

Journal de Poètes

Carlson, Stig 1920-   (Swedish)
PrEncyPP-1974

Poets of the Forties/
Fyrtiotalisterna

**Carman, (William) Bliss 1861-1929
(Canadian)**
BenReEncy-1987
CamGLE-1988
CasWL-1973
EncWL-1981
GdMWL-1985
LongCTCL-1975
OxAm-1983
OxCan-1983
OxEng-1985
PengAm-1971
PengEng-1971

Confederation Poets

**Carner i Puig-Oriol, Josep 1884-
1971 (Catalan-speaking Spanish)**
CasWL-1973
ClDMEuL-1980
EncWL-1981
GdMWL-1985
OxSpan-1978
PengEur-1969

Noucentismo

**Carnovsky, Morris 1897-
(American)**
BenReEncy-1987
OxAmThe-1984

Group Theater

Carossa, Hans 1878-1956 (German)
ClDMEuL-1980
EncWL-1981
GdMWL-1985
OxGer-1986

PengEur-1969

New Objectivity/Neue
Sachlichkeit

**Carpelan, Bo 1926-   (Swedish-
speaking Finnish)**
   EncWL-1981
   PengEur-1969
   PrEncyPP-1974

Swedish-Finnish Modernists

**Carpentier, Alejo 1904-1980
(Cuban)**
   BenReEncy-1987
   CamGLE-1988
   CaribWr-1979
   CasWL-1973
   EncWL-1981
   GdMWL-1985
   OxEng-1985
   OxSpan-1978
   PengAm-1971

Afro-Cubanism
Criollismo
Magic Realism
Naturalism

Carrà, Carlo 1881-1966 (Italian)
   EncWL-1981
   OxEng-1985

Futurism

**Carranza, Eduardo 1913-
(Columbian)**
   EncWL-1981
   OxSpan-1978

Stone and Sky Movement

**Carrión, Alejandro 1915-
(Ecuadorian)**
   EncWL-1981
   OxSpan-1978

Grupo Elan

**Carroll, Paul Vincent 1900-1968
(Irish)**
   BenReEncy-1987
   CasWL-1973
   EncWL-1981
   LongCTCL-1975
   McGWD-1984
   OxThe-1983

Irish Renaissance

Caruth, Hayden 1921-   (American)
   BenReEncy-1987
   OxAm-1983
   OxEng-1985

Poetry

Carter, Angela 1940-   (English)
   CamGLE-1988
   GdMWL-1985
   OxEng-1985

Magic Realism

**Carvalho, Ronald de 1893-1935
(Brazilian)**
   ClDMEuL-1980
   EncWL-1981
   GdMWL-1985
   PengAm-1971
   PrEncyPP-1974

Modernism
Orpheu Group

**Cary, (Arthur) Joyce 1888-1957
(Irish-born English)**
BenReEncy-1987
CamGLE-1988
CasWL-1973
CEnMWL-1963
EncWL-1981
GdMWL-1985
LongCTCL-1975
OxEng-1985
PengEng-1971

Modernism

**Casaccia, Gabriel 1907-
(Paraguayan)**
EncWL-1981
OxSpan-1978

Generation of 1940

Casal, Julián del 1863-1893 (Cuban)
BenReEncy-1987
CaribWr-1979
CasWL-1973
EncWL-1981
OxSpan-1978
PengAm-1971
PrEncyPP-1974

Modernismo

Caso, Antonio 1883-1946 (Mexican)
EncWL-1981
OxSpan-1978

Atheneum of Youth

**Cassady, Neal 1926-1968
(American)**
EncWL-1981

Beat Generation

Cassola, Carlo 1917-　　(Italian)
BenReEncy-1987
ClDMEuL-1980
EncWL-1981
GdMWL-1985
PengEur-1969

Neorealism

**Castellanos, Jésus 1879-1912
(Cuban)**
CaribWr-1979
OxSpan-1978

Realism

**Castelnuovo, Elías 1893-(?)
(Argentine)**
OxSpan-1978

Boedo Group

**Castro, Eugénio de 1869-1944
(Portuguese)**
CasWL-1973
EncWL-1981
GdMWL-1985
McGWD-1984
PengEur-1969

Modernismo
Symbolism

**Castro, José Antonio Fernández de
1897-1951 (Cuban)**
EncWL-1981

Afro-Cubanism

**Castro, José Maria Ferreira de 1898-
1974 (Portuguese)**
CasWL-1973
ClDMEuL-1980
EncWL-1981
GdMWL-1985

PengEur-1969

Neorealism
Seara Nova Group

**Castro, Luis 1909-1933
(Venezuelan)**
EncWL-1981

Generation of 1918

**Català, Victor (Catarina Albert i
Paradis) 1873-1966 (Catalan-
speaking Spanish)**
ClDMEuL-1980
EncWL-1981
GdMWL-1985
OxSpan-1978

Realism

Cather, Willa 1873-1947 (American)
BenReEncy-1987
CamGLE-1988
CasWL-1973
EncWL-1981
GdMWL-1985
LongCTCL-1975
OxAm-1983
OxCan-1983
OxEng-1985
PengAm-1971
RCom-1973

Realism

**Caudwell, Christopher 1907-1937
(English)**
CamGLE-1988
EncWL-1981
LongCTCL-1975
OxEng-1985
PengEng-1971

Marxist Criticism

**Cavacchioli, Enrico 1885-1954
(Italian)**
ClDMEuL-1980
GdMWL-1985

Theater of the Grotesque/Teatro
del grottescco

Céard, Henri 1851-1924 (French)
CasWL-1973
GdMWL-1985
OxFr-1959

Naturalism

Cecchi, Emilio 1884-1966 (Italian)
CasWL-1973
ClDMEuL-1980
EncWL-1981
PengEur-1969

Rondismo

**Cela, Camilio José 1916-
(Spanish)**
BenReEncy-1987
CasWL-1973
CEnMWL-1963
ClDMEuL-1980
EncWL-1981
GdMWL-1985
OxSpan-1978

Generation of 1936/Generación
del 1936
Tremendismo

**Celan, Paul (pseud. of Paul
Antschel) 1920-1970 (Romanian-
born Austrian)**
CasWL-1973
ClDMEuL-1980
EncWL-1981
OxEng-1985
OxGer-1986

PengEur-1969

Group 47/Gruppe 47

Celaya, Gabriel (Rafael Múgica)
1911-   (Spanish)
CasWL-1973
CIDMEuL-1980
EncWL-1981
GdMWL-1985
OxSpan-1978
PengEur-1969

Generation of 1936/Generación
del 1936
Grupo Espadaña

Cendrars, Blaise (pseud. of Frédéric
Louis Sauser) 1887-1961 (French-
speaking Swiss)
BenReEncy-1987
CasWL-1973
CIDMEuL-1980
EncWL-1981
GdMWL-1985
LongCTCL-1975
OxFr-1959
PengEur-1969

Cubism
Fantaisistes Group
Simultanéisme

Cerna, José n.d. (Peruvian)
OxSpan-1978

Estos 13/Hora Cero

Cernuda, Luis 1902-1963 (Spanish)
BenReEncy-1987
CasWL-1973
CIDMEuL-1980
EncWL-1981
GdMWL-1985
OxSpan-1978

PengEur-1969

Generation of 1927/Generación
del 1927
Surrealism
Ultraism/Ultraismo

Césaire, Aimé 1913- (Martinican)
BenReEncy-1987
CaribWr-1979
CasWL-1973
CIDMEuL-1980
EncWL-1981
GdMWL-1985
McGWD-1984
OxEng-1985
PengEur-1969
PrEncyPP-1974

Négritude
Surrealism

Cézanne, Paul 1839-1906 (French)
BenReEncy-1987
EncWL-1981
OxEng-1985
OxFr-1959

Cubism

Chabrol, Claude 1930-   (French)
BenReEncy-1987
EncWL-1981

New Wave/Nouvelle Vague

Chaiken, Joseph 1935-
(American)
McGWD-1984

Living Theater

Chairil Anwar 1922-1949
(Indonesian)
CasWL-1973

DOrLit-1974
EncWL-1981
GdMWL-1985
PengCOAL-1969
PrEncyPP-1974

Generation of 1945

Champfleury (pseud. of Jules Husson) 1821-1889 (French)
CamGLE-1988
CasWL-1973
OxEng-1985
OxFr-1959
PengEur-1969

Realism

Chang Tzu-p'ing n.d. (Chinese)
DOrLit-1974

Creation Society

Chapygin, Alexey Pavlovich 1870-1937 (Russian)
BenReEncy-1987
CasWL-1973
ClDMEuL-1980
EncWL-1981

Socialist Realism

Char, René 1907-   (French)
BenReEncy-1987
CasWL-1973
CEnMWL-1963
ClDMEuL-1980
EncWL-1981
GdMWL-1985
OxFr-1959
PengEur-1969
PrEncyPP-1974

Surrealism

Charbonneau, Jean 1875-1960 (French-speaking Canadian)
OxCan-1983

Literary School of Montreal/
École Littéraire de Montreal

Charik, Izy 1898-1937 (Yiddish-speaking Byelorussian)
CasWL-1973
ClDMEuL-1980

Minsk Group

Charnetsky, Stepan 1881-1945 (Ukrainian)
EncWL-1981

Young Muse Group/Moloda Muza

Chavée, Achille 1906-1969 (Belgian)
ClDMEuL-1980
EncWL-1981
GdMWL-1985

Surrealism

Chekhov, Anton Pavlovich 1860-1904 (Russian)
BenReEncy-1987
CasWL-1973
ClDMEuL-1980
EncWL-1981
GdMWL-1985
LongCTCL-1975
McGWD-1984
OxAmThe-1984
OxEng-1985
OxThe-1983
PengEur-1969
RCom-1973

Moscow Art Theater
Naturalism

Realism

Ch'ên Tu-hsiu 1879-1942 (Chinese)
CasWL-1973
DOrLit-1974
EncWL-1981

May Fourth Movement/Wu-
ssu yün-tung

Ch'eng Fang-wu n.d. (Chinese)
DOrLit-1974

Creation Society

**Chennevière, Georges 1884-1929
(French)**
OxFr-1959
PrEncyPP-1974

Unanimism/Unanisme

**Cheremshyna, Marko 1874-1927
(Ukrainian)**
EncWL-1981

Modernism

**Chernyavsky, Mykola 1867-1937
(Ukrainian)**
EncWL-1981

Modernism

Chi Hsien 1913-   (Chinese)
EncWL-1981

Modernist School

Chiarelli, Luigi 1880-1947 (Italian)
ClDMEuL-1980
GdMWL-1985
OxThe-1983

Theater of the Grotesque/Teatro
del grottescco

Chiaves, Carlo 1883-1919 (Italian)
ClDMEuL-1980

Crepuscolarismo

**Chikovani, Simone 1902/3-1966
(Georgian)**
DOrLit-1974
EncWL-1981

Futurism

**Chirico, Giorgio De 1888-1978
(Greek-born Italian)**
BenReEncy-1987
EncWL-1981
OxFr-1959
RCom-1973

Surrealism

**Chirikov, Evgeny Nikolayevich
1864-1932 (Russian)**
CasWL-1973
GdMWL-1985

Znanie Group

**Chmielowski, Piotr 1848-1904
(Polish)**
ClDMEuL-1980

Warsaw Positivism

**Chocano, José Santos 1875-1934
(Peruvian)**
CasWL-1973
EncWL-1981
PengAm-1971
PrEncyPP-1974

Modernismo

Ch'oe Nam-son 1890-1957 (Korean)
DOrLit-1974
EncWL-1981
GdMWL-1985

New Poetry Movement

Cholnoky, Viktor n.d. (Hungarian)
ClDMEuL-1980

Nyugat Group

**Chomsky, Noam 1928-
(American)**
BenReEncy-1987
CamGLE-1988
EncWL-1981
OxEng-1985
PengAm-1971

Structuralism

Chopin, Kate 1851-1904 (American)
BenReEncy-1987
CamGLE-1988
GdMWL-1985
OxAm-1983
OxEng-1985
PengAm-1971

Local Color School

**Chorny, Kuzma 1900-1944
(Byelorussian)**
ClDMEuL-1980
EncWL-1981
PrEncyPP-1974

Socialist Realism
Uzvyssa Group

Chou Li-po 1908-   (Chinese)
CasWL-1973
DOrLit-1974

EncWL-1981

League of Left-Wing Writers

Chou Tso-Jên 1885-1966 (Chinese)
CasWL-1973

Literary Research Association

**Chuprynka, Hryhoriy 1879-1921
(Ukrainian)**
ClDMEuL-1980
EncWL-1981

Ukrainian Home Group

**Churchill, Winston 1871-1947
(American)**
BenReEncy-1987
CasWL-1973
EncWL-1981
GdMWL-1985
LongCTCL-1975
OxAm-1983
OxEng-1985
PengAm-1971

Muckrakers

**Cihler-Nehajev, Milutin 1880-1931
(Croatian)**
ClDMEuL-1980
EncWL-1981

Moderna

**Cilloniz, Antonio 1944-
(Peruvian)**
OxSpan-1978

Estos 13/Hora Cero

**Cisneros, Antonio 1942-
(Peruvian)**
GdMWL-1985

OxSpan-1978

Los Nuevos

Cixous, Hélène 1937-   (Algerian-born French)
CamGLE-1988
ClDMEuL-1980
EncWL-1981
GdMWL-1985

Feminist Criticism

Clarín (pseud. of Leopoldo Enrique García Alas y Ureña) 1852-1901 (Spanish)
BenReEncy-1987
CasWL-1973
ClDMEuL-1980
GdMWL-1985
OxSpan-1978

Naturalism
Realism

Claudel, Paul 1868-1955 (French)
BenReEncy-1987
CasWL-1973
CEnMWL-1963
ClDMEuL-1980
EncWL-1981
GdMWL-1985
LongCTCL-1975
McGWD-1984
OxEng-1985
OxFr-1959
OxThe-1983
PengEur-1969
PrEncyPP-1974

Nouvelle Revue Française
   Group
Symbolism
Total Theater

Claus, Hugo 1929-   (Belgian)
CasWL-1973
ClDMEuL-1980
EncWL-1981
GdMWL-1985
McGWD-1984
OxThe-1983

Cobra
Fifties Poets/Vijftigers

Claussen, Sophus Niels Christen 1865-1931 (Danish)
CasWL-1973
ClDMEuL-1980
GdMWL-1985
PengEur-1969

Symbolism

Clurman, Harold 1901-1980 (American)
BenReEncy-1987
CamGLE-1988
OxAm-1983
OxAmThe-1984
OxThe-1983
PengAm-1971

Group Theater
Theater Guild

Cochofel, Joao José 1919-1982 (Portuguese)
EncWL-1981

Neorealism

Cocteau, Jean 1889-1963 (French)
BenReEncy-1987
CasWL-1973
CEnMWL-1963
ClDMEuL-1980
EncWL-1981
GdMWL-1985

LongCTCL-1975
McGWD-1984
OxEng-1985
OxFr-1959
OxThe-1983
PengEur-1969

Cubism
Surrealism

**Cody, Hiram Alfred 1872-1948
(Canadian)**
OxCan-1983

Local Color School

**Coimbra, Leonardo 1883-1936
(Portuguese)**
ClDMEuL-1980

Portuguese Renascence
Movement

Colinet, Paul 1898-1957 (Belgian)
ClDMEuL-1980
EncWL-1981

Surrealism

Coloma, Luis 1851-1915 (Spanish)
ClDMEuL-1980
OxSpan-1978

Realism

Colombo, Furio 1931-   (Italian)
ClDMEuL-1980

Group 63/Gruppo 63

Colum, Padraic 1881-1972 (Irish)
BenReEncy-1987
CamGLE-1988
CasWL-1973
EncWL-1981

GdMWL-1985
LongCTCL-1975
McGWD-1984
OxEng-1985
OxThe-1983
PengEng-1971
PrEncyPP-1974

Abbey Theater
Irish Renaissance

Comet, César A. n.d. (Spanish)
OxSpan-1978

Ultraism/Ultraismo

**Commisso, Giovanni 1895-1969
(Italian)**
ClDMEuL-1980

Solaria Group

**Connelly, Marc 1890-1980
(American)**
BenReEncy-1987
CamGLE-1988
EncWL-1981
GdMWL-1985
LongCTCL-1975
OxAm-1983
OxAmThe-1984
PengAm-1971

Expressionism

Connolly, Cyril 1903-1974 (English)
BenReEncy-1987
CamGLE-1988
CasWL-1973
CEnMWL-1963
EncWL-1981
GdMWL-1985
LongCTCL-1975
OxEng-1985

PengEng-1971

Modernism

Conquest, Robert 1917-   (English)
BenReEncy-1987
CamGLE-1988
EncWL-1981
LongCTCL-1975
OxEng-1985

The Movement
New Lines Poets

Conrad, Joseph (born Józef Teodor Konrad Korzeniowski) 1857-1924 (Polish-born English)
BenReEncy-1987
CamGLE-1988
CasWL-1973
CEnMWL-1963
EncWL-1981
GdMWL-1985
LongCTCL-1975
OxEng-1985
PengEng-1971
RCom-1973

Edwardian Literature
Georgian Literature
Modernism

Conrad, Michael Georg 1846-1927 (German)
OxGer-1986

Naturalism

Conradi, Hermann 1862-1890 (German)
BenReEncy-1987
CasWL-1973
OxGer-1986

Naturalism

Conroy, Jack 1899-1980 (American)
CamGLE-1988
OxAm-1983

Proletarian Literature

Contini, Gianfranco 1902- (Italian)
ClDMEuL-1980
EncWL-1981

Solaria Group

Cook, George Cram 1873-1924 (American)
BenReEncy-1987
LongCTCL-1975
OxAm-1983
OxAmThe-1984

Provincetown Players

Cooke, Rose Terry 1827-1892 (American)
OxAm-1983

Local Color School

Copeau, Jacques 1879-1949 (French)
ClDMEuL-1980
EncWL-1981
GdMWL-1985
OxFr-1959
OxThe-1983

Nouvelle Revue Française Group
Théâtre du Vieux-Colombier
Theater Guild

Coppée, Francis-Joachim-Édouard-François 1842-1907 (French)
CasWL-1973
OxFr-1959
PengEur-1969

163

PrEncyPP-1974

Realism

Corazzini, Sergio 1887-1907 (Italian)
CasWL-1973
ClDMEuL-1980
EncWL-1981
GdMWL-1985
PengEur-1969

Crepuscolarismo

Corbière, Edouard Joachim 1845-1875 (French)
BenReEncy-1987
CasWL-1973
OxFr-1959
PengEur-1969

Symbolism

Coronel Urtecho, José 1906- (Nicaraguan)
EncWL-1981
OxSpan-1978

Exteriorismo

Corral, Simón n.d. (Ecuadorian)
OxSpan-1978

Grupo Tzántzico

Correia, Romeu 1917- (Portuguese)
ClDMEuL-1980
GdMWL-1985

Neorealism

Corsen, Charles 1927-   (Curaçaon)
CaribWr-1979

Porch Group/De Stoep

Corsen, Yolanda (pseud. of Oda Blinder) 1918-1969 (Curaçaon)
CaribWr-1979

Porch Group/De Stoep

Corso, Gregory 1930-   (American)
BenReEncy-1987
CamGLE-1988
CasWL-1973
EncWL-1981
OxAm-1983
OxEng-1985
PengAm-1971
PrEncyPP-1974

Beat Generation
San Francisco School

Cortázar, Julio 1914-1984 (Belgian-born Argentine)
BenReEncy-1987
CamGLE-1988
CasWL-1973
EncWL-1981
GdMWL-1985
OxSpan-1978
PengAm-1971

Magic Realism

Cortesao, Jaime 1884-1960 (Portuguese)
ClDMEuL-1980
EncWL-1981
McGWD-1984

Portuguese Renascence Movement
Seara Nova Group

**Cosbuc, George 1866-1918
(Romanian)**
ClDMEuL-1980
GdMWL-1985
PengEur-1969

Samanatorism

**Cossío, José María 1893-
(Spanish)**
EncWL-1981
OxSpan-1978

Generation of 1927/Generación
del 1927

**Costa y Martínez, Joaquín 1846-
1911 (Spanish)**
CasWL-1973
ClDMEuL-1980
OxSpan-1978
PengEur-1969

Generation of 1898/Generación
del 1898

**Cournos, John 1881-1966
(American)**
LongCTCL-1975
OxAm-1983
OxEng-1985

Imagism

**Couto, Rui Ribeiro 1898-1963
(Brazilian)**
PengAm-1971

Modernism

Coward, Noël 1899-1973 (English)
BenReEncy-1987
CamGLE-1988
CasWL-1973
EncWL-1981

GdMWL-1985
LongCTCL-1975
McGWD-1984
OxAmThe-1984
OxEng-1985
OxThe-1983
PengEng-1971

Georgian Literature
Modernism

**Cowley, Malcolm 1898-1989
(American)**
BenReEncy-1987
EncWL-1981
OxAm-1983
PengAm-1971

Lost Generation

**Crane, (Harold) Hart 1899-1932
(American)**
BenReEncy-1987
CamGLE-1988
CasWL-1973
CEnMWL-1963
EncWL-1981
GdMWL-1985
LongCTCL-1975
OxAm-1983
OxEng-1985
PengAm-1971

Lost Generation
Poetry

**Crane, R(onald) S(almon) 1886-1967
(American)**
CasWL-1973
EncWL-1981
PengAm-1971
PrEncyPP-1974

Chicago Critics

Crane, Stephen 1871-1900 (American)
BenReEncy-1987
CamGLE-1988
CasWL-1973
EncWL-1981
GdMWL-1985
LongCTCL-1975
OxAm-1983
OxEng-1985
PengAm-1971
RCom-1973

Naturalism

Crawford, Cheryl 1902-1986 (American)
BenReEncy-1987
CamGLE-1988
OxAm-1983
OxAmThe-1984
OxThe-1983

Group Theater
Theater Guild

Crawford, Isabella Valancy 1850-1887 (Irish-born Canadian)
EncWL-1981
OxCan-1983
OxEng-1985

Confederation Poets

Creeley, Robert 1926- (American)
BenReEncy-1987
CamGLE-1988
CasWL-1973
EncWL-1981
GdMWL-1985
OxAm-1983
OxEng-1985
PengAm-1971

PrEncyPP-1974

Black Mountain Poets

Crémer, Victoriano 1908- (Spanish)
OxSpan-1978

Grupo Espadaña

Crevel, René 1900-1935 (French)
BenReEncy-1987
ClDMEuL-1980
EncWL-1981
OxEng-1985
PrEncyPP-1974

Surrealism

Croce, Benedetto 1866-1952 (Italian)
BenReEncy-1987
CasWL-1973
ClDMEuL-1980
EncWL-1981
GdMWL-1985
LongCTCL-1975
OxEng-1985
PengEur-1969

La Critica

Cruz, Viriato da 1928-1973 (Angolan)
EncWL-1981

Association of Angola's Native Sons

Cruz e Sousa, Joao de 1861-1898 (Brazilian)
CasWL-1973
EncWL-1981
PengAm-1971

Symbolism

Crystallis, Costas n.d. (Greek)
PrEncyPP-1974

New School of Athens/Greek
Parnassians

Csáth, Géza n.d. (Hungarian)
ClDMEuL-1980

Nyugat Group

Csuka, Zoltán 1901-   (Hungarian-speaking Yugoslavian)
EncWL-1981

Kalangya Group

Csurka, István n.d. (Hungarian)
ClDMEuL-1980

Generation of 1955

Cuadra, José de la 1903-1941 (Ecuadorian)
EncWL-1981
GdMWL-1985
OxSpan-1978
PengAm-1971

Group of Guayaquil/Grupo de
Guayaquil

Cuesta, Jorge n.d. (Mexican)
OxSpan-1978

Contemporaries/
Contemporáneos

Cuesta y Cuesta, Alfonso 1912- (Ecuadorian)
OxSpan-1978

Grupo Elan

Cullen, Countee 1903-1946 (American)
BenReEncy-1987
CamGLE-1988
CasWL-1973
EncWL-1981
OxAm-1983
PengAm-1971
PrEncyPP-1974

Harlem Renaissance

Culler, Jonathan 1944- (American)
CamGLE-1988
EncWL-1981

Structuralism

Cummings, E(dward) E(stlin) 1894-1962 (American)
BenReEncy-1987
CamGLE-1988
CasWL-1973
CEnMWL-1963
EncWL-1981
GdMWL-1985
LongCTCL-1975
McGWD-1984
OxAm-1983
OxEng-1985
PengAm-1971

Lost Generation
Modernism
Provincetown Players

Cuney, Waring 1906-1976 (American)
BenReEncy-1987
CamGLE-1988
PrEncyPP-1974

Harlem Renaissance

**Cunha, Euclides Rodrigues Pimenta
da 1866-1909 (Brazilian)**
  CasWL-1973
  EncWL-1981
  GdMWL-1985
  PengAm-1971

  Modernism
  Verde-Amarelismo

**Curel, François de 1854-1928
(French)**
  CasWL-1973
  ClDMEuL-1980
  EncWL-1981
  OxFr-1959
  PengEur-1969

  Théâtre Libre

Cutts, Simon 1944- (English)
  DCLT-1979

  Concrete Poetry

**Cvirka, Petras 1909-1947
(Lithuanian)**
  CasWL-1973
  ClDMEuL-1980
  EncWL-1981
  GdMWL-1985

  Third Front Movement/Trecias
    Frontas

**Czachorowski, Stanislaw Swen
  1920-   (Polish)**
  ClDMEuL-1980

Wspólczesnosc Generation

**Czaykowski, Bogdan 1923-
(Polish)**
  ClDMEuL-1980

  Kontynenty Group

**Czechowicz, Józef 1903-1939
(Polish)**
  CasWL-1973
  ClDMEuL-1980
  EncWL-1981
  GdMWL-1985
  PengEur-1969
  PrEncyPP-1974

  Cracow Avant-Garde

**Czerniawski, Adam 1934-
(Polish)**
  ClDMEuL-1980

  Kontynenty Group

**Czernik, Stanislaw 1899-1969
(Polish)**
  ClDMEuL-1980

  Authenticism

**Czuchnowski, Marian 1909-
(Polish)**
  ClDMEuL-1980
  EncWL-1981

  Cracow Avant-Garde

**Czyzewski, Tytus 1885-1945
(Polish)**
  ClDMEuL-1980

  Futurism

D

Dabit, Eugène 1898-1936 (French)
BenReEncy-1987
CasWL-1973
ClDMEuL-1980
EncWL-1981
GdMWL-1985
OxFr-1959

Populisme

**Dadourian, Aharon 1877-1965
(Armenian)**
EncWL-1981

Mehian Group

**Dagerman, Stig 1923-1954
(Swedish)**
CasWL-1973
ClDMEuL-1980
EncWL-1981
GdMWL-1985
OxThe-1983
PengEur-1969

Poets of the Forties/
Fyrtiotalisterna

**Dahlberg, Edward 1900-1977
(American)**
BenReEncy-1987
CamGLE-1988
GdMWL-1985
OxAm-1983

PengAm-1971

Proletarian Literature

**Daiches, David 1912-   (English-
born Scottish)**
BenReEncy-1987
EncWL-1981
LongCTCL-1975
OxEng-1985

Scottish Renaissance

**Daisne, Johan (pseud. of Herman
Thiery) 1912-1978 (Belgian)**
CasWL-1973
ClDMEuL-1980
EncWL-1981
GdMWL-1985
McGWD-1984

Magic Realism

Dalí, Salvador 1904-1989 (Spanish)
BenReEncy-1987
ClDMEuL-1980
EncWL-1981
OxEng-1985
OxFr-1959
OxSpan-1978

Surrealism

**Damas, Léon-Gontran 1912-1978
(French Guianese)**
BenReEncy-1987

CaribWr-1979
CasWL-1973
EncWL-1981
GdMWL-1985
OxEng-1985
PrEncyPP-1974

Négritude

Daoason, Sigfús 1928-   (Icelandic)
EncWL-1981

Modernism

Darío, Rubén (pseud. of Félix Rubén García Sarmiento) 1867-1916 (Nicaraguan)
BenReEncy-1987
CasWL-1973
EncWL-1981
GdMWL-1985
McGWD-1984
OxSpan-1978
PengAm-1971
PrEncyPP-1974

Modernismo

Darowski, Jan 1926-   (Polish)
ClDMEuL-1980

Kontynenty Group

Darvas, József 1912-   (Hungarian)
ClDMEuL-1980
EncWL-1981

Populist Movement

Daudet, Alphonse 1840-1897 (French)
BenReEncy-1987
CasWL-1973
ClDMEuL-1980
EncWL-1981

McGWD-1984
OxEng-1985
OxFr-1959
PengEur-1969
RCom-1973

Naturalism
Realism

Daumal, René 1908-1944 (French)
ClDMEuL-1980
EncWL-1981

Great Game Group/*Le Grand Jeu*

Dauthendey, Max 1867-1918 (German)
EncWL-1981
GdMWL-1985
PengEur-1969
PrEncyPP-1974

Jugendstil

Davey, Frank 1940-   (Canadian)
EncWL-1981
OxCan-1983

Tish Group

Davico, Oskar 1909-   (Serbian-speaking Yugoslavian)
CasWL-1973
ClDMEuL-1980
EncWL-1981
GdMWL-1985
PengEur-1969

Surrealism

Davidson, Donald 1893-1968 (American)
CamGLE-1988
EncWL-1981

170

OxAm-1983
PengAm-1971
PrEncyPP-1974

The Fugitives/Agrarians

Davie, Donald 1922- (English)
CamGLE-1988
CasWL-1973
EncWL-1981
GdMWL-1985
LongCTCL-1975
OxEng-1985

The Movement
New Lines Poets

**Davies, Hugh Sykes 1909-1984(?)
(English)**
BenReEncy-1987
EncWL-1981
OxEng-1985

Surrealism

**Davies, W(illiam) H(enry) 1871-
1940 (Welsh-born English)**
BenReEncy-1987
CamGLE-1988
CasWL-1973
CEnMWL-1963
EncWL-1981
GdMWL-1985
LongCTCL-1975
OxEng-1985
PengEng-1971
PrEncyPP-1974

Georgian Literature

**Dávila, Virgilio 1869-1943 (Puerto
Rican)**
CaribWr-1979
EncWL-1981
OxSpan-1978

PrEncyPP-1974

Modernismo

**Davis, Rebecca H(arding) 1831-1910
(American)**
BenReEncy-1987
CamGLE-1988
OxAm-1983

Realism

**Davis, Richard Harding 1864-1916
(American)**
BenReEncy-1987
CamGLE-1988
OxAm-1983
OxAmThe-1984

Local Color School

**Dawson, Fielding 1930-
(American)**
HandLit-1986

Black Mountain Poets

**Day-Lewis, C(ecil) 1904-1972
(Irish-born English)**
BenReEncy-1987
CamGLE-1988
CasWL-1973
CEnMWL-1963
EncWL-1981
GdMWL-1985
LongCTCL-1975
OxEng-1985
PengEng-1971

Pylon School

**Dazai Osamu (pseud. of Tsushima
Shuji) 1909-1948 (Japanese)**
CasWL-1973
CEnMWL-1963

DOrLit-1974
EncWL-1981
GdMWL-1985
PengCOAL-1969

Decadents/Burai-ha
I-Novel/Watakushi shosetsu

**DeAmicis, Edmondo 1846-1908
(Italian)**
CasWL-1973
PengEur-1969

Verismo

**Debelyanov, Dimcho 1887-1916
(Bulgarian)**
CasWL-1973
ClDMEuL-1980
EncWL-1981
GdMWL-1985
PengEur-1969
PrEncyPP-1974

Symbolism

**Debenedetti, Giacomo 1901-1967
(Italian)**
ClDMEuL-1980
EncWL-1981

Solaria Group

**Debreczeni, József 1905-
(Hungarian-speaking
Yugoslavian)**
EncWL-1981

Kalangya Group

Dedinac, Milan 1902-1966 (Serbian)
ClDMEuL-1980
EncWL-1981

Surrealism

**De Forest, John William 1826-1906
(American)**
BenReEncy-1987
CamGLE-1988
GdMWL-1985
OxAm-1983
PengAm-1971

Realism

**De Gasperi, Alcide 1881-1954
(Italian)**
ClDMEuL-1980

Neorealism

**Deglavs, Augusts 1862-1922
(Latvian)**
EncWL-1981

Realism

**Dehmel, Richard 1863-1920
(German)**
BenReEncy-1987
CasWL-1973
ClDMEuL-1980
EncWL-1981
GdMWL-1985
OxGer-1986
PengEur-1969
PrEncyPP-1974

Jugendstil
Naturalism

**De Kooning, Willem 1904-
(Dutch-born American)**
BenReEncy-1987

New York School

**De la Mare, Walter 1873-1956
(English)**
BenReEncy-1987

CamGLE-1988
CasWL-1973
CEnMWL-1963
EncWL-1981
GdMWL-1985
LongCTCL-1975
OxEng-1985
PengEng-1971
PrEncyPP-1974

Georgian Literature

Delaney, Shelagh 1939-   (English)
BenReEncy-1987
CamGLE-1988
LongCTCL-1975
McGWD-1984
OxEng-1985
PengEng-1971

Kitchen Sink Drama
Theater Workshop

**Delaunay, Sonia 1885-1979
(Ukrainian-born French)**
EncWL-1981

Cubism
Futurism

Del Buono, Oreste 1923-   (Italian)
ClDMEuL-1980
EncWL-1981

Group 63/Gruppo 63
Neorealism

Deledda, Grazia 1871-1936 (Italian)
CasWL-1973
ClDMEuL-1980
EncWL-1981
GdMWL-1985
OxEng-1985

PengEur-1969

Verismo

Dell, Floyd 1887-1969 (American)
BenReEncy-1987
CamGLE-1988
LongCTCL-1975
OxAm-1983
PengAm-1971

Chicago Group/Renaissance
Provincetown Players

**De Man, Paul 1919-1983 (Belgian-
born American)**
CamGLE-1988
EncWL-1981

Deconstructionism
Structuralism
Yale School of Critics

**De Marchi, Emilio 1851-1901
(Italian)**
ClDMEuL-1980
PengEur-1969

Verismo

Deml, Jakub 1878-1961 (Czech)
ClDMEuL-1980
EncWL-1981
GdMWL-1985

Expressionism

**Densusianu, Ovid 1873-1937
(Romanian)**
ClDMEuL-1980

Symbolism

**Derème, Tristan 1889-1942
(French)**
ClDMEuL-1980
OxFr-1959

Fantaisistes Group

**De Robertis, Giuseppe 1888-1963
(Italian)**
CasWL-1973
ClDMEuL-1980
EncWL-1981

Hermeticism/Poesia Ermetica

**De Roberto, Federico 1861-1927
(Italian)**
BenReEncy-1987
CasWL-1973
ClDMEuL-1980
PengEur-1969

Verismo

**Derrida, Jacques 1930- (Algerian-
born French)**
CamGLE-1988
ClDMEuL-1980
EncWL-1981
OxEng-1985
PrEncyPP-1974

Deconstructionism
Structuralism
Tel Quel Group
Yale School of Critics

Déry, Tibor 1884-1977 (Hungarian)
CasWL-1973
ClDMEuL-1980
EncWL-1981
GdMWL-1985
PengEur-1969

Today Group/*Ma*

**De Santis, Vincent P. 1918-
(American)**
HarDMT-1988

Neorealism

**De Sica, Vittorio 1901(?)-1974
(Italian)**
BenReEncy-1987
EncWL-1981
McGWD-1984
OxEng-1985

Neorealism

Desnos, Robert 1900-1945 (French)
BenReEncy-1987
CasWL-1973
ClDMEuL-1980
EncWL-1981
GdMWL-1985
OxEng-1985
PengEur-1969
PrEncyPP-1974

Surrealism

Dessau, Paul 1894-1979 (German)
OxGer-1986

Berlin Ensemble/Berliner
Ensemble

De Vries, Peter 1910-   (American)
BenReEncy-1987
HarDMT-1988
OxAm-1983

Poetry

**Deyssel, Lodewijk van (pseud. of
Karel Joan Lodewijk Albertdingk
Thijm) 1864-1952 (Dutch)**
CasWL-1973
ClDMEuL-1980

EncWL-1981
GdMWL-1985
PengEur-1969

Movement of the Eighties/
　Beweging van Tachtig

Dhrossinis, Yorghos 1859-1949
(Greek)
　EncWL-1981
　PrEncyPP-1974

　New School of Athens/Greek
　　Parnassians

Diakhaté, Lamine 1928-
(Senegalese)
　EncWL-1981

　Négritude

Díaz, Leopoldo 1862-1947
(Argentine)
　OxSpan-1978
　PrEncyPP-1974

　Modernismo

Díaz Casanueva, Humberto 1905-
(Chilean)
　OxSpan-1978
　PrEncyPP-1974

　Creationism/Creacionismo

Díaz Mirón, Salvador 1853-1928
(Mexican)
　CasWL-1973
　EncWL-1981
　OxSpan-1978
　PengAm-1971

　Modernismo

Díaz Rodríguez, Manuel 1868-1927
(Venezuelan)
　CasWL-1973
　EncWL-1981
　OxSpan-1978
　PengAm-1971

　Modernismo

Díaz Silveira, Francisco 1871-1924
(Cuban)
　CaribWr-1979

　Arpas Cubanas Group

Díaz Valcárcel, Emilio 1929-
(Puerto Rican)
　CaribWr-1979
　EncWL-1981

　Generation of 1940

Dib, Mohammed 1920-
(Algerian)
　CasWL-1973
　DOrLit-1974
　EncWL-1981

　Generation of 1952/54

Dickens, Charles 1812-1870
(English)
　BenReEncy-1987
　CamGLE-1988
　CasWL-1973
　EncWL-1981
　OxAm-1983
　OxEng-1985
　OxThe-1983
　PengAm-1971
　PengEng-1971
　RCom-1973

　Realism

Diego, Eliseo 1920-   (Cuban)
  CaribWr-1979
  OxSpan-1978

  Criollismo

**Diego (Cendoya), Gerardo 1896-
1987 (Spanish)**
  CasWL-1973
  ClDMEuL-1980
  EncWL-1981
  GdMWL-1985
  OxSpan-1978
  PengEur-1969
  PrEncyPP-1974

  Creationism/Creacionismo
  Generation of 1927/Generación
    del 1927
  Ultraism/Ultraismo

**Diego Padró, José I. de 1899-
(Puerto Rican)**
  OxSpan-1978

  Diepalismo

**Digges, Dudley 1879-1947 (Irish-
born American)**
  OxAmThe-1984
  OxThe-1983

  Theater Guild

**Di Giacomo, Salvatore 1860-1934
(Italian)**
  CasWL-1973
  ClDMEuL-1980
  EncWL-1981
  McGWD-1984

  Verismo

**Diktonius, Elmer Rafael 1896-1961
(Swedish-speaking Finnish)**
  CasWL-1973
  ClDMEuL-1980
  EncWL-1981
  GdMWL-1985
  PengEur-1969
  PrEncyPP-1974

  Swedish-Finnish Modernists

**Dimov, Dimitur 1909-1966
(Bulgarian)**
  CasWL-1973
  EncWL-1981
  GdMWL-1985

  Socialist Realism

Dimov, Leonid 1926-   (Romanian)
  EncWL-1981

  Oneiric Movement

**Dionísio, Mário 1916-
(Portuguese)**
  EncWL-1981

  Neorealism

**Diop, Alioune 1910-1980
(Senegalese)**
  EncWL-1981
  PrEncyPP-1974

  Négritude

**Diop, Birago Ismael 1906-
(Senegalese)**
  CasWL-1973
  ClDMEuL-1980
  EncWL-1981
  GdMWL-1985

PengCOAL-1969

Négritude

Diop, David 1927-1960 (Senegalese)
EncWL-1981
GdMWL-1985
PengCOAL-1969
PrEncyPP-1974

Négritude

Diop, Ousmane Socé 1911-
(Senegalese)
EncWL-1981
PengCOAL-1969

Négritude

Divoire, Fernand 1883-1951
(French-speaking Belgian)
OxFr-1959

Abbaye Group/Groupe de
l'Abbaye
Simultanéisme

Dix, Otto 1891-1969 (German)
BenReEncy-1987

New Objectivity/Neue
Sachlichkeit

Djabarly, Djafar 1899-1934
(Azerbaijani)
EncWL-1981

Socialist Realism

Döblin, Alfred 1878-1957 (German)
BenReEncy-1987
CasWL-1973
ClDMEuL-1980
EncWL-1981
GdMWL-1985

OxGer-1986
PengEur-1969

Expressionism
New Objectivity/Neue
Sachlichkeit
Storm Circle/*Der Sturm*
Surrealism

Doinas, Stefan Augustin (pseud. of
Stefan Popa) 1922-   (Romanian)
EncWL-1981

Sibiu Group

Domenchina, Juan José 1898-1959
(Spanish)
ClDMEuL-1980
OxSpan-1978

Generation of 1927/Generación
del 1927

Domínguez, Manuel 1869-1935
(Paraguayan)
EncWL-1981

Generation of 1900

Domjanic, Dragutin 1875-1933
(Croatian-speaking Yugoslavian)
ClDMEuL-1980
EncWL-1981
PrEncyPP-1974

Moderna

Donoso, José 1924-   (Chilean)
BenReEncy-1987
EncWL-1981
GdMWL-1985
OxSpan-1978
PengAm-1971

Generation of 1950

**Dontsov, Dmytro 1883-1973
(Ukrainian)**
ClDMEuL-1980
EncWL-1981

Visnyk

Dorn, Ed 1929- (American)
BenReEncy-1987
EncWL-1981
OxAm-1983
PengAm-1971
PrEncyPP-1974

Black Mountain Poets

**Dorosh, Yefim Yakovlevich 1908-
1972 (Russian)**
ClDMEuL-1980
EncWL-1981

Village Prose

Dorst, Tankred 1925-   (German)
EncWL-1981
OxGer-1986
OxThe-1983

Epic Theater/Episches Theater

**Dos Passos, John 1896-1970
(American)**
BenReEncy-1987
CamGLE-1988
CasWL-1973
EncWL-1981
GdMWL-1985
LongCTCL-1975
McGWD-1984
OxAm-1983
OxEng-1985
PengAm-1971

Jazz Age
Lost Generation

Naturalism
Proletarian Literature

**Dostoevski, Fedor Mikhailovich
1821-1881 (Russian)**
BenReEncy-1987
CamGLE-1988
CasWL-1973
ClDMEuL-1980
EncWL-1981
OxEng-1985
PengEur-1969
RCom-1973

Realism

**Dosvitny, Oles 1891-1934
(Ukrainian)**
ClDMEuL-1980
EncWL-1981

Free Academy of Proletarian
Literature/VAPLITE

Drach, Ivan 1936-   (Ukrainian)
ClDMEuL-1980
EncWL-1981
GdMWL-1985

Generation of the 1960s/
Shestydesyatnyky

**Drachmann, Holger Henrik
Herholdt 1846-1908 (Danish)**
CasWL-1973
ClDMEuL-1980
GdMWL-1985
PengEur-1969
PrEncyPP-1974

Naturalism
Realism
Vero Ani Group

Dray-Khmara, Mykhaylo 1889-1938 (Ukrainian)
ClDMEuL-1980
EncWL-1981

Neoclassic Group

Dreiser, Theodore 1871-1945 (American)
BenReEncy-1987
CamGLE-1988
CasWL-1973
CEnMWL-1963
EncWL-1981
GdMWL-1985
LongCTCL-1975
OxAm-1983
OxEng-1985
PengAm-1971
RCom-1973

Chicago Group/Renaissance
Naturalism

Drinkwater, John 1882-1937 (English)
BenReEncy-1987
CamGLE-1988
CasWL-1973
LongCTCL-1975
McGWD-1984
OxEng-1985
PengEng-1971
PrEncyPP-1974

Georgian Literature

Droguett, Carlos 1915-　(Chilean)
EncWL-1981
OxSpan-1978

Generation of 1938/Generación del 1938

Drummond de Andrade, Carlos 1902-1987 (Brazilian)
CasWL-1973
EncWL-1981
GdMWL-1985
PengAm-1971
PrEncyPP-1974

Modernism

Dsida, Jeno 1907-1938 (Hungarian-speaking Romanian)
ClDMEuL-1980
EncWL-1981

Nyugat Group
Transylvanian Helicon Group

D'Sola, Otto 1912-　(Venezuelan)
EncWL-1981
OxSpan-1978

Viernes Group

ad-Du'aji, 'Ali 1909-1949 (Tunisian)
DOrLit-1974
EncWL-1981

Under the Ramparts/Taht al-Sur Group

DuBois, William Edward Brown 1868-1963 (American)
BenReEncy-1987
CamGLE-1988
CasWL-1973
EncWL-1981
LongCTCL-1975
OxAm-1983
OxEng-1985
PengAm-1971

Harlem Renaissance

**Dubowka, Uladzimier 1900-1975
(Byelorussian)**
  ClDMEuL-1980
  EncWL-1981

  Uzvyssa Group

**Duchamp, Marcel 1887-1968
(French)**
  BenReEncy-1987
  EncWL-1981
  OxEng-1985
  OxFr-1959

  Dadaism
  Orphism
  Surrealism

**Ducic, Jovan 1871-1943 (Serbian-
speaking Yugoslavian)**
  CasWL-1973
  ClDMEuL-1980
  EncWL-1981
  GdMWL-1985
  PengEur-1969

  Moderna

**Dudás, Kálmán 1912-
(Hungarian-speaking
Yugoslavian)**
  EncWL-1981

  Kalangya Group

Dudek, Louis 1918-   (Canadian)
  CasWL-1973
  GdMWL-1985
  OxCan-1983

  First Statement Group

**Duffy, Charles Gavan 1816-1903
(Irish)**
  OxEng-1985

  PrEncyPP-1974

  Irish Renaissance

**Duhamel, Georges (pseud. of Denis
Thévenin) 1884-1966 (French)**
  BenReEncy-1987
  CasWL-1973
  ClDMEuL-1980
  EncWL-1981
  GdMWL-1985
  LongCTCL-1975
  OxFr-1959
  PengEur-1969

  Abbaye Group/Groupe de
    l'Abbaye
  Unanimism/Unanisme

**Dujardin, Édouard 1861-1949
(French)**
  BenReEncy-1987
  CamGLE-1988
  ClDMEuL-1980
  EncWL-1981
  GdMWL-1985
  OxEng-1985
  OxFr-1959

  Symbolism

Dullin, Charles 1885-1949 (French)
  OxFr-1959
  OxThe-1983

  Théâtre du Vieux-Colombier

**Dumitrescu, Geo 1920-
(Romanian)**
  EncWL-1981

  Bucharest Group

Duncan, Norman 1871-1916 (Canadian)
OxCan-1983

Local Color School

Duncan, Robert 1919-1988 (American)
BenReEncy-1987
CamGLE-1988
CasWL-1973
EncWL-1981
GdMWL-1985
OxAm-1983
OxEng-1985
PengAm-1971
PrEncyPP-1974

Black Mountain Poets
San Francisco School

Duncan, Sara Jeanette 1861-1922 (Canadian)
CamGLE-1988
OxCan-1983

Local Color School

Dunsany, Edward John Moreton Drax Plunkett 1878-1957 (Irish)
BenReEncy-1987
CasWL-1973
GdMWL-1985
LongCTCL-1975
McGWD-1984
OxEng-1985
OxThe-1983
PengEng-1971
RCom-1973

Abbey Theater
Edwardian Literature
Irish Renaissance

Du Plessys, Maurice 1864-1924 (French)
GdMWL-1985
OxFr-1959

École Romane

Durand, Luis 1895-1954 (Chilean)
EncWL-1981
OxSpan-1978

Criollismo

Durant, Rudo n.d. (Belgian)
ClDMEuL-1980

Fifties Poets/Vijftigers

Duranty, Louis 1833-1880 (French)
CamGLE-1988
OxFr-1959

Realism
Théâtre Libre

Duras, Marguerite (pseud. of Marguerite Donnadieu) 1914- (Indochinese-born French)
BenReEncy-1987
CasWL-1973
ClDMEuL-1980
EncWL-1981
GdMWL-1985
McGWD-1984
OxEng-1985
OxThe-1983
PengEur-1969

Deconstructionism
New Novel/Nouveau Roman

Dürrenmatt, Friedrich 1921- (German-speaking Swiss)
BenReEncy-1987
CasWL-1973

181

ClDMEuL-1980
EncWL-1981
GdMWL-1985
LongCTCL-1975
OxAmThe-1984
OxEng-1985
OxGer-1986
OxThe-1983
PengEur-1969

Epic Theater/Episches Theater

Durtain, Luc 1881-1959 (French)
ClDMEuL-1980
GdMWL-1985
OxFr-1959

Abbaye Group/Groupe de
l'Abbaye

Unanimism/Unanisme

Dutton, Paul 1934-   (Canadian)
OxCan-1983

Four Horsemen

**Dygasinski, Adolf 1839-1902
(Polish)**
ClDMEuL-1980

Naturalism

**Dzilums, Alfreds 1907-1966
(Latvian)**
EncWL-1981

Realism

E

Eagleton, Terry 1943- (English)
CamGLE-1988
EncWL-1981
OxEng-1985

Marxist Criticism

Eco, Umberto 1932- (Italian)
BenReEncy-1987
ClDMEuL-1980
EncWL-1981
OxEng-1985

Group 63/Gruppo 63

Edfelt, Bo Johannes 1904- (Swedish)
CasWL-1973
ClDMEuL-1980
EncWL-1981

New Objectivity/Neue
Sachlichkeit

Edschmid, Kasimir 1890-1966 (German)
CasWL-1973
ClDMEuL-1980
EncWL-1981
OxGer-1986
PengEur-1969
PrEncyPP-1974

Expressionism

Edwards, Jorge 1931- (Chilean)
EncWL-1981
OxSpan-1978

Generation of 1950

Edwards Bello, Joaquín 1887-1968 (Chilean)
CasWL-1973
EncWL-1981
OxSpan-1978
PengAm-1971

Criollismo

Eeden, Frederik Willem van 1860-1932 (Dutch)
CasWL-1973
ClDMEuL-1980
EncWL-1981
GdMWL-1985
McGWD-1984
PengEur-1969
PrEncyPP-1974

Movement of the Eighties/
Beweging van Tachtig

Efendiev, Ilyas 1914- (Azerbaijani)
EncWL-1981

Socialist Realism

**Eggleston, Edward 1837-1902
(American)**
   CamGLE-1988
   CasWL-1973
   GdMWL-1985
   OxAm-1983
   OxEng-1985
   PengAm-1971

   Local Color School
   Realism

**Eggleston, George Cary 1839-1911
(American)**
   CamGLE-1988
   OxAm-1983

   Local Color School

**Ehrenstein, Albert 1886-1950
(Austrian)**
   EncWL-1981
   OxGer-1986
   PengEur-1969

   Expressionism

Eich, Günter 1907-1972 (German)
   CasWL-1973
   ClDMEuL-1980
   EncWL-1981
   GdMWL-1985
   OxGer-1986
   PengEur-1969

   Group 47/Gruppe 47

**Eikhenbaum, Boris 1886-1959
(Russian)**
   EncWL-1981
   PrEncyPP-1974

   LEF
   Russian Formalism

Einstein, Carl 1885-1940 (German)
   EncWL-1981
   OxGer-1986

   Expressionism

Eisler, Hanns 1898-1962 (German)
   EncWL-1981
   OxGer-1986

   Berlin Ensemble/Berliner
   Ensemble

**Ekelöf, (Bengt) Gunnar 1907-1968
(Swedish)**
   BenReEncy-1987
   CasWL-1973
   ClDMEuL-1980
   EncWL-1981
   GdMWL-1985
   PengEur-1969

   Modernism
   Surrealism

**Eklund, R.R. 1894-1946 (Swedish-
speaking Finnish)**
   ClDMEuL-1980

   Swedish-Finnish Modernists

**Ekwenski, Cyprian 1921-
(Nigerian)**
   BenReEncy-1987
   CamGLE-1988
   CasWL-1973
   EncWL-1981
   GdMWL-1985
   LongCTCL-1975
   PengCOAL-1969

   Onitsha Novels/Chapbooks

Elburg, Jan 1919-   (Dutch)
EncWL-1981

Fifties Poets/Vijftigers

**Elger, Semyon V. 1894-1966
(Chuvash)**
EncWL-1981

Socialist Realism

**Eliot, George (pseud. of Mary Ann
Evans) 1819-1880 (English)**
BenReEncy-1987
CamGLE-1988
CasWL-1973
EncWL-1981
OxEng-1985
PengEng-1971
RCom-1973

Naturalism
Realism

**Eliot, T(homas) S(tearns) 1888-1965
(American-born English)**
BenReEncy-1987
CamGLE-1988
CasWL-1973
CEnMWL-1963
EncWL-1981
GdMWL-1985
LongCTCL-1975
McGWD-1984
OxAm-1983
OxAmThe-1984
OxEng-1985
OxThe-1983
PengAm-1971
PengEng-1971
PrEncyPP-1974
RCom-1973

Georgian Literature
Group Theater

Modernism
New Criticism
New Humanism
Poetry
Symbolism

Eliraz, Israel 1936-   (Israeli)
ClDMEuL-1980

Metarealism

Eloglu, Metin 1927-   (Turkish)
ClDMEuL-1980

The Second New

**Eloy Blanco, Andrés 1897-1955
(Venezuelan)**
EncWL-1981
OxSpan-1978

Generation of 1918

Elskamp, Max 1862-1931 (Belgian)
CasWL-1973
ClDMEuL-1980
EncWL-1981
GdMWL-1985
PrEncyPP-1974

Symbolism

**Elster, Kristian 1841-1881
(Norwegian)**
ClDMEuL-1980

Realism

**Éluard, Paul (pseud. of Eugène
Grindel) 1895-1952 (French)**
BenReEncy-1987
CasWL-1973
CEnMWL-1963
ClDMEuL-1980
EncWL-1981

GdMWL-1985
OxEng-1985
OxFr-1959
PengEur-1969
PrEncyPP-1974

Dadaism
Surrealism

**Elytis, Odysseus (pseud. of
Odysseus Alepoudhelis) 1911-
(Greek)**
BenReEncy-1987
ClDMEuL-1980
EncWL-1981
GdMWL-1985
PengEur-1969

Generation of 1930

**Embirikos, Andreas 1901-1975
(Greek)**
ClDMEuL-1980
EncWL-1981
GdMWL-1985
PengEur-1969

Generation of 1930

**Empson, William 1906-1984
(English)**
BenReEncy-1987
CamGLE-1988
CasWL-1973
CEnMWL-1963
EncWL-1981
GdMWL-1985
LongCTCL-1975
OxEng-1985
PengEng-1971
PrEncyPP-1974

Cambridge Group
Georgian Literature
Modernism

New Criticism

**Enckell, Rabbe Arnfinn 1903-1974
(Swedish-speaking Finnish)**
CasWL-1973
ClDMEuL-1980
EncWL-1981
GdMWL-1985
PengEur-1969
PrEncyPP-1974

Swedish-Finnish Modernists

Engel, Erich 1891-1966 (German)
McGWD-1984
OxGer-1986

Berlin Ensemble/Berliner
Ensemble
New Objectivity/Neue
Sachlichkeit

**Engonopoulos, Nikos 1910-
(Greek)**
ClDMEuL-1980
GdMWL-1985

Generation of 1930

Enno, Ernst 1875-1934 (Estonian)
ClDMEuL-1980
EncWL-1981
GdMWL-1985

Young Estonia Group

**Enright, D(ennis) J(oseph) 1920-
(English)**
CamGLE-1988
EncWL-1981
LongCTCL-1975
OxEng-1985
PengEng-1971

The Movement

New Lines Poets
Scrutiny

Enzensberger, Hans Magnus 1929-
(German)
  CasWL-1973
  ClDMEuL-1980
  EncWL-1981
  GdMWL-1985
  OxGer-1986
  PengEur-1969

Group 47/Gruppe 47

Epstein, Jacob 1880-1959
(American-born English)
  BenReEncy-1987
  CamGLE-1988
  LongCTCL-1975
  OxEng-1985

Vorticism

Erdei, Ferenc n.d. (Hungarian)
  ClDMEuL-1980

Populist Movement

Erdélyi, József 1896-1978
(Hungarian)
  ClDMEuL-1980
  EncWL-1981

Populist Movement

Erik, Max 1898-1937 (Yiddish-
speaking Byelorussian)
  ClDMEuL-1980
  EncWL-1981

Minsk Group

Erikson, Bernt 1918-   (Swedish)
  PrEncyPP-1974

Poets of the Forties/
Fyrtiotalisterna

Eristin, Erilik (pseud. of Semyon
Stepanovich Yakovlev) 1892-1942
(Yakut)
  EncWL-1981

Socialist Realism

Erlingsson, Thorsteinn 1858-1914
(Icelandic)
  ClDMEuL-1980

Realism

Ermanis, Peteris 1893-1969
(Latvian)
  EncWL-1981

Expressionism

Ernst, Max 1891-1976 (German)
  BenReEncy-1987
  ClDMEuL-1980
  EncWL-1981
  OxEng-1985
  OxFr-1959

Dadaism
Surrealism

Ernst, Otto 1862-1926 (German)
  OxGer-1986

Heimatkunst

Ernst, Paul 1866-1955 (German)
  CasWL-1973
  ClDMEuL-1980
  EncWL-1981
  OxGer-1986
  OxThe-1983

PengEur-1969

Expressionism

**Erro, Carlos Alberto 1899-
(Argentine)**
EncWL-1981

Criollismo

Ertl, Emil 1860-1935 (Austrian)
OxGer-1986

Heimatkunst

**Ervine, St. John Greer 1883-1971
(Irish)**
CamGLE-1988
CasWL-1973
LongCTCL-1975
McGWD-1984
OxEng-1985
OxThe-1983
PengEng-1971

Abbey Theater

**Esenin, Sergei Aleksandrovich 1895-
1925 (Russian)**
BenReEncy-1987
CasWL-1973
CEnMWL-1963
ClDMEuL-1980
EncWL-1981
GdMWL-1985
OxEng-1985
PengEur-1969
PrEncyPP-1974

Imaginists

**Espina García, Antonio 1894-
(Spanish)**
ClDMEuL-1980
GdMWL-1985

OxSpan-1978

Generation of 1927/Generación
del 1927
Surrealism

Esslin, Martin 1918- (American)
EncWL-1981

Theater of the Absurd

**Estrella, Ulises 1940-
(Ecuadorian)**
OxSpan-1978

Grupo Tzántzico

**Etchells, Frederick 1886-1973
(English)**
CamGLE-1988

Vorticism

**Evdoshvili, Irodion 1873-1916
(Georgian)**
EncWL-1981

Democratic Poets

**Everson, William 1912-
(American)**
EncWL-1981
OxAm-1983
PengAm-1971
PrEncyPP-1974

San Francisco School

**Eybers, Elisabeth 1915-   (South
African)**
CasWL-1973
EncWL-1981
GdMWL-1985

PengCOAL-1969

The Dertigers

**Eyck, Pieter Nicolaas Van 1887-
1954 (Dutch)**
   CasWL-1973
   ClDMEuL-1980

De Beweging

**Eyüboglu, Bedri Rahmi 1913-
(Turkish)**
   CasWL-1973
   PrEncyPP-1974

Garip Movement

F

Fábry, Rudolf 1915-   (Czech)
ClDMEuL-1980
EncWL-1981

Nadrealisti Movement

Fadeyev, Alexander Aleksandrovich
1901-1956 (Russian)
BenReEncy-1987
CasWL-1973
ClDMEuL-1980
EncWL-1981
GdMWL-1985
PengEur-1969

Socialist Realism

Fagus (pseud. of Georges Eugène
Faillet) 1872-1933 (Belgian-born
French)
ClDMEuL-1980

Fantaisistes Group

Fahlström, Öjvind 1928-1976
(Swedish)
ClDMEuL-1980

Concrete Poetry

Faiz, Faiz Ahmad (pseud. of Faiz
Ahmed) 1912(?)-1984 (Pakistani)
CasWL-1973
DOrLit-1974
EncWL-1981

GdMWL-1985

Progressive Writers' Movement

Fallada, Hans (pseud. of Rudolf
Ditzen) 1893-1947 (German)
CasWL-1973
ClDMEuL-1980
EncWL-1981
GdMWL-1985
LongCTCL-1975
OxGer-1986
PengEur-1969

New Objectivity/Neue
Sachlichkeit

Fangen, Ronald August 1895-1946
(Norwegian)
BenReEncy-1987
CasWL-1973
EncWL-1981
PengEur-1969

Oxford Group

Fanon, Frantz 1925-1961
(Martinican)
BenReEncy-1987
CaribWr-1979

Négritude

Fargue, Léon-Paul 1876(?)-1947
(French)
CasWL-1973

ClDMEuL-1980
EncWL-1981
GdMWL-1985
OxFr-1959
PengEur-1969

Cubism

Farhat, Ilyas 1893-   (Lebanese)
EncWL-1981

Andalusian League

**Farrell, James T(homas) 1904-1979
(American)**
BenReEncy-1987
CamGLE-1988
CasWL-1973
EncWL-1981
GdMWL-1985
LongCTCL-1975
OxAm-1983
OxEng-1985
PengAm-1971

Jazz Age
Naturalism
Proletarian Literature

**Farrokhzad, Forugh 1935-1967
(Iranian)**
CasWL-1973
DOrLit-1974
EncWL-1981

New Wave Movement

Farzad, Mas'ud 1906-   (Iranian)
CasWL-1973
DOrLit-1974

Rab'e Group

Fast, Howard 1914-   (American)
BenReEncy-1987

CamGLE-1988
EncWL-1981
OxAm-1983
PengAm-1971

Socialist Realism

**Fauset, Jessie Redmon 1884(?)-1961
(American)**
CamGLE-1988
OxAm-1983
PrEncyPP-1974

Harlem Renaissance

Fay, Frank J. 1870-1931 (Irish)
McGWD-1984
OxEng-1985
OxThe-1983

Abbey Theater
Irish Renaissance

**Fay, William George 1872-1947
(Irish)**
McGWD-1984
OxEng-1985
OxThe-1983

Abbey Theater
Irish Renaissance

Federer, Heinrich 1866-1928 (Swiss)
EncWL-1981
OxGer-1986

Heimatkunst

**Fedin, Konstantin Aleksandrovich
1892-1977 (Russian)**
BenReEncy-1987
CasWL-1973
ClDMEuL-1980
EncWL-1981
GdMWL-1985

PengEur-1969

Modernism
Serapion Brotherhood

Féjadarvas, Géza n.d. (Hungarian)
ClDMEuL-1980

Populist Movement

**Fêng, Hsüeh-Fêng 1906-
(Chinese)**
CasWL-1973
DOrLit-1974

Lakeside Society

Fenoglio, Beppe 1922-1963 (Italian)
ClDMEuL-1980
EncWL-1981
GdMWL-1985
OxEng-1985

Neorealism

Fenyo, Miksa n.d. (Hungarian)
ClDMEuL-1980

Nyugat Group

Ferber, Edna 1887-1968 (American)
BenReEncy-1987
LongCTCL-1975
OxAm-1983
OxAmThe-1984
PengAm-1971

Provincetown Players

Ferguson, Samuel 1810-1886 (Irish)
CamGLE-1988
CasWL-1973
EncWL-1981
OxEng-1985

PengEng-1971

Irish Renaissance

**Ferlinghetti, Lawrence 1919-
(American)**
BenReEncy-1987
CamGLE-1988
CasWL-1973
EncWL-1981
OxAm-1983
OxEng-1985
PengAm-1971
PrEncyPP-1974

Beat Generation
San Francisco School

**Fernández, Jorge 1912-
(Ecuadorian)**
OxSpan-1978

Grupo Elan

**Fernández, Macedonio 1874-1952
(Argentine)**
GdMWL-1985
OxSpan-1978
PengAm-1971

Ultraism/Ultraismo

**Fernández Alvarez, Luis 1902-1952
(Venezuelan)**
EncWL-1981

Generation of 1918

**Ferreira, José Gomes 1900-
(Portuguese)**
ClDMEuL-1980
EncWL-1981

Neorealism

Ferreira, Manuel 1917-
(Portuguese)
ClDMEuL-1980

Claridade Movement

Feydeau, Ernest 1821-1873 (French)
EncWL-1981
OxFr-1959
PengEur-1969

Realism

Ficke, Arthur Davison 1883-1945
(American)
OxAm-1983

Spectra

Field, Edward 1924-   (American)
EncWL-1981

New York School

Fierro, Humberto 1890-1929
(Ecuadorian)
EncWL-1981

Modernismo

Figes, Eva 1932-   (German-born
English)
CamGLE-1988
OxEng-1985

Feminist Criticism

Fikret, Tevfik 1867-1915 (Turkish)
CasWL-1973
DOrLit-1974
PrEncyPP-1974

Servet-i Fünun/Edebiyat-i
Cedide

Filyansky, Mykola 1873-1937
(Ukrainian)
ClDMEuL-1980
EncWL-1981

Symbolism

Finch, Robert 1900-   (American-
born Canadian)
EncWL-1981
OxCan-1983
PrEncyPP-1974

Montreal Movement

Finlay, Ian Hamilton 1925-
(Bahamian-born Scottish)
CamGLE-1988
EncWL-1981
OxEng-1985
PrEncyPP-1974

Concrete Poetry

Fischer, U.Chr. n.d. (German)
OxGer-1986

Cologne School of New
Realism/Kölner Schule des
neuen Realismus

Fisher, Roy 1930-   (English)
CamGLE-1988
OxEng-1985

Jazz Poetry

Fisher, Rudolph 1897-1934
(American)
CamGLE-1988

Harlem Renaissance

GdMWL-1985
PrEncyPP-1974

Hermeticism/Poesia Ermetica

Flores, Ángel 1900-   **(Puerto Rican)**
EncWL-1981

Magic Realism

Fodor, József n.d. (Hungarian)
ClDMEuL-1980

Nyugat Group

**Foerster, Norman 1887-1972
(American)**
EncWL-1981
OxAm-1983
PengAm-1971
PrEncyPP-1974

New Humanism

**Fogazzaro, Antonio 1842-1911
(Italian)**
BenReEncy-1987
ClDMEuL-1980
GdMWL-1985
OxEng-1985
PengEur-1969

Verismo

**Foix, J(osep)-V(icenç) 1893-
(Spanish)**
CasWL-1973
ClDMEuL-1980
EncWL-1981
GdMWL-1985
OxSpan-1978

Surrealism

**Fondane, Benjamin 1898-1944
(Swiss)**
˙ *EncWL-1981*

Existentialism

**Fonseca, António José Branquinho
1905-**   **(Portuguese)**
ClDMEuL-1980
EncWL-1981
GdMWL-1985

Presencistas Group

**Fonseca, Manuel da 1911-
(Portuguese)**
ClDMEuL-1980

Neorealism

**Fontane, Theodor 1819-1898
(German)**
BenReEncy-1987
CasWL-1973
ClDMEuL-1980
EncWL-1981
OxEng-1985
OxGer-1986
PengEur-1969

Realism

**Ford, Ford Madox 1873-1939
(English)**
BenReEncy-1987
CamGLE-1988
CasWL-1973
CEnMWL-1963
EncWL-1981
GdMWL-1985
LongCTCL-1975
OxEng-1985
PengEng-1971

Edwardian Literature

Imagism
Modernism
Poetry
Vorticism

Forster, E(dward) M(organ) 1879-1970 (English)
  BenReEncy-1987
  CamGLE-1988
  CasWL-1973
  CEnMWL-1963
  EncWL-1981
  GdMWL-1985
  LongCTCL-1975
  OxEng-1985
  PengEng-1971
  RCom-1973

Bloomsbury Group
Edwardian Literature
Modernism

Fort, Paul 1872-1960 (French)
  CasWL-1973
  ClDMEuL-1980
  EncWL-1981
  OxFr-1959
  OxThe-1983
  PengEur-1969

Naturism/Naturisme
Symbolism

Foucault, Michel 1926-1984 (French)
  BenReEncy-1987
  CamGLE-1988
  ClDMEuL-1980
  EncWL-1981
  OxEng-1985
  PrEncyPP-1974

Structuralism

Fox, John 1862(?)-1919 (American)
  OxAm-1983

Local Color School

Fox, Ralph 1900-1937 (English)
  EncWL-1981

Socialist Realism

Francisco, Ramón 1929- (Dominican Republican)
  CaribWr-1979

Promotion of 1948

Franco Oppenheimer, Félix 1912- (Puerto Rican)
  CaribWr-1979
  OxSpan-1978

Ensueñismo Group
Transcendentalist Group

Frank, Leonhard 1882-1961 (German)
  BenReEncy-1987
  ClDMEuL-1980
  GdMWL-1985
  McGWD-1984
  OxGer-1986
  PengEur-1969

Expressionism

Frank, Waldo 1889-1967 (American)
  CamGLE-1988
  EncWL-1981
  OxAm-1983
  PengAm-1971

Proletarian Literature

**Fraser, G(eorge) S(utherland) 1915-
1980 (Scottish)**
BenReEncy-1987
CamGLE-1988
CasWL-1973
GdMWL-1985
OxEng-1985
PengEng-1971

New Apocalypse

**Fraser, William Alexander 1857-
1933 (Canadian)**
OxCan-1983

Local Color School

**Fréchette, Louis 1839-1908
(Canadian)**
BenReEncy-1987
OxCan-1983

Literary School of Montreal/
    École Littéraire de Montreal

**Frederic, Harold 1856-1898
(American)**
CamGLE-1988
GdMWL-1985
OxAm-1983
PengAm-1971

Naturalism

**Freeman, Joseph 1897-1965
(American)**
OxAm-1983

Proletarian Literature

**Freeman, Mary E(leanor) Wilkins
1852-1930 (American)**
CamGLE-1988
CasWL-1973
EncWL-1981

LongCTCL-1975
OxAm-1983
OxEng-1985
PengAm-1971

Local Color School

**Freiligrath, Hermann Ferdinand
1810-1876 (German)**
BenReEncy-1987
OxGer-1986
PengEur-1969
PrEncyPP-1974

Realism

**Frensson, Gustav 1863-1945
(German)**
GdMWL-1985
OxGer-1986

Heimatkunst

**Freud, Sigmund 1856-1939
(Austrian)**
BenReEncy-1987
CasWL-1973
EncWL-1981
HandLit-1986
HarDMT-1988
LongCTCL-1975
OxEng-1985
OxGer-1986
PengEur-1969
RCom-1973

**Freyre, Gilberto de Melo 1900-1987
(Brazilian)**
BenReEncy-1987
CasWL-1973
EncWL-1981
PengAm-1971

Modernism
Region-Tradition Movement

**Fridegård, Jan 1897-1968
(Swedish)**
ClDMEuL-1980
EncWL-1981
GdMWL-1985
PengEur-1969

Proletarian Writers/
  Arbetardiktare

Fried, Erich 1921-1988 (Austrian)
ClDMEuL-1980
GdMWL-1985
OxGer-1986
PengEur-1969

Group 47/Gruppe 47

**Friedman, Norman 1925-
(American)**
PrEncyPP-1974

Chicago Critics

Frisch, Max 1911-   (Swiss)
BenReEncy-1987
CasWL-1973
ClDMEuL-1980
EncWL-1981
GdMWL-1985
McGWD-1984
OxEng-1985
OxGer-1986
OxThe-1983
PengEur-1969

Epic Theater/Episches Theater
Existentialism
Theater of the Absurd

**Fröding, Gustaf 1860-1911
(Swedish)**
BenReEncy-1987
CasWL-1973
ClDMEuL-1980

EncWL-1981
GdMWL-1985
PengEur-1969
PrEncyPP-1974

Nittiotalister

Frost, Robert 1874-1963 (American)
BenReEncy-1987
CamGLE-1988
CEnMWL-1963
EncWL-1981
GdMWL-1985
LongCTCL-1975
OxAm-1983
OxEng-1985
PengAm-1971
PrEncyPP-1974

Poetry

Fry, Christopher 1907-   (English)
BenReEncy-1987
CamGLE-1988
CasWL-1973
CEnMWL-1963
EncWL-1981
GdMWL-1985
LongCTCL-1975
McGWD-1984
OxAmThe-1984
OxEng-1985
OxThe-1983
PengEng-1971

Modernism

Fry, Roger 1866-1934 (English)
BenReEncy-1987
LongCTCL-1975
OxEng-1985

Bloomsbury Group

Fucini, Renato 1843-1921 (Italian)
ClDMEuL-1980
GdMWL-1985
PengEur-1969

Verismo

Fuentes, Carlos 1929-　(Mexican)
BenReEncy-1987
CamGLE-1988
CasWL-1973
EncWL-1981
GdMWL-1985
OxSpan-1978
PengAm-1971

Magic Realism

Fuller, Henry Blake 1857-1929 (American)
CamGLE-1988
CasWL-1973
OxAm-1983
PengAm-1971

Chicago Group/Renaissance Realism

Fuller, Roy 1912-　(English)
BenReEncy-1987
CamGLE-1988
CasWL-1973
EncWL-1981
GdMWL-1985
LongCTCL-1975
OxEng-1985
PengEng-1971

The Movement

Füst, Milán 1888-1967 (Hungarian)
CasWL-1973
ClDMEuL-1980
EncWL-1981
GdMWL-1985
PengEur-1969

Nyugat Group

Fylypovych, Pavlo 1891-1937 (Ukrainian)
EncWL-1981

Neoclassic Group

G

Gabo, Naum 1890-1977 (Russian)
HarDMT-1988

Constructivism

Gadda, Carlo Emilio 1893-1973 (Italian)
BenReEncy-1987
CasWL-1973
ClDMEuL-1980
EncWL-1981
GdMWL-1985
OxEng-1985
PengEur-1969

Solaria Group

Gailit, August 1891-1960 (Estonian)
ClDMEuL-1980
EncWL-1981
GdMWL-1985

Siuru Group

Gajcy, Tadeusz 1922-1944 (Polish)
CasWL-1973
EncWL-1981

Condemned Generation Poets

Gál, Laszló 1902-   (Hungarian-speaking Yugoslavian)
EncWL-1981

Hid Group

Galaction, Gala 1879-1961 (Romanian)
CasWL-1973
ClDMEuL-1980
EncWL-1981

Poporanism

Galczynski, Konstanty Ildefons 1905-1953 (Polish)
CasWL-1973
ClDMEuL-1980
EncWL-1981
GdMWL-1985
McGWD-1984
PengEur-1969
PrEncyPP-1974

Cracow Avant-Garde
Quadriga

Gale, Rita 1925-   (Latvian)
EncWL-1981

New York Group

Gale, Zona 1874-1938 (American)
BenReEncy-1987
CamGLE-1988
LongCTCL-1975
McGWD-1984
OxAm-1983
OxAmThe-1984
PengAm-1971

Local Color School

Washington Square Players

Gallardo, Salvador n.d. (Mexican)
OxSpan-1978

Estridentismo

**Gallegos, Rómulo 1884-1968
(Venezuelan)**
BenReEncy-1987
CasWL-1973
EncWL-1981
GdMWL-1985
OxSpan-1978
PengAm-1971

Realism

**Gallegos Lara, Joaquín 1911-1947
(Ecuadorian)**
EncWL-1981
GdMWL-1985
OxSpan-1978

Group of Guayaquil/Grupo de
Guayaquil

**Galovic, Fran 1887-1914 (Croatian-
speaking Yugoslavian)**
ClDMEuL-1980

Moderna

**Galsworthy, John 1867-1933
(English)**
BenReEncy-1987
CamGLE-1988
CasWL-1973
CEnMWL-1963
EncWL-1981
GdMWL-1985
LongCTCL-1975
McGWD-1984
OxAmThe-1984
OxEng-1985

OxThe-1983
PengEng-1971
RCom-1973

Edwardian Literature
Georgian Literature
Modernism
Naturalism
Realism

**Gálvez, Manuel 1882-1962
(Argentine)**
BenReEncy-1987
CasWL-1973
EncWL-1981
GdMWL-1985
OxSpan-1978
PengAm-1971

Realism

Gan, Alexei n.d. (Russian)
HarDMT-1988

Constructivism

**Ganghofer, Ludwig 1855-1920
(German)**
OxGer-1986

Heimatkunst

Ganivet, Angel 1865-1898 (Spanish)
ClDMEuL-1980
OxSpan-1978

Generation of 1898/Generación
del 1898

Gaos, Vicente 1919-   (Spanish)
ClDMEuL-1980
EncWL-1981
GdMWL-1985
OxSpan-1978
PengEur-1969

Generation of 1936/Generación
del 1936

**Gaprindashvili, Valerian 1889-1941
(Georgian)**
EncWL-1981
PrEncyPP-1974

Blue Horns Group/Tsispheri
q'antesbi

Garaudy, Roger 1913- (French)
ClDMEuL-1980
EncWL-1981

Marxist Criticism

Garay, Blas 1873-1899 (Paraguayan)
EncWL-1981

Generation of 1900

**Garborg, Arne 1851-1924
(Norwegian)**
BenReEncy-1987
CasWL-1973
ClDMEuL-1980
GdMWL-1985
PengEur-1969

Naturalism
Neoromanticism

**García Lorca, Federico 1898-1936
(Spanish)**
BenReEncy-1987
CasWL-1973
CEnMWL-1963
ClDMEuL-1980
EncWL-1981
GdMWL-1985
LongCTCL-1975
McGWD-1984
OxEng-1985
OxSpan-1978

OxThe-1983
PengEur-1969
PrEncyPP-1974
RCom-1973

Generation of 1927/Generación
del 1927
Surrealism
Ultraism/Ultraismo

**García Márquez, Gabriel 1928-
(Columbian)**
BenReEncy-1987
CamGLE-1988
CasWL-1973
EncWL-1981
GdMWL-1985
McGWD-1984
OxEng-1985
OxSpan-1978
PengAm-1971

Magic Realism

**García Marruz, Fina 1923-
(Cuban)**
CaribWr-1979
EncWL-1981

Orígenes Group

Garfias, Pedro n.d. (Spanish)
OxSpan-1978

Ultraism/Ultraismo

**Garioch, Robert (pseud. of R.G.
Sutherland) 1908-1981 (Scottish)**
CamGLE-1988
CasWL-1973
EncWL-1981
GdMWL-1985
OxEng-1985

Scottish Renaissance

Garland, (Hannibal) Hamlin 1860-1940 (American)
BenReEncy-1987
CamGLE-1988
CasWL-1973
EncWL-1981
GdMWL-1985
LongCTCL-1975
OxAm-1983
PengAm-1971

Local Color School
Naturalism
Realism

Garmendia, Salvador 1928- (Venezuelan)
EncWL-1981
OxSpan-1978

Sardio Group

Garnett, David 1892-1981 (English)
BenReEncy-1987
CamGLE-1988
CasWL-1973
EncWL-1981
GdMWL-1985
LongCTCL-1975
OxEng-1985
PengEng-1971

Bloomsbury Group

Gascoyne, David 1916- (English)
BenReEncy-1987
CamGLE-1988
EncWL-1981
GdMWL-1985
LongCTCL-1975
OxEng-1985
PengEng-1971

Surrealism

Gaskell, Elizabeth 1810-1865 (English)
BenReEncy-1987
CamGLE-1988
CasWL-1973
OxEng-1985
PengEng-1971

Realism

Gassol, Ventura 1893-1980 (Spanish)
EncWL-1981

Noucentismo

Gastelúm, Bernardo J. n.d. (Mexican)
OxSpan-1978

Contemporaries/
Contemporáneos

Gastev, Alexey Kapitonovich 1882- (Russian)
CasWL-1973
EncWL-1981
PrEncyPP-1974

Smithy Poets/Kuznitsa

Gatsos, Nikos 1915- (Greek)
ClDMEuL-1980
EncWL-1981
GdMWL-1985

Generation of 1930

Gatto, Alfonso 1909-1976 (Italian)
ClDMEuL-1980
EncWL-1981
GdMWL-1985
OxEng-1985
PengEur-1969

Hermeticism/Poesia Ermetica

Gaudier-Brzeska, Henri 1891-1915 (French)
EncWL-1981
OxEng-1985

Vorticism

Gay Calbó, Enrique 1889-(?) (Cuban)
CaribWr-1979

Cenáculo Group

Gelber, Jack 1932-   (American)
BenReEncy-1987
CamGLE-1988
EncWL-1981
GdMWL-1985
OxAm-1983
OxAmThe-1984
OxThe-1983
PengAm-1971

Living Theater
Theater of the Absurd

Gellért, Oszkár 1882-1967 (Hungarian)
EncWL-1981

Nyugat Group

Genet, Jean 1910-1986 (French)
BenReEncy-1987
CasWL-1973
CEnMWL-1963
ClDMEuL-1980
EncWL-1981
GdMWL-1985
LongCTCL-1975
McGWD-1984
OxAmThe-1984

OxEng-1985
OxThe-1983
PengEur-1969

New Wave/Nouvelle Vague
Theater of Cruelty/Théâtre de
la Cruauté
Theater of the Absurd

Genette, Gérard 1930-   (French)
CamGLE-1988
ClDMEuL-1980
EncWL-1981
OxEng-1985
PrEncyPP-1974

Structuralism

Gentile, Giovanni 1875-1944 (Italian)
CasWL-1973
ClDMEuL-1980

La Critica

George, Stefan 1868-1933 (German)
BenReEncy-1987
CasWL-1973
CEnMWL-1963
ClDMEuL-1980
EncWL-1981
GdMWL-1985
LongCTCL-1975
OxGer-1986
PengEur-1969
PrEncyPP-1974

Jugendstil
Symbolism

Georgiev, V. n.d. (Bulgarian)
CasWL-1973
PrEncyPP-1974

Socialist Realism

**Gerasimov, Mikhail 1889-1939
(Russian)**
EncWL-1981

Smithy Poets/Kuznitsa

**Gerbasi, Vicente 1912-
(Venezuelan)**
EncWL-1981

Viernes Group

Ghil, René 1862-1925 (French)
CasWL-1973
ClDMEuL-1980
OxFr-1959
PrEncyPP-1974

Symbolism

**Giacometti, Alberto 1901-1966
(Swiss)**
BenReEncy-1987
EncWL-1981

Surrealism

**Giacosa, Giuseppe 1847-1906
(Italian)**
BenReEncy-1987
CasWL-1973
ClDMEuL-1980
GdMWL-1985
OxThe-1983
PengEur-1969

Intimismo
Verismo

**Gibbon, Lewis Grassic (pseud. of
James Leslie Mitchell) 1901-1935
(Scottish)**
BenReEncy-1987
CamGLE-1988
CasWL-1973

CEnMWL-1963
EncWL-1981
LongCTCL-1975
OxEng-1985
PengEng-1971

Scottish Renaissance

**Gibran, Kahlil 1883-1931
(Lebanese-born American)**
BenReEncy-1987
CasWL-1973
DOrLit-1974
EncWL-1981

Society of the Pen

**Gibson, Wilfred Wilson 1878-1962
(English)**
CamGLE-1988
EncWL-1981
OxEng-1985
PrEncyPP-1974

Georgian Literature

Gide, André 1869-1951 (French)
BenReEncy-1987
CasWL-1973
CEnMWL-1963
ClDMEuL-1980
EncWL-1981
GdMWL-1985
LongCTCL-1975
McGWD-1984
OxEng-1985
OxFr-1959
OxThe-1983
PengEur-1969
RCom-1973

Nouvelle Revue Française
   Group
Total Theater

Giguère, Roland 1929-
(Canadian)
  BenReEncy-1987
  OxCan-1983

  Hexagone Group

Gijsen, Marnix (pseud. of Jan-
Albert Goris) 1899-   (Belgian)
  ClDMEuL-1980
  EncWL-1981
  GdMWL-1985

  Ruimte Group

Gilbert, Enrique Gil 1912-
(Ecuadorian)
  EncWL-1981
  GdMWL-1985
  OxSpan-1978
  PengAm-1971

  Group of Guayaquil/Grupo de
    Guayaquil

Gilbert, Sandra M. 1936-
(American)
  OxEng-1985

  Feminist Criticism

Gilbert-Lecomte, Roger 1907-1943
(French)
  EncWL-1981

  Great Game Group/*Le Grand
    Jeu*

Gill, Charles 1871-1918 (Canadian)
  OxCan-1983

  Literary School of Montreal/
    École Littéraire de Montreal

Gils, Gust 1924-   (Belgian)
  ClDMEuL-1980
  EncWL-1981

  Fifties Poets/Vijftigers
  Fifty-Five Poets/Vijfenvijftigers

Ginsberg, Allen 1926- (American)
  BenReEncy-1987
  CamGLE-1988
  CasWL-1973
  EncWL-1981
  GdMWL-1985
  LongCTCL-1975
  OxAm-1983
  OxEng-1985
  PengAm-1971
  PrEncyPP-1974

  Beat Generation
  Confessional Poetry
  San Francisco School

Gira, Liudas 1884-1946 (Lithuanian)
  PrEncyPP-1974

  Socialist Realism

Girard, René 1923-   (French)
  BenReEncy-1987

  Structuralism

Giraud, Albert 1860-1929 (Belgian)
  ClDMEuL-1980
  GdMWL-1985

  Jeune Belgique Group

Giraudoux, Jean 1882-1944 (French)
  BenReEncy-1987
  CasWL-1973
  CEnMWL-1963
  ClDMEuL-1980
  EncWL-1981

GdMWL-1985
LongCTCL-1975
McGWD-1984
OxAmThe-1984
OxEng-1985
OxFr-1959
OxThe-1983
PengEur-1969
RCom-1973

Nouvelle Revue Française
  Group

**Gissing, George 1857-1903
(English)**
BenReEncy-1987
CamGLE-1988
CasWL-1973
EncWL-1981
GdMWL-1985
LongCTCL-1975
OxEng-1985
PengEng-1971

Naturalism
Realism

Giuliani, Alfredo 1924-   (Italian)
ClDMEuL-1980
EncWL-1981

Group 63/Gruppo 63

**Gjellerup, Karl Adolph 1857-1919
(Danish)**
BenReEncy-1987
CasWL-1973
ClDMEuL-1980
GdMWL-1985
PengEur-1969
PrEncyPP-1974

Naturalism

**Gladkov, Fyodor Vasilyevich 1883-
1958 (Russian)**
BenReEncy-1987
CasWL-1973
ClDMEuL-1980
EncWL-1981
GdMWL-1985

Forge Group
Modernism
Socialist Realism

**Glanz-Leyeles, Aaron 1889-1966
(Yiddish-speaking American)**
ClDMEuL-1980
EncWL-1981

Introspectivists Movement/
  Inzikh

**Glasgow, Ellen 1873(?)-1945
(American)**
CamGLE-1988
CasWL-1973
EncWL-1981
GdMWL-1985
LongCTCL-1975
OxAm-1983
OxEng-1985
PengAm-1971

Realism

**Glaspell, Susan 1882-1948
(American)**
BenReEncy-1987
CamGLE-1988
GdMWL-1985
LongCTCL-1975
McGWD-1984
OxAm-1983
OxAmThe-1984
OxThe-1983

Provincetown Players

Glatstein, Jacob 1896-1971 (Polish-born Yiddish)
CasWL-1973
ClDMEuL-1980
EncWL-1981
GdMWL-1985
PrEncyPP-1974

Introspectivists Movement/
Inzikh

Gleizes, Albert 1881-1953 (French)
OxFr-1959

Abbaye Group/Groupe de
l'Abbaye
Cubism

Glik, Hirsh 1922-1944 (Yiddish-speaking Lithuanian)
ClDMEuL-1980

Young Vilna

Godard, Jean-Luc 1930- (French)
BenReEncy-1987
EncWL-1981

New Wave/Nouvelle Vague

Godfrey, Peter 1917-   (South African-born English)
HarDMT-1988

Gate Theater

Godoy, Juan 1911-   (Chilean)
EncWL-1981

Generation of 1938/Generación
del 1938

Godoy, Juan G. 1793-1864 (Argentine)
OxSpan-1978

Gaucho Literature

Goemans, Camille 1900-1960 (Belgian)
EncWL-1981

Surrealism

Goering, Reinhard 1887-1936 (German)
ClDMEuL-1980
OxGer-1986
OxThe-1983

Expressionism

Gogarty, Oliver St. John 1878-1957 (Irish)
BenReEncy-1987
CamGLE-1988
CasWL-1973
EncWL-1981
LongCTCL-1975
OxEng-1985
PengEng-1971
PrEncyPP-1974

Irish Renaissance

Gogol, Nikolay Vasilyevich 1809-1852 (Russian)
BenReEncy-1987
CasWL-1973
EncWL-1981
McGWD-1984
OxEng-1985
OxThe-1983
PengEur-1969
RCom-1973

Realism

**Gold, Michael 1893-1967
(American)**
CamGLE-1988
OxAm-1983
PengAm-1971

Proletarian Literature

**Goldmann, Lucien 1913-1970
(Romanian-born French)**
BenReEncy-1987
CamGLE-1988
ClDMEuL-1980
EncWL-1981
OxEng-1985

Marxist Criticism
Structuralism

**Goll, Yvan 1891-1950 (German-
speaking Yiddish)**
CasWL-1973
ClDMEuL-1980
EncWL-1981
GdMWL-1985
OxGer-1986
PengEur-1969

Expressionism

**Gomes, Joaquim Soeiro Pereira
1910-1949 (Portuguese)**
ClDMEuL-1980
EncWL-1981

Neorealism

**Gómez Carillo, Enrique 1873-1927
(Guatemalan)**
EncWL-1981
OxSpan-1978

Modernismo

**Gómez de la Serna, Ramón 1888-
1963 (Spanish)**
BenReEncy-1987
CasWL-1973
ClDMEuL-1980
EncWL-1981
GdMWL-1985
McGWD-1984
OxSpan-1978
PengEur-1969

Generation of 1898/Generación
del 1898
Surrealism

**Gomringer, Eugen 1925-
(Bolivian-born German)**
CamGLE-1988
CasWL-1973
EncWL-1981
OxGer-1986
PrEncyPP-1974

Concrete Poetry

**Gonçalves, António Aurélio 1901-
(Portuguese)**
ClDMEuL-1980

Claridade Movement

**Goncharov, Ivan Alexandrovich
1812-1891 (Russian)**
BenReEncy-1987
CasWL-1973
OxEng-1985
PengEur-1969

Realism

**Goncourt, Edmond de 1822-1896
(French)**
BenReEncy-1987
CasWL-1973
OxEng-1985

OxFr-1959
OxThe-1983
PengEur-1969
RCom-1973

Naturalism
Realism

**Goncourt, Jules de 1830-1870
(French)**
BenReEncy-1987
CasWL-1973
OxEng-1985
OxFr-1959
OxThe-1983
PengEur-1969
RCom-1973

Naturalism
Realism

**Gondra, Manuel 1871-1927
(Paraguayan)**
EncWL-1981

Generation of 1900

**González, Otto-Raúl 1921-
(Guatemalan)**
OxSpan-1978

Grupo Acento

**González Lanuza, Eduardo 1900-
(Spanish-born Argentine)**
OxSpan-1978

Florida Group

**González Martínez, Enrique 1871-
1952 (Mexican)**
CasWL-1973
EncWL-1981
OxSpan-1978
PengAm-1971

PrEncyPP-1974

Atheneum of Youth
Contemporaries/
   Contemporáneos
Modernismo

**González Prada, Manuel 1848-1918
(Peruvian)**
BenReEncy-1987
CasWL-1973
EncWL-1981
OxSpan-1978
PengAm-1971

Modernismo

**González Rojo, Enrique n.d.
(Mexican)**
OxSpan-1978

Contemporaries/
   Contemporáneos

**González Tuñón, Raúl n.d.
(Argentine)**
EncWL-1981
OxSpan-1978

Boedo Group

Goodman, Edward n.d. (American)
OxAmThe-1984

Washington Square Players

**Gordon, Charles W(illiam) 1860-
1937 (Canadian)**
OxCan-1983

Local Color School

Gorky, Arshile 1905-1948 (Armenian)
HarDMT-1988

New York School

Gorky, Maxim (pseud. of Alexey Maximovich Peshkov) 1868-1936 (Russian)
BenReEncy-1987
CasWL-1973
CEnMWL-1963
ClDMEuL-1980
EncWL-1981
GdMWL-1985
McGWD-1984
OxAmThe-1984
OxEng-1985
OxThe-1983
PengEur-1969
RCom-1973

Moscow Art Theater
Naturalism
Proletkult
Realism
Socialist Realism
Znanie Group

Gornick, Vivian 1935- (American)
HandLit-1986

Feminist Criticism

Gorodetsky, Sergei Mitrofanovich 1884-1967 (Russian)
CasWL-1973
ClDMEuL-1980
EncWL-1981
OxEng-1985
PrEncyPP-1974

Acmeism

Gorostiza, José 1901-1973 (Mexican)
CasWL-1973
EncWL-1981
GdMWL-1985
OxSpan-1978
PengAm-1971

Contemporaries/
Contemporáneos

Górski, Artur 1870-1959 (Polish)
ClDMEuL-1980

Young Poland/Mloda Polska

Gorter, Herman 1864-1927 (Dutch)
CasWL-1973
ClDMEuL-1980
EncWL-1981
GdMWL-1985
PengEur-1969
PrEncyPP-1974

Movement of the Eighties/
Beweging van Tachtig

Gossaert, Geerten 1884-1958 (Dutch)
CasWL-1973
ClDMEuL-1980

De Beweging

Gottlieb, Adolph 1903-1974 (American)
HarDMT-1988

New York School

Gourmont, Rémy de 1858-1915 (French)
CamGLE-1988
CasWL-1973
ClDMEuL-1980
EncWL-1981

LongCTCL-1975
OxFr-1959
PengEur-1969

Symbolism

Govoni, Corrado 1884-1965 (Italian)
CasWL-1973
EncWL-1981
GdMWL-1985
PengEur-1969
PrEncyPP-1974

Crepuscolarismo
Futurism

Goytisolo, Juan 1931-   (Spanish)
BenReEncy-1987
CasWL-1973
ClDMEuL-1980
EncWL-1981
GdMWL-1985
OxSpan-1978

Turia Group

Gozzano, Guido 1883-1916 (Italian)
CasWL-1973
ClDMEuL-1980
EncWL-1981
GdMWL-1985
PengEur-1969
PrEncyPP-1974

Crepuscolarismo

Gracq, Julien (pseud. of Louis Poirier) 1910-   (French)
CasWL-1973
ClDMEuL-1980
EncWL-1981
GdMWL-1985
PengEur-1969

PrEncyPP-1974

Surrealism

Grade, Chaim 1910-1982 (Yiddish-speaking Lithuanian)
CasWL-1973
ClDMEuL-1980
EncWL-1981

Young Vilna

Grainger, Martin Allerdale 1874-1941 (English-born Canadian)
OxCan-1983

Local Color School

Gramsci, Antonio 1891-1937 (Italian)
CasWL-1973
ClDMEuL-1980
EncWL-1981
OxEng-1985

Marxist Criticism
Neorealism

Grant, Duncan 1885-1978 (Scottish)
CamGLE-1988
EncWL-1981
OxEng-1985

Bloomsbury Group

Granville-Barker, Harley 1877-1946 (English)
BenReEncy-1987
CamGLE-1988
CasWL-1973
GdMWL-1985
LongCTCL-1975
McGWD-1984
OxEng-1985
OxThe-1983

PengEng-1971

Edwardian Literature

Gras, Felix 1884-1901 (Provençal-speaking French)
ClDMEuL-1980

Félibrige Movement

Grass, Günter 1927-   (German)
BenReEncy-1987
CasWL-1973
ClDMEuL-1980
EncWL-1981
GdMWL-1985
McGWD-1984
OxEng-1985
OxGer-1986
PengEur-1969

Group 47/Gruppe 47
Theater of the Absurd

Grave, Elsa 1918-   (Swedish)
ClDMEuL-1980

Poets of the Forties/
    Fyrtiotalisterna

Graves, Robert 1895-1985 (English)
BenReEncy-1987
CamGLE-1988
CasWL-1973
CEnMWL-1963
EncWL-1981
GdMWL-1985
LongCTCL-1975
OxEng-1985
PengEng-1971
PrEncyPP-1974

Georgian Literature

Gray, Alexander 1882-1968 (Scottish)
CamGLE-1988
EncWL-1981

Scottish Renaissance

Green, Henry (pseud. of Henry Vincent Yorke) 1905-1974 (English)
BenReEncy-1987
CamGLE-1988
CasWL-1973
CEnMWL-1963
EncWL-1981
GdMWL-1985
LongCTCL-1975
OxEng-1985
PengEng-1971

Modernism

Green, Paul Eliot 1894-1981 (American)
BenReEncy-1987
CamGLE-1988
EncWL-1981
LongCTCL-1975
McGWD-1984
OxAm-1983
OxAmThe-1984
OxThe-1983
PengAm-1971

Carolina Playmakers
Group Theater
Provincetown Players

Greenberg, Uri Zvi 1894-1981 (Yiddish-speaking Israeli)
CasWL-1973
ClDMEuL-1980
EncWL-1981
GdMWL-1985
PengCOAL-1969

PengEur-1969

Gang Group/Khalyastre

**Greene, (Henry) Graham 1904-
(English)**
BenReEncy-1987
CamGLE-1988
CasWL-1973
CEnMWL-1963
EncWL-1981
GdMWL-1985
LongCTCL-1975
McGWD-1984
OxEng-1985
OxThe-1983
PengEng-1971

Georgian Literature
Modernism

**Greenwood, Walter 1903-1974
(English)**
CamGLE-1988
LongCTCL-1975
OxEng-1985
PengEng-1971

Proletarian Literature

**Greer, Germaine 1939-
(Australian)**
HandLit-1986

Feminist Criticism

Gregh, Fernand 1873-1960 (French)
EncWL-1981
OxFr-1959

Humanisme

**Gregory, Lady Isabella Augusta
1852-1932 (Irish)**
BenReEncy-1987

CamGLE-1988
CasWL-1973
EncWL-1981
GdMWL-1985
LongCTCL-1975
McGWD-1984
OxAmThe-1984
OxEng-1985
OxThe-1983
PengEng-1971

Abbey Theater
Edwardian Literature
Irish Literary Theater
Irish Renaissance

Greimas, A.J. 1917-   (French)
CamGLE-1988
EncWL-1981
PrEncyPP-1974

Semiotics
Structuralism

**Grenfell, Wilfred 1865-1940
(English)**
CamGLE-1988
LongCTCL-1975
OxCan-1983

Local Color School

**Grenier, Paul-Louis 1879-1954
(French)**
EncWL-1981

Society for Occitan Studies

**Griese, Friedrich 1890-1975
(German)**
GdMWL-1985
OxGer-1986

Heimatkunst

**Grignon, Claude-Henri 1894-1976
(French-speaking Canadian)**
CasWL-1973
OxCan-1983

Literary School of Montreal/
École Littéraire de Montreal

**Grímsson, Stefán Hördur 1919-
(Icelandic)**
EncWL-1981

Modernism

Gris, Juan 1887-1927 (Spanish)
BenReEncy-1987

Cubism

**Grochowiak, Stanislaw 1934-1976
(Polish)**
CasWL-1973
ClDMEuL-1980
EncWL-1981

Theater of the Absurd
Wspólczesnosc Generation

**Grosz, Georg 1893-1959 (German-
born American)**
BenReEncy-1987
OxGer-1986

Dadaism
New Objectivity/Neue
Sachlichkeit

Grotowski, Jerzy 1933-   (Polish)
EncWL-1981
McGWD-1984
OxThe-1983

Theater Laboratory

**Grün, Max von der 1926-
(German)**
ClDMEuL-1980
OxGer-1986

Group 61/Gruppe 61

Grünthal, Ivar 1924-   (Estonian)
EncWL-1981

Soothsayers Movement/
Arbujad

Gruszecki, Artur 1853-1929 (Polish)
ClDMEuL-1980

Naturalism

Gruzdev, Illya n.d. (Russian)
HarDMT-1988

Serapion Brotherhood

**Grydzewski, Mieczyslaw 1894-1970
(Polish)**
ClDMEuL-1980

Skamander Group

**Gryparis, George (Ioannis) 1872-
1942 (Greek)**
GdMWL-1985
PrEncyPP-1974

New School of Athens/Greek
Parnassians

**Guanes, Alejandro 1872-1925
(Paraguayan)**
EncWL-1981
OxSpan-1978

Generation of 1900

Gubar, Susan 1944-   (American)
OxEng-1985

Feminist Criticism

Guest, Barbara 1920-   (American)
EncWL-1981

New York School

Guglielmi, Angelo 1924-   (Italian)
EncWL-1981

Group 63/Gruppo 63

Guillén, Jorge 1893-1984 (Spanish)
BenReEncy-1987
CasWL-1973
CEnMWL-1963
ClDMEuL-1980
EncWL-1981
GdMWL-1985
OxSpan-1978
PengEur-1969

Generation of 1927/Generación
   del 1927

Guillén Batista, Nicolás 1902-
(Cuban)
BenReEncy-1987
CaribWr-1979
CasWL-1973
EncWL-1981
GdMWL-1985
OxSpan-1978
PengAm-1971

Afro-Cubanism
Negrismo

Guilloux, Louis 1899-1980 (French)
BenReEncy-1987
CasWL-1973
ClDMEuL-1980

EncWL-1981
GdMWL-1985

Populisme

Güiraldes, Ricardo 1886-1927
(Argentine)
BenReEncy-1987
CasWL-1973
CEnMWL-1963
EncWL-1981
GdMWL-1985
OxSpan-1978
PengAm-1971

Criollismo
Gaucho Literature
Realism
Ultraism/Ultraismo

Guirao, Ramón 1908-1949 (Cuban)
CaribWr-1979
EncWL-1981
OxSpan-1978
PengAm-1971

Afro-Cubanism

Gumilyov, Nikolai Stepanovich
1886-1921 (Russian)
BenReEncy-1987
CasWL-1973
ClDMEuL-1980
EncWL-1981
GdMWL-1985
OxEng-1985
PengEur-1969
PrEncyPP-1974

Acmeism

Gunasinghe, Siri n.d. (Sri Lankan)
EncWL-1981

Free Verse Group

Gunn, Thom 1929-   (English)
BenReEncy-1987
CamGLE-1988
CasWL-1973
EncWL-1981
GdMWL-1985
LongCTCL-1975
OxEng-1985
PengEng-1971

The Movement
New Lines Poets

**Guro, Yelena Genrikhovna 1877-
1913 (Russian)**
CasWL-1973
ClDMEuL-1980
GdMWL-1985

Cubo-Futurism

**Gusein, Mehti 1909-1965
(Azerbaijani)**
EncWL-1981

Socialist Realism

**Gutiérrez, Eduardo 1853-1890
(Argentine)**
BenReEncy-1987
OxSpan-1978

Gaucho Literature

**Gutiérrez Nájera, Manuel 1859-
1895 (Mexican)**
BenReEncy-1987
CasWL-1973
EncWL-1981
OxSpan-1978
PengAm-1971
PrEncyPP-1974

Modernismo

**Guzmán, Martín Luis 1887-1976
(Mexican)**
BenReEncy-1987
CasWL-1973
EncWL-1981
GdMWL-1985
OxSpan-1978
PengAm-1971

Realism

**Guzmán, Nicomedes 1914-1964
(Chilean)**
EncWL-1981

Generation of 1938/Generación
del 1938

**Gwala, Mafika Pascal 1946-
(South African)**
EncWL-1981

Black Consciousness Movement

**Gyergyai, Albert 1893-
(Hungarian)**
ClDMEuL-1980

Nyugat Group

Gyseghem, André van n.d.
HarDMT-1988

Unity Theater

Gysen, René n.d. (Belgian)
ClDMEuL-1980

Komma Group

Gyulai, Pál 1826-1909 (Hungarian)
ClDMEuL-1980
GdMWL-1985

Popular National School

H

Haan, Jacob Israël de 1881-1924
(Dutch)
CasWL-1973
ClDMEuL-1980

De Beweging

Haasbroek, P.J. 1943-   (South
African)
EncWL-1981

The Sestigers

Haavardsholm, Espen 1945-
(Norwegian)
ClDMEuL-1980
EncWL-1981

Profil Group

Haavikko, Paavo 1931-   (Finnish)
ClDMEuL-1980
EncWL-1981
GdMWL-1985
PengEur-1969

Modernism

Hacks, Peter 1928-   (German)
ClDMEuL-1980
EncWL-1981
GdMWL-1985
OxGer-1986
PengEur-1969

Berlin Ensemble

Deutsches Theater
Epic Theater/Episches Theater

Haertski, Maksim 1893-1939
(Byelorussian)
EncWL-1981

Our Soil Group/Nasaniustva

Hafstein, Hannes 1861-1922
(Icelandic)
GdMWL-1985

Realism
Vero Ani Group

Halas, Frantisek 1901-1949 (Czech)
CasWL-1973
ClDMEuL-1980
EncWL-1981
GdMWL-1985
PengEur-1969

Poeticism

Halász, Gábor n.d. (Hungarian)
ClDMEuL-1980

Nyugat Group

Halbe, Max 1865-1944 (German)
BenReEncy-1987
ClDMEuL-1980
OxGer-1986

PengEur-1969

Naturalism

Hallström, Per 1866-1960 (Swedish)
CasWL-1973
ClDMEuL-1980
EncWL-1981
OxThe-1983

Nittiotalister

**Halper, Albert 1904-1984
(American)**
CamGLE-1988
OxAm-1983

Proletarian Literature

**Halpern, Moishe Leib 1886-1932
(Yiddish-speaking American)**
CasWL-1973
ClDMEuL-1980
EncWL-1981
GdMWL-1985

Young Ones/Die Yunge

**Hamilton, Cuthbert 1884-1959
(Indian-born English)**
CamGLE-1988

Vorticism

Hamilton, Ian 1925- (Scottish)
CamGLE-1988
EncWL-1981
OxEng-1985

Concrete Poetry

**Hamsun, Knut (pseud. of Knud
Pedersen) 1859-1952 (Norwegian)**
BenReEncy-1987
CasWL-1973

ClDMEuL-1980
EncWL-1981
GdMWL-1985
LongCTCL-1975
OxEng-1985
OxThe-1983
PengEur-1969

Neoromanticism

**Hamzah Hussein 1927-
(Malaysian)**
EncWL-1981

Generation of the 1950s/Asas
'50

**Hàn Mac Tu 1913-1940
(Vietnamese)**
DOrLit-1974
EncWL-1981

Self-Reliant Group

**Hansjakob, Heinrich 1837-1916
(German)**
OxGer-1986

Heimatkunst

**Harasymowicz, Jerzy 1933-
(Polish)**
ClDMEuL-1980

Wspólczesnosc Generation

**Harden, Maximilian 1861-1927
(German)**
OxGer-1986

Freie Bühne

**Harding, D(enys) W(yatt) 1906-
(English)**
CamGLE-1988

OxEng-1985

Scrutiny

Hardwick, Elizabeth 1916-
(American)
EncWL-1981
OxAm-1983
OxEng-1985

Feminist Criticism

Hardy, Thomas 1840-1928 (English)
BenReEncy-1987
CamGLE-1988
CasWL-1973
CEnMWL-1963
EncWL-1981
GdMWL-1985
LongCTCL-1975
OxEng-1985
PengEng-1971
PrEncyPP-1974
RCom-1973

Edwardian Literature
Naturalism
Realism

Harecki, Maksim 1893-1939
(Byelorussian)
ClDMEuL-1980

Renaissance Group/
  Adradzenstva

Harig, Ludwig n.d. (German)
OxGer-1986

Cologne School of New
  Realism/Kölner Schule des
  neuen Realismus

Harris, Joel Chandler 1848-1908
(American)
BenReEncy-1987
CamGLE-1988
CasWL-1973
OxAm-1983
OxEng-1985
PengAm-1971

Local Color School

Hart, Heinrich 1855-1906 (German)
BenReEncy-1987
CasWL-1973
OxGer-1986

Naturalism

Hart, Julius 1859-1930 (German)
BenReEncy-1987
OxGer-1986

Freie Bühne
Naturalism

Harte, (Francis) Bret 1836(?)-1902
(American)
BenReEncy-1987
CamGLE-1988
CasWL-1973
OxAm-1983
OxAmThe-1984
OxEng-1985
PengAm-1971

Local Color School
Realism

Hartlaub, G.F. 1884-1963 (German)
HarDMT-1988

New Objectivity/Neue
  Sachlichkeit

**Hartleben, Otto Erich 1864-1905
(German)**
  CasWL-1973
  OxGer-1986

  Naturalism

**Hartman, Geoffrey 1929-
(German-born American)**
  CamGLE-1988
  EncWL-1981

  Deconstructionism
  Yale School of Critics

**Harun, Ales 1887-1920
(Byelorussian)**
  ClDMEuL-1980
  EncWL-1981

  Our Soil Group/Nasaniustva
  Renaissance Group/
    Adradzenstva

Hasan, Isma'il (?)-1982 (Sudanese)
  EncWL-1981

  Realism

**Hasenclever, Walter 1890-1940
(German)**
  CamGLE-1988
  CasWL-1973
  ClDMEuL-1980
  EncWL-1981
  GdMWL-1985
  McGWD-1984
  OxGer-1986
  OxThe-1983
  PengEur-1969

  Expressionism

**Hasim, Ahmet 1884-1933 (Iraqi-
born Turkish)**
  CasWL-1973
  ClDMEuL-1980
  DOrLit-1974
  EncWL-1981
  GdMWL-1985

  Dawn of the Future/Fecr-i Ati

**Hatvany, Lajos 1880-1961
(Hungarian)**
  ClDMEuL-1980
  EncWL-1981

  Nyugat Group

**Hatzopoulos, Constantine 1871-
1920 (Greek)**
  EncWL-1981
  GdMWL-1985
  PrEncyPP-1974

  New School of Athens/Greek
    Parnassians

**Haugen, Paal-Helge 1945-
(Norwegian)**
  ClDMEuL-1980
  EncWL-1981

  Profil Group

Hauková, Jirina 1919-   (Czech)
  ClDMEuL-1980

  Group 42

Haulot, Arthur n.d. (Belgian)
  ClDMEuL-1980

  Journal de Poètes

**Hauptmann, Carl 1858-1921
(German)**
CasWL-1973
ClDMEuL-1980
GdMWL-1985
McGWD-1984
OxGer-1986

Naturalism

**Hauptmann, Gerhart 1862-1946
(German)**
BenReEncy-1987
CamGLE-1988
CasWL-1973
ClDMEuL-1980
EncWL-1981
GdMWL-1985
LongCTCL-1975
McGWD-1984
OxEng-1985
OxGer-1986
OxThe-1983
PengEur-1969
RCom-1973

Deutsches Theater
Freie Bühne
Naturalism
Neoromanticism/Neuromantik
Symbolism
Théâtre Libre

**Hausmann, Raoul 1886-1971
(Austrian)**
EncWL-1981

Dadaism

Havel, Václav 1936-   (Czech)
BenReEncy-1987
CasWL-1973
ClDMEuL-1980
EncWL-1981
GdMWL-1985

McGWD-1984

Theater of the Absurd

Hawkins, Spike 1942-   (English)
OxEng-1985

Jazz Poetry

Hay, Elijah

See **Marjorie Allen Seiffert**

**Hay, George Campbell 1915-
(Scottish)**
EncWL-1981
PengEng-1971
PrEncyPP-1974

Scottish Renaissance

Hay, John 1838-1905 (American)
OxAm-1983
PengAm-1971

Local Color School

**Haya de la Torre, Victor Raúl 1895-
1979 (Peruvian)**
EncWL-1981
OxSpan-1978

Aprismo

**H.D. (pseud. of Hilda Doolittle)
1886-1961 (American)**
BenReEncy-1987
CamGLE-1988
CasWL-1973
EncWL-1981
GdMWL-1985
LongCTCL-1975
OxAm-1983
OxEng-1985
PengAm-1971

PrEncyPP-1974

Bloomsbury Group
Imagism
Poetry

Hearn, Lafcadio 1850-1904 (Greek-born American)
BenReEncy-1987
CamGLE-1988
CasWL-1973
GdMWL-1985
OxAm-1983
OxEng-1985
PengAm-1971
PengEng-1971

Local Color School

Heartfield, John 1891-1968 (German)
EncWL-1981

Dadaism

Hecht, Ben 1894-1964 (American)
BenReEncy-1987
CamGLE-1988
LongCTCL-1975
McGWD-1984
OxAm-1983
OxAmThe-1984
PengAm-1971

Chicago Group/Renaissance

Heckel, Erich 1883-1970 (German)
OxGer-1986

Expressionism

Hedayat, Sadeq 1903-1951 (Iranian)
DOrLit-1974

EncWL-1981

Rab'e Group

Hedenvind-Eriksson, Gustav 1880-1967 (Swedish)
ClDMEuL-1980
GdMWL-1985
PengEur-1969

Proletarian Writers/
Arbetardiktare

Heer, Jakob Christoph 1859-1925 (Swiss)
EncWL-1981
OxGer-1986

Heimatkunst

Heidegger, Martin 1889-1976 (German)
BenReEncy-1987
CasWL-1973
ClDMEuL-1980
EncWL-1981
LongCTCL-1975
OxEng-1985
OxFr-1959
OxGer-1986
RCom-1973

Existentialism

Heidenstam, (Carl Gustaf) Verner von 1859-1940 (Swedish)
BenReEncy-1987
CasWL-1973
ClDMEuL-1980
EncWL-1981
GdMWL-1985
PengEur-1969
PrEncyPP-1974

Nittiotalister

Heikkilä, Lasse 1925-1961 (Finnish)
ClDMEuL-1980

Modernism

Heiremans, Luis Alberto 1928-1964 (Chilean)
EncWL-1981
GdMWL-1985
McGWD-1984
OxSpan-1978

Generation of 1950

Heissenbüttel, Helmut 1921- (German)
CasWL-1973
ClDMEuL-1980
EncWL-1981
GdMWL-1985
OxGer-1986
PengEur-1969
PrEncyPP-1974

Concrete Poetry

Helburn, Theresa 1887-1959 (American)
OxAmThe-1984

Theater Guild

Held, John 1889-1958 (American)
OxAm-1983

Jazz Age

Hellaakoski, Aaro 1893-1952 (Finnish)
EncWL-1981
PengEur-1969
PrEncyPP-1974

Flame Bearers Group/
  Tulenkantajat

Hellström, Gustaf 1882-1953 (Swedish)
CasWL-1973
ClDMEuL-1980
EncWL-1981
GdMWL-1985
PengEur-1969

Tiotalister

Hemingway, Ernest 1899-1961 (American)
BenReEncy-1987
CamGLE-1988
CasWL-1973
CEnMWL-1963
EncWL-1981
GdMWL-1985
LongCTCL-1975
OxAm-1983
OxEng-1985
PengAm-1971
RCom-1973

Lost Generation

Hemmer, Jarl 1893-1944 (Finnish)
ClDMEuL-1980
EncWL-1981

Loafers/Dagdrivarna

Hémon, Roparz 1900-1978 (Breton-speaking French)
EncWL-1981
GdMWL-1985
PengEur-1969
PrEncyPP-1974

Breton Movement

Hénault, Gilles 1920-   (Canadian)
OxCan-1983

Hexagone Group

Hendry, James Findlay 1912-
(Scottish)
   BenReEncy-1987
   CamGLE-1988
   OxEng-1985
   PengEng-1971

New Apocalypse

Henri, Adrian 1932-   **(English)**
   CamGLE-1988
   OxEng-1985

Liverpool Poets

Hennique, Léon 1851-1935
(Gaudeloupean-born French)
   CaribWr-1979
   GdMWL-1985
   OxFr-1959

Théâtre Libre

Henry, O. (pseud. of William
Sydney Porter) 1862-1910
(American)
   BenReEncy-1987
   CamGLE-1988
   EncWL-1981
   GdMWL-1985
   LongCTCL-1975
   OxAm-1983
   OxEng-1985
   PengAm-1971

Local Color School

Heppenstall, Rayner 1911-1981
(English)
   EncWL-1981
   GdMWL-1985
   LongCTCL-1975
   PengEng-1971

New Novel/Nouveau Roman

Herbert, Zbigniew 1924-   **(Polish)**
   BenReEncy-1987
   ClDMEuL-1980
   EncWL-1981
   GdMWL-1985
   OxEng-1985
   PengEur-1969

Theater of the Absurd
Wspólczesnosc Generation

Herbst, Josephine 1897-1969
(American)
   CamGLE-1988
   OxAm-1983

Proletarian Literature

Herburger, Günter 1932-
(German)
   ClDMEuL-1980
   EncWL-1981
   GdMWL-1985
   OxGer-1986

Cologne School of New
   Realism/Kölner Schule des
   neuen Realismus

Herceg, János 1909-   **(Hungarian-**
speaking Yugoslavian)
   EncWL-1981

Kalangya Group

Hernández, Felisberto 1902-1964
(Uruguayan)
   EncWL-1981
   OxSpan-1978

Generation of 1945

Hernández, José 1834-1886
(Argentine)
   BenReEncy-1987

CasWL-1973
EncWL-1981
OxSpan-1978
PengAm-1971
PrEncyPP-1974

Gaucho Literature

Hernández, Miguel de 1910-1942 (Spanish)
BenReEncy-1987
CasWL-1973
ClDMEuL-1980
EncWL-1981
GdMWL-1985
McGWD-1984
OxSpan-1978
PengEur-1969

Generation of 1936/Generación del 1936

Hernández Catá, Alfonso 1884-1940 (Cuban)
CaribWr-1979
CasWL-1973
OxSpan-1978
PengAm-1971

Realism

Hernández Miyares, Enrique 1859-1915 (Cuban)
CaribWr-1979

Arpas Cubanas Group

Hernández Rueda, Lupo 1930- (Dominican Republican)
CaribWr-1979
EncWL-1981

Surprised Poetry Movement

Herreman, Raymond 1896- (Belgian)
ClDMEuL-1980
EncWL-1981

Het Fonteintje Group

Herrera y Reissig, Julio 1875-1910 (Uruguayan)
BenReEncy-1987
CasWL-1973
EncWL-1981
GdMWL-1985
OxSpan-1978
PengAm-1971
PrEncyPP-1974

Modernismo

Herrick, Robert Welch 1868-1938 (American)
BenReEncy-1987
CamGLE-1988
CasWL-1973
GdMWL-1985
LongCTCL-1975
OxAm-1983
OxEng-1985
PengAm-1971

Naturalism

Herwegh, Georg 1817-1875 (German)
OxGer-1986
PengEur-1969
PrEncyPP-1974

Realism

Hesse, Hermann 1877-1962 (German)
BenReEncy-1987
CasWL-1973
ClDMEuL-1980

EncWL-1981
GdMWL-1985
OxEng-1985
OxGer-1986
PengEur-1969
RCom-1973

Neoromanticism/Neuromantik

Heyke, Leon 1885-1939 (Kashubian-speaking Polish)
EncWL-1981

Young Kashubian Movement

Heym, Georg 1887-1912 (German)
BenReEncy-1987
CasWL-1973
ClDMEuL-1980
EncWL-1981
GdMWL-1985
OxGer-1986
PengEur-1969
PrEncyPP-1974

Expressionism

Hicks, Granville 1901-1982 (American)
EncWL-1981
OxAm-1983
PengAm-1971

Marxist Criticism
Proletarian Literature

Hidalgo, Bartolomé 1788-1822 (Uruguayan)
ClDMEuL-1980
OxSpan-1978
PengAm-1971
PrEncyPP-1974

Gaucho Literature

Hierro, José 1922-　　(Spanish)
CasWL-1973
ClDMEuL-1980
EncWL-1981
GdMWL-1985
OxSpan-1978
PengEur-1969

Generation of 1936/Generación del 1936

Higgins, Frederick Robert 1896-1941 (Irish)
GdMWL-1985
OxEng-1985
PrEncyPP-1974

Irish Renaissance

Hildesheimer, Wolfgang 1916- (German)
CasWL-1973
ClDMEuL-1980
EncWL-1981
GdMWL-1985
McGWD-1984
OxGer-1986
PengEur-1969

Epic Theater/Episches Theater
Group 47/Gruppe 47
Theater of the Absurd

Hiller, Kurt 1885-1972 (German)
EncWL-1981
PengEur-1969

Expressionism

Hilpert, Heinz 1890-1967 (German)
OxThe-1983

Deutsches Theater

Hinostroza, Rodolfo 1941-
(Peruvian)
OxSpan-1978

Los Nuevos

Hippius, Zinaida Nikolayevna 1869-
1945 (Russian)
CasWL-1973
ClDMEuL-1980
EncWL-1981
GdMWL-1985
PengEur-1969
PrEncyPP-1974

Symbolism

Hipple, Walter J., Jr. 1921-
(American)
PrEncyPP-1974

Chicago Critics

Hirschfeld, Georg 1873-1942
(German)
BenReEncy-1987
OxGer-1986

Naturalism

Hirth, George n.d. (German)
PrEncyPP-1974

Jugendstil

Hlavácek, Karel 1874-1898 (Czech)
CasWL-1973
ClDMEuL-1980
EncWL-1981
PengEur-1969

Symbolism

Hlebka, P. n.d. (Byelorussian)
PrEncyPP-1974

Socialist Realism

Hoàng Dao 1907-1948 (Vietnamese)
DOrLit-1974
EncWL-1981

Ngày nay Group

Hobsbaum, Philip 1932-
(English)
CamGLE-1988
OxEng-1985

The Group

Hoddis, Jakob van 1887-1942
(German)
EncWL-1981
GdMWL-1985
OxGer-1986
PengEur-1969

Expressionism

Hodgson, Ralph 1871-1962
(English)
BenReEncy-1987
CamGLE-1988
GdMWL-1985
LongCTCL-1975
OxEng-1985
PengEng-1971
PrEncyPP-1974

Georgian Literature

Hoel, Sigurd 1890-1960
(Norwegian)
CasWL-1973
ClDMEuL-1980
EncWL-1981
GdMWL-1985

McGWD-1984
PengEur-1969

Expressionism

Hofmann, Hans 1923-   **(Swiss)**
HarDMT-1988

New York School

**Hofmannsthal, Hugo von 1874-1929
(Austrian)**
BenReEncy-1987
CasWL-1973
CEnMWL-1963
ClDMEuL-1980
EncWL-1981
GdMWL-1985
McGWD-1984
OxEng-1985
OxGer-1986
OxThe-1983
PengEur-1969
PrEncyPP-1974

Jugendstil
Neoromanticism/Neuromantik
Symbolism
Young Vienna Group/Jungwien

**Hofstein, David 1889-1952
(Yiddish-speaking Ukrainian)**
CasWL-1973
ClDMEuL-1980
EncWL-1981
GdMWL-1985

Kiev Group

Holan, Vladimír 1905-   **(Czech)**
CasWL-1973
ClDMEuL-1980
EncWL-1981

GdMWL-1985

Poeticism

Holappa, Pentti 1927-   **(Finnish)**
ClDMEuL-1980
EncWL-1981

Modernism

Höllerer, Walter 1922-   **(German)**
ClDMEuL-1980
EncWL-1981
OxGer-1986
PengEur-1969

Group 47/Gruppe 47

Holloway, John 1920-   **(English)**
CamGLE-1988
EncWL-1981

The Movement
New Lines Poets

**Holm, Peter R. 1931-
(Norwegian)**
EncWL-1981

Symbolic Modernism

**Holmes, John Clellon 1926-
(American)**
CamGLE-1988
OxAm-1983
OxEng-1985
PengAm-1971

Beat Generation

Holmsen, Bjarne P.

> **See Arno Holz and Johannes
> Schlaf**

229

Holub, Miroslav 1923-   (Czech)
CasWL-1973
ClDMEuL-1980
EncWL-1981
GdMWL-1985

May Group/Kveten

Holz, Arno 1863-1929 (German)
BenReEncy-1987
CasWL-1973
ClDMEuL-1980
EncWL-1981
GdMWL-1985
OxGer-1986
OxThe-1983
PengEur-1969
PrEncyPP-1974

Freie Bühne
Naturalism

Holzamer, W. n.d. (German)
OxGer-1986

Heimatkunst

Hopkins, Gerard Manley 1844-1889 (English)
BenReEncy-1987
CamGLE-1988
CasWL-1973
CEnMWL-1963
EncWL-1981
GdMWL-1985
LongCTCL-1975
OxEng-1985
PengEng-1971
RCom-1973

Modernism

Hora, Josef 1891-1945 (Czech)
CasWL-1973
ClDMEuL-1980

EncWL-1981
GdMWL-1985
PengEur-1969

Poeticism
Proletarian Literature

Hordynsky, Svyatoslav 1909- (Ukrainian)
ClDMEuL-1980
EncWL-1981

Nazustrich

Horejsí, Jindrich 1886-1941 (Czech)
EncWL-1981

Proletarian Literature

Horne, Frank 1899-1974 (American)
CamGLE-1988
PrEncyPP-1974

Harlem Renaissance

Horniman, Annie Elizabeth 1860-1937 (English)
EncWL-1981
LongCTCL-1975
McGWD-1984
OxAmThe-1984
OxEng-1985

Abbey Theater

Horovitz, Michael 1935-   (English)
CamGLE-1988
OxEng-1985

Jazz Poetry

Horta, Maria Teresa 1937- (Portuguese)
EncWL-1981

GdMWL-1985

Poetry 61 Movement

Horváth, Ödön von 1901-1938 (Austrian)
CasWL-1973
ClDMEuL-1980
EncWL-1981
GdMWL-1985
OxGer-1986

New Objectivity/Neue
Sachlichkeit

Houedard, Dom Sylvester 1924- (English)
DCLT-1979

Concrete Poetry

Houghton, William Stanley 1881-1913 (English)
OxEng-1985
OxThe-1983

Realism

Housman, A(lfred) E(dward) 1859-1936 (English)
BenReEncy-1987
CamGLE-1988
CasWL-1973
CEnMWL-1963
EncWL-1981
GdMWL-1985
LongCTCL-1975
OxEng-1985
PengEng-1971
RCom-1973

Georgian Literature

Howe, E(dgar) W(atson) 1853-1937 (American)
BenReEncy-1987
CamGLE-1988
OxAm-1983

Local Color School
Realism

Howells, William Dean 1837-1920 (American)
BenReEncy-1987
CamGLE-1988
CasWL-1973
EncWL-1981
GdMWL-1985
McGWD-1984
OxAm-1983
OxAmThe-1984
OxEng-1985
PengAm-1971
RCom-1973

Realism

Hrynevych, Katrya 1875-1947 (Ukrainian)
EncWL-1981

Modernism

Hsü Chih-mo 1897-1931 (Chinese)
CasWL-1973
DOrLit-1974
EncWL-1981
GdMWL-1985
PengCOAL-1969

Crescent Society

Huch, Ricarda 1864-1947 (German)
BenReEncy-1987
CasWL-1973
ClDMEuL-1980
EncWL-1981

GdMWL-1985
OxGer-1986
PengEur-1969

Neoromanticism/Neuromantik

Hudson, W(illiam) H(enry) 1841-1922 (Argentine-born English)
BenReEncy-1987
CamGLE-1988
CasWL-1973
EncWL-1981
GdMWL-1985
LongCTCL-1975
OxEng-1985
PengEng-1971

Edwardian Literature

Huelsenbeck, Richard 1892-1974 (German)
EncWL-1981
GdMWL-1985
OxGer-1986
PrEncyPP-1974

Dadaism

Huerta, Efraín 1914-1982 (Mexican)
EncWL-1981
OxSpan-1978

Taller Group

Hu Feng 1903-   (Chinese)
CasWL-1973
DOrLit-1974

Hu-Feng Group

Hughes, (James) Langston 1902-1967 (American)
BenReEncy-1987
CamGLE-1988
CasWL-1973

EncWL-1981
GdMWL-1985
LongCTCL-1975
McGWD-1984
OxAm-1983
OxAmThe-1984
OxEng-1985
PengAm-1971
PrEncyPP-1974

Harlem Renaissance
Jazz Poetry

Hughes, Ted 1930-   (English)
BenReEncy-1987
CamGLE-1988
CasWL-1973
EncWL-1981
GdMWL-1985
LongCTCL-1975
McGWD-1984
OxEng-1985
PengEng-1971

The Group

Hugo, Valentine 1890-1968 (French)
EncWL-1981

Surrealism

Huidobro, Vincente 1893-1948 (Chilean)
CasWL-1973
ClDMEuL-1980
EncWL-1981
GdMWL-1985
OxSpan-1978
PengAm-1971
PrEncyPP-1974

Creationism/Creacionismo
Ultraism/Ultraismo

Hulewicz, Jerzy 1886-1941 (Polish)
ClDMEuL-1980

Zdroj Group

Hulme, T(homas) E(rnest) 1883-1917 (English)
BenReEncy-1987
CamGLE-1988
CasWL-1973
EncWL-1981
GdMWL-1985
LongCTCL-1975
OxAm-1983
OxEng-1985
PengEng-1971
PrEncyPP-1974
RCom-1973

Georgian Literature
Imagism
Modernism
Symbolism
Vorticism

Hunt, Hugh 1911-   (English)
OxThe-1983

Abbey Theater

Hurston, Zora Neale 1903-1960 (American)
BenReEncy-1987
CamGLE-1988
OxAm-1983

Harlem Renaissance

Hüser, Fritz 1908-1979 (German)
OxGer-1986

Group 61/Gruppe 61

Hu Shih 1891-1962 (Chinese)
BenReEncy-1987

CasWL-1973
DOrLit-1974
EncWL-1981
GdMWL-1985

May Fourth Movement/Wu-ssu yün-tung
Vernacular Movement

Husserl, Edmund 1859-1938 (German)
BenReEncy-1987
EncWL-1981

Existentialism

Huxley, Aldous 1894-1963 (English)
BenReEncy-1987
CamGLE-1988
CasWL-1973
CEnMWL-1963
EncWL-1981
GdMWL-1985
LongCTCL-1975
OxEng-1985
PengEng-1971

Georgian Literature
Modernism

Huysmans, Joris-Karl 1848-1907 (French)
BenReEncy-1987
CamGLE-1988
CasWL-1973
ClDMEuL-1980
EncWL-1981
GdMWL-1985
OxEng-1985
OxFr-1959
PengEur-1969
PrEncyPP-1974

Naturalism
Symbolism

Hyde, Douglas 1860-1949 (Irish)
BenReEncy-1987
CamGLE-1988
CasWL-1973
EncWL-1981
LongCTCL-1975
McGWD-1984
OxEng-1985
OxThe-1983
PengEng-1971

PrEncyPP-1974

Edwardian Literature
Irish Literary Theater
Irish Renaissance

Hyon Chin-gon 1900-1943 (Korean)
EncWL-1981

Naturalism

I

Iashvili, Paolo 1894-1937
(Georgian)
DOrLit-1974
EncWL-1981
GdMWL-1985
PrEncyPP-1974

Blue Horns Group/Tsispheri
q'antesbi

Ibrahimov, Mirza 1911-
(Azerbaijani)
DOrLit-1974
EncWL-1981

Socialist Realism

Ibraileanu, Garabet 1871-1936
(Romanian)
CasWL-1973
ClDMEuL-1980
EncWL-1981

Poporanism
Populist Literature Movement

Ibsen, Henrik 1828-1906
(Norwegian)
BenReEncy-1987
CamGLE-1988
CasWL-1973
ClDMEuL-1980
EncWL-1981
GdMWL-1985
LongCTCL-1975
McGWD-1984

OxAmThe-1984
OxEng-1985
OxGer-1986
OxThe-1983
PengEur-1969
RCom-1973

Naturalism
Realism
Théâtre Libre

Ibuse Masuji 1898-   **(Japanese)**
CasWL-1973
DOrLit-1974
EncWL-1981
GdMWL-1985
PengCOAL-1969

I-Novel/Watakushi shosetsu

Icaza Coronel, Jorge 1906-1979
(Ecuadorian)
BenReEncy-1987
CasWL-1973
EncWL-1981
GdMWL-1985
OxSpan-1978
PengAm-1971

Realism

Iceland, Reuben 1884-1955
(Yiddish-speaking American)
ClDMEuL-1980

EncWL-1981

Young Ones/Die Yunge

al 'Id Al Khalifa, Muhammad 1904-1979 (Algerian)
DOrLit-1974
EncWL-1981

Al-Shihab

Ignatov, David 1885-1953 (Yiddish-speaking American)
ClDMEuL-1980
EncWL-1981
GdMWL-1985

Young Ones/Die Yunge

Ignotus, Paul (pseud. of Hugó Veigelsberg) 1869-1949 (Hungarian)
ClDMEuL-1980
EncWL-1981
GdMWL-1985

Nyugat Group

Iida Dakotsu 1885-1962 (Japanese)
DOrLit-1974

Hototogisu Poets

Ilhan, Attilâ 1925-   (Turkish)
EncWL-1981
PrEncyPP-1974

Abstract Movement

Illakowicz, Jaroslaw 1894- (Polish)
PrEncyPP-1974

Skamander Group

Illakowiczówna, Kazimiera 1892- (Polish)
CasWL-1973
ClDMEuL-1980

Skamander Group

Illescas, Carlos n.d. (Guatemalan)
OxSpan-1978

Grupo Acento

Illyés, Gyula 1902-   (Hungarian)
CasWL-1973
ClDMEuL-1980
EncWL-1981
GdMWL-1985
PengEur-1969

Today Group/*Ma*
Populist Movement

Inber, Vera Mikhaylovna 1893-1972 (Russian)
CasWL-1973
ClDMEuL-1980
EncWL-1981
PengEur-1969
PrEncyPP-1974

Constructivism

Ingamells, Rex 1913-1955 (Australian)
BenReEncy-1987
GdMWL-1985
PrEncyPP-1974

Jindyworobak Movement

Insingel, Mark 1935-   (Belgian)
EncWL-1981

Concrete Poetry

Ionesco, Eugène 1912- (Romanian-born French)
BenReEncy-1987
CasWL-1973
CEnMWL-1963
ClDMEuL-1980
EncWL-1981
GdMWL-1985
LongCTCL-1975
McGWD-1984
OxAmThe-1984
OxEng-1985
OxThe-1983
PengEur-1969
RCom-1973

New Wave/Nouvelle Vague
Theater of the Absurd

Iorga, Nicolae 1871-1940 (Romanian)
CasWL-1973
ClDMEuL-1980
EncWL-1981
GdMWL-1985
PengEur-1969

Populist Literature Movement
Samanatorism

Irigaray, Luce n.d. (French)
CamGLE-1988

Feminist Criticism

Irzykowski, Karol 1873-1944 (Polish)
CasWL-1973
ClDMEuL-1980
GdMWL-1985
PengEur-1969

Young Poland/Mloda Polska

Isaksson, Ulla 1916-   (Swedish)
ClDMEuL-1980
EncWL-1981

Poets of the Forties/
Fyrtiotalisterna

Isayev, Mladen n.d. (Bulgarian)
PrEncyPP-1974

Socialist Realism

Isherwood, Christopher 1904-1986 (English-born American)
BenReEncy-1987
CamGLE-1988
CasWL-1973
CEnMWL-1963
EncWL-1981
GdMWL-1985
LongCTCL-1975
McGWD-1984
OxAm-1983
OxEng-1985
PengEng-1971

Group Theater

Ishida Hakyo 1913-1969 (Japanese)
DOrLit-1974

Hototogisu Poets

Ishikawa Takuboku 1885-1912 (Japanese)
BenReEncy-1987
CasWL-1973
DOrLit-1974
EncWL-1981
GdMWL-1985
PengCOAL-1969

Myojo Group

Isou, Isidore (pseud. of Isidore Goldmann) 1925-   (French)
 GdMWL-1985
 OxFr-1959

 Lettrism

Ito Sei 1905-1970 (Japanese)
 DOrLit-1974

 New Psychological School/
 Shinshinrigaku-ha

Ivanov, Georgy Vladimirovich 1894-1958 (Russian)
 ClDMEuL-1980
 EncWL-1981
 GdMWL-1985

 Acmeism

Ivanov, Vsevolod Vyacheslavovich 1895-1963 (Russian)
 BenReEncy-1987
 CasWL-1973
 CEnMWL-1963
 ClDMEuL-1980
 EncWL-1981
 GdMWL-1985
 McGWD-1984
 OxThe-1983
 PengEur-1969

 Modernism
 Moscow Art Theater

 Serapion Brotherhood

Ivanov, Vyacheslav Ivanovich 1866-1949 (Russian)
 BenReEncy-1987
 CasWL-1973
 ClDMEuL-1980
 EncWL-1981
 GdMWL-1985
 PengEur-1969
 PrEncyPP-1974

 Symbolism

Ivnik, Ivan 1914-1942 (Chuvash)
 EncWL-1981

 Socialist Realism

Ivo, Lêdo 1924-   (Brazilian)
 PrEncyPP-1974

 Generation of 1945

Iwaszkiewicz, Jaroslaw 1894-1980 (Ukrainian-born Polish)
 CasWL-1973
 ClDMEuL-1980
 EncWL-1981
 GdMWL-1985
 PengEur-1969
 PrEncyPP-1974

 Skamander Group

J

Jacinto, António 1924-   (Angolan)
EncWL-1981

Association of Angola's Native
Sons

Jackson, Laura (Riding) 1901-
(American)
BenReEncy-1987
CamGLE-1988
EncWL-1981
GdMWL-1985
LongCTCL-1975
OxAm-1983
OxEng-1985
PengAm-1971

The Fugitives/Agrarians
New Criticism

Jacob, Max 1876-1944 (French)
BenReEncy-1987
CasWL-1973
CEnMWL-1963
ClDMEuL-1980
EncWL-1981
GdMWL-1985
OxFr-1959
PengEur-1969

Cubism
Surrealism

Jacob, Violet 1863-1946 (Scottish)
CamGLE-1988
CasWL-1973

EncWL-1981
PengEng-1971

Scottish Renaissance

Jacobsen, Jens Peter 1847-1885
(Danish)
BenReEncy-1987
CasWL-1973
ClDMEuL-1980
EncWL-1981
PengEur-1969
PrEncyPP-1974

Naturalism

Jæger, Frank 1926-1977 (Danish)
CasWL-1973
ClDMEuL-1980
EncWL-1981

Heretica Poets
Naturalism

Jahnn, Hans Henny 1894-1959
(German)
CasWL-1973
ClDMEuL-1980
EncWL-1981
GdMWL-1985
OxGer-1986
OxThe-1983
PengEur-1969

Expressionism

Jaimes Freyre, Ricardo 1868-1933
(Bolivian)
  CasWL-1973
  EncWL-1981
  GdMWL-1985
  OxSpan-1978
  PengAm-1971
  PrEncyPP-1974

  Modernismo

Jain, Nemicandra n.d. (Indian)
  DOrLit-1974

  New Poetry Movement/Nayi
  Kavita

Jakobson, Roman 1896-1982
(Russian-born American)
  CamGLE-1988
  ClDMEuL-1980
  EncWL-1981
  OxEng-1985
  PrEncyPP-1974

  Prague Linguistic Circle
  Russian Formalism
  Structuralism

James, Henry 1843-1916 (American-
born English)
  BenReEncy-1987
  CamGLE-1988
  CasWL-1973
  CEnMWL-1963
  EncWL-1981
  GdMWL-1985
  LongCTCL-1975
  McGWD-1984
  OxAm-1983
  OxAmThe-1984
  OxEng-1985
  OxThe-1983
  PengAm-1971
  PengEng-1971

  RCom-1973

  Edwardian Literature
  Modernism
  Realism

Jamma', Idris 1922-1980 (Sudanese)
  EncWL-1981

  Romantic Poets

Jammes, Francis 1868-1938 (French)
  BenReEncy-1987
  CasWL-1973
  ClDMEuL-1980
  EncWL-1981
  GdMWL-1985
  OxFr-1959
  PengEur-1969

  Naturism/Naturisme

Jandl, Ernst 1925-   (Austrian)
  CasWL-1973
  ClDMEuL-1980
  EncWL-1981
  OxGer-1986

  Concrete Poetry
  Vienna Group/Wiener Gruppe

Jansevskis, Jekabs (pseud. of
Jekabs Janovskis) 1865-1931
(Latvian)
  CasWL-1973
  EncWL-1981

  Realism

Jarnés Millán, Benjamín 1888-1949
(Spanish)
  CasWL-1973
  ClDMEuL-1980
  EncWL-1981
  GdMWL-1985

OxSpan-1978

Generation of 1927/Generación
del 1927
Surrealism

Jasienski, Bruno 1901-1939 (Polish)
ClDMEuL-1980
EncWL-1981
McGWD-1984

Futurism

Jaspers, Karl 1883-1969 (German)
BenReEncy-1987
CasWL-1973
EncWL-1981
OxEng-1985
OxFr-1959
OxGer-1986
RCom-1973

Existentialism

**Jaunsudrabins, Janis 1877-1962
(Latvian)**
EncWL-1981

Realism

Jeanson, Francis n.d. (French)
ClDMEuL-1980

Existentialism

Jékely, Zoltán n.d. (Hungarian)
ClDMEuL-1980

Nyugat Group

**Jennings, Elizabeth 1926-
(English)**
CamGLE-1988
EncWL-1981
GdMWL-1985

LongCTCL-1975
OxEng-1985
PengEng-1971

The Movement
New Lines Poets

Jens, Walter 1923-   (German)
OxGer-1986
PengEur-1969

Group 47/Gruppe 47

**Jensen, Wilhelm 1837-1911
(German)**
OxGer-1986

Heimatkunst

Jesensky, Janko 1874-1945 (Czech)
CasWL-1973
ClDMEuL-1980
EncWL-1981
GdMWL-1985
PengEur-1969

Modernism

**Jewett, Sarah Orne 1849-1909
(American)**
BenReEncy-1987
CamGLE-1988
CasWL-1973
EncWL-1981
GdMWL-1985
OxAm-1983
OxEng-1985
PengAm-1971

Local Color School
Realism

Jilemnicky, Peter 1901-1949 (Czech)
CasWL-1973
ClDMEuL-1980

EncWL-1981
GdMWL-1985
PengEur-1969

DAV Group

**Jiménez, Juan Ramón 1881-1958
(Spanish)**
BenReEncy-1987
CasWL-1973
CEnMWL-1963
ClDMEuL-1980
EncWL-1981
GdMWL-1985
OxSpan-1978
PengEur-1969
PrEncyPP-1974

Modernismo

**Jiribine, Kün (pseud. of S. Savin)
1903-1970 (Yakut)**
EncWL-1981

Socialist Realism

Joans, Ted 1928-   **(American)**
OxEng-1985

Jazz Poetry

**Jóhannes, úr Kötlum 1899-1972
(Icelandic)**
CasWL-1973
ClDMEuL-1980
EncWL-1981

Form Revolution

**Johnson, B(ryan) S(tanley) 1933-
1973 (English)**
CamGLE-1988
OxEng-1985

The Group

New Wave/Nouvelle Vague

Johnson, Barbara n.d. (American)
CamGLE-1988

Deconstructionism

**Johnson, Bengt Emil 1936-
(Swedish)**
ClDMEuL-1980

Concrete Poetry

Johnson, Eyvind 1900-   **(Swedish)**
BenReEncy-1987
CasWL-1973
ClDMEuL-1980
EncWL-1981
GdMWL-1985
PengEur-1969

Proletarian Writers/
Arbetardiktare

**Johnson, Georgia Douglas 1886-
1966 (American)**
PrEncyPP-1974

Harlem Renaissance

**Johnson, Helene 1907-
(American)**
CamGLE-1988
PrEncyPP-1974

Harlem Renaissance

**Johnson, James Weldon 1871-1938
(American)**
BenReEncy-1987
CamGLE-1988
CasWL-1973
EncWL-1981
OxAm-1983
OxAmThe-1984

PengAm-1971
PrEncyPP-1974

Harlem Renaissance

Johnson, Uwe 1934-1984 (German)
BenReEncy-1987
CasWL-1973
ClDMEuL-1980
EncWL-1981
GdMWL-1985
OxGer-1986
PengEur-1969

Group 47/Gruppe 47

Johnston, Denis 1901-1984 (Irish)
CamGLE-1988
CasWL-1973
EncWL-1981
GdMWL-1985
LongCTCL-1975
McGWD-1984
OxEng-1985
OxThe-1983

Irish Renaissance

Johst, Hanns 1890-1978 (German)
EncWL-1981
GdMWL-1985
OxGer-1986

Expressionism

Jókai, Mór 1825-1904 (Hungarian)
ClDMEuL-1980
EncWL-1981
GdMWL-1985
PengEur-1969

Popular National School

Jones, Alice 1853-1933 (Canadian)
OxCan-1983

Local Color School

**Jones, Henry Arthur 1851-1929
(English)**
BenReEncy-1987
CamGLE-1988
CasWL-1973
EncWL-1981
LongCTCL-1975
McGWD-1984
OxAmThe-1984
OxEng-1985
OxThe-1983
PengEng-1971

Georgian Literature
Modernism

Jones, LeRoi

See **Imamu Amiri Baraka**

**Jones, Robert Edmund 1887-1954
(American)**
OxAm-1983
OxAmThe-1984
OxThe-1983

Provincetown Players
Washington Square Players

**Jonker, Ingrid 1933-1965 (South
African)**
EncWL-1981
GdMWL-1985

The Sestigers

Jorgensen, Jens Johannes 1866-1956 (Danish)
CasWL-1973
ClDMEuL-1980
GdMWL-1985
PengEur-1969

Symbolism

Jorn, Asger 1914-1973 (Danish)
HarDMT-1988

Cobra
Experimentalists/
  Experimentelen

Jouve, Pierre-Jean 1887-1976 (French)
BenReEncy-1987
CasWL-1973
CEnMWL-1963
ClDMEuL-1980
EncWL-1981
GdMWL-1985
OxFr-1959
PengEur-1969

Abbaye Group/Group de
  l'Abbaye

Jouvet, Louis 1887-1951 (French)
OxEng-1985
OxFr-1959

Théâtre du Vieux-Colombier

Jovine, Francesco 1902-1950 (Italian)
CasWL-1973
ClDMEuL-1980
EncWL-1981
GdMWL-1985
PengEur-1969

Neorealism

Verismo

Joyce, James 1882-1941 (Irish)
BenReEncy-1987
CamGLE-1988
CasWL-1973
CEnMWL-1963
EncWL-1981
GdMWL-1985
LongCTCL-1975
McGWD-1984
OxEng-1985
OxThe-1983
PengEng-1971
RCom-1973

Edwardian Literature
Georgian Literature
Imagism
Irish Renaissance
Modernism

Juhász, Gyula 1883-1937 (Hungarian)
CasWL-1973
ClDMEuL-1980
EncWL-1981
GdMWL-1985
PengEur-1969

Nyugat Group

Jung, Carl Gustav 1875-1961 (Swiss)
BenReEncy-1987
CasWL-1973
EncWL-1981
HandLit-1986
HarDMT-1988
LongCTCL-1975
OxEng-1985
OxGer-1986
RCom-1973

Juvonen, Helvi 1919-1959 (Finnish)
ClDMEuL-1980
EncWL-1981
GdMWL-1985
PengEur-1969

Modernism

Jylhä, Yrjö 1903-1956 (Finnish)
ClDMEuL-1980
EncWL-1981

Flame Bearers Group/
Tulenkantajat

K

Kaalep, Ain 1926-　　(Estonian)
  EncWL-1981

  Soothsayers Movement/
    Arbujad

**Kachalov, Vasili Ivanovich 1875-
1948 (Russian)**
  OxThe-1983

  Moscow Art Theater

**Kaczerginski, Schmerke 1908-1954
(Yiddish-speaking Lithuanian)**
  ClDMEuL-1980

  Young Vilna

**Kaden Bandrowski, Juliusz 1885-
1944 (Polish)**
  CasWL-1973
  ClDMEuL-1980
  EncWL-1981
  PengEur-1969

  Expressionism

**Kaffka, Margit 1880-1918
(Hungarian)**
  CasWL-1973
  ClDMEuL-1980
  EncWL-1981
  GdMWL-1985
  PengEur-1969

  Nyugat Group

Kafka, Franz 1883-1924 (Austrian)
  BenReEncy-1987
  CasWL-1973
  CEnMWL-1963
  ClDMEuL-1980
  EncWL-1981
  GdMWL-1985
  LongCTCL-1975
  OxEng-1985
  OxGer-1986
  PengEur-1969
  RCom-1973

  Expressionism

Kahn, Gustave 1859-1936 (French)
  CasWL-1973
  ClDMEuL-1980
  EncWL-1981
  McGWD-1984
  OxFr-1959
  PengEur-1969
  PrEncyPP-1974

  Symbolism

Kailas, Uuno 1901-1933 (Finnish)
  ClDMEuL-1980
  EncWL-1981
  GdMWL-1985
  PengEur-1969
  PrEncyPP-1974

  Flame Bearers Group/
    Tulenkantajat

Kainer, Josef 1917-1972 (Czech)
ClDMEuL-1980

Group 42

Kainz, Josef 1858-1910 (German)
OxThe-1983

Deutsches Theater

Kaiser, Georg 1878-1945 (German)
BenReEncy-1987
CamGLE-1988
CasWL-1973
ClDMEuL-1980
EncWL-1981
GdMWL-1985
LongCTCL-1975
McGWD-1984
OxEng-1985
OxGer-1986
OxThe-1983
PengEur-1969
RCom-1973

Expressionism

Kajava, Viljo 1909-   (Finnish)
ClDMEuL-1980
EncWL-1981

Kiila Group

Kalachynski, M. n.d. (Byelorussian)
PrEncyPP-1974

Socialist Realism

Kallas, Aino 1878-1956 (Finnish)
EncWL-1981
GdMWL-1985
PengEur-1969

Young Estonia Group

Kalma, Douwe 1896-1953 (Dutch)
CasWL-1973
EncWL-1981
PrEncyPP-1974

Young Frisian Movement

Kálnoky, László n.d. (Hungarian)
ClDMEuL-1980

Nyugat Group
Ujhold Group

Kamalesvar 1932-   (Indian)
DOrLit-1974

New Short Story Movement/
Nayi Kahani

**Kambas, Nikolaos 1857-1932
(Greek)**
EncWL-1981

New School of Athens/Greek
Parnassians

**Kamensky, Vasily Vasilyevich 1884-
1961 (Russian)**
CasWL-1973
ClDMEuL-1980
EncWL-1981
PrEncyPP-1974

Cubo-Futurism

Kamondy, László n.d. (Hungarian)
ClDMEuL-1980

Generation of 1955

**Kandinsky, Wassily 1866-1944
(Russian)**
BenReEncy-1987
EncWL-1981
OxGer-1986

PrEncyPP-1974

Expressionism

Kangro, Bernard 1910- (Estonian)
CasWL-1973
ClDMEuL-1980
EncWL-1981
GdMWL-1985
PrEncyPP-1974

Soothsayers Movement/
Arbujad

**Kanik, Orhan Veli 1914-1950
(Turkish)**
ClDMEuL-1980
DOrLit-1974
EncWL-1981
GdMWL-1985
PrEncyPP-1974

Garip Movement
Poetic Realism

Kaplinski, Jaan 1941-   (Estonian)
EncWL-1981
GdMWL-1985

Soothsayers Movement/
Arbujad

**Karaosmanoglu, Yakup Kadri 1888-
1974 (Turkish)**
ClDMEuL-1980
DOrLit-1974
EncWL-1981
GdMWL-1985
PengCOAL-1969

Dawn of the Future/Fecr-i Ati

**Karaslavov, Georgi 1904-
(Bulgarian)**
CasWL-1973

EncWL-1981

Socialist Realism

**Karinthy, Frigyes 1887-1938
(Hungarian)**
CasWL-1973
ClDMEuL-1980
EncWL-1981
GdMWL-1985
PengEur-1969

Nyugat Group

**Karlfeldt, Erik Axel 1864-1931
(Swedish)**
BenReEncy-1987
CasWL-1973
ClDMEuL-1980
EncWL-1981
GdMWL-1985
PengEur-1969
PrEncyPP-1974

Nittiotalister

**Karmansky, Petro 1878-1956
(Ukrainian)**
ClDMEuL-1980
EncWL-1981

Young Muse Group/Moloda
Muza

**Karnowski, Jan 1886-1939
(Kashubian-speaking Polish)**
EncWL-1981

Young Kashubian Movement

**Karpowicz, Tymoteusz 1921-
(Polish)**
CasWL-1973
ClDMEuL-1980
EncWL-1981

Theater of the Absurd
Wspólczesnosc Generation

**Kasack, Hermann 1896-1966
(German)**
CasWL-1973
ClDMEuL-1980
EncWL-1981
GdMWL-1985
OxGer-1986
PengEur-1969

Surrealism

Kasai Zenzo 1887-1928 (Japanese)
DOrLit-1974

I-Novel/Watakushi shosetsu

Kasprowicz, Jan 1860-1926 (Polish)
CasWL-1973
ClDMEuL-1980
EncWL-1981
GdMWL-1985
PengEur-1969
PrEncyPP-1974

Young Poland/Mloda Polska
Zdroj Group

**Kassák, Lajos 1887-1967
(Hungarian)**
CasWL-1973
ClDMEuL-1980
EncWL-1981
GdMWL-1985
PengEur-1969

Today Group/*Ma*

Kästner, Erich 1899-1974 (German)
CasWL-1973
ClDMEuL-1980
EncWL-1981
GdMWL-1985

OxGer-1986
PengEur-1969

New Objectivity/Neue
Sachlichkeit

**Katayev, Valentin Petrovich 1897-
1986 (Russian)**
BenReEncy-1987
CasWL-1973
ClDMEuL-1980
EncWL-1981
GdMWL-1985
McGWD-1984
OxThe-1983
PengEur-1969

Odessa School
Socialist Realism

Kato Shuson 1905-   (Japanese)
DOrLit-1974

Hototogisu Poets

**Kaverin, Venyamin Aleksandrovich
(pseud. of Veniamin Zilber) 1902-
(Russian)**
BenReEncy-1987
CasWL-1973
ClDMEuL-1980
EncWL-1981
GdMWL-1985
PengEur-1969

Serapion Brotherhood

**Kawabata Yasunari 1899-1972
(Japanese)**
BenReEncy-1987
CasWL-1973
CEnMWL-1963
DOrLit-1974
EncWL-1981
GdMWL-1985

PengCOAL-1969
RCom-1973

New Sensationalist School

**Kawahigashi Hekigodo 1873-1937
(Japanese)**
DOrLit-1974
EncWL-1981

Hototogisu Poets

**Kazakov, Yury Pavlovich 1927-
(Russian)**
BenReEncy-1987
ClDMEuL-1980
EncWL-1981
PengEur-1969

Village Prose

**Kazan, Elia 1909-   (Turkish-born
American)**
BenReEncy-1987
EncWL-1981
OxAm-1983
OxAmThe-1984
OxThe-1983

Group Theater

**Kazin, Vasily Vasilyevich 1898-
(Russian)**
CasWL-1973
PrEncyPP-1974

Smithy Poets/Kuznitsa

**Keast, William R. 1914-
(American)**
PengAm-1971
PrEncyPP-1974

Chicago Critics

Keller, Gottfried 1819-1890 (Swiss)
BenReEncy-1987
EncWL-1981
OxGer-1986
PengEur-1969
PrEncyPP-1974

Realism

Kemal, Yashar 1922-   (Turkish)
ClDMEuL-1980
DOrLit-1974
EncWL-1981
GdMWL-1985

Village Fiction

**Kemény, Simon 1883-1945
(Hungarian)**
EncWL-1981

Nyugat Group

**Kennedy, Leo 1907-   (English-
born Canadian)**
EncWL-1981
OxCan-1983
PrEncyPP-1974

Montreal Movement

Keris Mas 1922-   (Malaysian)
EncWL-1981

Generation of the 1950s/Asas
'50

Kerouac, Jack 1922-1969 (American)
BenReEncy-1987
CamGLE-1988
CasWL-1973
CEnMWL-1963
EncWL-1981
GdMWL-1985
LongCTCL-1975

OxAm-1983
OxEng-1985
PengAm-1971
PrEncyPP-1974

Beat Generation

Kerr, Alfred 1867-1948 (German)
CIDMEuL-1980
EncWL-1981
OxGer-1986
OxThe-1983

Expressionism

Kette, Dragotin 1876-1899 (Slovene-speaking Yugoslavian)
CIDMEuL-1980
EncWL-1981

Moderna

Keynes, John Maynard 1883-1946 (English)
BenReEncy-1987
CamGLE-1988
EncWL-1981
LongCTCL-1975
OxEng-1985

Bloomsbury Group

Khadi, Mukhamedi 1879-1920 (Azerbaijani)
EncWL-1981

Füyüzat Movement

Khái Hung 1896-1947 (Vietnamese)
DOrLit-1974
EncWL-1981

Ngày nay Group

Kharms, Daniil Ivanovich (pseud. of Daniil Yuvachov) 1905-1942 (Russian)
CIDMEuL-1980
EncWL-1981
GdMWL-1985
McGWD-1984

OBEIRIU

Khlebnikov, Velemir Vladimirovich 1885-1922 (Russian)
BenReEncy-1987
CasWL-1973
CIDMEuL-1980
EncWL-1981
GdMWL-1985
PengEur-1969
PrEncyPP-1974

Cubo-Futurism

Khotkevych, Hnat 1877-1942 (Ukrainian)
EncWL-1981

Modernism

Khvylovy, Mykola 1893-1933 (Ukrainian)
CIDMEuL-1980
EncWL-1981
GdMWL-1985
PengEur-1969

Free Academy of Proletarian Literature/VAPLITE

Kielland, Alexander Lange 1849-1906 (Norwegian)
BenReEncy-1987
CIDMEuL-1980
EncWL-1981
GdMWL-1985
OxThe-1983

PengEur-1969

Realism

Kiestra, Douwe Hermans 1899-1970 (Dutch)
EncWL-1981
PrEncyPP-1974

Young Frisian Movement

Kilpi, Volter 1874-1939 (Finnish)
ClDMEuL-1980
EncWL-1981
GdMWL-1985
PengEur-1969

National Neoromanticism

Kim Tong-in 1900-1951 (Korean)
DOrLit-1974
EncWL-1981

Naturalism

King, Basil 1859-1929 (Canadian)
OxCan-1983

Local Color School

Kingsley, Sidney 1906- (American)
CamGLE-1988
GdMWL-1985
OxAm-1983
OxAmThe-1984

Group Theater

Kipling, (Joseph) Rudyard 1865-1936 (Indian-born English)
BenReEncy-1987
CamGLE-1988
CasWL-1973
CEnMWL-1963

EncWL-1981
GdMWL-1985
LongCTCL-1975
OxAm-1983
OxEng-1985
PengEng-1971
PrEncyPP-1974
RCom-1973

Edwardian Literature
Realism

Kipphardt, Heinar 1922-1982 (German)
BenReEncy-1987
ClDMEuL-1980
EncWL-1981
OxGer-1986
OxThe-1983

Theater of Fact

Kirchner, Ernst Ludwig 1880-1938 (German)
OxGer-1986

Expressionism

Kirillov, Vladimir 1890-1943 (Russian)
EncWL-1981
PrEncyPP-1974

Smithy Poets/Kuznitsa

Kirkland, Joseph 1830-1893 (American)
OxAm-1983

Realism

Kirsa, Faustas 1891-1964 (Lithuanian)
EncWL-1981

PrEncyPP-1974

Symbolism

**Kirshon, Vladimir Mikhaylovich
1902-1938 (Russian)**
CasWL-1973
ClDMEuL-1980
GdMWL-1985
PengEur-1969

Russian Association of
Proletarian Writers

**Kisch, Egon Erwin 1885-1948
(German)**
PengEur-1969

New Objectivity/Neue
Sachlichkeit

Kivikkaho, Eila 1921-   (Finnish)
ClDMEuL-1980

Modernism

Kivimaa, Arvi 1904-   (Finnish)
ClDMEuL-1980
PengEur-1969

Flame Bearers Group/
Tulenkantajat

Klee, Paul 1879-1940 (Swiss)
BenReEncy-1987
OxGer-1986

Expressionism
Surrealism

**Klein, A(braham) M(oses) 1909-
1972 (Canadian)**
BenReEncy-1987
CamGLE-1988
CasWL-1973

EncWL-1981
GdMWL-1985
LongCTCL-1975
OxCan-1983
PengEng-1971
PrEncyPP-1974

Montreal Movement

Klidzejs, Janis 1914-   (Latvian)
EncWL-1981

Realism

Kline, Franz 1910-1962 (American)
BenReEncy-1987
EncWL-1981

New York School

**Klingsor, Tristan 1874-1966
(French)**
OxFr-1959
PengEur-1969

Fantaisistes Group

**Kloos, Willem Johannes Theodorus
1859-1938 (Dutch)**
CasWL-1973
ClDMEuL-1980
EncWL-1981
GdMWL-1985
PengEur-1969
PrEncyPP-1974

Movement of the Eighties/
Beweging van Tachtig

**Klyuyev, Nikolay Alexeyevich 1887-
1937 (Russian)**
CasWL-1973
ClDMEuL-1980
EncWL-1981
GdMWL-1985

PengEur-1969

Imaginists
Symbolism

Knights, L(ionel) C(harles) 1906-
(English)
CamGLE-1988
HarDMT-1988
OxEng-1985
PengEng-1971

Scrutiny

Knipper-Chekhova, Olga
Leonardovna 1870-1959 (Russian)
OxThe-1983

Moscow Art Theater

Knish, Anne

See **Arthur Davison Ficke**

Knowles, Robert E. 1868-1946
(Canadian)
OxCan-1983

Local Color School

Knudsen, Erik 1922-   (Danish)
CasWL-1973
ClDMEuL-1980
EncWL-1981
GdMWL-1985
McGWD-1984
OxThe-1983
PengEur-1969

Heretica Poets

Krleza, Miroslav 1893- (Croatian)
CasWL-1973
ClDMEuL-1980
EncWL-1981

GdMWL-1985
McGWD-1984
PengEur-1969

Marxist Criticism

Kobylyansky, Volodymyr 1895-
1919 (Ukrainian)
EncWL-1981

Symbolism

Kocagöz, Samim 1916-   (Turkish)
ClDMEuL-1980

Village Fiction

Koch, Frederick Henry 1877-1944
(American)
OxAm-1983

Carolina Playmakers

Koch, Kenneth 1925-   (American)
BenReEncy-1987
CamGLE-1988
EncWL-1981
GdMWL-1985
McGWD-1984
OxAm-1983
PengAm-1971
PrEncyPP-1974

New York School

Koch, Martin 1882-1940 (Swedish)
CasWL-1973
ClDMEuL-1980
EncWL-1981
GdMWL-1985
PengEur-1969

Proletarian Writers/
    Arbetardiktare

Kodolányi, János 1899-1969 (Hungarian)
ClDMEuL-1980
EncWL-1981

Populist Movement

Kokoschka, Oskar 1886-1980 (Austrian-born English)
BenReEncy-1987
CamGLE-1988
ClDMEuL-1980
EncWL-1981
GdMWL-1985
OxGer-1986

Expressionism
Jugendstil
Storm Circle/*Der Sturm*

Kolas, Yakub 1882-1956 (Byelorussian)
CasWL-1973
ClDMEuL-1980
EncWL-1981
GdMWL-1985
PrEncyPP-1974

Flame Group
Our Soil Group/Nasaniustva
Renaissance Group/
  Adradzenstva

Kolbenhoff, Walter 1908- (German)
OxGer-1986

Group 47/Gruppe 47

Komját, Aladár n.d. (Hungarian)
ClDMEuL-1980

Today Group/*Ma*

Kopit, Arthur 1937-   (American)
BenReEncy-1987
CamGLE-1988
CasWL-1973
EncWL-1981
McGWD-1984
OxAm-1983
OxAmThe-1984
OxThe-1983
PengAm-1971

Theater of the Absurd

Köprülü, Mehmed Fuad 1890-1966 (Turkish)
ClDMEuL-1980

Dawn of the Future/Fecr-i Ati

Kornacki, Jerzy 1908-   (Polish)
ClDMEuL-1980

Przedmiescie Group

Körner, Wolfgang n.d. (German)
OxGer-1986

Group 61/Gruppe 61

Kornhauser, Julian 1946-   (Polish)
ClDMEuL-1980

Teraz Group

Koroleva, Natalena 1889-1966 (Ukrainian)
EncWL-1981

Logos Group

Korotych, Vitaly 1936- (Ukrainian)
ClDMEuL-1980
EncWL-1981

Generation of the 1960s/
Shestydesyatnyky

Korsakas, Kostas 1909-
(Lithuanian)
EncWL-1981

Third Front Movement/Trecias
Frontas

Koryurek, Enis Behiç 1891-1949
(Turkish)
ClDMEuL-1980
EncWL-1981

Syllabists/Hececiler

Kosach, Yury 1909-   (Ukrainian)
ClDMEuL-1980
EncWL-1981

Nazustrich

Kosmac, Ciril 1910-   (Slovene-
speaking Yugoslavian)
ClDMEuL-1980
EncWL-1981

Socialist Realism

Kosor, Josip 1879-1961 (Croatian-
speaking Yugoslavian)
CasWL-1973
ClDMEuL-1980
GdMWL-1985
PengEur-1969

Moderna

Kostenko, Lina 1930-   (Ukrainian)
ClDMEuL-1980
EncWL-1981

Generation of the 1960s/
Shestydesyatnyky

Kosynka, Hryhoriy 1899-1934
(Ukrainian)
ClDMEuL-1980
EncWL-1981

Link/Lanka

Kosztolányi, Dezso 1885-1936
(Hungarian)
CasWL-1973
ClDMEuL-1980
EncWL-1981
GdMWL-1985
PengEur-1969

Nyugat Group

Kötlum, Jóhannes úr 1899-1972
(Icelandic)
ClDMEuL-1980

Form Revolution

Kotsyubyns'ky, Mykhaylo 1864-
1913 (Ukrainian)
CasWL-1973
ClDMEuL-1980
EncWL-1981
GdMWL-1985
PengEur-1969

Modernism

Koun, Karolos 1908-1987 (Greek)
McGWD-1984
OxThe-1983

Celebratory Theater

Kouwenaar, Gerrit 1923-   (Dutch)
CasWL-1973
EncWL-1981

Fifties Poets/Vijftigers

Kovács, Imre n.d. (Hungarian)
ClDMEuL-1980

Populist Movement

Koziol, Urszula 1931-   (Polish)
ClDMEuL-1980
GdMWL-1985

Wspólczesnosc Generation

Kraajiete, Aina 1923-   (Latvian)
EncWL-1981

New York Group

Kramer, Theodor 1897-1958 (Austrian)
EncWL-1981
PengEur-1969

New Objectivity/Neue Sachlichkeit

Kranjcevic, Silvije Strahimir 1865-1908 (Croatian-speaking Yugoslavian)
CasWL-1973
ClDMEuL-1980
GdMWL-1985
PengEur-1969

Moderna

Kranjec, Misko 1908-   (Slovene-speaking Yugoslavian)
CasWL-1973
ClDMEuL-1980
EncWL-1981

Socialist Realism

Krapiva, Kandrat 1896- (Byelorussian)
ClDMEuL-1980

EncWL-1981
PrEncyPP-1974

Socialist Realism
Uzvyssa Group

Krasko, Ivan (pseud. of Ján Botto) 1876-1958 (Czech)
CasWL-1973
ClDMWEuL-1980
EncWL-1981
GdMWL-1985
PengEur-1969

Modernism

Kraus, Karl 1874-1936 (Austrian)
BenReEncy-1987
CamGLE-1988
CasWL-1973
CEnMWL-1963
ClDMEuL-1980
EncWL-1981
GdMWL-1985
OxGer-1986
PengEur-1969

Expressionism

Kravtsiv, Bohdan 1904-1975 (Ukrainian)
ClDMEuL-1980
EncWL-1981

Visnyk

Kretzer, Max 1854-1941 (German)
ClDMEuL-1980
OxGer-1986

Naturalism

Krieger, Murray 1923-
(American)
EncWL-1981

New Criticism

Krige, Uys 1910-   (South African)
CasWL-1973
EncWL-1981
GdMWL-1985
PengCOAL-1969
PengEng-1971

The Dertigers

Kristeva, Julia 1941- (Bulgarian-
born French)
ClDMEuL-1980
EncWL-1981
PrEncyPP-1974

Feminist Criticism
Semiotics
Structuralism
Tel Quel Group

Kroetsch, Robert 1927-
(Canadian)
BenReEncy-1987
CamGLE-1988
OxCan-1983

Tish Group

Kröger, T. 1844-1918 (German)
OxGer-1986

Heimatkunst

Kruchyonykh, Alexey Eliseyevich
1886-1968 (Russian)
CasWL-1973
ClDMEuL-1980
EncWL-1981

PrEncyPP-1974

Cubo-Futurism

Krúdy, Gyula 1878-1933
(Hungarian)
CasWL-1973
ClDMEuL-1980
EncWL-1981
GdMWL-1985
PengEur-1969

Nyugat Group

Krustev, Krustyo 1866-1919
(Bulgarian)
CasWL-1973
ClDMEuL-1980
EncWL-1981

Misul Group

Krynicki, Ryszard 1943-   (Polish)
ClDMEuL-1980

Teraz Group

Kubin, Alfred 1877-1959 (Austrian)
CasWL-1973
ClDMEuL-1980
EncWL-1981

Expressionism

Kulbak, Moshe 1896-1940 (Yiddish-
speaking Byelorussian)
ClDMEuL-1980
EncWL-1981

Minsk Group

Külebi, Cahit 1917-   (Turkish)
PrEncyPP-1974

Garip Movement

Kulish, Mykola 1892-1937 (Ukrainian)
ClDMEuL-1980
EncWL-1981
GdMWL-1985
PengEur-1969

Free Academy of Proletarian
Literature/VAPLITE

Künde (pseud. of Alexey Andreevich Ivanov) 1898-1934 (Yakut)
EncWL-1981

Socialist Realism

Kundera, Milan 1929-   (Czech)
BenReEncy-1987
CamGLE-1988
CasWL-1973
ClDMEuL-1980
EncWL-1981
GdMWL-1985
OxEng-1985
PengEur-1969

Magic Realism

Kunikida Doppo (pseud. of Kunikida Tetsuo) 1871-1908 (Japanese)
CasWL-1973
DOrLit-1974
EncWL-1981

Naturalist Poets/
Shizenshugisha

Kuo Mo-Jo 1892-1978 (Chinese)
CasWL-1973
DOrLit-1974
EncWL-1981
GdMWL-1985

All-China Federation of
Literary and Art Circles
Creation Society

Kupala, Yanka 1882-1942 (Byelorussian)
CasWL-1973
ClDMEuL-1980
EncWL-1981
GdMWL-1985
PrEncyPP-1974

Flame Group
Our Soil Group/Nasaniustva
Renaissance Group/
Adradzenstva

Kuprin, Alexander Ivanovich 1870-1938 (Russian)
BenReEncy-1987
CasWL-1973
ClDMEuL-1980
EncWL-1981
GdMWL-1985

Znanie Group

Kurek, Jalu 1904-   (Polish)
ClDMEuL-1980
EncWL-1981
GdMWL-1985

Cracow Avant-Garde

Kuzmin, Mikhail Alekseyevich 1875-1935 (Russian)
CasWL-1973
ClDMEuL-1980
EncWL-1981
GdMWL-1985
PengEur-1969
PrEncyPP-1974

Acmeism

Kvaran, Einar Hjörleifsson 1859-1938 (Icelandic)
  CasWL-1973
  ClDMEuL-1980
  EncWL-1981

  Realism
  Vero Ani Group

Kvitko, Leib 1890-1952 (Yiddish-speaking Ukrainian)
  CasWL-1973
  ClDMEuL-1980
  EncWL-1981
  GdMWL-1985

  Kiev Group

L

Laaban, Ilmar 1921-   (Estonian)
EncWL-1981
GdMWL-1985

Soothsayers Movement/
Arbujad

Laberge, Albert 1877-1960
(Canadian)
CasWL-1973
OxCan-1983

Literary School of Montreal/
École Littéraire de Montreal

Lacan, Jacques 1901-1981 (French)
CamGLE-1988
ClDMEuL-1980
EncWL-1981
OxEng-1985
PrEncyPP-1974

Deconstructionism
Structuralism

La Capria, Raffaele 1922-
(Italian)
ClDMEuL-1980

Group 63/Gruppo 63

Laforet Díaz, Carmen 1921-
(Spanish)
CasWL-1973
ClDMEuL-1980
EncWL-1981

GdMWL-1985
OxSpan-1978

Tremendismo

Laforgue, Jules 1860-1887 (French)
BenReEncy-1987
CamGLE-1988
CasWL-1973
ClDMEuL-1980
EncWL-1981
OxEng-1985
OxFr-1959
PengEur-1969
PrEncyPP-1974

Symbolism

Lafourcade, Enrique 1927-
(Chilean)
EncWL-1981

Generation of 1950

Lagerkvist, Pär 1891-1974 (Swedish)
BenReEncy-1987
CasWL-1973
ClDMEuL-1980
EncWL-1981
GdMWL-1985
McGWD-1984
OxThe-1983
PengEur-1969
PrEncyPP-1974

Modernism

Lagerlöf, Selma Ottila Lovisa 1858-1940 (Swedish)
BenReEncy-1987
CasWL-1973
ClDMEuL-1980
EncWL-1981
GdMWL-1985
LongCTCL-1975
PengEur-1969

Nittiotalister

Lama, Antonio G. de n.d. (Spanish)
OxSpan-1978

Grupo Espadaña

Lamantia, Philip 1927- (American)
EncWL-1981
OxAm-1983
PengAm-1971

Beat Generation
San Francisco School

Lamontagne, Blanche 1889-1958 (Canadian)
PrEncyPP-1974

Terroir School

Lampman, Archibald 1861-1899 (Canadian)
CamGLE-1988
CasWL-1973
EncWL-1981
OxCan-1983
PengEng-1971

Confederation Poets

Lampo, Hubert 1920- (Belgian)
CasWL-1973
ClDMEuL-1980

EncWL-1981

Magic Realism

Lams-Eglons, Visvaldis 1923- (Latvian)
EncWL-1981

Socialist Realism

Landau, Zishe 1889-1937 (Yiddish-speaking American)
ClDMEuL-1980
EncWL-1981
GdMWL-1985
PrEncyPP-1974

Young Ones/Die Yunge

Landsbergis, Algirdas 1924- (Lithuanian)
CasWL-1973
EncWL-1981
GdMWL-1985

Earth Movement

Lang, Fritz 1890-1976 (Austrian-born American)
BenReEncy-1987
EncWL-1981

Expressionism

Lange, Antoni 1861-1929 (Polish)
CasWL-1973
ClDMEuL-1980
GdMWL-1985

Young Poland/Mloda Polska

Lange, Norah 1906- (Argentine)
OxSpan-1978

Florida Group

Langendonck, Prosper van 1862-1920 (Belgian)
ClDMEuL-1980

Van nu en straks Group

Langhoff, Wolfgang 1901-1966 (German)
HarDMT-1988

Deutsches Theater

Langner, Lawrence 1890-1962 (Welsh-born American)
OxAmThe-1984
OxThe-1983

Provincetown Players
Theater Guild
Washington Square Players

Lao Shê (pseud. of Shu Ch'ing-ch'un) 1899-1966 (Chinese)
BenReEncy-1987
CasWL-1973
DOrLit-1974
EncWL-1981
GdMWL-1985
McGWD-1984
PengCOAL-1969

All-China Anti-Aggression
   Federation of Writers and
   Artists
New Literature Movement

Lapido, Duro 1931-1978 (Nigerian)
EncWL-1981

Mbari Club
Yoruba Opera

Lapointe, Paul-Marie 1929- (Canadian)
BenReEncy-1987

OxCan-1983

Hexagone Group

Larbaud, Valéry-Nicholas 1881-1957 (French)
CasWL-1973
ClDMEuL-1980
EncWL-1981
GdMWL-1985
OxFr-1959
PengEur-1969

Fantaisistes Group

Larionov, Mikhail 1881-1964 (Russian)
HarDMT-1988

Cubo-Futurism

Larkin, Philip 1922-1985 (English)
BenReEncy-1987
CamGLE-1988
CasWL-1973
CEnMWL-1963
EncWL-1981
GdMWL-1985
LongCTCL-1975
OxEng-1985
PengEng-1971

The Movement
New Lines Poets

Larrea, Juan 1895-1982 (Spanish)
CasWL-1973
ClDMEuL-1980
EncWL-1981
GdMWL-1985
OxSpan-1978
PrEncyPP-1974

Creationism/Creacionismo
Surrealism

Ultraism/Ultraismo

Larrea, Rafael n.d. (Ecuadorian)
OxSpan-1978

Grupo Tzántzico

**L'Arronge, Adolf 1838-1908
(German)**
OxGer-1986
OxThe-1983

Deutsches Theater

Larsen, Alf 1885-1967 (Norwegian)
ClDMEuL-1980
EncWL-1981

Generation of 1905

Larsen, Karl 1860-1927 (Danish)
EncWL-1981

Realism

Larsen, Nella 1891-1964 (American)
CamGLE-1988

Harlem Renaissance

**Lasker-Schüller, Else 1869-1945
(German)**
CasWL-1973
ClDMEuL-1980
EncWL-1981
GdMWL-1985
OxGer-1986
PengEur-1969
PrEncyPP-1974

Expressionism
Storm Circle/*Der Sturm*

Laso, Jaime 1926-   (Chilean)
EncWL-1981

Generation of 1950

Lasso, Ignacio n.d. (Ecuadorian)
OxSpan-1978

Grupo Elan

**La Tailhède, Raymond de 1867-
1938 (French)**
OxFr-1959

École Romane

**Laták, István 1910-   (Hungarian-
speaking Yugoslavian)**
EncWL-1981

Hid Group

**Latorre, Mariano 1886-1955
(Chilean)**
CasWL-1973
EncWL-1981
GdMWL-1985
OxSpan-1978
PengAm-1971

Criollismo

Lattuada, Alberto 1914-   (Italian)
HarDMT-1988

Neorealism

**Lauer, Mirko 1947-   (Czech-born
Peruvian)**
OxSpan-1978

Los Nuevos

Laurens, Henri 1885-1954 (French)
HarDMT-1988

Cubism

Lavrenyov, Boris Andreyevich 1894-1959 (Russian)
CasWL-1973
ClDMEuL-1980
EncWL-1981
PengEur-1969

Modernism

Lawrence, D(avid) H(erbert) 1885-1930 (English)
BenReEncy-1987
CamGLE-1988
CasWL-1973
CEnMWL-1963
EncWL-1981
GdMWL-1985
LongCTCL-1975
McGWD-1984
OxAm-1983
OxEng-1985
OxThe-1983
PengEng-1971
PrEncyPP-1974
RCom-1973

Georgian Literature
Imagism
Modernism

Lawrynowicz, Zygmunt 1925- (Polish)
ClDMEuL-1980

Kontynenty Group

Lawson, John Howard 1894-1977 (American)
CamGLE-1988
GdMWL-1985

OxAm-1983
OxAmThe-1984
PengAm-1971

Group Theater
Proletarian Literature

Lawson, Thomas W(illiam) 1857-1925 (American)
OxAm-1983

Muckrakers

Layton, Irving 1912-   (Romanian-born Canadian)
BenReEncy-1987
CamGLE-1988
CasWL-1973
EncWL-1981
GdMWL-1985
OxCan-1983
PengEng-1971

First Statement Group

Leacock, Stephen 1869-1944 (Canadian)
BenReEncy-1987
CamGLE-1988
CasWL-1973
EncWL-1981
GdMWL-1985
LongCTCL-1975
OxCan-1983
OxEng-1985
PengEng-1971

Local Color School

Leavis, F(rank) R(aymond) 1895-1978 (English)
BenReEncy-1987
CamGLE-1988
CasWL-1973
EncWL-1981

LongCTCL-1975
OxEng-1985
PengEng-1971

Modernism
New Criticism
Scrutiny

Leavis, Q(ueenie) D. 1906-1981
(English)
CamGLE-1988
EncWL-1981
HarDMT-1988
OxEng-1985

Scrutiny

Lechón, Jan (pseud. of Leszek
Serafinowicz) 1899-1956 (Polish)
CasWL-1973
ClDMEuL-1980
EncWL-1981
GdMWL-1985
PrEncyPP-1974

Skamander Group

Lecomte, Marcel 1900-1966
(Belgian)
ClDMEuL-1980
EncWL-1981

Surrealism

Leeuw, Aart van der 1876-1932
(Dutch)
CasWL-1973
ClDMEuL-1980
PengEur-1969

De Beweging

Léger, Fernand 1881-1955 (French)
BenReEncy-1987
EncWL-1981

Cubism
Futurism
Orphism
Surrealism

Leguizamón, Martiniano 1858-1935
(Argentine)
CasWL-1973
OxSpan-1978
PengAm-1971

Gaucho Literature

Lehtonen, Joel 1881-1934 (Finnish)
CasWL-1973
ClDMEuL-1980
EncWL-1981
GdMWL-1985
PengEur-1969

National Neoromanticism

Leino, Eino (pseud. of Eino
Lönnbohm) 1878-1926 (Finnish)
CasWL-1973
ClDMEuL-1980
EncWL-1981
GdMWL-1985
PengEur-1969

National Neoromanticism

Leiris, Michel 1901-   (French)
CasWL-1973
ClDMEuL-1980
EncWL-1981
GdMWL-1985
PrEncyPP-1974

Surrealism

Leiva, Raúl 1916-   (Guatemalan)
OxSpan-1978

Grupo Acento

Lemaître, Maurice n.d. (French)
HarDMT-1988

Lettrism

**Lemonnier, Camille 1845-1913
(French)**
OxFr-1959

Symbolism

**Lemonnier, Léon 1892-1953
(French)**
BenReEncy-1987
ClDMEuL-1980
EncWL-1981
GdMWL-1985

Populisme

Lengyel, József 1896- (Hungarian)
ClDMEuL-1980
EncWL-1981
PengEur-1969

Today Group/*Ma*

Lenz, Siegfried 1926- (German)
BenReEncy-1987
CasWL-1973
ClDMEuL-1980
EncWL-1981
GdMWL-1985
OxGer-1986

Group 47/Gruppe 47

**Leonhard, Rudolf 1889-1953
(German)**
EncWL-1981
OxGer-1986

Expressionism

**Leonidze, Giorgi 1899-1966
(Georgian)**
DOrLit-1974
EncWL-1981
GdMWL-1985

Blue Horns Group/Tsispheri
q'antesbi

**Leonov, Leonid Maksimovich 1899-
(Russian)**
BenReEncy-1987
CasWL-1973
ClDMEuL-1980
EncWL-1981
GdMWL-1985
McGWD-1984
OxEng-1985
OxThe-1983
PengEur-1969

Serapion Brotherhood
Socialist Realism

**Lerberghe, Charles Van 1861-1907
(Belgian)**
CasWL-1973
ClDMEuL-1980
EncWL-1981
GdMWL-1985
OxFr-1959
PengEur-1969
PrEncyPP-1974

Symbolism

**Leroux, Étienne 1922-   (South
African)**
CasWL-1973
EncWL-1981
GdMWL-1985
PengCOAL-1969

The Sestigers

**Lesmian, Boleslaw 1879-1937
(Polish)**
CasWL-1973
ClDMEuL-1980
EncWL-1981
GdMWL-1985
PengEur-1969

Skamander Group
Young Poland/Mloda Polska

**Lesznai, Anna 1885-1966
(Hungarian)**
EncWL-1981

Nyugat Group

**Levertin, Oscar Ivar 1862-1906
(Swedish)**
CasWL-1973
ClDMEuL-1980
EncWL-1981
PengEur-1969
PrEncyPP-1974

Nittiotalister

**Levertov, Denise 1923-   (English-
born American)**
BenReEncy-1987
CamGLE-1988
EncWL-1981
OxAm-1983
OxEng-1985
PengAm-1971
PrEncyPP-1974

Black Mountain Poets

Levi, Carlo 1902-1975 (Italian)
BenReEncy-1987
CasWL-1973
CEnMWL-1963
ClDMEuL-1980
EncWL-1981

GdMWL-1985
OxEng-1985
PengEur-1969

Neorealism

Levi, Primo 1919-   (Italian)
BenReEncy-1987
ClDMEuL-1980
OxEng-1985

Neorealism

**Lévi-Strauss, Claude 1908-
(French)**
BenReEncy-1987
CamGLE-1988
CasWL-1973
ClDMEuL-1980
EncWL-1981
OxEng-1985
PrEncyPP-1974

Semiotics
Structuralism

Levy, Melvin n.d. (American)
OxThe-1983

Group Theater

**Lewis, C(live) S(taples) 1898-1963
(Irish-born English)**
BenReEncy-1987
CamGLE-1988
CasWL-1973
EncWL-1981
LongCTCL-1975
OxEng-1985
PengEng-1971

The Inklings

Lewis, (Percy) Wyndham 1882-1957 (English)
BenReEncy-1987
CamGLE-1988
CasWL-1973
CEnMWL-1963
EncWL-1981
GdMWL-1985
LongCTCL-1975
OxCan-1983
OxEng-1985
PengEng-1971
PrEncyPP-1974

Georgian Literature
Modernism
Vorticism

Lewis, Sinclair 1885-1951 (American)
BenReEncy-1987
CamGLE-1988
CasWL-1973
CEnMWL-1963
EncWL-1981
GdMWL-1985
LongCTCL-1975
McGWD-1984
OxAm-1983
OxEng-1985
PengAm-1971
RCom-1973

Realism

Lewis, Stephen n.d. (English)
OxThe-1983

Theater Workshop

Leyb, Mani (pseud. of Mani Leyb Brahinsky) 1883-1953 (Yiddish-speaking American)
ClDMEuL-1980

PrEncyPP-1974

Young Ones/Die Yunge

Leyeles, A. (pseud. of Aaron Glanz) 1899-1966 (Yiddish-speaking American)
CasWL-1973
GdMWL-1985
PrEncyPP-1974

Introspectivists

Lezama Lima, José 1910-1976 (Cuban)
BenReEncy-1987
CaribWr-1979
CasWL-1973
EncWL-1981
GdMWL-1985
OxSpan-1978
PengAm-1971

Criollismo
Orígenes Group
Transcendentalist Group

Libedinsky, Yury Nikolayevich 1898- (Russian)
CasWL-1973
ClDMEuL-1980

October Group

Lichtenstein, Alfred 1889-1914 (German)
EncWL-1981
GdMWL-1985
OxGer-1986
PengEur-1969

Expressionism

Lidman, Sven 1882-1960 (Swedish)
CasWL-1973

ClDMEuL-1980
EncWL-1981

Tiotalister

**Lie, Jonas Lauritz Idemil 1833-1908
(Norwegian)**
BenReEncy-1987
CasWL-1973
ClDMEuL-1980
EncWL-1981
GdMWL-1985
PengEur-1969

Naturalism
Neoromanticism
Realism

**Lienhard, Friedrich 1865-1929
(German)**
OxGer-1986

Heimatkunst

**Liliencron, Detlev von 1844-1909
(German)**
BenReEncy-1987
CasWL-1973
EncWL-1981
GdMWL-1985
OxGer-1986
PengEur-1969

Naturalism

**Liliev, Nikolay 1885-1960
(Bulgarian)**
CasWL-1973
EncWL-1981
GdMWL-1985
PengEur-1969
PrEncyPP-1974

Symbolism

**Lima, Jorge de 1893-1953
(Brazilian)**
CasWL-1973
EncWL-1981
GdMWL-1985
PengAm-1971
PrEncyPP-1974

Modernism

**Linares Rivas, Manuel 1878-1938
(Spanish)**
CasWL-1973
ClDMEuL-1980
GdMWL-1985
OxSpan-1978

Novecentismo

**Lindegren, Erik 1910-1968
(Swedish)**
CasWL-1973
ClDMEuL-1980
EncWL-1981
GdMWL-1985
PengEur-1969
PrEncyPP-1974

Poets of the Forties/
Fyrtiotalisterna

**Lindsay, (John) Maurice 1918-
(Scottish)**
CasWL-1973
EncWL-1981
PengEng-1971

Scottish Renaissance

**Lindsay, Vachel 1879-1931
(American)**
BenReEncy-1987
CamGLE-1988
CasWL-1973
CEnMWL-1963

EncWL-1981
GdMWL-1985
LongCTCL-1975
OxAm-1983
OxEng-1985
PengAm-1971

Chicago Group/Renaissance
Jazz Age
Jazz Poetry

**Lins de Rêgo Cavalcanti, José 1901-
1957 (Brazilian)**
BenReEncy-1987
CasWL-1973
EncWL-1981
GdMWL-1985
PengAm-1971

Modernism
Region-Tradition Movement

**Liost, Guerau de 1873-1933
(Spanish)**
EncWL-1981
GdMWL-1985
OxSpan-1978

Noucentismo

**Lipchitz, Jacques 1891-1973
(Lithuanian)**
HarDMT-1988

Cubism

**Lisboa, António Maria 1928-1953
(Portuguese)**
EncWL-1981
GdMWL-1985

Surrealism

**Lisboa, Irene 1892-1958
(Portuguese)**
CIDMEuL-1980
EncWL-1981

Presencistas Group

Littlewood, Joan 1914-　　(English)
EncWL-1981
LongCTCL-1975
OxThe-1983

Theater of Fact
Theater Workshop
Total Theater

Liu Ya-tzu 1887-1958 (Chinese)
EncWL-1981

Southern Society/Nan-shê
　Group

**Livshits, Benedikt Konstantinovich
1887-1939 (Russian)**
CIDMEuL-1980
EncWL-1981

Cubo-Futurism

**Livytska-Kholodna, Natalia 1902-
　(Ukrainian)**
EncWL-1981

Tank Group

**Llerena, José Alfredo n.d.
(Ecuadorian)**
OxSpan-1978

Grupo Elan

**Lloréns Torres, Luis 1878-1944
(Puerto Rican)**
CaribWr-1979
OxSpan-1978

PrEncyPP-1974

Modernismo

**Lluch Mora, Francisco 1924-
(Puerto Rican)**
CaribWr-1979

Transcendentalist Group

**Lobato, José Bento Monteiro 1882-
1948 (Brazilian)**
CasWL-1973
EncWL-1981
GdMWL-1985
PengAm-1971

Modernism

**Lobsien, Wilhelm 1872-1947
(German)**
OxGer-1986

Heimatkunst

Locke, Alain 1886-1954 (American)
BenReEncy-1987
CamGLE-1988
PrEncyPP-1974

Harlem Renaissance

Lodeizen, Hans 1924-1950 (Dutch)
CasWL-1973
EncWL-1981

Experimentelen

Lodge, David 1935-   (English)
CamGLE-1988
EncWL-1981
OxEng-1985

Structuralism

**Lodovici, Cesare Vico 1885-1968
(Italian)**
OxThe-1983

Crepuscolarismo

Loerke, Oskar 1884-1941 (German)
CasWL-1973
EncWL-1981
GdMWL-1985
OxGer-1986
PengEur-1969

Expressionism

**Loewinsohn, Ron 1937-
(American)**
EncWL-1981

Beat Generation

**Logue, Christopher 1926-
(English)**
CamGLE-1988
OxEng-1985

Jazz Poetry

**Lo-Johansson, Ivar 1901-
(Swedish)**
CasWL-1973
ClDMEuL-1980
EncWL-1981
GdMWL-1985
PengEur-1969

Proletarian Writers/
Arbetardiktare

London, Jack 1876-1916 (American)
BenReEncy-1987
CamGLE-1988
CasWL-1973
EncWL-1981
GdMWL-1985

LongCTCL-1975
OxAm-1983
OxCan-1983
OxEng-1985
PengAm-1971
RCom-1973

Naturalism

Löns, Hermann 1866-1914 (German)
ClDMEuL-1980
OxGer-1986

Heimatkunst

Lopes, Manuel 1907-   (Cape Verdean)
ClDMEuL-1980
EncWL-1981

Claridade Movement

Loranger, Jean-Aubert 1896-1942 (French-speaking Canadian)
OxCan-1983

Literary School of Montreal/
    École Littéraire de Montreal

Lotman, Yury 1922-   (Russian)
EncWL-1981

Semiotics

Lotz, Ernst Wilhelm 1890-1914 (German)
EncWL-1981

Expressionism

Louw, Nicholaas Petrus Van Wyck 1906-1970 (South African)
CasWL-1973
EncWL-1981
GdMWL-1985

PengCOAL-1969
PrEncyPP-1974

The Dertigers

Louw, W(illiam) E(wart) G(ladstone) 1913-   (South African)
CasWL-1973
EncWL-1981
PrEncyPP-1974

The Dertigers

Loveira y Chirino, Carlos 1882-1928 (Cuban)
CaribWr-1979
CasWL-1973
EncWL-1981
OxSpan-1978
PengAm-1971

Realism

Lovinescu, Eugen 1881-1943 (Romanian)
CasWL-1973
ClDMEuL-1980
EncWL-1981

Sburatorul Group

Lowell, Amy 1874-1925 (American)
BenReEncy-1987
CamGLE-1988
CasWL-1973
EncWL-1981
LongCTCL-1975
OxAm-1983
OxEng-1985
PengAm-1971
PrEncyPP-1974
RCom-1973

Imagism

Poetry

**Lowell, Robert 1917-1977
(American)**
  BenReEncy-1987
  CamGLE-1988
  CasWL-1973
  CEnMWL-1963
  EncWL-1981
  GdMWL-1985
  LongCTCL-1975
  McGWD-1984
  OxAm-1983
  OxEng-1985
  PengAm-1971
  PrEncyPP-1974
  RCom-1973

Confessional Poetry

**Lozeau, Albert 1878-1924
(Canadian)**
  GdMWL-1985
  OxCan-1983

Literary School of Montreal/
  École Littéraire de Montreal

**Lozinsky, Mikhail 1886-1955
(Russian)**
  ClDMEuL-1980

Acmeism

**Lucebert (pseud. of Lubertys
Jacobus Swaanswijk) 1924-
(Dutch)**
  CasWL-1973
  ClDMEuL-1980
  EncWL-1981
  GdMWL-1985
  PengEur-1969

Fifties Poets/Vijftigers

**Lucie-Smith, Edward 1933-
(Jamaican-born English)**
  CamGLE-1988
  CaribWr-1979
  OxEng-1985

The Group

**Lugones, Leopoldo 1873-1938
(Argentine)**
  BenReEncy-1987
  CasWL-1973
  EncWL-1981
  GdMWL-1985
  OxSpan-1978
  PengAm-1971
  PrEncyPP-1974

Modernismo

**Lu Hsün (pseud. of Chou Shu-jen)
1881-1936 (Chinese)**
  BenReEncy-1987
  CasWL-1973
  CEnMWL-1963
  DOrLit-1974
  EncWL-1981
  GdMWL-1985
  PengCOAL-1969

League of Left-Wing Writers
May Fourth Movement/Wu-
  ssu yün-tung

**Luis, Leopoldo de 1918-
(Spanish)**
  OxSpan-1978

Grupo Espadaña

**Lukács, Gyorgy 1885-1971
(Hungarian)**
  BenReEncy-1987
  CamGLE-1988
  CasWL-1973

ClDMEuL-1980
EncWL-1981
McGWD-1984
OxEng-1985
OxGer-1986
PengEur-1969

Marxist Criticism
Socialist Realism

Lumpkin, Grace n.d. (American)
OxAm-1983

Proletarian Literature

Lunacharsky, Anatoli Vasilyevich 1875-1933 (Russian)
CasWL-1973
GdMWL-1985
ClDMEuL-1980
EncWL-1981
McGWD-1984
OxThe-1983
PengEur-1969

Moscow Art Theater
Proletkult
Socialist Realism

Lundkvist, Artur 1906-   (Swedish)
CasWL-1973
ClDMEuL-1980
EncWL-1981
GdMWL-1985
PengEur-1969
PrEncyPP-1974

Five Young Men/Fem Unga
Surrealism

Lunts, Lev Natanovich 1901-1924 (Russian)
CasWL-1973
ClDMEuL-1980

EncWL-1981

Serapion Brotherhood

Lutsky, Ostap n.d. (Ukrainian)
ClDMEuL-1980

Young Muse Group/Moloda
Muza

Luzi, Mario 1914-   (Italian)
CasWL-1973
ClDMEuL-1980
EncWL-1981
GdMWL-1985
OxEng-1985
PengEur-1969

Hermeticism/Poesia Ermetica

Luznytsky, Hryhory 1903- (Ukrainian)
EncWL-1981

Logos Group

Lyaturynska, Oksana 1902-1970 (Ukrainian)
ClDMEuL-1980
EncWL-1981

Visnyk

Lynch, Benito 1885-1951 (Argentine)
BenReEncy-1987
CasWL-1973
EncWL-1981
GdMWL-1985
OxSpan-1978
PengAm-1971

Gaucho Literature

Lyn'kow, M. n.d. (Byelorussian)
PrEncyPP-1974

   Socialist Realism

Lypa, Yury 1900-1944 (Ukrainian)
ClDMEuL-1980
EncWL-1981

   Tank Group

   Visnyk

Lytle, Andrew 1902-   (American)
BenReEncy-1987
EncWL-1981
OxAm-1983
PengAm-1971

   The Fugitives/Agrarians

M

McAuley, James Phillip 1917-1976 (Australian)
BenReEncy-1987
CamGLE-1988
CasWL-1973
GdMWL-1985
PengEng-1971
PrEncyPP-1974

Angry Penguins

MacBeth, George 1932-   (Scottish)
BenReEncy-1987
CamGLE-1988
OxEng-1985

The Group
New Lines Poets

MacCaffery, Steven n.d. (Canadian)
OxCan-1983

Four Horsemen

MacCaig, Norman 1910- (Scottish)
CamGLE-1988
CasWL-1973
EncWL-1981
OxEng-1985
PengEng-1971

New Apocalypse

MacCarthy, Desmond 1878-1952 (English)
BenReEncy-1987
CamGLE-1988
EncWL-1981
LongCTCL-1975
OxEng-1985
PengEng-1971

Bloomsbury Group

MacClellan, Keith n.d. (Canadian)
OxCan-1983

First Statement Group

McClung, Nellie 1873-1951 (Canadian)
OxCan-1983

Local Color School

McClure, Michael 1932- (American)
BenReEncy-1987
McGWD-1984
OxAm-1983
PengAm-1971

Beat Generation

McClure, Samuel Sidney 1857-1949 (Irish-born American)
BenReEncy-1987

Muckrakers

MacColl, Ewan 1915- (Scottish)
OxThe-1983

Theater Workshop

MacDiarmid, Hugh (pseud. of Christopher Murray Grieve) 1892-1978 (Scottish)
BenReEncy-1987
CamGLE-1988
CasWL-1973
CEnMWL-1963
EncWL-1981
GdMWL-1985
LongCTCL-1975
OxEng-1985
PengEng-1971
PrEncyPP-1974

Scottish Renaissance

Macedonski, Alexandru 1854-1920 (Romanian)
CasWL-1973
ClDMEuL-1980
EncWL-1981
GdMWL-1985
PengEur-1969

Symbolism

McGough, Roger 1937- (English)
CamGLE-1988
OxEng-1985

Liverpool Poets

Macgowan, Kenneth 1888-1963 (American)
OxAm-1983
OxAmThe-1984
OxThe-1983

Provincetown Players

MacGregor, Mary Esther 1876-1961 (Canadian)
OxCan-1983

Local Color School

Machado, Bernardino 1851-1944 (Portuguese)
ClDMEuL-1980

Portuguese Renascence Movement

Machado y Ruiz, Antonio 1875-1939 (Spanish)
BenReEncy-1987
CasWL-1973
CEnMWL-1963
ClDMEuL-1980
EncWL-1981
GdMWL-1985
McGWD-1984
OxSpan-1978
PengEur-1969
PrEncyPP-1974

Generation of 1898/Generación del 1898
Modernismo

Machado y Ruiz, Manuel 1874-1947 (Spanish)
CasWL-1973
ClDMEuL-1980
EncWL-1981
GdMWL-1985
McGWD-1984
OxSpan-1978
PengEur-1969
PrEncyPP-1974

Modernismo

Machery, Pierre n.d. (French)
CamGLE-1988

EncWL-1981
OxEng-1985

Marxist Criticism

**McKay, Claude 1889-1948
(Jamaican-born American)**
BenReEncy-1987
CamGLE-1988
CaribWr-1979
CasWL-1973
GdMWL-1985
OxAm-1983
PrEncyPP-1974

Harlem Renaissance

**McKeon, Richard 1900-1985
(American)**
PengAm-1971
PrEncyPP-1974

Chicago Critics

McLaughlin, C.A. n.d. (American)
PrEncyPP-1974

Chicago Critics

**Mclean, Norman 1902-
(American)**
PengAm-1971
PrEncyPP-1974

Chicago Critics

MacLean, Sorley 1911-　(Scottish)
CamGLE-1988
OxEng-1985

Scottish Renaissance

**MacLeish, Archibald 1892-1982
(American)**
BenReEncy-1987

CamGLE-1988
CasWL-1973
CEnMWL-1963
EncWL-1981
GdMWL-1985
LongCTCL-1975
OxAm-1983
OxAmThe-1984
OxEng-1985
PengAm-1971

Lost Generation

**MacLow, Jackson 1922-
(American)**
OxThe-1983

Living Theater

**MacNamara, Brinsley 1890-1963
(Irish)**
LongCTCL-1975
OxThe-1983

Abbey Theater

MacNeice, Louis 1907-1963 (Irish-born English)
BenReEncy-1987
CamGLE-1988
CasWL-1973
CEnMWL-1963
EncWL-1981
GdMWL-1985
LongCTCL-1975
OxEng-1985
PengEng-1971

Pylon School

Macrì, Oreste 1913-　(Italian)
ClDMEuL-1980

Hermeticism/Poesia Ermetica

Macve, Prabhakar n.d. (Indian)
DOrLit-1974

New Poetry Movement/Nayi
Kavita

**Madge, Charles Henry 1912-
(South African-born English)**
CamGLE-1988
EncWL-1981
GdMWL-1985
LongCTCL-1975
OxEng-1985
PengEng-1971

Cambridge Group

**Maeterlinck, Maurice 1862-1949
(Belgian)**
BenReEncy-1987
CamGLE-1988
CasWL-1973
ClDMEuL-1980
EncWL-1981
GdMWL-1985
LongCTCL-1975
McGWD-1984
OxAmThe-1984
OxEng-1985
OxFr-1959
OxThe-1983
PengEur-1969
PrEncyPP-1974

Symbolism
Theater of Silence/Théâtre de
l'Inexprimé

**Maeztu y Whitney, Ramiro de 1874-
1936 (Spanish)**
BenReEncy-1987
CasWL-1973
ClDMEuL-1980
EncWL-1981
OxSpan-1978

Generation of 1898/Generación
del 1898

**Magallanes Moure, Manuel 1878-
1924 (Chilean)**
CasWL-1973
GdMWL-1985
OxSpan-1978
PrEncyPP-1974

Modernismo

Magritte, René 1898-1967 (Belgian)
BenReEncy-1987
ClDMEuL-1980
EncWL-1981

Surrealism

**Mahjub, Muhammad Ahmad 1910-
1976 (Sudanese)**
EncWL-1981

Romantic Poets

**Mahsuri Salikon 1927-
(Malaysian)**
EncWL-1981

Generation of the 1950s/Asas
'50

**al-Majdhub, Muhammad al-Mahdi
1919-   (Sudanese)**
EncWL-1981

Realism

Majerová, Marie 1882-1967 (Czech)
CasWL-1973
ClDMEuL-1980
EncWL-1981
GdMWL-1985

PengEur-1969

Socialist Realism

**Majowski, Alexander 1876-1938
(Kashubian-speaking Polish)**
EncWL-1981

Young Kashubian Movement

Makal, Mahmut 1930-   (Turkish)
CasWL-1973
ClDMEuL-1980
DOrLit-1974

Village Fiction

Makayanka, A. n.d. (Byelorussian)
PrEncyPP-1974

Socialist Realism

Málaga, Oscar n.d. (Peruvian)
OxSpan-1978

Estos 13/Hora Cero

**Malakasis, Miltiadis 1869-1943
(Greek)**
EncWL-1981
PrEncyPP-1974

New School of Athens/Greek
Parnassians

**Malanyuk, Yevhen 1897-1968
(Ukrainian)**
ClDMEuL-1980
EncWL-1981
GdMWL-1985

Visnyk

Malerba, Luigi 1927-   (Italian)
ClDMEuL-1980

EncWL-1981

Group 63/Gruppo 63

**Malevich, Kazimir Severinovich
1878-1935 (Russian)**
BenReEncy-1987
EncWL-1981

Cubo-Futurism

Malina, Judith 1926- (German)
OxAmThe-1984

Living Theater

**Maliszweski, Aleksander 1901-1978
(Polish)**
ClDMEuL-1980

Quadriga

**Mallarmé, Stéphane 1842-1898
(French)**
BenReEncy-1987
CamGLE-1988
CasWL-1973
ClDMEuL-1980
EncWL-1981
OxEng-1985
OxFr-1959
PengEur-1969
PrEncyPP-1974
RCom-1973

Symbolism

Malle, Louis 1932-   (French)
BenReEncy-1987

New Wave/Nouvelle Vague

**Malmanche, Tanguy 1875-1953
(Breton-speaking French)**
EncWL-1981

GdMWL-1985
PengEur-1969

Breton Movement

Malraux, André 1901-1976 (French)
BenReEncy-1987
CasWL-1973
CEnMWL-1963
ClDMEuL-1980
EncWL-1981
GdMWL-1985
LongCTCL-1975
McGWD-1984
OxEng-1985
OxFr-1959
PengEur-1969
RCom-1973

Existentialism

**al-Ma'luf, Fawzi 1889-1930
(Lebanese)**
EncWL-1981

Andalusian League

**al-Ma'luf, Shafiq 1905-
(Lebanese)**
EncWL-1981

Andalusian League

**Mamedkulizade, Djalil 1866-1932
(Azerbaijani)**
EncWL-1981

Molla Nasreddin Movement

**Mammeri, Mouloud 1917-
(Algerian)**
ClDMEuL-1980
DOrLit-1974

EncWL-1981

Generation of 1954

**Mandelshtam, Osip 1891-1938(?)
(Russian)**
BenReEncy-1987
CasWL-1973
CEnMWL-1963
ClDMEuL-1980
EncWL-1981
GdMWL-1985
OxEng-1985
PengEur-1969
PrEncyPP-1974

Acmeism

Mándy, Iván 1918- (Hungarian)
ClDMEuL-1980
GdMWL-1985

Ujhold Group

**Manganelli, Giorgio 1922-
(Italian)**
ClDMEuL-1980

Group 63/Gruppo 63

Mann, Thomas 1875-1955 (German)
BenReEncy-1987
CasWL-1973
CEnMWL-1963
ClDMEuL-1980
EncWL-1981
GdMWL-1985
LongCTCL-1975
OxEng-1985
OxGer-1986
PengEur-1969
RCom-1973

Modernism
Realism

Manner, Eeva Liisa 1921-
(Finnish)
   ClDMEuL-1980
   EncWL-1981
   GdMWL-1985
   PengEur-1969

   Modernism

Mansfield, Katherine (pseud. of
Kathleen Beauchamp) 1888-1923
(New Zealand-born English)
   BenReEncy-1987
   CamGLE-1988
   CasWL-1973
   CEnMWL-1963
   EncWL-1981
   GdMWL-1985
   LongCTCL-1975
   OxEng-1985
   PengEng-1971

   Modernism

Manzini, Gianna 1896-   **(Italian)**
   CasWL-1973
   ClDMEuL-1980

   Solaria Group

Mao Tun (pseud. of Shen Yen-
ping) 1896-1981 (Chinese)
   CasWL-1973
   DOrLit-1974
   EncWL-1981
   GdMWL-1985
   PengCOAL-1969

   League of Left-Wing Writers
   Literary Research Association
   New Literature Movement

Maples Arce, Manuel 1898-
(Mexican)
   GdMWL-1985
   OxSpan-1978

   Estridentismo

Márai, Sándor 1900-   **(Hungarian)**
   CasWL-1973
   ClDMEuL-1980
   EncWL-1981
   GdMWL-1985
   PengEur-1969

   Nyugat Group

Maran, René 1887-1960
(Martinican)
   CasWL-1973
   EncWL-1981
   GdMWL-1985

   Négritude

Marc, Franz 1880-1916 (German)
   BenReEncy-1987
   EncWL-1981
   OxGer-1986

   Expressionism
   Storm Circle/*Der Sturm*

Marcel, Gabriel 1889-1973 (French)
   BenReEncy-1987
   CasWL-1973
   ClDMEuL-1980
   EncWL-1981
   McGWD-1984
   OxEng-1985
   OxFr-1959
   OxThe-1983
   PengEur-1969
   RCom-1973

   Existentialism

Marchand, Olivier n.d. (Canadian)
OxCan-1983

Hexagone Group

Marcinkevicius, Justinas 1930-
(Lithuanian)
EncWL-1981
PrEncyPP-1974

Socialist Realism

Marcos Suárez, Miguel de 1894-
1954 (Cuban)
CaribWr-1979

Realism

Marechal, Leopoldo 1900-1970
(Argentine)
CasWL-1973
EncWL-1981
GdMWL-1985
OxSpan-1978
PengAm-1971

Florida Group
Ultraism/Ultraismo

Mariano, Gabriel 1928-   (Cape
Verdean)
EncWL-1981

Antievasion Group/Anti-
Evasao

Marien, Marcel n.d. (Belgian)
ClDMEuL-1980

Surrealism

Marinello Vidaurreta, Juan 1898-
(Cuban)
CaribWr-1979
EncWL-1981

OxSpan-1978

Afro-Cubanism

Marinetti, Filippo Tommaso 1876-
1944 (Italian)
BenReEncy-1987
CasWL-1973
ClDMEuL-1980
EncWL-1981
GdMWL-1985
LongCTCL-1975
McGWD-1984
OxEng-1985
OxFr-1959
OxThe-1983
PengEur-1969
PrEncyPP-1974

Futurism

Maritain, Jacques 1882-1973
(French)
BenReEncy-1987
CasWL-1973
ClDMEuL-1980
EncWL-1981
OxFr-1959

Existentialism

Marjanovic, Milan 1879-1955
(Croatian-speaking Yugoslavian)
ClDMEuL-1980
EncWL-1981

Moderna

Marker, Chris 1921-   (French)
HarDMT-1988

New Wave/Nouvelle Vague

Markish, Peretz 1895-1952
(Yiddish-speaking Ukrainian)
CasWL-1973
ClDMEuL-1980
EncWL-1981
GdMWL-1985
PengEur-1969

Gang Group/Khalyastre
Kiev Group

Marks, Percy 1891-1956 (American)
OxAm-1983

Jazz Age

Marlatt, Daphne 1942-
(Australian-born Canadian)
OxCan-1983

Tish Group

Marquand, John P(hillips) 1893-
1960 (American)
BenReEncy-1987
CasWL-1973
EncWL-1981
GdMWL-1985
LongCTCL-1975
McGWD-1984
OxAm-1983
PengAm-1971

Realism

Marsh, Edward 1872-1953 (English)
BenReEncy-1987
CamGLE-1988
EncWL-1981
LongCTCL-1975
OxEng-1985
PengEng-1971
PrEncyPP-1974

Georgian Literature

Marsh, Robert H. 1926-
(American)
PrEncyPP-1974

Chicago Critics

Marshall, Herbert 1906-   (English)
HarDMT-1988

Unity Theater

Marshall, Norman 1901-1980
(English)
HarDMT-1988
OxThe-1983

Gate Theater

Marsman, Hendrik 1889-1940
(Dutch)
CasWL-1973
ClDMEuL-1980
EncWL-1981
GdMWL-1985
PengEur-1969

Expressionism

Martí, José 1853-1895 (Cuban)
BenReEncy-1987
CaribWr-1979
CasWL-1973
EncWL-1981
McGWD-1984
OxSpan-1978
PengAm-1971
PrEncyPP-1974

Modernismo

Martin du Gard, Roger 1881-1958
(French)
BenReEncy-1987
CasWL-1973
CEnMWL-1963

ClDMEuL-1980
EncWL-1981
GdMWL-1985
McGWD-1984
OxEng-1985
OxFr-1959
PengEur-1969

Nouvelle Revue Française
Group

Martin Montes, José Luis 1921-
(Puerto Rican)
CaribWr-1979

Ensueñismo Group

Martínez Estrada, Ezequiel 1895-
1964 (Argentine)
EncWL-1981
OxSpan-1978
PengAm-1971

Ultraism/Ultraismo

Martínez Moreno, Carlos 1917-
(Uruguayan)
EncWL-1981
OxSpan-1978

Generation of 1945

Martínez Ruiz, José

See **Azorín**

Martínez Sierra, Gregorio 1881-
1947 (Spanish)
BenReEncy-1987
CasWL-1973
ClDMEuL-1980
EncWL-1981
GdMWL-1985
LongCTCL-1975
OxSpan-1978

OxThe-1983
PengEur-1969

Novecentismo

Martínez Torres, Olga n.d.
(Guatemalan)
OxSpan-1978

The Dawn Group/Grupo Saker
Ti

Martini, Fausto Maria 1886-1931
(Italian)
ClDMEuL-1980
OxThe-1983

Crepuscolarismo

Martins, Ovídio 1928-   (Cape
Verdean)
EncWL-1981

Antievasion Group/Anti-
Evasao

Martinson, Harry (Edmund) 1904-
1978 (Swedish)
BenReEncy-1987
CasWL-1973
ClDMEuL-1980
EncWL-1981
GdMWL-1985
OxThe-1983
PengEur-1969
PrEncyPP-1974

Five Young Men/Fem Unga

Martinson, Moa 1890-1964
(Swedish)
ClDMEuL-1980
EncWL-1981

Proletarian Writers/
Arbetardiktare

Martovych, Les (Olexandr) 1871-1916 (Ukrainian)
EncWL-1981

Modernism

Martyn, Edward 1859-1923 (Irish)
CamGLE-1988
CasWL-1973
EncWL-1981
LongCTCL-1975
McGWD-1984
OxEng-1985
OxThe-1983

Abbey Theater
Irish Literary Theater
Irish Renaissance

Marugg, Tip 1923-   (Curaçaon)
CaribWr-1979
EncWL-1981

Porch Group/De Stoep

Marx, (Heinrich) Karl 1818-1883 (German)
BenReEncy-1987
CasWL-1973
EncWL-1981
HandLit-1986
HarDMT-1988
LongCTCL-1975
OxEng-1985
OxFr-1959
OxGer-1986
RCom-1973

Masamune Hakucho 1879-1962 (Japanese)
CasWL-1973
DOrLit-1974

GdMWL-1985

Naturalist Poets/
Shizenshugisha

Masaoka Shiki (pseud. of Masaoka Tsunenori) 1867-1902 (Japanese)
BenReEncy-1987
CasWL-1973
DOrLit-1974
EncWL-1981
GdMWL-1985

Hototogisu Poets

Masaryk, Tomás Garrigue 1850-1937 (Czech)
ClDMEuL-1980
EncWL-1981
GdMWL-1985
PengEur-1969

Moderna

Mascagni, Pietro 1863-1945 (Italian)
HarDMT-1988

Verismo

Masefield, John 1878-1967 (English)
BenReEncy-1987
CamGLE-1988
CasWL-1973
CEnMWL-1963
EncWL-1981
GdMWL-1985
LongCTCL-1975
McGWD-1984
OxEng-1985
PengEng-1971

Edwardian Literature
Georgian Literature
Modernism

Masing, Uku 1909-   (Estonian)
ClDMEuL-1980
EncWL-1981
GdMWL-1985
PrEncyPP-1974

Soothsayers Movement/
Arbujad

Masson, André 1897-1987 (French)
ClDMEuL-1980
EncWL-1981
OxEng-1985

Surrealism

**Masters, Edgar Lee 1869(?)-1950
(American)**
BenReEncy-1987
CamGLE-1988
CasWL-1973
CEnMWL-1963
EncWL-1981
GdMWL-1985
LongCTCL-1975
OxAm-1983
OxEng-1985
PengAm-1971
PrEncyPP-1974

Chicago Group/Renaissance
Realism

Mathur, Girijakumar n.d. (Indian)
DOrLit-1974

New Poetry Movement/Nayi
Kavita

**Matic, Dusan 1898-   (Serbian-
speaking Yugoslavian)**
CasWL-1973
ClDMEuL-1980
EncWL-1981

PengEur-1969

Surrealism

**Matos, Anton Gustav 1873-1914
(Croatian-speaking Yugoslavian)**
ClDMEuL-1980
EncWL-1981
GdMWL-1985
PengEur-1969

Moderna

**Matos Paoli, Francisco 1915-
(Puerto Rican)**
CaribWr-1979
EncWL-1981
OxSpan-1978

Transcendentalist Group

**Matsas, Alexandros 1911-1969
(Greek)**
ClDMEuL-1980

Generation of 1930

**Matthews, Brander 1852-1929
(American)**
BenReEncy-1987
OxAm-1983
OxAmThe-1984
OxThe-1983
PengAm-1971

Local Color School

**Matuszewski, Ignacy 1858-1919
(Polish)**
ClDMEuL-1980

Young Poland/Mloda Polska

Matute, Ana María 1925-
(Spanish)
BenReEncy-1987
CasWL-1973
ClDMEuL-1980
EncWL-1981
GdMWL-1985
OxSpan-1978
PengEur-1969

Turia Group

Maugham, W(illiam) Somerset 1874-
1965 (English)
BenReEncy-1987
CamGLE-1988
CasWL-1973
CEnMWL-1963
EncWL-1981
GdMWL-1985
LongCTCL-1975
McGWD-1984
OxAmThe-1984
OxEng-1985
OxThe-1983
PengEng-1971

Georgian Literature
Modernism
Naturalism
Realism

Maupassant, Guy de 1850-1893
(French)
BenReEncy-1987
CasWL-1973
EncWL-1981
OxEng-1985
OxFr-1959
PengEur-1969
RCom-1973

Naturalism
Realism

Mauriac, Claude 1914-   **(French)**
BenReEncy-1987
CasWL-1973
ClDMEuL-1980
EncWL-1981
GdMWL-1985

New Novel/Nouveau Roman
New Wave/Nouvelle Vague

Mauriac, François 1885-1970
(French)
BenReEncy-1987
CasWL-1973
CEnMWL-1963
ClDMEuL-1980
EncWL-1981
GdMWL-1985
LongCTCL-1975
McGWD-1984
OxEng-1985
OxFr-1959
PengEur-1969
RCom-1973

Nouvelle Revue Française
Group

Maurras, Charles 1868-1952
(French)
BenReEncy-1987
CasWL-1973
ClDMEuL-1980
EncWL-1981
GdMWL-1985
OxFr-1959
PengEur-1969

École Romane

Mayakovsky, Vladimir
Vladimirovich 1893-1930
(Russian)
BenReEncy-1987
CasWL-1973

CEnMWL-1963
ClDMEuL-1980
EncWL-1981
GdMWL-1985
LongCTCL-1975
McGWD-1984
OxEng-1985
OxThe-1983
PengEur-1969
PrEncyPP-1974

Cubo-Futurism
LEF
Socialist Realism

Mayer, Hans 1907-   (German)
HarDMT-1988

Group 47/Gruppe 47

**Mayröcker, Friederike 1924-
(Austrian)**
ClDMEuL-1980
OxGer-1986

Vienna Group/Wiener Gruppe

**al-Mazini, Ibrahim 'Abdalqadir
1890-1949 (Egyptian)**
CasWL-1973
DOrLit-1974
EncWL-1981

Diwan School of Poets

Mehren, Stein 1935-   (Norwegian)
ClDMEuL-1980
EncWL-1981
GdMWL-1985

Symbolic Modernism

**Mehring, Walter 1896-1981
(German)**
EncWL-1981

OxGer-1986
PengEur-1969

Dadaism

Mehta, Nares n.d. (Indian)
DOrLit-1974

New Poetry Movement/Nayi
Kavita

**Meireles, Cecília 1901-1964
(Brazilian)**
CasWL-1973
EncWL-1981
GdMWL-1985
PengAm-1971
PrEncyPP-1974

Festa Group
Modernism

Mejía, Feliciano n.d. (Peruvian)
OxSpan-1978

Estos 13/Hora Cero

**Melo e Castro, E.M. de 1932-
(Portuguese)**
EncWL-1981
GdMWL-1985

Poetry 61 Movement

Meltzer, David 1937-   (American)
EncWL-1981
OxAm-1983
PengAm-1971

Beat Generation

Mendelsohn, Erich 1887-1953 (German)
HarDMT-1988

Expressionism

Mendes, Murilo 1902- (Brazilian)
EncWL-1981
GdMWL-1985
PengAm-1971
PrEncyPP-1974

Modernism

Merezhkovsky, Dmitry Sergeyevich 1865-1941 (Russian)
BenReEncy-1987
CasWL-1973
ClDMEuL-1980
EncWL-1981
GdMWL-1985
LongCTCL-1975
PengEur-1969

Symbolism

Meriluoto, Aila 1924- (Finnish)
ClDMEuL-1980
EncWL-1981
PengEur-1969

Modernism

Merleau-Ponty, Maurice 1908-1961 (French)
BenReEncy-1987
ClDMEuL-1980
EncWL-1981
OxEng-1985
OxFr-1959

Existentialism

Merrill, Stuart 1863-1915 (American-born French)
CasWL-1973
ClDMEuL-1980
EncWL-1981
GdMWL-1985
OxAm-1983
OxFr-1959
PengAm-1971
PengEur-1969
PrEncyPP-1974

Symbolism

Mesa y Rosales, Enrique de 1878-1929 (Spanish)
CasWL-1973
ClDMEuL-1980
OxSpan-1978

Modernismo

Mesens, E.L.T. 1903-1970 (Belgian)
ClDMEuL-1980
EncWL-1981

Surrealism

Metzinger, Jean 1883-1956 (French)
HarDMT-1988

Cubism

Meyerhold, Vsevolod Emilievich 1874-1940 (Russian)
BenReEncy-1987
EncWL-1981
McGWD-1984
OxThe-1983

Agitprop Theater
Constructivism
Moscow Art Theater

Michaux, Henri 1899-1984 (Belgian-born French)
BenReEncy-1987
CasWL-1973
CEnMWL-1963
ClDMEuL-1980
EncWL-1981
GdMWL-1985
OxFr-1959
PengEur-1969

Surrealism

Micheli, Silvio 1911-   (Italian)
EncWL-1981

Neorealism

Micinski, Tadeusz 1873-1918 (Polish)
CasWL-1973
ClDMEuL-1980
GdMWL-1985

Young Poland/Mloda Polska

Mieses Burgos, Franklin 1907- (Dominican Republican)
CaribWr-1979
EncWL-1981

Surprised Poetry Movement

Miezelaitis, Eduardas 1919- (Lithuanian)
EncWL-1981
GdMWL-1985
PrEncyPP-1974

Socialist Realism

Miguéis, José Rodrigues 1901- (Portuguese)
ClDMEuL-1980

EncWL-1981

Seara Nova Group

Mikulásek, Oldrich 1910-   (Czech)
ClDMEuL-1980

Group 42

Miles, John 1938-   (South African)
EncWL-1981

The Sestigers

Milev, Geo(rge) 1895-1925 (Bulgarian)
CasWL-1973
EncWL-1981
GdMWL-1985

Symbolism

Millay, Edna St. Vincent 1892-1950 (American)
BenReEncy-1987
CamGLE-1988
CasWL-1973
CEnMWL-1963
EncWL-1981
GdMWL-1985
LongCTCL-1975
OxAm-1983
OxAmThe-1984
OxEng-1985
PengAm-1971

Provincetown Players

Miller, Henry 1891-1980 (American)
BenReEncy-1987
CamGLE-1988
CasWL-1973
CEnMWL-1963
EncWL-1981
GdMWL-1985

LongCTCL-1975
OxAm-1983
OxEng-1985
PengAm-1971

Beat Generation
Surrealism

Miller, J. Hillis 1928-   (American)
CamGLE-1988
EncWL-1981
PrEncyPP-1974

Deconstructionism
Geneva School of Critics
Yale School of Critics

**Miller, Joachin 1837-1913
(American)**
BenReEncy-1987
CamGLE-1988
CasWL-1973
LongCTCL-1975
OxAm-1983
OxAmThe-1984
PengAm-1971

Local Color School

Millett, Kate 1934-   (American)
OxAm-1983

Feminist Criticism

Milligan, Alice 1866-1953 (Irish)
OxThe-1983

Irish Literary Theater

**Milosz, Czeslaw 1911-
(Lithuanian-born Polish)**
BenReEncy-1987
CasWL-1973
ClDMEuL-1980
EncWL-1981

GdMWL-1985
OxAm-1983
OxEng-1985
PengEur-1969
PrEncyPP-1974

Cracow Avant-Garde
Zagary Group

**Minkoff, Nokhum Borekh 1898-
1958 (Yiddish-speaking
American)**
ClDMEuL-1980
EncWL-1981
GdMWL-1985
PrEncyPP-1974

Introspectivists Movement/
Inzikh

Minovi, M. n.d. (Iranian)
DOrLit-1974

Rab'e Group

**Minulescu, Ion 1881-1944
(Romanian)**
CasWL-1973
ClDMEuL-1980
EncWL-1981
McGWD-1984

Symbolism

Miraji 1913-1950 (Pakistani)
EncWL-1981

Assembly of the Men of Good
Taste

Miró, Gabriel 1879-1930 (Spanish)
CasWL-1973
CEnMWL-1963
ClDMEuL-1980
EncWL-1981

GdMWL-1985
PengEur-1969

Generation of 1927/Generación
del 1927

Miró, Joan 1893-1983 (Spanish)
BenReEncy-1987
ClDMEuL-1980
EncWL-1981
OxEng-1985
RCom-1973

Surrealism

Miron, Gaston 1928-   (Canadian)
CasWL-1973
EncWL-1981
OxCan-1983

Hexagone Group

**Miskinis, Antanas 1905-
(Lithuanian)**
EncWL-1981
PrEncyPP-1974

Socialist Realism

**Mistral, Frédéric 1830-1914
(Provençal-speaking French)**
BenReEncy-1987
CasWL-1973
ClDMEuL-1980
EncWL-1981
GdMWL-1985
OxEng-1985
OxFr-1959
PengEur-1969
PrEncyPP-1974

Félibrige Movement

Mitchell, Adrian 1932-   (English)
CamGLE-1988

OxEng-1985

Underground Poetry

**Mizuhara Shuoshi 1892-
(Japanese)**
DOrLit-1974

Hototogisu Poets

**Mlodozeniec, Stanislaw 1895-1959
(Polish)**
ClDMEuL-1980
PengEur-1969

Futurism

**Moberg, Vilhelm 1898-1973
(Swedish)**
BenReEncy-1987
CasWL-1973
ClDMEuL-1980
EncWL-1981
GdMWL-1985
OxThe-1983
PengEur-1969

Proletarian Writers/
Arbetardiktare

Mockel, Albert 1866-1945 (Belgian)
CasWL-1973
ClDMEuL-1980
GdMWL-1985
OxFr-1959

Symbolism

**Modersohn-Becker, Paula 1876-
1953 (German)**
OxGer-1986

Expressionism

Moeller, Philip 1880-1958
(American)
  OxAm-1983
  OxAmThe-1984

  Theater Guild
  Washington Square Players

Moens, Wies 1898-   **(Belgian)**
  CasWL-1973
  ClDMEuL-1980
  EncWL-1981

  Ruimte Group

Moers, Ellen 1928-1979 (American)
  OxEng-1985

  Feminist Criticism

Moldova, György 1934-
(Hungarian)
  ClDMEuL-1980
  EncWL-1981

  Generation of 1955

Molinari, Ricardo E. 1898-
(Argentine)
  EncWL-1981
  OxSpan-1978

  Florida Group

Mon, Franz 1926-   **(German)**
  CasWL-1973
  ClDMEuL-1980
  EncWL-1981
  OxGer-1986

  Concrete Poetry

Monro, H(arold) E. 1879-1932
(English)
  BenReEncy-1987

  CamGLE-1988
  GdMWL-1985
  LongCTCL-1975
  OxEng-1985
  PengEng-1971
  PrEncyPP-1974

  Georgian Literature

Monroe, Harriet 1860-1936
(American)
  BenReEncy-1987
  CamGLE-1988
  CasWL-1973
  EncWL-1981
  LongCTCL-1975
  OxAm-1983
  OxEng-1985
  PengAm-1971

  Chicago Group/Renaissance
  Poetry

Montale, Eugenio 1896-1981
(Italian)
  BenReEncy-1987
  CasWL-1973
  CEnMWL-1963
  ClDMEuL-1980
  EncWL-1981
  GdMWL-1985
  OxEng-1985
  PengEur-1969
  PrEncyPP-1974

  Crepuscolarismo
  Hermeticism/Poesia Ermetica
  Solaria Group

Monteiro, Adolfo Casais 1908-1972
(Portuguese)
  ClDMEuL-1980
  EncWL-1981

PrEncyPP-1974

Presencistas Group

Montgomery, Lucy Maud 1874-1942 (Canadian)
CamGLE-1988
OxCan-1983

Local Color School

Mooney, Ria 1903-1973 (Irish)
OxThe-1983

Abbey Theater

Moore, G(eorge) E(dward) 1873-1958 (English)
BenReEncy-1987
CamGLE-1988
EncWL-1981
LongCTCL-1975
OxEng-1985

Bloomsbury Group

Moore, George Augustus 1852-1933 (Irish)
BenReEncy-1987
CamGLE-1988
CasWL-1973
EncWL-1981
LongCTCL-1975
McGWD-1984
OxEng-1985
OxThe-1983
PengEng-1971
PrEncyPP-1974
RCom-1973

Irish Literary Theater
Irish Renaissance
Naturalism
Realism

Moore, Marianne 1887-1972 (American)
CamGLE-1988
CEnMWL-1963
EncWL-1981
GdMWL-1985
LongCTCL-1975
OxAm-1983
OxEng-1985
PengAm-1971

Poetry

Moore, Merrill 1903-1957 (American)
BenReEncy-1987
GdMWL-1985
OxAm-1983
PengAm-1971

The Fugitives/Agrarians

Moore, Nicholas 1918- (English)
HarDMT-1988

New Apocalypse

Mora, Tulio n.d. (Peruvian)
OxSpan-1978

Estos 13/Hora Cero

Morais, Vinícius de 1913-1980 (Brazilian)
EncWL-1981
PengAm-1971
PrEncyPP-1974

Modernism

Morante, Elsa 1918-1985 (Italian)
BenReEncy-1987
CEnMWL-1963
ClDMEuL-1980
EncWL-1981

GdMWL-1985
PengEur-1969

Neorealism

Moravia, Alberto 1907-1990
(Italian)
BenReEncy-1987
CasWL-1973
CEnMWL-1963
ClDMEuL-1980
EncWL-1981
GdMWL-1985
LongCTCL-1975
McGWD-1984
OxEng-1985
PengEur-1969

Neorealism

More, Paul Elmer 1864-1937
(American)
CasWL-1973
EncWL-1981
LongCTCL-1975
OxAm-1983
PengAm-1971
PrEncyPP-1974

New Humanism

Moréas, Jean (pseud. of Yannis
Papadiamantopoulos) 1856-1910
(Greek-born French)
CasWL-1973
ClDMEuL-1980
EncWL-1981
GdMWL-1985
OxFr-1959
PengEur-1969
PrEncyPP-1974

École Romane
Symbolism

Moreno, Fulgencio R. 1872-1935
(Paraguayan)
EncWL-1981

Generation of 1900

Moreno Jiménes, Domingo 1894-
(Dominican Republican)
CaribWr-1979

Posthumanismo

Moreno Villa, José 1887-1955
(Spanish)
ClDMEuL-1980
OxSpan-1978

Surrealism

Moretti, Marino 1885-1979 (Italian)
CasWL-1973
ClDMEuL-1980
GdMWL-1985
PengEur-1969

Crepuscolarismo

Morgan, Edwin 1920-   (Scottish)
CasWL-1973
EncWL-1981
OxEng-1985

Concrete Poetry

Morgan, Emanuel

See **Witter Bynner**

Morgan, Robin 1941-   (American)
HandLit-1986

Feminist Criticism

Mori Ogai (pseud. of Mori Rintaro) 1862-1922 (Japanese)
BenReEncy-1987
CasWL-1973
DOrLit-1974
EncWL-1981
GdMWL-1985
PengCOAL-1969

Romanticism/Bungakkai

Móricz, Zsigmond 1879-1942 (Hungarian)
CasWL-1973
ClDMEuL-1980
EncWL-1981
GdMWL-1985
McGWD-1984
PengEur-1969

Nyugat Group

Mörike, Eduard 1804-1875 (German)
BenReEncy-1987
CasWL-1973
EncWL-1981
OxGer-1986
PengEur-1969
PrEncyPP-1974
RCom-1973

Realism

Moro, César (pseud. of Alfredo César Quíspez Asín) 1903-1956 (Peruvian)
BenReEncy-1987
EncWL-1981
OxSpan-1978
PengAm-1971

Surrealism

Morrell, Ottoline 1873-1938 (English)
CamGLE-1988
EncWL-1981
OxEng-1985

Bloomsbury Group

Morrison, Arthur 1863-1945 (English)
CamGLE-1988
LongCTCL-1975
OxEng-1985

Realism

Morselli, Ercole Luigi 1882-1921 (Italian)
OxThe-1983

Crepuscolarismo

Mosendz, Leonid 1897-1948 (Ukrainian)
ClDMEuL-1980
EncWL-1981

Visnyk

Moskvin, Ivan Mikhailovich 1874-1946 (Russian)
OxThe-1983

Moscow Art Theater

Mota, Mauro 1912-   (Brazilian)
EncWL-1981

Generation of 1945

Mouw, Johan Andreas der n.d. (Dutch)
ClDMEuL-1980

De Beweging

Mozhayev, Boris Andreyevich 1923-
 (Russian)
ClDMEuL-1980
GdMWL-1985

Village Prose

Mrozek, Slawomir 1930-   (Polish)
BenReEncy-1987
CasWL-1973
ClDMEuL-1980
EncWL-1981
GdMWL-1985
McGWD-1984
OxThe-1983
PengEur-1969

Theater of the Absurd

Mtshali, Oswald Mbuyiseni 1940-
 (South African)
CamGLE-1988
EncWL-1981

Black Consciousness Movement

Müftüoglu, Ahmet Hikmet 1870-
1927 (Turkish)
ClDMEuL-1980

National Literature Movement/
Millî Edebiyat

Mukarovsky, Jan 1891-1975 (Czech)
ClDMEuL-1980
EncWL-1981

Prague Linguistic Circle

Muktibodh, Gajanan Madhav n.d.
 (Indian)
DOrLit-1974

New Poetry Movement/Nayi
Kavita

Murakami Kijo 1865-1938
 (Japanese)
DOrLit-1974

Hototogisu Poets

Murfree, Mary Noailles 1850-1922
 (American)
BenReEncy-1987
OxAm-1983

Local Color School

Murn-Aleksandrov, Josip 1879-
1901 (Slovene-speaking
Yugoslavian)
ClDMEuL-1980
EncWL-1981

Moderna

Murray, Thomas Cornelius 1873-
1959 (Irish)
CamGLE-1988
LongCTCL-1975

Abbey Theater

Murriagui, Alfonso 1930-
 (Ecuadorian)
OxSpan-1978

Grupo Tzántzico

Musgrave, Susan 1951-
 (American-born Canadian)
OxCan-1983

Tish Group

Mushanokoji Saneatsu 1885-
 (Japanese)
CasWL-1973
DOrLit-1974
EncWL-1981

GdMWL-1985
PengCOAL-1969

I-Novel/Watakushi shosetsu
White Birch School/Shirakaba-
ha

**Müsrepov, Ghabit Makhmud-ulï
1902-   (Kazakh)**
DOrLit-1974
EncWL-1981

Socialist Realism

**Mussche, Achilles 1896-
(Belgian)**

CIDMEuL-1980

Ruimte Group

**Mustapää, P. (pseud. of Martti
Haavio) 1899-   (Finnish)**
GdMWL-1985
PengEur-1969
PrEncyPP-1974

Flame Bearers Group/
Tulenkantajat

Mykolaitis, Vincas

See **Putinas**

N

Nadir, Moyshe (pseud. of Isaac
Reis) 1885-1943 (Yiddish-
speaking American)
ClDMEuL-1980
EncWL-1981

Young Ones/Die Yunge

Nadiradse, K. n.d. (Georgian)
PrEncyPP-1974

Blue Horns Group/Tsispheri
q'antesbi

Nagarjun (pseud. of Vaidyanath
Misra) 1911-   (Indian)
DOrLit-1974
EncWL-1981

Realism/Pragati-vada

Nagy, Ágnes Nemes n.d.
(Hungarian)
ClDMEuL-1980

Ujhold Group

Nagys, Henrikas 1920-
(Lithuanian)
ClDMEuL-1980

Earth Movement

Na'ima, Mikha'il 1889-(?)
(Lebanese-born American)
CasWL-1973

DOrLit-1974
EncWL-1981

Society of the Pen

Nájar, Jorge n.d. (Peruvian)
OxSpan-1978

Estos 13/Hora Cero

Naji, Ibrahim 1893-1953 (Egyptian)
CasWL-1973
DOrLit-1974
EncWL-1981

Apollo School of Poets

Nakamura Kusatao 1901-
(Japanese)
DOrLit-1974

Hototogisu Poets

Nakamura Shin'ichiro 1918-
(Japanese)
DOrLit-1974

Matinée Poétique

Nalkowska, Zofia 1884-1954
(Polish)
CasWL-1973
ClDMEuL-1980
EncWL-1981

GdMWL-1985

Young Poland/Mloda Polska

**Namora, Fernando 1919-1989
(Portuguese)**
ClDMEuL-1980
EncWL-1981
GdMWL-1985

Neorealism

Nandino, Elías n.d. (Mexican)
OxSpan-1978

Contemporaries/
Contemporáneos

**Napierski, Stefan 1899-1940
(Polish)**
ClDMEuL-1980

Skamander Group

**Navarro Luna, Manuel 1894-
(Cuban)**
CaribWr-1979

Manzanillo Group

**Naydus, Leyb 1890-1918 (Yiddish-
speaking American)**
EncWL-1981

Young Ones/Die Yunge

**Nayir, Yasar Nabi 1908-
(Turkish)**
ClDMEuL-1980
DOrLit-1974

Seven Torches/Yedi Mes'ale

**Nazor, Vladimir 1876-1949
(Croatian)**
ClDMEuL-1980
EncWL-1981
GdMWL-1985
PengEur-1969

Moderna

**Negoitescu, Ion 1921-
(Romanian)**
EncWL-1981

Sibiu Group

Negri, Ada 1870-1945 (Italian)
CasWL-1973
EncWL-1981
PengEur-1969

Verismo

Neher, Caspar 1897-1962 (German)
OxGer-1986
OxThe-1983

Berlin Ensemble/Berliner
Ensemble

**Nelligan, Émile 1879-1941
(Canadian)**
CasWL-1973
EncWL-1981
GdMWL-1985
OxCan-1983
PrEncyPP-1974

Literary School of Montreal/
École Littéraire de Montreal

**Nemésio, Vitorino 1901-1978
(Portuguese)**
ClDMEuL-1980

EncWL-1981

Presencistas Group

Németh, Andor n.d. (Hungarian)
ClDMEuL-1980

Today Group/*Ma*

**Németh, László 1901-1975
(Hungarian)**
ClDMEuL-1980
EncWL-1981
PengEur-1969

Populist Movement

**Nemirovich-Danchenko, Vladimir
Ivanovich 1858-1943 (Russian)**
BenReEncy-1987
CasWL-1973
ClDMEuL-1980
McGWD-1984
OxAmThe-1984
OxThe-1983

Moscow Art Theater

**Neris, Salomeja 1904-1945
(Lithuanian)**
CasWL-1973
ClDMEuL-1980
EncWL-1981
GdMWL-1985
PrEncyPP-1974

Socialist Realism
Third Front Movement/Trecias
    Frontas

**Neruda, Pablo (pseud. of Neftalí
Reyes Basualto) 1904-1973
(Chilean)**
BenReEncy-1987
CasWL-1973

CEnMWL-1963
EncWL-1981
GdMWL-1985
McGWD-1984
OxEng-1985
OxSpan-1978
PengAm-1971

Neoromanticism/Neuromantik
Surrealism

Nervo, Amado 1870-1919 (Mexican)
BenReEncy-1987
CasWL-1973
EncWL-1981
OxSpan-1978
PengAm-1971
PrEncyPP-1974

Modernismo

**Neto, António Agostinho 1922-1979
(Angolan)**
EncWL-1981
PengCOAL-1969

Association of Angola's Native
    Sons

Neuhuys, Paul 1897-   (Belgian)
ClDMEuL-1980
EncWL-1981

Dadaism
Surrealism

**Nevinson, Christopher 1889-1946
(English)**
OxEng-1985

Vorticism

303

**Newman, Barnett 1905-1970
(American)**
HarDMT-1988

New York School

**Nexo, Martin Andersen 1869-1954
(Danish)**
CasWL-1973
ClDMEuL-1980
EncWL-1981
PengEur-1969

Socialist Realism

Nezval, Vítezslav 1900-1958 (Czech)
BenReEncy-1987
CasWL-1973
ClDMEuL-1980
EncWL-1981
GdMWL-1985
McGWD-1984
PengEur-1969
PrEncyPP-1974

Nine Powers Group/Devêtsil
Poeticism
Surrealism

**Nhât-Linh (pseud. of Nguyen
Tuong-Tam) 1906-1963
(Vietnamese)**
CasWL-1973
DOrLit-1974
EncWL-1981

Ngày nay Group
Self-Reliant Group
Tu'Luc School

**Niang, Lamine 1928-
(Senegalese)**
EncWL-1981

Négritude

**Nichol, B(arrie) P(hillip) 1944-
(Canadian)**
CamGLE-1988
OxCan-1983

Four Horsemen

**Niedecker, Lorine 1903-1970
(American)**
PrEncyPP-1974

Objectivism

Niedra, Aida 1898-1972 (Latvian)
EncWL-1981

Realism

Nieri, Ildefonso 1853-1920 (Italian)
ClDMEuL-1980

Verismo

**Nieuwenhuys, Constant 1920-
(Dutch)**
HarDMT-1988

Cobra

**Nijhoff, Martinus 1894-1953
(Dutch)**
CasWL-1973
ClDMEuL-1980
EncWL-1981
GdMWL-1985
PengEur-1969

De Beweging
Het Getij

**Nikitin, Nikolay Nikolayevich 1895-
1963 (Russian)**
ClDMEuL-1980

Serapion Brotherhood

Nin, Anaïs 1903-1977 (French-born American)
BenReEncy-1987
CamGLE-1988
EncWL-1981
OxAm-1983
PengAm-1971

Surrealism

Nirala, S.T. 1898-1961 (Indian)
DOrLit-1974
EncWL-1981
PrEncyPP-1974

Realism/Pragati-vada
Romanticism/Chhaya-vada

Nister, Der (pseud. of Pinkhes Kahanovitsh) 1884-1950 (Yiddish-speaking Ukrainian)
CasWL-1973
ClDMEuL-1980
EncWL-1981
GdMWL-1985

Kiev Group

Niven, Frederick 1878-1944 (Chilean-born Canadian)
OxCan-1983

Local Color School

Noailles, Comtesse Anna Mathieu de 1876-1933 (French)
BenReEncy-1987
CasWL-1973
ClDMEuL-1980
EncWL-1981
OxFr-1959

Naturism/Naturisme

Nolasko, Sócrates 1884-(?) (Cuban)
CaribWr-1979

Oriente Group

Nolde, Emil 1867-1956 (German)
BenReEncy-1987
OxGer-1986

Expressionism

Nora, Eugenio G. de 1923- (Spanish)
GdMWL-1985
OxSpan-1978

Grupo Espadaña

Nordström, Ludvig Anshelm 1882-1942 (Swedish)
CasWL-1973
ClDMEuL-1980
EncWL-1981
GdMWL-1985
PengEur-1969

Tiotalister

Norman, Frank 1930-1980 (English)
BenReEncy-1987

Naturalism
Theater Workshop

Norris, Frank 1870-1902 (American)
BenReEncy-1987
CamGLE-1988
CasWL-1973
EncWL-1981
GdMWL-1985
LongCTCL-1975
OxAm-1983
OxEng-1985
PengAm-1971

RCom-1973

Naturalism

**Nossack, Hans Erich 1901-1977
(German)**
ClDMEuL-1980
EncWL-1981
GdMWL-1985
OxGer-1986
PengEur-1969

Surrealism

Nougé, Paul 1895-1967 (Belgian)
ClDMEuL-1980
EncWL-1981

Surrealism

**Novo López, Salvador 1904-1974
(Mexican)**
CasWL-1973
EncWL-1981
GdMWL-1985
OxSpan-1978
PengAm-1971

Contemporaries/
Contemporáneos

**Novomesky, Ladislav (Laco) 1904-
1976 (Slovak-speaking Czech)**
CasWL-1973
ClDMEuL-1980
EncWL-1981
GdMWL-1985
PengEur-1969

DAV Group

**Nowaczynski, Adolf 1876-1944
(Polish)**
ClDMEuL-1980

Young Poland/Mloda Polska

Nowak, Tadeusz 1930- (Polish)
ClDMEuL-1980
EncWL-1981
GdMWL-1985

Wspólczesnosc Generation

**Nugroho Notosutanto n.d.
(Indonesian)**
PrEncyPP-1974

Generation of 1950

Nummi, Lassi 1928- (Finnish)
ClDMEuL-1980

Modernism

Nusinov, Isak 1889-1950 (Russian)
EncWL-1981

Socialist Realism

Nuttall, Jeff 1933- (English)
OxEng-1985

Underground Poetry

Nwana, Peter n.d. (Nigerian)
EncWL-1981

Onitsha Novels/Chapbooks

**Nygard, Olav 1884-1924
(Norwegian)**
ClDMEuL-1980
EncWL-1981

Generation of 1905

Earth Movement

Nyka-Niliunas, Alfonsas (pseud. of Alfonsas Cipkus) 1920- (Lithuanian)
CIDMEuL-1980
EncWL-1981

Nzuji, Clémentine 1944-　(Zairian)
EncWL-1981

Pléiade du Congo Group

O

Obrestad, Tor 1938-   (Norwegian)
ClDMEuL-1980
EncWL-1981

Profil Group

O'Brien, Flann 1911-1966 (Irish)
BenReEncy-1987
CamGLE-1988
CasWL-1973
EncWL-1981
GdMWL-1985
LongCTCL-1975
OxEng-1985

Modernism

Obstfelder, Sigbjorn 1866-1900 (Norwegian)
CasWL-1973
ClDMEuL-1980
GdMWL-1985
PengEur-1969

Neoromanticism

O'Casey, Sean 1880-1964 (Irish)
BenReEncy-1987
CamGLE-1988
CasWL-1973
CEnMWL-1963
EncWL-1981
GdMWL-1985
LongCTCL-1975
McGWD-1984
OxAmThe-1984

OxEng-1985
OxThe-1983
PengEng-1971
RCom-1973

Abbey Theater
Irish Renaissance
Modernism
Realism
Symbolism

O'Connor, Frank (pseud. of Michael O'Donovan) 1903-1966 (Irish)
BenReEncy-1987
CamGLE-1988
CasWL-1973
LongCTCL-1975
OxEng-1985
PengEng-1971

Abbey Theater
Irish Renaissance

Odets, Clifford 1906-1963 (American)
BenReEncy-1987
CamGLE-1988
CasWL-1973
CEnMWL-1963
EncWL-1981
GdMWL-1985
LongCTCL-1975
McGWD-1984
OxAm-1983
OxAmThe-1984

OxEng-1985
OxThe-1983
PengAm-1971

Group Theater
Proletarian Literature
Theater Guild

O'Faoláin, Sean 1900-   (Irish)
BenReEncy-1987
CamGLE-1988
CasWL-1973
EncWL-1981
GdMWL-1985
LongCTCL-1975
OxEng-1985
PengEng-1971

Irish Renaissance

O'Flaherty, Liam 1896-1984 (Irish)
BenReEncy-1987
CamGLE-1988
CasWL-1973
EncWL-1981
GdMWL-1985
LongCTCL-1975
OxEng-1985
PengEng-1971

Irish Renaissance

O'Grady, Standish 1846-1928 (Irish)
CamGLE-1988
CasWL-1973
OxEng-1985
PengEng-1971

Irish Renaissance

**Ogrizovic, Milan 1877-1923
(Croatian-speaking Yugoslavian)**
ClDMEuL-1980

Moderna

Ogunde, Hubert 1916-   (Nigerian)
EncWL-1981
McGWD-1984
PengCOAL-1969

Yoruba Opera

**Ogunmola, E. Kola 1925-1973
(Nigerian)**
EncWL-1981
McGWD-1984
PengCOAL-1969

Yoruba Opera

**O'Hara, Frank 1926-1966
(American)**
BenReEncy-1987
CamGLE-1988
EncWL-1981
GdMWL-1985
OxAm-1983
PengAm-1971
PrEncyPP-1974

New York School

Okland, Einar 1940-   (Norwegian)
ClDMEuL-1980
EncWL-1981

Profil Group

Oks, Jaan 1884-1918 (Estonian)
ClDMEuL-1980
EncWL-1981
GdMWL-1985

Young Estonia Group

Olbracht, Ivan 1882-1952 (Czech)
CasWL-1973
ClDMEuL-1980
EncWL-1981
GdMWL-1985

PengEur-1969

Socialist Realism

**O'Leary, Juan E. 1879-1969
(Paraguayan)**
EncWL-1981
OxSpan-1978

Generation of 1900

**Oles, Oleksander (pseud. of
Oleksander Kandyba) 1878-1944
(Ukrainian)**
ClDMEuL-1980
EncWL-1981
PengEur-1969

Ukrainian Home Group

**Olesha, Yury Karlovich 1899-1960
(Russian)**
BenReEncy-1987
CasWL-1973
ClDMEuL-1980
EncWL-1981
GdMWL-1985
PengEur-1969

Modernism

**Olivares Figueroa, Rafael 1893-1972
(Venezuelan)**
EncWL-1981

Viernes Group

**Oliveira, Carlos de 1921-1981
(Portuguese)**
ClDMEuL-1980
EncWL-1981

Neorealism

**Olkhivsky, Borys 1908-1944
(Ukrainian)**
ClDMEuL-1980

My Group

**Oller y Moragues, Narcís 1846-1930
(Catalan-speaking Spanish)**
CasWL-1973
ClDMEuL-1980
EncWL-1981
GdMWL-1985
OxSpan-1978

Realism

Ollier, Claude 1922-   (French)
ClDMEuL-1980
EncWL-1981
GdMWL-1985

New Novel/Nouveau Roman

Olmi, Ermanno 1931-   (Italian)
OxEng-1985

Neorealism

**Ölöksüöyebis, Bylatan 1893-1939
(Yakut)**
EncWL-1981

Socialist Realism

**Olson, Charles 1910-1970
(American)**
BenReEncy-1987
CamGLE-1988
CasWL-1973
EncWL-1981
GdMWL-1985
OxAm-1983
OxEng-1985
PengAm-1971

PrEncyPP-1974

Black Mountain Poets

Olson, Elder 1909- (American)
EncWL-1981
OxAm-1983
PengAm-1971
PrEncyPP-1974

Chicago Critics

Olsson, Hagar 1893-1978 (Finnish)
CasWL-1973
ClDMEuL-1980
EncWL-1981
GdMWL-1985
McGWD-1984
PengEur-1969

Swedish-Finnish Modernists

Olzhych, Oleh (pseud. of Oleh Kandyba) 1909-1944 (Ukrainian)
ClDMEuL-1980
EncWL-1981

Visnyk

Ömer Seyfeddin 1884-1920 (Turkish)
CasWL-1973
ClDMEuL-1980
DOrLit-1974
EncWL-1981
GdMWL-1985

Genç Kalemler

O'Neill, Alexandre 1924- (Portuguese)
ClDMEuL-1980
EncWL-1981

GdMWL-1985

Surrealism

O'Neill, Eugene 1888-1953 (American)
BenReEncy-1987
CamGLE-1988
CasWL-1973
CEnMWL-1963
EncWL-1981
GdMWL-1985
LongCTCL-1975
McGWD-1984
OxAm-1983
OxAmThe-1984
OxEng-1985
OxThe-1983
PengAm-1971
PrEncyPP-1974
RCom-1973

Expressionism
Group Theater
Naturalism
Provincetown Players
Realism
Theater Guild

Onetti, Juan Carlos 1909- (Uruguayan)
BenReEncy-1987
CasWL-1973
EncWL-1981
GdMWL-1985
OxSpan-1978
PengAm-1971

Generation of 1945

Onís y Sánchez, Federico de 1886- (?) (Spanish)
OxSpan-1978

Generation of 1898/Generación
del 1898

Onofri, Arturo 1885-1928 (Italian)
  CasWL-1973
  ClDMEuL-1980
  GdMWL-1985

  Hermeticism/Poesia Ermetica

Opatoshu, Josef 1886-1954
  (Yiddish-speaking American)
  CasWL-1973
  ClDMEuL-1980
  EncWL-1981
  GdMWL-1985
  PengEur-1969

  Young Ones/Die Yunge

Oppen, George 1908-1984
  (American)
  BenReEncy-1987
  CamGLE-1988
  GdMWL-1985
  OxAm-1983
  PengAm-1971
  PrEncyPP-1974

  Objectivism

Oppenheimer, Joel 1930-1988
  (American)
  EncWL-1981
  PengAm-1971
  PrEncyPP-1974

  Black Mountain Poets

Opperman, Diederik Johannes 1914-
  (South African)
  CasWL-1973
  EncWL-1981
  GdMWL-1985
  PengCOAL-1969

PrEncyPP-1974

The Dertigers

Oras, Ants 1900-   (Estonian)
  ClDMEuL-1980
  EncWL-1981

  Soothsayers Movement/
    Arbujad

Ordóñez, Antonio n.d. (Ecuadorian)
  OxSpan-1978

  Grupo Tzántzico

Ordubady, Mamed Said 1872-1950
  (Azerbaijani)
  EncWL-1981
  GdMWL-1985

  Socialist Realism

Orhon, Orhan Seyfi 1890-1972
  (Turkish)
  ClDMEuL-1980
  EncWL-1981

  Syllabists/Hececiler

Orjasæter, Tore 1886-1968
  (Norwegian)
  CasWL-1973
  ClDMEuL-1980
  EncWL-1981
  GdMWL-1985
  McGWD-1984
  OxThe-1983

  Generation of 1905

Orkan, Wladyslaw 1875-1930
  (Polish)
  CasWL-1973
  ClDMEuL-1980

EncWL-1981
GdMWL-1985

Young Poland/Mloda Polska
Zdroj Group

Ornsbo, Jess 1932-   (Danish)
  ClDMEuL-1980
  EncWL-1981
  McGWD-1984

  Modernism

Orpaz, Yitzhak 1923-   (Russian-born Israeli)
  CasWL-1973
  ClDMEuL-1980

  Metarealism

Ors y Rovira, Eugenio d' 1882-1954 (Spanish)
  CasWL-1973
  ClDMEuL-1980
  EncWL-1981
  GdMWL-1985
  OxSpan-1978

  Noucentismo

Ortaç, Yusuf Ziya 1895-1967 (Turkish)
  ClDMEuL-1980
  EncWL-1981

  Syllabists/Hececiler

Ortega, Julio 1942-   (Peruvian)
  OxSpan-1978

  Los Nuevos

Ortega Munilla, José 1856-1922 (Spanish)
  CasWL-1973

EncWL-1981
OxSpan-1978

Generation of 1898/Generación
  del 1898

Ortega y Gasset, José 1883-1955 (Spanish)
  BenReEncy-1987
  CasWL-1973
  CEnMWL-1963
  ClDMEuL-1980
  EncWL-1981
  GdMWL-1985
  LongCTCL-1975
  OxEng-1985
  OxSpan-1978
  PengEur-1969

  Existentialism
  Generation of 1898/Generación
    del 1898
  Generation of 1927/Generación
    del 1927
  Novecentismo

Ortese, Anna Maria 1915- (Italian)
  EncWL-1981
  GdMWL-1985

  Neorealism

Ortiz, Adalberto 1914- (Ecuadorian)
  EncWL-1981
  PengAm-1971
  OxSpan-1978

  Naturalism

Ortiz, Fernando 1881-1969 (Cuban)
  EncWL-1981

OxSpan-1978

Afro-Cubanism

**Ortiz de Montellano, Bernardo
1899-1949 (Mexican)**
OxSpan-1978

Contemporaries/
Contemporáneos

**Orzeszkowa, Eliza 1841-1910
(Polish)**
CasWL-1973
ClDMEuL-1980
EncWL-1981
GdMWL-1985
PengEur-1969

Realism
Warsaw Positivism

Osborne, John 1929-   (English)
BenReEncy-1987
CamGLE-1988
CasWL-1973
CEnMWL-1963
EncWL-1981
GdMWL-1985
LongCTCL-1975
McGWD-1984
OxAmThe-1984
OxEng-1985
OxThe-1983
PengEng-1971
RCom-1973

Angry Young Men
Kitchen Sink Drama

**Oshagan, Hagop 1883-1948
(Armenian)**
EncWL-1981

Mehian Group

Osipov, Petr N. 1900-   (Chuvash)
EncWL-1981

Socialist Realism

Óskar, Jón 1921-   (Icelandic)
EncWL-1981

Modernism

**Osmachka, Todos 1895-1962
(Ukrainian)**
EncWL-1981

Modernism

**Osmonov, Alïkul 1915-1950
(Kirgiz)**
EncWL-1981

Socialist Realism

**Ostaijen, Paul van 1896-1928
(Belgian)**
CasWL-1973
ClDMEuL-1980
EncWL-1981
GdMWL-1985
PengEur-1969

Expressionism
Ruimte Group

**Ostrovsky, Nikolay Alexeyevich
1904-1936 (Russian)**
BenReEncy-1987
CasWL-1973
ClDMEuL-1980
EncWL-1981
McGWD-1984

Socialist Realism

Osvát, Erno 1877-1929 (Hungarian)
ClDMEuL-1980

EncWL-1981

Nyugat Group

Oswald, Gösta 1926-1950 (Swedish)
ClDMEuL-1980

Poets of the Forties/
Fyrtiotalisterna

Otero, Blas de 1916-   (Spanish)
CasWL-1973
CEnMWL-1963
ClDMEuL-1980
EncWL-1981
GdMWL-1985
OxSpan-1978
PengEur-1969

Generation of 1936/Generación
del 1936
Grupo Espadaña

Otero Silva, Miguel 1908-
(Venezuelan)
EncWL-1981
OxSpan-1978

Generation of 1918

Otten, Karl 1889-1963 (German)
EncWL-1981

Expressionism

Ottieri, Ottiero 1896-   (Italian)
EncWL-1981
GdMWL-1985

Literature and Industry

Ottlik, Géza n.d. (Hungarian)
ClDMEuL-1980

Ujhold Group

Ouellette, Fernand 1930-
(Canadian)
OxCan-1983

Hexagone Group

Ovalle López, Werner n.d.
(Guatemalan)
OxSpan-1978

The Dawn Group/Grupo Saker
Ti

Ovechkin, Valentin Vladimirovich
1904-1968 (Russian)
CasWL-1973
ClDMEuL-1980

Village Prose

Owen, Alun 1926-   (Welsh)
McGWD-1984

Kitchen Sink Drama

Owen, Gilberto 1905-1952
(Mexican)
OxSpan-1978

Contemporaries/
Contemporáneos

Owen, Wilfred 1893-1918 (English)
BenReEncy-1987
CamGLE-1988
CasWL-1973
CEnMWL-1963
EncWL-1981
GdMWL-1985
LongCTCL-1975
OxEng-1985
PengEng-1971

PrEncyPP-1974

Georgian Literature
Modernism

Ozaki Koyo 1868-1903 (Japanese)
CasWL-1973
DOrLit-1974
EncWL-1981

Friends of the Inkstone/
　Ken'yusha

**Ozansoy, Halit Fahri 1891-1971
(Turkish)**
CIDMEuL-1980
EncWL-1981

Syllabists/Hececiler

**Ozóg, Jan Boleslaw 1913-
(Polish)**
CIDMEuL-1980

Authenticism

P

Paap, Willem Anthony 1856-1923 (Dutch)
CasWL-1973
ClDMEuL-1980

Movement of the Eighties/
Beweging van Tachtig

Paavolainen, Olavi 1903-1964 (Finnish)
ClDMEuL-1980
EncWL-1981
PengEur-1969

Flame Bearers Group/
Tulenkantajat

Pachovsky, Vasyl 1878-1942 (Ukrainian)
ClDMEuL-1980
EncWL-1981

Young Muse Group/Moloda
Muza

Page, Thomas Nelson 1853-1922 (American)
BenReEncy-1987
CamGLE-1988
CasWL-1973
OxAm-1983
PengAm-1971

Local Color School

Pagliarini, Elio 1927-   (Italian)
ClDMEuL-1980
EncWL-1981

Group 63/Gruppo 63

Palamas, Kostis 1859-1943 (Greek)
BenReEncy-1987
CasWL-1973
ClDMEuL-1980
EncWL-1981
GdMWL-1985
McGWD-1984
PengEur-1969
PrEncyPP-1974

New School of Athens/Greek
Parnassians

Palazzeschi, Aldo (pseud. of Aldo Giurlani) 1885-1974 (Italian)
CasWL-1973
ClDMEuL-1980
EncWL-1981
GdMWL-1985
PengEur-1969

Crepuscolarismo
Futurism

Palencia, Oscar Arturo n.d. (Guatemalan)
OxSpan-1978

The Dawn Group/Grupo Saker
Ti

Palés Matos, Luis 1899-1959 (Puerto Rican)
CaribWr-1979
CasWL-1973
EncWL-1981
GdMWL-1985
OxSpan-1978
PengAm-1971
PrEncyPP-1974

Afro-Cubanism
Diepalismo
Modernismo
Negrismo

Palitzsch, Peter 1918-   (German)
OxThe-1983

Berlin Ensemble/Berliner
Ensemble

Palma, Clemente 1875-1946 (Peruvian)
EncWL-1981

Modernismo

Palma, Oscar Edmundo n.d. (Guatemalan)
OxSpan-1978

The Dawn Group/Grupo Saker
Ti

Pálsson, Gestur 1852-1891 (Icelandic)
ClDMEuL-1980

Realism
Vero Ani Group

Panagiotopoulos, Ioannis M. 1901- (Greek)
ClDMEuL-1980

Generation of 1930

Panchenko, P. n.d. (Byelorussian)
PrEncyPP-1974

Socialist Realism

Panedas, J. Rivas n.d. (Spanish)
OxSpan-1978

Ultraism/Ultraismo

Panero Torbado, Leopoldo 1909-1962 (Spanish)
BenReEncy-1987
CasWL-1973
ClDMEuL-1980
OxSpan-1978
PengEur-1969

Generation of 1936/Generación
del 1936

Panneton, Philippe 1895-1960 (French-speaking Canadian)
CasWL-1973
EncWL-1981
OxCan-1983

Literary School of Montreal/
École Littéraire de Montreal

Panova, Vera Fëdorovna 1905-1973 (Russian)
CasWL-1973
ClDMEuL-1980
EncWL-1981
McGWD-1984
PengEur-1969

Socialist Realism

**Pansaers, Clément 1885-1922
(Belgian)**
  ClDMEuL-1980
  EncWL-1981

  Dadaism

**Pant, Sumitranandan 1900-
(Indian)**
  DOrLit-1974
  EncWL-1981

  Realism/Pragati-vada
  Romanticism/Chhaya-vada

Pap, Károly n.d. (Hungarian)
  ClDMEuL-1980

  Populist Movement

**Papini, Giovanni 1881-1956
(Italian)**
  CasWL-1973
  CEnMWL-1963
  ClDMEuL-1980
  EncWL-1981
  GdMWL-1985
  LongCTCL-1975
  PengEur-1969
  PrEncyPP-1974

  Futurism

Pappas, Nikos 1906-   (Greek)
  ClDMEuL-1980

  Generation of 1930

Paquet, Alfons 1881-1944 (German)
  OxGer-1986

  Epic Theater/Episches Theater

**Pardo Bazán, Emilia 1852-1921
(Spanish)**
  BenReEncy-1987
  CasWL-1973
  ClDMEuL-1980
  EncWL-1981
  GdMWL-1985
  OxSpan-1978
  PengEur-1969

  Naturalism
  Realism

**Pareja Diezcanseco, Alfredo 1908-
(Ecuadorian)**
  EncWL-1981
  GdMWL-1985
  OxSpan-1978
  PengAm-1971

  Group of Guayaquil/Grupo de
  Guayaquil

**Parker, Gilbert 1862-1932
(Canadian)**
  BenReEncy-1987
  LongCTCL-1975
  OxCan-1983

  Local Color School

**Parland, Henry 1908-1930
(Swedish-speaking Finnish)**
  ClDMEuL-1980
  PrEncyPP-1974

  Swedish-Finnish Modernists

**Parland, Ralf 1914- (Swedish-
speaking Finnish)**
  PrEncyPP-1974

  Swedish-Finnish Modernists

Parronchi, Alessandro 1914-
(Italian)
    ClDMEuL-1980

    Hermeticism/Poesia Ermetica

Pascoaes, Joaquim Teixeira de
(pseud. of Joaquim Pereira
Teixeira de Vasconcelos) 1877-
1952 (Portuguese)
    CasWL-1973
    ClDMEuL-1980
    EncWL-1981
    GdMWL-1985
    PengEur-1969
    PrEncyPP-1974

    Portuguese Renascence
    Movement

Pascoli, Giovanni 1855-1912
(Italian)
    CasWL-1973
    ClDMEuL-1980
    EncWL-1981
    GdMWL-1985
    OxEng-1985
    PengEur-1969

    Crepuscolarismo

Pasolini, Pier Paolo 1922-1975
(Italian)
    BenReEncy-1987
    CasWL-1973
    ClDMEuL-1980
    EncWL-1981
    GdMWL-1985
    OxEng-1985
    PengEur-1969

    Neorealism

Pasternak, Boris Leonidovich 1890-
1960 (Russian)
    BenReEncy-1987
    CasWL-1973
    CEnMWL-1963
    ClDMEuL-1980
    EncWL-1981
    GdMWL-1985
    LongCTCL-1975
    OxEng-1985
    PengEur-1969
    RCom-1973

    Centrifuge
    Cubo-Futurism

Patchen, Kenneth 1911-1972
(American)
    CamGLE-1988
    EncWL-1981
    OxAm-1983
    OxEng-1985

    Jazz Poetry

Patock, Jan 1886-1940 (Kashubian-
speaking Polish)
    EncWL-1981

    Young Kashubian Movement

Patrício, António 1878-1930
(Portuguese)
    ClDMEuL-1980
    EncWL-1981
    McGWD-1984

    Symbolism

Patten, Brian 1946-   (English)
    CamGLE-1988
    OxEng-1985

    Liverpool Poets

Paul, Leslie 1905-1985 (Irish)
LongCTCL-1975
OxEng-1985

Angry Young Men

Paulhan, Jean 1884-1968 (French)
CasWL-1973
ClDMEuL-1980
EncWL-1981
OxFr-1959
PengEur-1969

Cubism
Surrealism

Pavese, Cesare 1908-1950 (Italian)
BenReEncy-1987
CasWL-1973
CEnMWL-1963
ClDMEuL-1980
EncWL-1981
GdMWL-1985
OxEng-1985
PengEur-1969

Neorealism
Solaria Group

Pavlenko, Peter Andreyevich 1899-1951 (Russian)
CasWL-1973
EncWL-1981
GdMWL-1985

Socialist Realism

Pawlikowska-Jasnorzewska, Maria 1891-1945 (Polish)
ClDMEuL-1980
GdMWL-1985
PrEncyPP-1974

Skamander Group

Paz, Octavio 1914-   **(Mexican)**
BenReEncy-1987
CasWL-1973
CEnMWL-1963
EncWL-1981
GdMWL-1985
OxSpan-1978
PengAm-1971

Postvanguardist Poetry
Surrealism
Taller Group

Pedroso, Reginio 1896- (Cuban)
CaribWr-1979
EncWL-1981

Afro-Cubanism

Peel, Adriaan n.d. (Belgian)
ClDMEuL-1980

Fifties Poets/Vijftigers

Péguy, Charles Pierre 1873-1914 (French)
BenReEncy-1987
CasWL-1973
CEnMWL-1963
ClDMEuL-1980
EncWL-1981
GdMWL-1985
LongCTCL-1975
OxEng-1985
OxFr-1959
PengEur-1969

Nouvelle Revue Française
Group

Peiper, Tadeusz 1891-1969 (Polish)
ClDMEuL-1980
EncWL-1981
GdMWL-1985

McGWD-1984

Cracow Avant-Garde

Pellicer, Carlos 1899-1977 (Mexican)
CasWL-1973
EncWL-1981
GdMWL-1985
OxSpan-1978
PengAm-1971

Contemporaries/
  Contemporáneos

**Pennanen, Jarno 1906-1969
(Finnish)**
ClDMEuL-1980

Kiila Group

**Penrose, Roland 1900-1984
(English)**
OxEng-1985

Surrealism

**Perbosc, Antonin 1861-1944
(Breton-speaking French)**
EncWL-1981
GdMWL-1985

Félibrige Movement

**Pereda Valdés, Ildefonso 1899-
(Uruguayan)**
EncWL-1981
OxSpan-1978

Afro-Cubanism
Negrismo

**Pereda y Sánchez de Porrúa, José
María de 1833-1906 (Spanish)**
BenReEncy-1987
CasWL-1973

ClDMEuL-1980
OxSpan-1978
PengEur-1969

Realism

Péret, Benjamin 1899-1959 (French)
ClDMEuL-1980
EncWL-1981
OxEng-1985
OxFr-1959
PengEur-1969
PrEncyPP-1974

Surrealism

**Pérez de Ayala, Ramón 1881-1962
(Spanish)**
BenReEncy-1987
CasWL-1973
CEnMWL-1963
ClDMEuL-1980
EncWL-1981
GdMWL-1985
OxSpan-1978
PengEur-1969

Generation of 1898/Generación
  del 1898
Novecentismo

**Pérez Galdós, Benito 1843-1920
(Spanish)**
BenReEncy-1987
CasWL-1973
ClDMEuL-1980
EncWL-1981
OxSpan-1978
OxThe-1983
PengEur-1969

Realism

Pérez Valiente, Salvador n.d.
(Spanish)
  OxSpan-1978

  Grupo Espadaña

Perk, Jacques Fabrice Herman 1859-
1881 (Dutch)
  CasWL-1973
  ClDMEuL-1980
  EncWL-1981
  PengEur-1969
  PrEncyPP-1974

  Movement of the Eighties/
    Beweging van Tachtig

Perkonig, Josef Friedrich 1890-1959
(Austrian)
  EncWL-1981
  OxGer-1986

  Heimatkunst

Pernath, Hugues C. 1931-1975
(Belgian)
  ClDMEuL-1980
  EncWL-1981

  Fifties Poets/Vijftigers
  Fifty-Five Poets/Vijfenvijftigers

Perron, Edgar Du 1899-1940
(Javanese-born Dutch)
  CasWL-1973
  ClDMEuL-1980
  EncWL-1981
  GdMWL-1985
  PengEur-1969

  Forum Group

Pessanha, Camilo 1867-1926
(Portuguese)
  CasWL-1973

  ClDMEuL-1980
  EncWL-1981
  GdMWL-1985

  Symbolism

Pessoa, Fernando 1888-1935
(Portuguese)
  CasWL-1973
  CEnMWL-1963
  ClDMEuL-1980
  EncWL-1981
  GdMWL-1985
  McGWD-1984
  PengEur-1969
  PrEncyPP-1974

  Orpheu Group
  Portuguese Renascence
    Movement
  Presencistas Group

Peters, Rollo 1892-1967 (French-
born American)
  OxAmThe-1984

  Theater Guild
  Washington Square Players

Petlyura, Symon 1879-1926
(Ukrainian)
  ClDMEuL-1980
  EncWL-1981

  Today Group/*Ma*

Petofi, Sándor 1823-1849
(Hungarian)
  ClDMEuL-1980
  EncWL-1981

  Popular National School

**Petrenas-Tarulis, Juozas 1896-1980
(Lithuanian)**
EncWL-1981

Four Winds Movement/Keturi
Vejai

**Petrescu, Cezar 1892-1961
(Romanian)**
CasWL-1973
EncWL-1981
GdMWL-1985
PengEur-1969

Gîndirea

**Pevsner, Antoine 1886-1962
(Russian)**
BenReEncy-1987

Constructivism

**Pezoa Véliz, Carlos 1879-1908
(Chilean)**
CasWL-1973
OxSpan-1978
PengAm-1971
PrEncyPP-1974

Modernismo

Pfemfert, Franz 1879-1954 (German)
EncWL-1981
OxGer-1986

Expressionism

**Phan Bôi Châu 1867-1940
(Vietnamese)**
DOrLit-1974
EncWL-1981

Dông-kinh School of the Just
Cause

**Phan Châu Trinh 1872-1926
(Vietnamese)**
EncWL-1981

Dông-kinh School of the Just
Cause

**Philippide, Alexandru 1900-1979
(Romanian)**
EncWL-1981

Gîndirea

**Phillips, David Graham 1867-1911
(American)**
BenReEncy-1987
LongCTCL-1975
OxAm-1983

Muckrakers

**Picabia, Francis 1879-1953 (French-
born Cuban Spaniard)**
EncWL-1981
OxFr-1959
PrEncyPP-1974

Dadaism
Surrealism

Picasso, Pablo 1881-1973 (Spanish)
BenReEncy-1987
EncWL-1981
OxEng-1985
OxFr-1959
PrEncyPP-1974

Cubism
Surrealism

**Picchia, Paulo Menotti del 1892-
(Brazilian)**
PengAm-1971
PrEncyPP-1974

Modernism
Verde-Amarelismo

Pickard, Tom 1946-   (English)
OxEng-1985

Underground Poetry

**Pidmohylny, Valeriyan 1901-1941
(Ukrainian)**
ClDMEuL-1980
EncWL-1981
GdMWL-1985

Link/Lanka

Piechal, Marian 1905-   (Polish)
ClDMEuL-1980

Quadriga

Pignatari, Décio 1927-   (Brazilian)
EncWL-1981

Concrete Poetry

**Pilinszky, János 1921-
(Hungarian)**
ClDMEuL-1980
EncWL-1981
GdMWL-1985

Ujhold Group

Pillat, Ion 1891-1945 (Romanian)
CasWL-1973
EncWL-1981

Gîndirea

**Pilnyak, Boris (pseud. of Boris
Andreevich Vogau) 1894-1938(?)
(Russian)**
BenReEncy-1987
CasWL-1973

CEnMWL-1963
ClDMEuL-1980
EncWL-1981
GdMWL-1985
PengEur-1969

Modernism
Socialist Realism

**Pilon, Jean-Guy 1930-
(Canadian)**
CasWL-1973
GdMWL-1985
OxCan-1983

Hexagone Group

**Pin i Soler, Josep 1842-1927
(Catalan-speaking Spanish)**
ClDMEuL-1980

Realism

**Pinero, Arthur Wing 1855-1934
(English)**
BenReEncy-1987
CamGLE-1988
CasWL-1973
EncWL-1981
GdMWL-1985
LongCTCL-1975
McGWD-1984
OxAmThe-1984
OxEng-1985
OxThe-1983
PengEng-1971

Georgian Literature
Modernism

**Pinget, Robert 1919-   (Swiss-born
French)**
CasWL-1973
ClDMEuL-1980
EncWL-1981

GdMWL-1985
McGWD-1984
OxEng-1985

New Novel/Nouveau Roman
Theater of the Absurd

Pinski, David 1872-1959 (Yiddish-speaking Israeli)
CasWL-1973
ClDMEuL-1980
EncWL-1981
GdMWL-1985
PengCOAL-1969
PengEur-1969

Young Israel

Pinter, Harold 1930-   (English)
BenReEncy-1987
CamGLE-1988
CasWL-1973
EncWL-1981
GdMWL-1985
LongCTCL-1975
McGWD-1984
OxAmThe-1984
OxEng-1985
OxThe-1983
PengEng-1971
RCom-1973

Comedy of Menace
New Wave/Nouvelle Vague
Theater of Cruelty/Théâtre de
    la Cruauté
Theater of the Absurd

Pinthus, Kurt 1886-1975 (German)
EncWL-1981

Expressionism

Piovene, Guido 1907-1974 (Italian)
CasWL-1973

ClDMEuL-1980
EncWL-1981
GdMWL-1985
PengEur-1969

Neorealism

Pirandello, Luigi 1867-1936 (Italian)
BenReEncy-1987
CasWL-1973
CEnMWL-1963
ClDMEuL-1980
EncWL-1981
GdMWL-1985
LongCTCL-1975
McGWD-1984
OxAmThe-1984
OxEng-1985
OxThe-1983
PengEur-1969
RCom-1973

Theater of the Grotesque/Teatro
    del grottescco
Verismo

Piscator, Erwin 1893-1966 (German)
BenReEncy-1987
EncWL-1981
McGWD-1984
OxGer-1986
OxThe-1983

Berlin Ensemble/Berliner
    Ensemble
Epic Theater/Episches Theater
Total Theater

Plá, Josefina 1909-   (Paraguayan)
EncWL-1981
OxSpan-1978

Generation of 1940

Plath, Sylvia 1932-1963 (American)
BenReEncy-1987
CamGLE-1988
CasWL-1973
EncWL-1981
GdMWL-1985
LongCTCL-1975
OxAm-1983
OxEng-1985
PengAm-1971
PrEncyPP-1974

Confessional Poetry

Platonov, Andrey Platonovich 1899-1951 (Russian)
BenReEncy-1987
ClDMEuL-1980
EncWL-1981
GdMWL-1985
OxEng-1985
PengEur-1969

Modernism

Pluzhnyk, Yevhen 1898-1936 (Ukrainian)
ClDMEuL-1980
EncWL-1981

Link/Lanka

Podbevsek, Anton 1898- (Slovene-speaking Yugoslavian)
EncWL-1981

Expressionism

Pogodin, Nikolay Fyodorovich 1900-1962 (Russian)
CasWL-1973
ClDMEuL-1980
EncWL-1981
GdMWL-1985
McGWD-1984

OxThe-1983
PengEur-1969

Socialist Realism

Polemis, John (Ioannis) 1862-1925 (Greek)
EncWL-1981
GdMWL-1985
PrEncyPP-1974

New School of Athens/Greek Parnassians

Polenz, Wilhelm von 1861-1903 (German)
OxGer-1986

Heimatkunst
Naturalism

Polevoy, Boris Nikolayevich (pseud. of Boris Kampov) 1908-1981 (Russian)
CasWL-1973
EncWL-1981

Socialist Realism

Politis, Kosmas 1888-1974 (Greek)
ClDMEuL-1980
GdMWL-1985

Generation of 1930

Politis, Nikolaos 1852-1921 (Greek)
EncWL-1981

New School of Athens/Greek Parnassians

Pollack, Jackson 1912-1956 (American)
BenReEncy-1987

New York School

Polonskaya, Elizaveta n.d. (Russian)
HarDMT-1988

Serapion Brotherhood

Ponge, Francis 1899-1988 (French)
CasWL-1973
CEnMWL-1963
ClDMEuL-1980
EncWL-1981
GdMWL-1985
PengEur-1969
PrEncyPP-1974

Existentialism
Nouvelle Revue Française
  Group
Surrealism

Ponican, Ján (pseud. of Ján Rob-Ponican) 1902-   (Czech)
CasWL-1973

DAV Group

Pons, Josep Sebastià 1886-1962 (Spanish)
EncWL-1981
OxSpan-1978

Noucentismo

Poole, Ernest 1880-1950 (American)
OxAm-1983

Realism

Popova, Liubov 1889-1924 (Russian)
HarDMT-1988

Cubo-Futurism

Porfyras, Lambros 1879-1932 (Greek)
EncWL-1981
PrEncyPP-1974

New School of Athens/Greek
  Parnassians

Porta, Antonio 1935-   (Italian)
ClDMEuL-1980
EncWL-1981
GdMWL-1985

Group 63/Gruppo 63

Porter, Peter 1929-   (Australian-born English)
CamGLE-1988
CasWL-1973
GdMWL-1985
OxEng-1985

The Group

Pörtner, Paul n.d. (German)
OxGer-1986

Cologne School of New
  Realism/Kölner Schule des
  neuen Realismus

Poruks, Janis 1871-1911 (Latvian)
CasWL-1973
EncWL-1981
GdMWL-1985

Neoromanticism

Pougny, Jean 1894-1956 (French)
HarDMT-1988

Cubo-Futurism

Poulaille, Henri 1896-   (French)
ClDMEuL-1980
GdMWL-1985

Populisme

Poulet, Georges 1902-   (Belgian)
CasWL-1973
ClDMEuL-1980
EncWL-1981
PengEur-1969
PrEncyPP-1974

Geneva School of Critics

Pound, Ezra 1885-1972 (American)
BenReEncy-1987
CamGLE-1988
CasWL-1973
CEnMWL-1963
EncWL-1981
GdMWL-1985
LongCTCL-1975
OxAm-1983
OxEng-1985
PengAm-1971
PrEncyPP-1974
RCom-1973

Imagism
Lost Generation
Modernism
New Criticism
Poetry
Vorticism

Pozner, Vladimir 1905-   (Russian)
CasWL-1973

Acmeism

Serapion Brotherhood

Prado, Pedro 1886-1952 (Chilean)
CasWL-1973
EncWL-1981
GdMWL-1985
OxSpan-1978
PengAm-1971

Los Diez Group

**Prados Such, Emilio 1899-1962
(Spanish)**
ClDMEuL-1980
GdMWL-1985
OxSpan-1978
PengEur-1969

Generation of 1927/Generación
del 1927
Surrealism

**Prasad, Jaysankar 1889-1937
(Indian)**
DOrLit-1974

Romanticism/Chhaya-vada

**Pratella, Francesco 1880-1955
(Italian)**
HarDMT-1988

Futurism

Pratesi, Mario 1842-1921 (Italian)
ClDMEuL-1980

Verismo

Pratolini, Vasco 1913-   (Italian)
CasWL-1973
CEnMWL-1963
ClDMEuL-1980
EncWL-1981
GdMWL-1985

PengEur-1969

Neorealism

**Pratt, E(dwin) J(ohn) 1883-1964
(Canadian)**
BenReEncy-1987
CamGLE-1988
CasWL-1973
EncWL-1981
GdMWL-1985
OxCan-1983
PengEng-1971
PrEncyPP-1974

Montreal Movement

**Premchand (pseud. of Dhanpat Rai
Srivastav) 1880-1936 (Indian)**
BenReEncy-1987
CasWL-1973
DOrLit-1974
EncWL-1981
GdMWL-1985
PengCOAL-1969

Realism/Pragati-vada
Progressive Writers' Movement

Prévert, Jacques 1900-1977 (French)
BenReEncy-1987
CasWL-1973
CEnMWL-1963
ClDMEuL-1980
EncWL-1981
GdMWL-1985
OxFr-1959
PengEur-1969

Surrealism

**Prezihov, Voranc (pseud. of Lovro
Kuhar) 1893-1950 (Slovene-
speaking Yugoslavian)**
CasWL-1973

ClDMEuL-1980
EncWL-1981

Socialist Realism

**Prezzolini, Giuseppi 1882-1982
(Italian)**
CasWL-1973
ClDMEuL-1980
EncWL-1981
PrEncyPP-1974

Futurism

**Price-Mars, Jean 1876-1969
(Haitian)**
CaribWr-1979
EncWL-1981

Revue Indigène Group

Prins, Jan n.d. (Dutch)
ClDMEuL-1980

De Beweging

Prisco, Michele 1920-   (Italian)
ClDMEuL-1980
EncWL-1981

Neorealism

**Prishvin, Mikhail Mikhailovich
1873-1954 (Russian)**
CasWL-1973
CEnMWL-1963
ClDMEuL-1980
EncWL-1981
GdMWL-1985
PengEur-1969

Zavety (Behests) School
Znanie Group

Priyamvada, Usa n.d. (Indian)
DOrLit-1974

New Short Story Movement/
Nayi Kahani

Prus, Boleslaw 1845-1912 (Polish)
CasWL-1973
ClDMEuL-1980
EncWL-1981
PengEur-1969

Realism
Warsaw Positivism

**Przesmycki, Zenon 1861-1944
(Polish)**
CasWL-1973
EncWL-1981
GdMWL-1985

Young Poland/Mloda Polska

Przybos, Julian 1901-1970 (Polish)
CasWL-1973
ClDMEuL-1980
EncWL-1981
GdMWL-1985
PrEncyPP-1974

Cracow Avant-Garde

**Przybyszewski, Stanislaw 1868-
1927 (Polish)**
CasWL-1973
ClDMEuL-1980
EncWL-1981
GdMWL-1985
McGWD-1984
PengEur-1969

Young Poland/Mloda Polska
Zdroj Group

**Psykharis, Ioannis 1854-1929
(Greek)**
EncWL-1981
GdMWL-1985
PengEur-1969

New School of Athens/Greek
Parnassians

Ptácník, Karel 1921-   (Czech)
EncWL-1981

Socialist Realism

**Pujmanová, Marie 1893-1958
(Czech)**
CasWL-1973
EncWL-1981
PengEur-1969

Socialist Realism

**Pushcha, Yazep 1902-1964
(Byelorussian)**
ClDMEuL-1980
EncWL-1981

Uzvyssa Group

**Putinas (pseud. of Vincas
Mykolaitis) 1893-1967
(Lithuanian)**
CasWL-1973
ClDMEuL-1980
EncWL-1981
PrEncyPP-1974

Socialist Realism
Symbolism

Putrament, Jerzy 1910-   (Polish)
ClDMEuL-1980
EncWL-1981

Socialist Realism

Zagary Group

**Pylypenko, Serhiy 1891-1943
(Ukrainian)**
ClDMEuL-1980

Plough/Pluh

Q

Qasmi, Ahmad Nadim 1916-
(Pakistani)
DOrLit-1974
EncWL-1981

Progressive Writers' Movement

Quasímodo, Salvatore 1901-1968
(Italian)
BenReEncy-1987
CasWL-1973
CEnMWL-1963
ClDMEuL-1980
EncWL-1981
GdMWL-1985
LongCTCL-1975
OxEng-1985
PengEur-1969
PrEncyPP-1974

Hermeticism/Poesia Ermetica
Solaria Group

Queneau, Raymond 1903-1976
(French)
BenReEncy-1987
CasWL-1973

CEnMWL-1963
ClDMEuL-1980
EncWL-1981
GdMWL-1985
OxFr-1959
PengEur-1969
PrEncyPP-1974

Existentialism
Surrealism

Quintanilla, Luis n.d. (Mexican)
OxSpan-1978

Estridentismo

Quiroga, Horacio 1878-1937
(Uruguayan)
BenReEncy-1987
CasWL-1973
EncWL-1981
GdMWL-1985
OxSpan-1978
PengAm-1971

Council of Brilliant Knowledge
Generation of 1900
Realism

R

Raabe, Wilhelm (pseud. of Jakob
   Corvinus) 1831-1910 (German)
   BenReEncy-1987
   CasWL-1973
   EncWL-1981
   GdMWL-1985
   OxGer-1986
   PengEur-1969

   Realism

Rába, György n.d. (Hungarian)
   ClDMEuL-1980

   Ujhold Group

Rabie, Jan Sebastiaan 1920-
   (South African)
   EncWL-1981
   PengCOAL-1969

   The Sestigers

Raboy, Isaac 1882-1944 (Yiddish-
   speaking American)
   ClDMEuL-1980
   EncWL-1981

   Young Ones/Die Yunge

Radek, Karl 1885-1939 (Russian)
   EncWL-1981

   Socialist Realism

Radevski, Hristo 1903-
   (Bulgarian)
   CasWL-1973
   PrEncyPP-1974

   Socialist Realism

Radnóti, Miklós 1904-1944
   (Hungarian)
   CasWL-1973
   ClDMEuL-1980
   EncWL-1981
   GdMWL-1985
   PengEur-1969

   Nyugat Group

Raffles, Gerald n.d. (English)
   OxThe-1983

   Theater Workshop

Raghav, Rangey 1923-1962 (Indian)
   DOrLit-1974

   Realism/Pragati-vada

Ragimov, Suleiman 1900-
   (Azerbaijani)
   EncWL-1981

   Socialist Realism

334

al-Rahman, 'Abdallah 'abd 1891-1964 (Sudanese)
EncWL-1981

Neoclassicism

Raimondi, Giuseppe 1898-(Italian)
ClDMEuL-1980

Solaria Group

Raine, Kathleen 1908-   (English)
BenReEncy-1987
CamGLE-1988
CasWL-1973
EncWL-1981
GdMWL-1985
LongCTCL-1975
OxEng-1985
PengEng-1971

Cambridge Group

Rainis, Aspazija 1868-1943 (Latvian)
EncWL-1981

New Current Movement

Rainis, Janis (Janis Plieksans) 1865-1929 (Latvian)
CasWL-1973
ClDMEuL-1980
EncWL-1981
GdMWL-1985

New Current Movement

Rakesh, Mohan 1925-1972 (Indian)
DOrLit-1974
EncWL-1981
McGWD-1984

New Short Story Movement/
Nayi Kahani

Rakic, Milan 1876-1938 (Serbian)
ClDMEuL-1980
EncWL-1981
GdMWL-1985
PengEur-1969

Moderna

Rákos, Sándor n.d. (Hungarian)
ClDMEuL-1980

Ujhold Group

Rakosi, Carl 1903-   (American)
BenReEncy-1987
GdMWL-1985

Objectivism

Rama, Angel 1926-   (Uruguayan)
EncWL-1981

Generation of 1945

Ramat, Silvio 1939-   (Italian)
EncWL-1981

Hermeticism/Poesia Ermetica

Ramos, Graciliano 1892-1953 (Brazilian)
BenReEncy-1987
CasWL-1973
EncWL-1981
GdMWL-1985
PengAm-1971

Modernism

Ramos, José Antonio 1885-1946 (Cuban)
CaribWr-1979

GdMWL-1985
OxSpan-1978

Realism

Ransom, John Crowe 1888-1974
(American)
BenReEncy-1987
CamGLE-1988
CasWL-1973
CEnMWL-1963
EncWL-1981
GdMWL-1985
LongCTCL-1975
OxAm-1983
OxEng-1985
PengAm-1971
PrEncyPP-1974

The Fugitives/Agrarians
New Criticism

Rasp, Renate n.d. (German)
OxGer-1986

Cologne School of New
    Realism/Kölner Schule des
    neuen Realismus

Rasputin, Valentin Grigoryevich
1937-   (Russian)
ClDMEuL-1980
EncWL-1981
GdMWL-1985

Village Prose

Rattigan, Terence 1911-1977
(English)
BenReEncy-1987
CamGLE-1988
CasWL-1973
GdMWL-1985
LongCTCL-1975
McGWD-1984

OxAmThe-1984
OxEng-1985
OxThe-1983
PengEng-1971

Modernism

Ravitch, Meilech 1893-1976 (Polish-
born Yiddish)
CasWL-1973
ClDMEuL-1980
EncWL-1981

Gang Group/Khalyastre

Ray, Man 1890-1976 (American)
BenReEncy-1987
EncWL-1981
OxEng-1985
OxFr-1959

Dadaism
Lost Generation
Surrealism

Ray, Satyajit Amrt 1921-   (Indian)
BenReEncy-1987
DOrLit-1974

Realism/Pragati-vada

Raychev, Georgi 1882-1947
(Bulgarian)
CasWL-1973
ClDMEuL-1980
EncWL-1981
GdMWL-1985

Golden Horn Movement/
    Zlatorog

Raymond, Marcel 1897-1957 (Swiss)
CasWL-1973
EncWL-1981

PrEncyPP-1974

Geneva School of Critics

Raynaud, Ernest 1864-1936 (French)
OxFr-1959

École Romane

Rázus, Martin 1888-1937 (Czech)
ClDMEuL-1980
EncWL-1981

Modernism

Rea, Domenico 1921-   (Italian)
ClDMEuL-1980
EncWL-1981

Neorealism

Read, Herbert 1893-1968 (English)
BenReEncy-1987
CamGLE-1988
CasWL-1973
EncWL-1981
GdMWL-1985
LongCTCL-1975
OxEng-1985
PengEng-1971

Georgian Literature
Modernism
New Apocalypse
Surrealism

**Rèbora, Clemente 1885-1957
(Italian)**
CasWL-1973
ClDMEuL-1980
EncWL-1981
GdMWL-1985
PengEur-1969

Crepuscolarismo

**Rebreanu, Liviu 1885-1944
(Romanian)**
ClDMEuL-1980
EncWL-1981
GdMWL-1985
PengEur-1969

Sburatorul Group

Redgrove, Peter 1932-   (English)
CamGLE-1988
OxEng-1985

The Group

Reding, Josef 1929-   (German)
OxGer-1986

Group 61/Gruppe 61

**Redol, António Alves 1911-1969
(Portuguese)**
ClDMEuL-1980
EncWL-1981
GdMWL-1985
McGWD-1984

Neorealism

Reed, John 1887-1920 (American)
OxAmThe-1984

Provincetown Players

**Régio, José (pseud. of José Maria
dos Reis Pereira) 1901-1969
(Portuguese)**
CasWL-1973
ClDMEuL-1980
EncWL-1981
GdMWL-1985
McGWD-1984
PrEncyPP-1974

Presencistas Group

Regman, Cornel 1919-
(Romanian)
EncWL-1981

Sibiu Group

Régnier, Henri de 1864-1936
(French)
BenReEncy-1987
CasWL-1973
ClDMEuL-1980
EncWL-1981
LongCTCL-1975
OxFr-1959
PengEur-1969
PrEncyPP-1974

Symbolism

Reinhardt, Max 1873-1943
(German)
EncWL-1981
LongCTCL-1975
McGWD-1984
OxAmThe-1984
OxGer-1986
OxThe-1983

Deutsches Theater

Reis, Marcos Konder 1922-
(Brazilian)
EncWL-1981

Generation of 1945

Reisel, Vladimír 1919-   (Czech)
CasWL-1973
ClDMEuL-1980
EncWL-1981

Nadrealisti Movement

Reményik, Sándor 1890-1941
(Hungarian-speaking Romanian)
EncWL-1981
GdMWL-1985
PengEur-1969

Transylvanian Helicon Group

Remizov, Alexey Mikhailovich
1877-1957 (Russian)
BenReEncy-1987
CasWL-1973
CEnMWL-1963
ClDMEuL-1980
EncWL-1981
GdMWL-1985
McGWD-1984
PengEur-1969

Zavety (Behests) School

Rendra, W.S. 1935-   (Indonesian)
EncWL-1981
GdMWL-1985
PrEncyPP-1974

Generation of 1950

Renn, Ludwig 1889-1979 (German)
CEnMWL-1963
ClDMEuL-1980
EncWL-1981
GdMWL-1985
OxGer-1986
PengEur-1969

New Objectivity/Neue
    Sachlichkeit

Rentas Lucas, Eugenio 1910-
(Puerto Rican)
CaribWr-1979

Ensueñismo Group
Transcendentalist Group

Resnais, Alain 1922-   (French)
 BenReEncy-1987
 EncWL-1981

 New Wave/Nouvelle Vague

Reuterswärd, Carl Fredrik 1934-
(Swedish)
 ClDMEuL-1980

 Concrete Poetry

Révai, József n.d. (Hungarian)
 ClDMEuL-1980

 Today Group/*Ma*

Reverdy, Jacques 1889-1960
(French)
 BenReEncy-1987
 CasWL-1973
 ClDMEuL-1980
 EncWL-1981
 GdMWL-1985
 OxFr-1959
 OxSpan-1978
 PengEur-1969
 PrEncyPP-1974

 Creationism/Creacionismo
 Cubism

Rexroth, Kenneth 1905-1982
(American)
 BenReEncy-1987
 CamGLE-1988
 EncWL-1981
 OxAm-1983
 PengAm-1971
 PrEncyPP-1974

 Beat Generation
 Cubism
 Jazz Poetry
 San Francisco School

Reyes, Alfonso 1889-1959 (Mexican)
 BenReEncy-1987
 CasWL-1973
 EncWL-1981
 GdMWL-1985
 OxSpan-1978
 PengAm-1971

 Atheneum of Youth

Reyles Gutiérrez, Carlos Claudio
1868-1938 (Uruguayan)
 BenReEncy-1987
 CasWL-1973
 EncWL-1981
 GdMWL-1985
 OxSpan-1978
 PengAm-1971

 Generation of 1900

Reymont, Wladyslaw Stanislaw
1867-1925 (Polish)
 BenReEncy-1987
 CasWL-1973
 ClDMEuL-1980
 EncWL-1981
 GdMWL-1985
 PengEur-1969

 Young Poland/Mloda Polska

Reznikoff, Charles 1894-1976
(American)
 BenReEncy-1987
 CamGLE-1988
 GdMWL-1985
 OxAm-1983
 PengAm-1971
 PrEncyPP-1974

 Objectivism

Riba, Enric Prat de la 1870-1917
(Spanish)
ClDMEuL-1980

Noucentismo

Riba Bracóns, Carles 1893-1959
(Catalan-speaking Spanish)
CasWL-1973
CEnMWL-1963
ClDMEuL-1980
EncWL-1981
GdMWL-1985
OxSpan-1978
PengEur-1969

Noucentismo

Ribeiro, Aquilino 1885-1963
(Portuguese)
CasWL-1973
ClDMEuL-1980
EncWL-1981
GdMWL-1985
PengEur-1969

Seara Nova Group

Ribeiro, José Rosas n.d. (Peruvian)
OxSpan-1978

Estos 13/Hora Cero

Ribemont-Dessaignes, Georges
1884-1974 (French)
ClDMEuL-1980
PrEncyPP-1974

Dadaism

Ribera-Chevremont, Evaristo 1896-
(Puerto Rican)
PrEncyPP-1974

Modernismo

Ricardo, Cassiano 1895-1974
(Brazilian)
EncWL-1981
PengAm-1971
PrEncyPP-1974

Anta (Tapir) Group
Modernism
Verde-Amarelismo

Ricardou, Jean 1932-   (French)
ClDMEuL-1980
EncWL-1981

New Novel/Nouveau Roman
Structuralism
Tel Quel Group

Rice, Elmer (pseud. of Elmer
Leopold Reizenstein) 1892-1967
(American)
BenReEncy-1987
CamGLE-1988
CasWL-1973
EncWL-1981
GdMWL-1985
LongCTCL-1975
McGWD-1984
OxAm-1983
OxAmThe-1984
OxEng-1985
OxThe-1983
PengAm-1971
PrEncyPP-1974

Expressionism
Theater Guild

Rich, Adrienne 1929-   (American)
BenReEncy-1987
CamGLE-1988
EncWL-1981
OxAm-1983

PengAm-1971

Confessional Poetry

Richard, Jean-Pierre 1922-
(French)
ClDMEuL-1980
EncWL-1981
PrEncyPP-1974

Geneva School of Critics

Richards, I(vor) A(rmstrong) 1893-
1979 (English)
BenReEncy-1987
CamGLE-1988
CasWL-1973
EncWL-1981
LongCTCL-1975
OxEng-1985
PengEng-1971
PrEncyPP-1974

Georgian Literature
Modernism
New Criticism

Richardson, Dorothy 1873-1957
(English)
BenReEncy-1987
CamGLE-1988
CasWL-1973
EncWL-1981
GdMWL-1985
LongCTCL-1975
OxEng-1985
PengEng-1971

Georgian Literature
Modernism

Richter, Hans Werner 1908-
(German)
BenReEncy-1987
CasWL-1973

ClDMEuL-1980
EncWL-1981
GdMWL-1985
OxGer-1986
PengEur-1969

Group 47/Gruppe 47

Rickword, Edgell 1898-1982
(English)
OxEng-1985

Scrutiny

Ridala, Villem 1885-1942 (Estonian)
ClDMEuL-1980
EncWL-1981

Young Estonia Group

Ridder, Alfons de n.d. (Belgian)
ClDMEuL-1980

Het Fonteintje Group

Ridruejo, Dionisio 1912-1975
(Spanish)
BenReEncy-1987
CasWL-1973
ClDMEuL-1980
EncWL-1981
GdMWL-1985
OxSpan-1978

Generation of 1936/Generación
del 1936
Generación de la Guerra

Rifat, Oktay 1914-   (Turkish)
ClDMEuL-1980
DOrLit-1974
EncWL-1981
GdMWL-1985
PrEncyPP-1974

Garip Movement
Poetic Realism
The Second New

Rifbjerg, Klaus 1931-   (Danish)
  CasWL-1973
  ClDMEuL-1980
  EncWL-1981
  GdMWL-1985
  McGWD-1984
  OxThe-1983
  PengEur-1969

Modernism

Rigaut, Jacques 1899-1929 (French)
  ClDMEuL-1980
  GdMWL-1985

Surrealism

**al-Rihani, Amin 1876-1940
(Lebanese)**
  EncWL-1981

Society of the Pen

**Riley, James Whitcomb 1849-1916
(American)**
  BenReEncy-1987
  CamGLE-1988
  CasWL-1973
  LongCTCL-1975
  OxAm-1983
  PengAm-1971

Local Color School

**Rilke, Rainer Maria 1875-1926
(Austrian)**
  BenReEncy-1987
  CasWL-1973
  CEnMWL-1963
  ClDMEuL-1980
  EncWL-1981

  GdMWL-1985
  LongCTCL-1975
  OxEng-1985
  OxGer-1986
  PengEur-1969
  RCom-1973

Jugendstil
Symbolism

Rimanelli, Giose 1926-   (Italian)
  ClDMEuL-1980

Neorealism

**Rimbaud, Arthur 1854-1891
(French)**
  BenReEncy-1987
  CamGLE-1988
  CasWL-1973
  ClDMEuL-1980
  EncWL-1981
  LongCTCL-1975
  OxEng-1985
  OxFr-1959
  PengEur-1969
  PrEncyPP-1974
  RCom-1973

Symbolism

**Riou, Jakez 1899-1937 (Breton-
speaking French)**
  EncWL-1981
  GdMWL-1985
  PengEur-1969

Breton Movement

Ristic, Marko 1902-   (Serbian)
  ClDMEuL-1980
  EncWL-1981

Surrealism

Ritsos, Yannis 1909-   (Greek)
BenReEncy-1987
ClDMEuL-1980
EncWL-1981
GdMWL-1985
PengEur-1969

Generation of 1930

Rivai Apin n.d. (Indonesian)
PrEncyPP-1974

Generation of 1950

**Rivera, José Eustasio 1889-1928
(Columbian)**
BenReEncy-1987
CasWL-1973
EncWL-1981
GdMWL-1985
OxSpan-1978
PengAm-1971

Realism

Rivette, Jacques 1928-   (French)
HarDMT-1988

New Wave/Nouvelle Vague

Rivière, Jacques 1886-1925 (French)
CasWL-1973
ClDMEuL-1980
EncWL-1981
OxFr-1959
PengEur-1969

Nouvelle Revue Française
Group

**Roa Bastos, Augusto 1917-
(Paraguayan)**
CasWL-1973
EncWL-1981
GdMWL-1985

OxSpan-1978
PengAm-1971

Generation of 1940

**Robakidse, Grigol 1884-1962
(Georgian)**
EncWL-1981
PrEncyPP-1974

Blue Horns Group/Tsispheri
q'antesbi

**Robbe-Grillet, Alain 1922-
(French)**
BenReEncy-1987
CasWL-1973
CEnMWL-1963
ClDMEuL-1980
EncWL-1981
GdMWL-1985
OxEng-1985
PengEur-1969
RCom-1973

New Novel/Nouveau Roman
New Wave/Nouvelle Vague
Theater of the Absurd

**Roberts, Charles G(eorge) D(ouglas)
1860-1943 (Canadian)**
BenReEncy-1987
CamGLE-1988
EncWL-1981
LongCTCL-1975
OxAm-1983
OxCan-1983
PengEng-1971

Confederation Poets
Local Color School

Roberts, Theodore Goodridge 1877-1953 (Canadian)
OxCan-1983

Local Color School

Roberts, William 1895-1980 (English)
HarDMT-1988

Vorticism

Robinson, Edwin Arlington 1869-1935 (American)
BenReEncy-1987
CamGLE-1988
CasWL-1973
CEnMWL-1963
EncWL-1981
GdMWL-1985
LongCTCL-1975
OxAm-1983
OxEng-1985
PengAm-1971
PrEncyPP-1974

Realism

Robinson, Lennox 1886-1958 (Irish)
CamGLE-1988
CasWL-1973
GdMWL-1985
LongCTCL-1975
McGWD-1984
OxEng-1985
OxThe-1983

Abbey Theater
Edwardian Literature
Irish Renaissance

Roblès, Emmanuel 1914- (Algerian-born French)
BenReEncy-1987
CasWL-1973

ClDMEuL-1980
EncWL-1981
GdMWL-1985

North Africa Group of Writers

Rodchenko, Alexander 1891-1956 (Russian)
HarDMT-1988

Constructivism
LEF

Rode, Helge 1870-1937 (Danish)
ClDMEuL-1980
GdMWL-1985
PengEur-1969

Symbolism

Rodenbach, Georges 1855-1898 (Belgian)
ClDMEuL-1980
OxFr-1959
PrEncyPP-1974

Symbolism

Rodó, José Enrique 1871-1917 (Uruguayan)
BenReEncy-1987
CasWL-1973
EncWL-1981
OxSpan-1978
PengAm-1971
PrEncyPP-1974

Modernismo

Rodríguez, Luis Felipe 1888-1947 (Cuban)
CaribWr-1979
OxSpan-1978

Manzanillo Group

Rodríguez Cárdenas, Manuel 1912-
(Venezuelan)
EncWL-1981

Generation of 1918

Rodríguez Feo, José 1920-
(Cuban)
EncWL-1981

Orígenes Group

Roelants, Maurice 1895-1966
(Belgian)
ClDMEuL-1980
EncWL-1981
GdMWL-1985

Forum Group

Roethke, Theodore 1908-1963
(American)
BenReEncy-1987
CamGLE-1988
CasWL-1973
EncWL-1981
GdMWL-1985
OxAm-1983
OxEng-1985
PengAm-1971

Confessional Poetry

Roggeman, Willy 1934-   (Belgian)
ClDMEuL-1980
EncWL-1981

Komma Group

Rohmer, Eric 1920-   (French)
BenReEncy-1987

New Wave/Nouvelle Vague

Rojas, Jorge 1911-   (Colombian)
EncWL-1981

Stone and Sky Movement

Rojas Sepúlveda, Manuel 1896-1973
(Chilean)
BenReEncy-1987
EncWL-1981
OxSpan-1978
PengAm-1971

Realism

Roland de Renéville, André 1903-
1962 (French)
EncWL-1981

Great Game Group/*Le Grand
Jeu*

Roland Holst-Van den Schalk,
Henriette Goverdina Anna 1869-
1952 (Dutch)
CasWL-1973
ClDMEuL-1980
EncWL-1981
PengEur-1969

Movement of the Eighties/
Beweging van Tachtig

Rolicz-Lieder, Waclaw 1866-1912
(Polish)
ClDMEuL-1980
GdMWL-1985

Young Poland/Mloda Polska

Rolland, Romain 1866-1944
(French)
BenReEncy-1987
CasWL-1973
CEnMWL-1963
ClDMEuL-1980

EncWL-1981
GdMWL-1985
LongCTCL-1975
McGWD-1984
OxEng-1985
OxFr-1959
OxThe-1983
PengEur-1969
RCom-1973

Abbaye Group/Groupe de
   l'Abbaye

**Romains, Jules (pseud. of Louis
Farigoule) 1885-1972 (French)**
BenReEncy-1987
CasWL-1973
CEnMWL-1963
ClDMEuL-1980
EncWL-1981
GdMWL-1985
LongCTCL-1975
McGWD-1984
OxEng-1985
OxFr-1959
OxThe-1983
PengEur-1969
PrEncyPP-1974

Abbaye Group/Groupe de
   l'Abbaye
Nouvelle Revue Française
   Group
Unanimism/Unanisme

**Romero, Elvio 1926-
(Paraguayan)**
EncWL-1981
OxSpan-1978

Generation of 1940

**Romero, José Rubén 1890-1952
(Mexican)**
EncWL-1981

GdMWL-1985
OxSpan-1978
PengAm-1971

Realism

Romero, Luis 1916-   (Spanish)
ClDMEuL-1980
EncWL-1981
OxSpan-1978

Tremendismo

**Romero García, Vicente 1865-1917
(Venezuelan)**
EncWL-1981
OxSpan-1978

Criollismo

Rónay, György n.d. (Hungarian)
ClDMEuL-1980

Nyugat Group

Ronconi, Luca 1913-   (Italian)
OxThe-1983

Total Theater

Roover, Adriaan de n.d. (Belgian)
ClDMEuL-1980

Fifties Poets/Vijftigers

**Rosa, Faure da 1912-
(Portuguese)**
ClDMEuL-1980

Neorealism

**Rosa, Joao Guimaraes 1908-1967
(Brazilian)**
EncWL-1981

GdMWL-1985

Modernism

Rosales Camacho, Luis 1910-
(Spanish)
BenReEncy-1987
CasWL-1973
ClDMEuL-1980
GdMWL-1985
OxSpan-1978

Generation of 1936/Generación
del 1936
Generación de la Guerra

Rosa-Nieves, Cesáreo 1901-
(Puerto Rican)
CaribWr-1979

Ensueñismo Group

Rosegger, Peter 1843-1918
(Austrian)
OxGer-1986
PengEur-1969

Heimatkunst

Rosenberg, Isaac 1890-1918
(English)
BenReEncy-1987
CamGLE-1988
EncWL-1981
GdMWL-1985
LongCTCL-1975
OxEng-1985
PengEng-1971
PrEncyPP-1974

Georgian Literature

Rosi, Francesco 1922-   (Italian)
OxEng-1985

Neorealism

Rossellini, Roberto 1906-1977
(Italian)
BenReEncy-1987
ClDMEuL-1980
EncWL-1981
OxEng-1985

Neorealism

Roumain, Jacques 1907-1944
(Haitian)
CaribWr-1979
CasWL-1973
EncWL-1981
GdMWL-1985

Négritude
Revue Indigène Group

Roumanille, Joseph 1818-1891
(Provençal-speaking French)
CasWL-1973
ClDMEuL-1980
EncWL-1981
OxFr-1959
PengEur-1969
PrEncyPP-1974

Félibrige Movement

Roussel, Raymond 1877-1933
(French)
ClDMEuL-1980
EncWL-1981
GdMWL-1985
PengEur-1969

Surrealism

Rousset, Jean 1910-   (Swiss)
PrEncyPP-1974

Geneva School of Critics

Roy, Vladimír 1885-1936 (Czech)
CasWL-1973
ClDMEuL-1980
EncWL-1981

Modernism

Rózewicz, Tadeusz 1921-   (Polish)
BenReEncy-1987
CasWL-1973
ClDMEuL-1980
EncWL-1981
McGWD-1984

Theater of the Absurd

Rozhkov, P. n.d. (Russian)
EncWL-1981

Socialist Realism

Rubchak, Bohdan 1935-
(Ukrainian)
EncWL-1981

New York Group

Ruben, A(dresen) 1920-1975
(Portuguese)
EncWL-1981

Surrealism

Rudnytsky, Mykhaylo 1889-1975
(Ukrainian)
ClDMEuL-1980
EncWL-1981

Nazustrich

Rueda, Manuel 1921-   (Dominican
Republican)
CaribWr-1979
EncWL-1981

Pluralist Movement
Surprised Poetry Movement

Rueda Santos, Salvador 1857-1933
(Spanish)
CasWL-1973
ClDMEuL-1980
GdMWL-1985
OxSpan-1978
PengEur-1969

Modernismo

Rühm, Gerhard 1930-   (Austrian)
ClDMEuL-1980
EncWL-1981
McGWD-1984
OxGer-1986

Concrete Poetry
Vienna Group/Wiener Gruppe

Ruiz, Juan Ramírez n.d. (Peruvian)
OxSpan-1978

Estos 13/Hora Cero

Rulfo, Juan 1918-1986 (Mexican)
BenReEncy-1987
CasWL-1973
EncWL-1981
GdMWL-1985
OxSpan-1978
PengAm-1971

Magic Realism

Rumaker, Michael 1932-
(American)
PengAm-1971

PrEncyPP-1974

Beat Generation

Rushdie, Salman 1947-   (Indian-born English)
BenReEncy-1987
CamGLE-1988
OxEng-1985

Magic Realism

Russell, Bertrand 1872-1970 (English)
BenReEncy-1987
CamGLE-1988
CasWL-1973
EncWL-1981
LongCTCL-1975
OxEng-1985
PengEng-1971

Bloomsbury Group

Russell, George William

See Æ

Russolo, Luigi 1885-1947 (Italian)
EncWL-1981
OxEng-1985

Futurism

Ruyra i Ohms, Joachim 1858-1939 (Catalan-speaking Spanish)
ClDMEuL-1980

EncWL-1981
GdMWL-1985

Noucentismo
Realism

Rylsky, Maxym 1895-1964 (Ukrainian)
ClDMEuL-1980
EncWL-1981
PengEur-1969

Generation of the 1960s/
Shestydesyatnyky
Neoclassic Group

Rymkiewicz, Aleksander 1913- (Polish)
ClDMEuL-1980

Zagary Group

Rymkiewicz, Jaroslaw Marek 1934- (Polish)
ClDMEuL-1980
GdMWL-1985

Theater of the Absurd
Wspólczesnosc Generation

S

Saba, Umberto (pseud. of Umberto Poli) 1883-1957 (Italian)
CasWL-1973
ClDMEuL-1980
EncWL-1981
GdMWL-1985
OxEng-1985
PengEur-1969

Crepuscolarismo
Solaria Group

Sabir, Mirza Alekper 1862-1911 (Azerbaijani)
DOrLit-1974
EncWL-1981

Molla Nasreddin Movement

Sá-Carneiro, Mário de 1890-1916 (Portuguese)
CasWL-1973
ClDMEuL-1980
EncWL-1981
GdMWL-1985
PengEur-1969

Orpheu Group
Presencistas Group
Symbolism

Sack, Gustav 1885-1916 (German)
OxGer-1986

Expressionism

Sackville-West, Victoria 1892-1962 (English)
BenReEncy-1987
CamGLE-1988
EncWL-1981
LongCTCL-1975
OxEng-1985
PengEng-1971

Edwardian Literature

Sahay, Raghuvir (Firaq Gorakhpuri) 1896-   (Indian)
DOrLit-1974

New Poetry Movement/Nayi Kavita

Saint Georges de Bouhélier 1889-1942 (French)
ClDMEuL-1980
EncWL-1981
OxFr-1959

Naturism/Naturisme

Saint-John Perse (pseud. of Alexis Saint-Léger Léger) 1887-1975 (Guadeloupean-born French)
BenReEncy-1987
CaribWr-1979
CasWL-1973
CEnMWL-1963
EncWL-1981
GdMWL-1985
OxEng-1985

OxFr-1959
PengEur-1969

Nouvelle Revue Française
Group
Surrealism

Sainz, Gustavo 1940-   (Mexican)
EncWL-1981
OxSpan-1978

Wave Movement/Onda

Sakaguchi Ango 1906-1955
(Japanese)
DOrLit-1974

Decadents/Burai-ha

Saksena ao, Sarvesvardayal n.d.
(Indian)
DOrLit-1974

New Poetry Movement/Nayi
Kavita

Salda, Frantisek Xaver 1867-1937
(Czech)
CasWL-1973
ClDMEuL-1980
EncWL-1981
McGWD-1984

Modernism

Saleh, Christiane n.d. (Lebanese)
EncWL-1981

Surrealism

Salgado, Plínio 1901-1975
(Brazilian)
EncWL-1981
GdMWL-1985
PengAm-1971

PrEncyPP-1974

Modernism
Verde-Amarelismo

Salinas, Pedro 1891(?)-1951
(Spanish)
BenReEncy-1987
CasWL-1973
CEnMWL-1963
ClDMEuL-1980
EncWL-1981
GdMWL-1985
McGWD-1984
OxSpan-1978
PengEur-1969

Generation of 1927/Generación
del 1927
Novecentismo
Ultraism/Ultraismo

Salins, Gunars 1924-   (Latvian)
EncWL-1981
GdMWL-1985
PengEur-1969

New York Group

Salmon, André 1881-1969 (French)
CasWL-1973
ClDMEuL-1980
EncWL-1981
GdMWL-1985
OxFr-1959

Cubism

Salten, Felix 1869-1945 (Hungarian-
born Austrian)
EncWL-1981
OxGer-1986
PrEncyPP-1974

Young Vienna Group/Jungwien

San Secondo, Rossi di 1887-1956
(Italian)
  ClDMEuL-1980
  OxThe-1983

  Theater of the Grotesque/Teatro
  del grottescco

Sánchez Ferlosio, Rafael 1927-
(Italian-born Spanish)
  CasWL-1973
  ClDMEuL-1980
  EncWL-1981
  GdMWL-1985
  OxSpan-1978
  PengEur-1969

  Objectivism

Sánchez León, Abelardo n.d.
(Peruvian)
  OxSpan-1978

  Estos 13/Hora Cero

Sand, August 1914-1969 (Estonian)
  ClDMEuL-1980

  Soothsayers Movement/
    Arbujad

Sandburg, Carl 1878-1967
(American)
  BenReEncy-1987
  CamGLE-1988
  CasWL-1973
  CEnMWL-1963
  EncWL-1981
  GdMWL-1985
  LongCTCL-1975
  OxAm-1983
  OxEng-1985
  PengAm-1971
  PrEncyPP-1974

  Chicago Group/Renaissance
  Poetry
  Realism

Sandgren, Gustav 1904-
(Swedish)
  CasWL-1973
  GdMWL-1985

  Five Young Men/Fem Unga

Sanguineti, Edoardo 1930-
(Italian)
  ClDMEuL-1980
  EncWL-1981
  GdMWL-1985

  Group 63/Gruppo 63

Sankrtyayan, Rahul n.d. (Indian)
  DOrLit-1974

  Realism/Pragati-vada

Sánta, Ferenc 1927-   (Hungarian)
  ClDMEuL-1980
  EncWL-1981

  Generation of 1955

Sant'Elia, Antonio 1888-1916
(Italian)
  HarDMT-1988

  Futurism

Santic, Aleksa 1868-1924 (Serbian)
  ClDMEuL-1980
  PengEur-1969

  Moderna

Santos, Políbio Gomes dos 1911-
1939 (Portuguese)
ClDMEuL-1980

Neorealism

Santos Chocano, José 1875-1934
(Peruvian)
BenReEncy-1987
EncWL-1981
GdMWL-1985
OxSpan-1978

Modernismo

Sanusi Pané 1905-   (Indonesian)
PrEncyPP-1974

New Writers' Circle/Pudjangga
  Baru

Sarandaris, Giorgos 1908-1941
(Greek)
ClDMEuL-1980

Generation of 1930

Sarduy, Severo 1937-   (Cuban)
CaribWr-1979
EncWL-1981
GdMWL-1985
OxSpan-1978

Semiotics
Tel Quel Group

Sarkia, Kaarlo 1902-1945 (Finnish)
EncWL-1981
PengEur-1969

Flame Bearers Group/
  Tulenkantajat

Sárközi, György n.d. (Hungarian)
ClDMEuL-1980

Nyugat Group

Sarma, N. n.d. (Indian)
DOrLit-1974

Realism/Pragati-vada

Sarma, Ramvilas n.d. (Indian)
DOrLit-1974

New Poetry Movement/Nayi
  Kavita

Sarmiento, Domingo Faustino 1811-
1888 (Argentine)
BenReEncy-1987
CasWL-1973
EncWL-1981
OxSpan-1978
PengAm-1971

Gaucho Literature

Saroyan, William 1908-1981
(American)
BenReEncy-1987
CamGLE-1988
CasWL-1973
CEnMWL-1963
EncWL-1981
GdMWL-1985
LongCTCL-1975
McGWD-1984
OxAm-1983
OxAmThe-1984
OxThe-1983
PengAm-1971

Group Theater

Sarraute, Nathalie 1900-
(Russian-born French)
BenReEncy-1987
CasWL-1973
ClDMEuL-1980
EncWL-1981
GdMWL-1985
OxEng-1985
PengEur-1969

New Novel/Nouveau Roman
New Wave/Nouvelle Vague

Sartre, Jean-Paul 1905-1980
(French)
BenReEncy-1987
CasWL-1973
CEnMWL-1963
ClDMEuL-1980
EncWL-1981
GdMWL-1985
LongCTCL-1975
McGWD-1984
OxAm-1983
OxEng-1985
OxFr-1959
OxGer-1986
OxThe-1983
PengEur-1969
RCom-1973

Existentialism

Sarvig, Ole 1921-1981 (Danish)
CasWL-1973
ClDMEuL-1980
EncWL-1981
GdMWL-1985
PrEncyPP-1974

Heretica Poets

Sassoon, Siegfried 1886-1967
(English)
BenReEncy-1987

CamGLE-1988
CasWL-1973
CEnMWL-1963
EncWL-1981
GdMWL-1985
LongCTCL-1975
OxEng-1985
PengEng-1971
PrEncyPP-1974

Georgian Literature
Realism

Satomi Ton 1888-(?) (Japanese)
CasWL-1973
DOrLit-1974
EncWL-1981

White Birch School/Shirakaba-ha

Saussure, Ferdinand de 1857-1913
(Swiss)
BenReEncy-1987
CamGLE-1988
EncWL-1981
OxEng-1985
PrEncyPP-1974

Semiotics
Structuralism

Savchencko, Yakiv 1890-1937
(Ukrainian)
EncWL-1981

Symbolism

Sbarbaro, Camillo 1888-1967
(Italian)
CasWL-1973
ClDMEuL-1980
EncWL-1981

GdMWL-1985

Crepuscolarismo

Scannell, Vernon 1922-   (English)
CamGLE-1988
OxEng-1985

New Lines Poets

**Schäfer, Wilhelm 1868-1952
(German)**
OxGer-1986

Heimatkunst

Schallück, Paul 1922-1976 (German)
ClDMEuL-1980
EncWL-1981
OxGer-1986

Group 47/Gruppe 47

**Schaukal, Richard von 1874-1942
(Austrian)**
ClDMEuL-1980
OxGer-1986
PrEncyPP-1974

Jugendstil

**Schickele, René 1883-1940
(German)**
CasWL-1973
ClDMEuL-1980
EncWL-1981
GdMWL-1985
OxGer-1986
PengEur-1969

Expressionism

Schierbeek, Bert 1918-   (Dutch)
EncWL-1981

Fifties Poets/Vijftigers

Schildt, Runar 1888-1925 (Finnish)
ClDMEuL-1980
EncWL-1981

Loafers/Dagdrivarna

**Schlaf, Johannes 1862-1941
(German)**
BenReEncy-1987
CasWL-1973
ClDMEuL-1980
GdMWL-1985
OxGer-1986

Freie Bühne
Naturalism

Schlenther, P. 1854-1916 (German)
OxGer-1986

Freie Bühne

**Schlichter, Rudolf 1890-1955(?)
(German)**
HarDMT-1988

New Objectivity/Neue
Sachlichkeit

**Schlumberger, Jean 1877-1968
(French)**
CasWL-1973
GdMWL-1985
OxFr-1959

Nouvelle Revue Française
Group

Schmidt, Augusto Frederico 1906-
(Brazilian)
EncWL-1981
PengAm-1971
PrEncyPP-1974

Modernism

Schmidt-Rottluff, Karl 1884-1976
(German)
OxGer-1986

Expressionism

Schnack, Friedrich 1888-1977
(German)
OxGer-1986

Expressionism

Schneir, Miriam 1933-
(American)
HandLit-1986

Feminist Criticism

Schnell, Robert Wolfgang n.d.
(German)
OxGer-1986

Cologne School of New
Realism/Kölner Schule des
neuen Realismus

Schnitzler, Arthur 1862-1931
(Austrian)
BenReEncy-1987
CasWL-1973
ClDMEuL-1980
EncWL-1981
GdMWL-1985
LongCTCL-1975
McGWD-1984
OxGer-1986
OxThe-1983

PengEur-1969
PrEncyPP-1974

Deutsches Theater
Young Vienna Group/Jungwien

Schnurre, Wolfdietrich 1920-
(German)
CasWL-1973
ClDMEuL-1980
EncWL-1981
GdMWL-1985
OxGer-1986
PengEur-1969

Group 47/Gruppe 47

Schönherr, Karl 1867-1952
(Austrian)
OxGer-1986
OxThe-1983

Heimatkunst

Schöpflin, Aladár 1872-1950
(Hungarian)
ClDMEuL-1980
EncWL-1981

Nyugat Group

Schoultz, Solveig von 1907-
(Swedish-speaking Finnish)
EncWL-1981
PengEur-1969
PrEncyPP-1974

Swedish-Finnish Modernists

Schroer, G. n.d. (German)
OxGer-1986

Heimatkunst

Schurer, Fedde 1898-1968 (Frisian-speaking Dutch)
CasWL-1973
EncWL-1981
PrEncyPP-1974

Young Frisian Movement

Schuyler, George 1895-1977 (American)
CamGLE-1988
PrEncyPP-1974

Harlem Renaissance

Schuyler, James 1923-   (American)
BenReEncy-1987
EncWL-1981
OxAm-1983

New York School

Schwartz, Israel Jacob 1885-1971 (Yiddish-speaking American)
ClDMEuL-1980
EncWL-1981

Young Ones/Die Yunge

Schwitters, Kurt 1887-1948 (German)
EncWL-1981
GdMWL-1985
OxGer-1986
PengEur-1969

Dadaism
Merz

Schwob, Marcel 1867-1905 (French)
CamGLE-1988
ClDMEuL-1980
OxFr-1959

Symbolism

Sciascia, Leonardo 1921-   (Italian)
ClDMEuL-1980
EncWL-1981
GdMWL-1985
McGWD-1984

Neorealism

Scott, Duncan Campbell 1862-1947 (Canadian)
BenReEncy-1987
CamGLE-1988
CasWL-1973
EncWL-1981
LongCTCL-1975
McGWD-1984
OxCan-1983
PengEng-1971

Confederation Poets

Scott, F(rancis) R(eginald) 1899-1985 (Canadian)
BenReEncy-1987
CamGLE-1988
EncWL-1981
GdMWL-1985
OxCan-1983
PengEng-1971
PrEncyPP-1974

Montreal Movement

Scott, Tom 1918-   (Scottish)
EncWL-1981
GdMWL-1985

Scottish Renaissance

Scutenaire, Louis 1905-   (Belgian)
ClDMEuL-1980
EncWL-1981

Surrealism

**Sebyla, Wladyslaw 1902-1941
(Polish)**
ClDMEuL-1980

Quadriga

**Sedzicki, Franciszek 1882-1957
(Kashubian-speaking Polish)**
EncWL-1981

Young Kashubian Movement

Seeberg, Peter 1925-   (Danish)
ClDMEuL-1980
EncWL-1981
GdMWL-1985

Modernism

**Seferis, George (pseud. of Giorgios
Seferiadis) 1900-1971 (Greek)**
BenReEncy-1987
CasWL-1973
CEnMWL-1963
ClDMEuL-1980
EncWL-1981
GdMWL-1985
OxEng-1985
PengEur-1969

Generation of 1930

**Seghers, Anna (pseud. of Netty
Reiling Radványi) 1900-1983
(German)**
BenReEncy-1987
CasWL-1973
ClDMEuL-1980
EncWL-1981
GdMWL-1985
OxGer-1986
PengEur-1969

New Objectivity/Neue
    Sachlichkeit

**Sehabettin, Cenap 1870-1934
(Turkish)**
ClDMEuL-1980
PrEncyPP-1974

Servet-i Fünun/Edebiyat-i
    Cedide

Seifert, Jaroslav 1901-1986 (Czech)
BenReEncy-1987
CasWL-1973
ClDMEuL-1980
EncWL-1981
GdMWL-1985
PengEur-1969
PrEncyPP-1974

Poeticism
Proletarian Literature

**Seiffert, Marjorie Allen 1885-(?)
(American)**
OxAm-1983

Spectra

**Seisensui Ogiwara 1884-1976
(Japanese)**
EncWL-1981

New Tendency School

**Selvinsky, Ilya Lvovich 1899-1968
(Russian)**
CasWL-1973
ClDMEuL-1980
EncWL-1981
GdMWL-1985
PengEur-1969
PrEncyPP-1974

Constructivism

Semenko, Mykhaylo 1892-1939
(Ukrainian)
ClDMEuL-1980
EncWL-1981
GdMWL-1985

Futurism

Semper, Johannes 1892-1970
(Estonian)
CasWL-1973
ClDMEuL-1980

Siuru Group

Senghor, Leopold Sedar 1906-
(Senegalese)
BenReEncy-1987
CasWL-1973
ClDMEuL-1980
EncWL-1981
GdMWL-1985
OxEng-1985
PengCOAL-1969
PrEncyPP-1974

Négritude

Sepamla, Sydney Sipho 1932-
(South African)
CamGLE-1988
EncWL-1981

Black Consciousness Movement

Seppänen, Unto 1904-1955
(Finnish)
ClDMEuL-1980
EncWL-1981

Flame Bearers Group/
Tulenkantajat

Serafimovich, Aleksandr 1863-1949
(Russian)
ClDMEuL-1980
GdMWL-1985
PengEur-1969

Znanie Group

Serao, Matilde 1850-1927 (Greek-
born Italian)
BenReEncy-1987
CasWL-1973
ClDMEuL-1980
EncWL-1981
GdMWL-1985
PengEur-1969

Verismo

Sereni, Vittorio 1913-1983 (Italian)
CasWL-1973
ClDMEuL-1980
EncWL-1981
GdMWL-1985
OxEng-1985
PengEur-1969

Hermeticism/Poesia Ermetica

Serote, Mongane Wally 1944-
(South African)
CamGLE-1988
EncWL-1981

Black Consciousness Movement

Serpa, Alberto de 1906-
(Portuguese)
PrEncyPP-1974

Presencistas Group

Service, Robert W(illiam) 1874-1958
(English-born Canadian)
BenReEncy-1987

CamGLE-1988
OxCan-1983
OxEng-1985
PengEng-1971

Local Color School

Seuren, Günter n.d. (German)
OxGer-1986

Cologne School of New
Realism/Kölner Schule des
neuen Realismus

Severini, Gino 1883-1966 (Italian)
BenReEncy-1987
EncWL-1981
OxEng-1985

Futurism

Severyanin, Igor (Igor Vasilyevich Lotaryov) 1887-1942 (Russian)
CasWL-1973
ClDMEuL-1980
EncWL-1981
GdMWL-1985
PrEncyPP-1974

Ego-Futurism

Sexton, Anne 1928-1974 (American)
BenReEncy-1987
CamGLE-1988
CasWL-1973
EncWL-1981
GdMWL-1985
OxAm-1983
PengAm-1971
PrEncyPP-1974

Confessional Poetry

Shafer, Robert 1889-1956 (American)
HandLit-1986

New Humanism

Shaginyan, Marietta Sergeyevna 1888-1982 (Russian)
CasWL-1973
ClDMEuL-1980
EncWL-1981

Symbolism

Shah, Sayyid Nasir Ahmad n.d. (Pakistani)
EncWL-1981

Assembly of the Men of Good
Taste

Shahar, David 1926-   (Israeli)
ClDMEuL-1980

Metarealism

Shapiro, David 1947-   (American)
EncWL-1981

New York School

Shapiro, Karl 1913-   (American)
BenReEncy-1987
OxAm-1983

Poetry

Shaw, George Bernard 1856-1950 (Irish-born English)
BenReEncy-1987
CamGLE-1988
CasWL-1973
CEnMWL-1963
EncWL-1981
GdMWL-1985

LongCTCL-1975
McGWD-1984
OxAmThe-1984
OxEng-1985
OxThe-1983
PengEng-1971
RCom-1973

Abbey Theater
Edwardian Literature
Georgian Literature
Irish Renaissance
Modernism
Theater Guild

Shaw, Irwin 1913-1984 (American)
BenReEncy-1987
CamGLE-1988
LongCTCL-1975
OxAm-1983
OxAmThe-1984
PengAm-1971

Group Theater
Proletarian Literature

**Shchurat, Vasyl 1872-1948
(Ukrainian)**
EncWL-1981

Young Muse Group/Moloda
Muza

**Shengalaia, Demna 1896-
(Georgian)**
EncWL-1981

Futurism

**Sherman, Stuart 1881-1926
(American)**
OxAm-1983
PengAm-1971

PrEncyPP-1974

New Humanism

**Shershenevich, Vadim Alexeyevich
1893-1942 (Russian)**
ClDMEuL-1980
EncWL-1981

Imaginists
Mezzanine of Poetry

**Sherwood, Robert E(mmet) 1896-
1955 (American)**
BenReEncy-1987
CamGLE-1988
EncWL-1981
GdMWL-1985
LongCTCL-1975
OxAm-1983
OxAmThe-1984
PengAm-1971

Theater Guild

Shiels, George 1881-1949 (Irish)
CamGLE-1988
OxThe-1983

Abbey Theater

Shiga Naoya 1883-1971 (Japanese)
CasWL-1973
DOrLit-1974
EncWL-1981
GdMWL-1985
PengCOAL-1969

I-Novel/Watakushi shosetsu
White Birch School/Shirakaba-
ha

**Shimazaki Toson 1872-1943
(Japanese)**
BenReEncy-1987

CasWL-1973
DOrLit-1974
EncWL-1981
GdMWL-1985
PengCOAL-1969

Naturalism/Shizenshugi
Romanticism/Bungakkai

Shklovsky, Viktor Borisovich 1893-1984 (Russian)
BenReEncy-1987
CasWL-1973
ClDMEuL-1980
EncWL-1981
PengEur-1969
PrEncyPP-1974

LEF
Modernism
Russian Formalism
Serapion Brotherhood

Shkurupy, Geo 1903-1934 (Ukrainian)
EncWL-1981

Futurism

Shmelyov, Ivan Sergeyevich 1873-1950 (Russian)
CasWL-1973
ClDMEuL-1980
EncWL-1981
PengEur-1969

Znanie Group

Sholokov, Mikail Aleksandrovich 1905-1984 (Russian)
BenReEncy-1987
CasWL-1973
CEnMWL-1963
ClDMEuL-1980
EncWL-1981

GdMWL-1985
LongCTCL-1975
OxEng-1985
PengEur-1969

Socialist Realism

Shove, Gerald 1887-1947 (English)
HarDMT-1988

Bloomsbury Group

Showalter, Elaine 1941- (American)
OxEng-1985

Feminist Criticism

Shukla, Rameshawar 1915- (Indian)
EncWL-1981

Realism/Pragati-vada

Shukri, 'Abd al-Rahman 1886-1958 (Egyptian)
CasWL-1973
DOrLit-1974
EncWL-1981

Diwan School of Poets

Shukshin, Vasily Makarovich 1929-1974 (Russian)
BenReEncy-1987
ClDMEuL-1980
EncWL-1981
GdMWL-1985

Village Prose

Sïdïkbekov, Tügelbay 1912-
(Kirgiz)
  EncWL-1981

  Socialist Realism

Sienkiewicz, Henryk 1846-1916
(Polish)
  BenReEncy-1987
  CasWL-1973
  ClDMEuL-1980
  EncWL-1981
  GdMWL-1985
  LongCTCL-1975
  PengEur-1969

  Realism
  Warsaw Positivism

Sieroszweski, Waclaw 1858-1945
(Polish)
  ClDMEuL-1980
  PengEur-1969

  Young Poland/Mloda Polska

Sigurjónsson, Jóhann 1880-1919
(Icelandic)
  ClDMEuL-1980
  EncWL-1981
  OxThe-1983

  Progressive Romanticism

Sigússon, Hannes 1922-
(Icelandic)
  ClDMEuL-1980
  EncWL-1981

  Form Revolution
  Modernism

Sikelianos, Angelos 1884-1951
(Greek)
  CasWL-1973

  ClDMEuL-1980
  EncWL-1981
  GdMWL-1985
  PengEur-1969
  PrEncyPP-1974

  New School of Athens/Greek
  Parnassians

Sikhat, Abbas 1874-1918
(Azerbaijani)
  EncWL-1981

  Füyüzat Movement

Sill, Edward Roland 1841-1887
(American)
  OxAm-1983

  Genteel Tradition

Sillitoe, Alan 1928-   (English)
  BenReEncy-1987
  CamGLE-1988
  EncWL-1981
  GdMWL-1985
  LongCTCL-1975
  OxEng-1985
  PengEng-1971

  Angry Young Men

Silone, Ignazio (pseud. of Secondo
Tranquilli) 1900-1978 (Italian)
  BenReEncy-1987
  CasWL-1973
  CEnMWL-1963
  ClDMEuL-1980
  EncWL-1981
  GdMWL-1985
  LongCTCL-1975
  OxEng-1985
  PengEur-1969

  Neorealism

Proletarian Literature
Verismo

Silva, Domingos Carvalho da 1915-
(Brazilian)
EncWL-1981
PrEncyPP-1974

Generation of 1945

Silva, José Asunción 1865-1896
(Columbian)
BenReEncy-1987
CasWL-1973
OxSpan-1978
PengAm-1971
PrEncyPP-1974

Modernismo

Silva, José Marmelo e 1913-
(Portuguese)
EncWL-1981

Neorealism

Silva, Medardo Angel 1898-1919
(Ecuadorian)
EncWL-1981

Modernism

Silveira, Onésimo 1937-   (Cape
Verdean)
EncWL-1981

Antievasion Group/Anti-
Evasao

Silveira, Tasso da 1895-1968
(Brazilian)
EncWL-1981

Festa Group
Modernism

Sima, Joseph 1891-1971 (Czech-
born French)
EncWL-1981

Great Game Group/*Le Grand*
Jeu

Simh, Kedarnath n.d. (Indian)
DOrLit-1974

New Poetry Movement/Nayi
Kavita

Simh, Samserbahadur n.d. (Indian)
DOrLit-1974

New Poetry Movement/Nayi
Kavita

Simic, Antun Branko 1898-1925
(Croatian-speaking Yugoslavian)
EncWL-1981
PengEur-1969

Expressionism

Simoes, Joao Gaspar 1903-
(Portuguese)
ClDMEuL-1980
EncWL-1981

Presencistas Group

Simon, Claude 1913-
(Madagascar-born French)
BenReEncy-1987
CasWL-1973
ClDMEuL-1980
EncWL-1981
GdMWL-1985
OxEng-1985
PengEur-1969

New Novel/Nouveau Roman

Simonson, Lee 1888-1967
  (American)
  OxAmThe-1984
  OxThe-1983

  Theater Guild
  Washington Square Players

Simpson, N(orman) F(rederick)
  1919-   (English)
  BenReEncy-1987
  CamGLE-1988
  EncWL-1981
  GdMWL-1985
  McGWD-1984
  OxEng-1985

  New Wave/Nouvelle Vague
  Theater of the Absurd

Simpson, Robert n.d. (Canadian)
  OxCan-1983

  First Statement Group

Simunovic, Dinko 1893-1933
  (Croatian-speaking Yugoslavian)
  ClDMEuL-1980
  EncWL-1981
  GdMWL-1985

  Moderna

Sinclair, Arthur n.d. (Irish)
  OxAmThe-1984

  Abbey Theater

Sinclair, Upton 1878-1968
  (American)
  BenReEncy-1987
  CamGLE-1988
  CasWL-1973
  EncWL-1981
  GdMWL-1985

LongCTCL-1975
OxAm-1983
OxEng-1985
PengAm-1971

Muckrakers
Realism

Sinervo, Elvi 1912-   (Finnish)
  ClDMEuL-1980
  PrEncyPP-1974

  Kiila Group

Sinisgalli, Leonardo 1908-1981
  (Italian)
  CasWL-1973
  EncWL-1981
  PrEncyPP-1974

  Hermeticism/Poesia Ermetica

Sinka, István n.d. (Hungarian)
  ClDMEuL-1980

  Populist Movement

Sinkó, Ervin 1898-   (Hungarian-
  speaking Yugoslavian)
  EncWL-1981

  Hid Group

Sito, Jerzy S. n.d. (Polish)
  ClDMEuL-1980

  Kontynenty Group

Sitor Situmorang 1923-
  (Indonesian)
  EncWL-1981
  GdMWL-1985
  PrEncyPP-1974

  Generation of 1950

Sitwell, Edith 1887-1964 (English)
BenReEncy-1987
CamGLE-1988
CasWL-1973
CEnMWL-1963
EncWL-1981
GdMWL-1985
LongCTCL-1975
OxEng-1985
PengEng-1971

Modernism

Siwertz, Sigfrid 1882-1970 (Swedish)
CasWL-1973
ClDMEuL-1980
EncWL-1981
GdMWL-1985
PengEur-1969

Tiotalister

Siyavusgil, Sabri Esat (?)-1968 (Turkish)
ClDMEuL-1980

Seven Torches/Yedi Mes'ale

Sjöberg, Birger 1885-1929 (Swedish)
CasWL-1973
ClDMEuL-1980
EncWL-1981
GdMWL-1985
PengEur-1969
PrEncyPP-1974

Modernism
Swedish-Finnish Modernists

Sjödin, Stig 1917-   (Swedish)
PrEncyPP-1974

Poets of the Forties/
Fyrtiotalisterna

Skema, Antanas 1911-1961 (Lithuanian)
EncWL-1981

Earth Movement

Skram, Amalie 1846-1905 (Norwegian)
ClDMEuL-1980
GdMWL-1985
PengEur-1969

Naturalism

Skujins, Zigmunds 1926- (Latvian)
EncWL-1981

Socialist Realism

Slauerhoff, Jan Jacob 1898-1936 (Dutch)
ClDMEuL-1980
EncWL-1981
GdMWL-1985

Forum Group
Het Getij

Slaveykov, Pencho 1866-1912 (Bulgarian)
CasWL-1973
ClDMEuL-1980
EncWL-1981
GdMWL-1985
PengEur-1969

Misul Group

Slisarenko, Oleska 1891-1937 (Ukrainian)
ClDMEuL-1980

EncWL-1981

Free Academy of Proletarian
Literature/VAPLITE

**Slobodnik, Wlodzimierz 1900-
(Polish)**
  ClDMEuL-1980

Quadriga

**Slonimsky, Antoni 1895-1976
(Polish)**
  CasWL-1973
  ClDMEuL-1980
  EncWL-1981
  GdMWL-1985
  PengEur-1969
  PrEncyPP-1974

Skamander Group

**Slonimsky, Mikhail Leonidovich
1897-1972 (Russian)**
  ClDMEuL-1980

Serapion Brotherhood

**Small, Adam 1936- (South
African)**
  EncWL-1981

The Sestigers

Smieja, Florian 1925- (Polish)
  ClDMEuL-1980

Kontynenty Group

**Smit, Bartho 1924- (South
African)**
  EncWL-1981

The Sestigers

**Smith, A(rthur) J(ames) M(arshall)
1902-1980 (Canadian)**
  BenReEncy-1987
  CamGLE-1988
  CasWL-1973
  EncWL-1981
  GdMWL-1985
  LongCTCL-1975
  OxCan-1983
  PengEng-1971
  PrEncyPP-1974

Montreal Movement

Smith, Bernard 1906- (American)
  EncWL-1981

Marxist Criticism

**Smith, Francis Hopkinson 1838-
1915 (American)**
  OxAm-1983

Local Color School
Realism

**Smith, Sydney Goodsir 1915-1974
(New Zealand-born Scottish)**
  CamGLE-1988
  CasWL-1973
  EncWL-1981
  GdMWL-1985
  OxEng-1985
  PengEng-1971

Scottish Renaissance

**Smolych, Yury 1900-1976
(Ukrainian)**
  ClDMEuL-1980
  EncWL-1981

Free Academy of Proletarian
Literature/VAPLITE

**Snodgrass, W(illiam) D(eWitt) 1926-
(American)**
CamGLE-1988
CasWL-1973
EncWL-1981
GdMWL-1985
OxAm-1983
PengAm-1971
PrEncyPP-1974

Confessional Poetry

**Snoek, Paul (pseud. of Edmond
Schietekat) 1933-   (Belgian)**
ClDMEuL-1980
EncWL-1981
GdMWL-1985

Fifties Poets/Vijftigers
Fifty-Five Poets/Vijfenvijftigers

Snyder, Gary 1930-   (American)
BenReEncy-1987
CamGLE-1988
CasWL-1973
EncWL-1981
GdMWL-1985
OxAm-1983
OxEng-1985
PengAm-1971
PrEncyPP-1974

Beat Generation

**Södergran, Edith 1892-1923
(Swedish-speaking Finnish)**
CasWL-1973
ClDMEuL-1980
EncWL-1981
GdMWL-1985
PengEur-1969
PrEncyPP-1974

Swedish-Finnish Modernists

Sodums, Dzintars 1922-   (Latvian)
EncWL-1981

Modernism

Soffici, Ardengo 1879-1964 (Italian)
CasWL-1973
EncWL-1981
PengEur-1969
PrEncyPP-1974

Futurism

Sohnrey, H. 1859-1948 (German)
OxGer-1986

Heimatkunst

Soldati, Mario 1906-   (Italian)
ClDMEuL-1980
EncWL-1981
GdMWL-1985
PengEur-1969

Neorealism

Sollers, Philippe 1936-   (French)
BenReEncy-1987
ClDMEuL-1980
EncWL-1981
GdMWL-1985

New Novel/Nouveau Roman
Structuralism
Tel Quel Group

**Sologub, Fyodor (pseud. of Fyodor
Kuzmich Teternikov) 1863-1927
(Russian)**
BenReEncy-1987
CasWL-1973
CEnMWL-1963
ClDMEuL-1980
EncWL-1981
McGWD-1984

PengEur-1969
PrEncyPP-1974

Symbolism

**Soloukhin, Vladimir Alexeyevich
1924- (Russian)**
BenReEncy-1987
ClDMEuL-1980
EncWL-1981
GdMWL-1985
PengEur-1969

Village Prose

**Solovyov, Vladimir Sergeyevich
1853-1900 (Russian)**
BenReEncy-1987
ClDMEuL-1980
EncWL-1981
GdMWL-1985
PengEur-1969

Symbolism

Solstad, Dag 1943- (Norwegian)
ClDMEuL-1980
EncWL-1981

Profil Group

**Solt, Mary Ellen 1920-
(American)**
PrEncyPP-1974

Concrete Poetry

Sorensen, Villy 1929- (Danish)
CasWL-1973
ClDMEuL-1980
EncWL-1981
GdMWL-1985
PengEur-1969

Modernism

**Sorge, Reinhard 1892-1916
(German)**
CamGLE-1988
CasWL-1973
EncWL-1981
GdMWL-1985
McGWD-1984
OxGer-1986
OxThe-1983
PengEur-1969

Expressionism

Sorma, Agnes 1865-1927 (German)
OxThe-1983

Deutsches Theater
Freie Bühne

Sosa, Rafael n.d. (Guatemalan)
OxSpan-1978

The Dawn Group/Grupo Saker
Ti

**Sosyra, Volodymyr 1894-1965
(Ukrainian)**
EncWL-1981

Neoromanticism

**Soto, Pedro Juan 1928- (Puerto
Rican)**
CaribWr-1979
EncWL-1981
McGWD-1984

Generation of 1940

Sotola, Jiri 1924- (Czech)
ClDMEuL-1980

May Group/Kveten

Soupault, Philippe 1897-   (French)
BenReEncy-1987
CasWL-1973
ClDMEuL-1980
EncWL-1981
GdMWL-1985
OxFr-1959
PrEncyPP-1974

Dadaism
Surrealism

Souris, André 1899-1970 (Belgian)
EncWL-1981

Surrealism

**Sousa, António Sergio 1883-1968
(Portuguese)**
CasWL-1973
ClDMEuL-1980

Portuguese Renascence
  Movement
Seara Nova Group

**Soutar, William 1898-1943
(Scottish)**
CamGLE-1988
CasWL-1973
EncWL-1981
GdMWL-1985
OxEng-1985
PrEncyPP-1974

Scottish Renaissance

Sova, Antonín 1864-1928 (Czech)
ClDMEuL-1980
EncWL-1981
PengEur-1969
PrEncyPP-1974

Symbolism

Speliers, Hedwig n.d. (Belgian)
ClDMEuL-1980

Fifties Poets/Vijftigers

Spence, Lewis 1874-1955 (Scottish)
CamGLE-1988
EncWL-1981
PengEng-1971

Scottish Renaissance

**Spencer, Anne 1882-1975
(American)**
PrEncyPP-1974

Harlem Renaissance

Spender, Stephen 1909-   (English)
BenReEncy-1987
CamGLE-1988
CasWL-1973
CEnMWL-1963
EncWL-1981
GdMWL-1985
LongCTCL-1975
OxEng-1985
PengEng-1971

Group Theater
Pylon School

**Spingarn, Joel 1875-1939
(American)**
BenReEncy-1987
EncWL-1981
OxAm-1983

New Criticism

**Spurgeon, Caroline 1869-1942
(American)**
BenReEncy-1987
LongCTCL-1975

OxEng-1985

New Criticism

Squire, J(ohn) C(ollings) 1884-1958 (English)
BenReEncy-1987
CamGLE-1988
GdMWL-1985
LongCTCL-1975
OxEng-1985
PengEng-1971
PrEncyPP-1974

Georgian Literature

Sruoga, Balys 1896-1947 (Lithuanian)
EncWL-1981
PrEncyPP-1974

Symbolism

Stadler, Ernst 1883-1914 (German)
BenReEncy-1987
CasWL-1973
ClDMEuL-1980
EncWL-1981
GdMWL-1985
OxGer-1986
PengEur-1969
PrEncyPP-1974

Expressionism

Staff, Leopold 1878-1957 (Polish)
ClDMEuL-1980
EncWL-1981
GdMWL-1985
PengEur-1969

Skamander Group
Young Poland/Mloda Polska

Stanca, Radu 1920-1962 (Romanian)
EncWL-1981

Sibiu Group

Stancu, Zaharia 1902-1974 (Romanian)
ClDMEuL-1980
EncWL-1981
GdMWL-1985

Gîndirea

Stanislovsky, Konstantin Sergeivich 1863-1938 (Russian)
BenReEncy-1987
ClDMEuL-1980
EncWL-1981
LongCTCL-1975
McGWD-1984
OxAmThe-1984
OxThe-1983

Moscow Art Theater
Realism

Starobinsky, Jean 1920-   (Swiss)
ClDMEuL-1980
EncWL-1981
PrEncyPP-1974

Geneva School of Critics

Stavenhagen, Fritz 1876-1906 (German)
CasWL-1973
OxGer-1986

Heimatkunst

Stead, Robert 1880-1959 (Canadian)
OxCan-1983

Local Color School

**Stedman, Edmund Clarence 1833-
1908 (American)**
BenReEncy-1987
OxAm-1983

Genteel Tradition

**Stefenovych, Oleska 1900-1970
(Ukrainian)**
ClDMEuL-1980
EncWL-1981

Visnyk

Steffen, Günter n.d. (German)
OxGer-1986

Cologne School of New
Realism/Kölner Schule des
neuen Realismus

**Steffens, Lincoln 1866-1936
(American)**
BenReEncy-1987
LongCTCL-1975
OxAm-1983
PengAm-1971

Muckrakers

**Stehr, Hermann 1864-1940
(German)**
ClDMEuL-1980
OxGer-1986

Heimatkunst

**Stein, Gertrude 1874-1946
(American)**
BenReEncy-1987
CamGLE-1988
CasWL-1973
CEnMWL-1963
EncWL-1981
GdMWL-1985

LongCTCL-1975
McGWD-1984
OxAm-1983
OxAmThe-1984
OxEng-1985
PengAm-1971
RCom-1973

Cubism
Lost Generation

**Steinarr, Steinn (pseud. of
Adalsteinn Kristmundsson) 1908-
1958 (Icelandic)**
ClDMEuL-1980
EncWL-1981

Form Revolution
Modernism

**Steinbeck, John 1902-1968
(American)**
BenReEncy-1987
CamGLE-1988
CasWL-1973
CEnMWL-1963
EncWL-1981
GdMWL-1985
LongCTCL-1975
McGWD-1984
OxAm-1983
OxAmThe-1984
OxEng-1985
OxThe-1983
PengAm-1971

Naturalism
Proletarian Literature

**Stelaru, Dimitrie 1917-1971
(Romanian)**
EncWL-1981

Bucharest Group

Stepanova, Varvara 1894-1958 (Russian)
HarDMT-1988

Constructivism

Stephansson, Stephan Gudmundsson 1853-1927 (Icelandic)
BenReEncy-1987
CasWL-1973
ClDMEuL-1980
GdMWL-1985

Realism

Stephens, James 1882(?)-1950 (Irish)
BenReEncy-1987
CamGLE-1988
CasWL-1973
EncWL-1981
GdMWL-1985
LongCTCL-1975
McGWD-1984
OxEng-1985
PengEng-1971
PrEncyPP-1974
RCom-1973

Edwardian Literature
Georgian Literature
Irish Renaissance

Stere, Constantin 1865-1936 (Romanian)
CasWL-1973
EncWL-1981
GdMWL-1985

Populist Literature Movement

Stern, Anatole 1899-1968 (Polish)
ClDMEuL-1980

EncWL-1981

Futurism

Stern, Mario Rigoni 1921- (Italian)
ClDMEuL-1980

Neorealism

Sternheim, Carl 1878-1942 (German)
CasWL-1973
ClDMEuL-1980
EncWL-1981
GdMWL-1985
McGWD-1984
OxGer-1986
OxThe-1983
PengEur-1969

Expressionism

Stevens, Wallace 1879-1955 (American)
CamGLE-1988
CasWL-1973
CEnMWL-1963
EncWL-1981
GdMWL-1985
LongCTCL-1975
OxAm-1983
OxEng-1985
PengAm-1971

Poetry

Stewart, Harold 1916- (Australian)
PrEncyPP-1974

Angry Penguins

**Stifter, Adalbert 1805-1868
(Austrian)**
  BenReEncy-1987
  EncWL-1981
  OxGer-1986
  PengEur-1969
  PrEncyPP-1974

  Realism

Stil, André 1921-   (French)
  EncWL-1981

  Socialist Realism

**Stoddard, Richard Henry 1825-1903
(American)**
  GdMWL-1985
  OxAm-1983

  Genteel Tradition

**Stoppard, Tom 1937-   (Czech-
born English)**
  BenReEncy-1987
  CamGLE-1988
  EncWL-1981
  GdMWL-1985
  McGWD-1984
  OxAmThe-1984
  OxEng-1985
  OxThe-1983

  Theater of the Absurd

**Storm, Theodor 1817-1888
(German)**
  OxGer-1986
  PengEur-1969

  Impressionism

**Stowe, Harriet Beecher 1811-1896
(American)**
  BenReEncy-1987

  CamGLE-1988
  CasWL-1973
  OxAm-1983
  OxEng-1985
  PengAm-1971

  Local Color School
  Realism

**Stoyanov, Lyudmil (pseud. of
Georgi Zlatarev) 1888-(?)
(Bulgarian)**
  CasWL-1973
  PrEncyPP-1974

  Socialist Realism

Strachey, James 1887-1967 (English)
  HarDMT-1988

  Bloomsbury Group

**Strachey, (Giles) Lytton 1880-1932
(English)**
  BenReEncy-1987
  CamGLE-1988
  CasWL-1973
  CEnMWL-1963
  EncWL-1981
  LongCTCL-1975
  OxEng-1985
  PengEng-1971

  Bloomsbury Group

**Strachey, Marjorie 1882-1964
(English)**
  HarDMT-1988
  LongCTCL-1975

  Bloomsbury Group

**Straittigis, Yorghos 1860-1938
(Greek)**
  EncWL-1981

PrEncyPP-1974

New School of Athens/Greek Parnassians

Stramm, August 1874-1915 (German)
ClDMEuL-1980
EncWL-1981
GdMWL-1985
OxGer-1986
PengEur-1969
PrEncyPP-1974

Expressionism
Storm Circle/*Der Sturm*
Surrealism

Strasberg, Lee 1901-1982 (American)
BenReEncy-1987
CamGLE-1988
EncWL-1981
OxAm-1983
OxAmThe-1984
OxThe-1983

Group Theater
Theater Guild

Strauss und Torney, Lulu von 1873-1956 (German)
EncWL-1981
OxGer-1986

Heimatkunst

Streuvels, Stijn (pseud. of Frank Lateur) 1871-1969 (Belgian)
CasWL-1973
ClDMEuL-1980
EncWL-1981
GdMWL-1985

Van nu en straks Group

Strindberg, August 1849-1912 (Swedish)
BenReEncy-1987
CamGLE-1988
CasWL-1973
ClDMEuL-1980
EncWL-1981
GdMWL-1985
LongCTCL-1975
McGWD-1984
OxAmThe-1984
OxEng-1985
OxGer-1986
OxThe-1983
PengEur-1969
PrEncyPP-1974
RCom-1973

Expressionism
Freie Bühne
Naturalism
Realism
Théâtre Libre

Stringer, Arthur John Arbuthnott 1874-1950 (Canadian)
CasWL-1973
OxCan-1983

Local Color School

Strittmatter, Erwin 1912- (German)
CasWL-1973
EncWL-1981
GdMWL-1985
OxGer-1986
PengEur-1969

Berlin Ensemble/Berliner Ensemble

**Stroinski, Zdzisslaw 1920-1943
(Polish)**
  EncWL-1981

Condemned Generation Poets

Strug, Andrzej 1871-1937 (Polish)
  ClDMEuL-1980
  EncWL-1981
  GdMWL-1985

Young Poland/Mloda Polska

**Stuckenberg, Viggo 1863-1905
(Danish)**
  BenReEncy-1987
  ClDMEuL-1980
  GdMWL-1985

Symbolism

**Sudermann, Hermann 1857-1928
(German)**
  BenReEncy-1987
  CasWL-1973
  ClDMEuL-1980
  LongCTCL-1975
  McGWD-1984
  OxGer-1986
  OxThe-1983
  PengEur-1969

Deutsches Theater
Naturalism

Suits, Gustav 1883-1956 (Estonian)
  CasWL-1973
  ClDMEuL-1980
  EncWL-1981
  GdMWL-1985
  PrEncyPP-1974

Young Estonia Group

**Sullivan, Mark 1874-1952
(American)**
  BenReEncy-1987
  OxAm-1983

Muckrakers

Suman, S. n.d. (Indian)
  DOrLit-1974

Realism/Pragati-vada

**Su Man-Shu 1884-1918 (Japanese-
born Chinese)**
  CasWL-1973
  DOrLit-1974
  EncWL-1981

Southern Society/Nan-shê
Group

**Suratman Markasan 1930-
(Malaysian)**
  EncWL-1981

Generation of the 1950s/Asas
'50

Süreya, Cemal 1931-   (Turkish)
  ClDMEuL-1980
  DOrLit-1974
  EncWL-1981
  GdMWL-1985
  PrEncyPP-1974

Abstract Movement
The Second New

Sutherland, Betty n.d. (Canadian)
  OxCan-1983

First Statement Group

Sutherland, John 1919-1956 (Canadian)
OxCan-1983

First Statement Group

Sutzkever, Abraham 1913- (Yiddish-speaking Lithuanian)
CasWL-1973
ClDMEuL-1980
EncWL-1981
GdMWL-1985
PengEur-1969

Young Vilna

Svevo, Italo (pseud. of Ettore Schmitz) 1861-1928 (Italian)
BenReEncy-1987
CasWL-1973
CEnMWL-1963
ClDMEuL-1980
EncWL-1981
GdMWL-1985
LongCTCL-1975
OxEng-1985
PengEur-1969

Naturalism
Solaria Group

Svidzinsky, Volodymyr 1885-1941 (Ukrainian)
EncWL-1981

Symbolism

Swietochowski, Alexander 1849-1938 (Polish)
CasWL-1973
ClDMEuL-1980
GdMWL-1985

Warsaw Positivism

Sybesma, Rintsje Piter 1894-1975 (Dutch)
EncWL-1981
PrEncyPP-1974

Young Frisian Movement

Sydney-Turner, Saxon 1880-1962 (English)
CamGLE-1988

Bloomsbury Group

Sygietynski, Antoni 1850-1923 (Polish)
ClDMEuL-1980
EncWL-1981

Naturalism

Symonenko, Vasyl 1935-1963 (Ukrainian)
ClDMEuL-1980
EncWL-1981

Generation of the 1960s/ Shestydesyatnyky

Symons, Arthur 1865-1945 (English)
BenReEncy-1987
CamGLE-1988
CasWL-1973
EncWL-1981
LongCTCL-1975
OxEng-1985
PengEng-1971

Symbolism

Synge, John Millington 1871-1909 (Irish)
BenReEncy-1987
CamGLE-1988
CasWL-1973
CEnMWL-1963

EncWL-1981
GdMWL-1985
LongCTCL-1975
McGWD-1984
OxAmThe-1984
OxEng-1985
OxThe-1983
PengEng-1971
PrEncyPP-1974
RCom-1973

Abbey Theater
Edwardian Literature
Irish Literary Theater
Irish Renaissance
Naturalism
Realism
Symbolism

**Szabó, Dezso 1879-1945
(Hungarian)**
CasWL-1973
ClDMEuL-1980
EncWL-1981
GdMWL-1985
PengEur-1969

Populist Movement

Szábo, István n.d. (Hungarian)
ClDMEuL-1980

Generation of 1955

Szabó, László n.d. (Hungarian)
ClDMEuL-1980

Nyugat Group

**Szabó, Lorinc 1900-1957
(Hungarian)**
CasWL-1973
ClDMEuL-1980
EncWL-1981
GdMWL-1985

PengEur-1969

Nyugat Group

Szábo, Magda 1917-   (Hungarian)
ClDMEuL-1980
EncWL-1981

Ujhold Group

Szabó, Pál 1893-1970 (Hungarian)
ClDMEuL-1980
EncWL-1981

Populist Movement

Szabó, Zoltán n.d. (Hungarian)
ClDMEuL-1980

Populist Movement

**Szenteleky, Kornél 1893-1933
(Hungarian-speaking
Yugoslavian)**
EncWL-1981

Kalangya Group

Szép, Erno 1884-1953 (Hungarian)
CasWL-1973
ClDMEuL-1980
EncWL-1981

Nyugat Group

Szerb, Antal 1901-1945 (Hungarian)
CasWL-1973
ClDMEuL-1980
GdMWL-1985
PengEur-1969

Nyugat Group

**Szomory, Dezso 1869-1944
(Hungarian)**
ClDMEuL-1980
EncWL-1981

Nyugat Group

**Szymborska, Wislawa 1923-
(Polish)**
ClDMEuL-1980
EncWL-1981

Wspólczesnosc Generation

T

**Tabidze, Galaktion 1892-1959
(Georgian)**
DOrLit-1974
EncWL-1981
GdMWL-1985
PrEncyPP-1974

Blue Horns Group/Tsispheri
q'antesbi

**Tabidze, Titsian 1895-1937
(Georgian)**
DOrLit-1974
EncWL-1981
GdMWL-1985
PrEncyPP-1974

Blue Horns Group/Tsispheri
q'antesbi

**Tablada, José Juan 1871-1945
(Mexican)**
CasWL-1973
EncWL-1981
OxSpan-1978

Modernismo

Taborski, Boleslaw 1927-   (Polish)
ClDMEuL-1980

Kontynenty Group

**Tagore, Rabindranath 1861-1941
(Indian)**
BenReEncy-1987

CasWL-1973
DOrLit-1974
EncWL-1981
GdMWL-1985
LongCTCL-1975
OxEng-1985
PengCOAL-1969
PengEng-1971

Romanticism/Chhaya-vada

**Taha, 'Ali Mahmud 1902-1949
(Egyptian)**
CasWL-1973
DOrLit-1974
EncWL-1981

Apollo School of Poets

**Taine, Hippolyte 1828-1893
(French)**
BenReEncy-1987
EncWL-1981
OxEng-1985
OxFr-1959
PengEur-1969

Naturalism
Realism

**Takahama Kyoshi 1874-1959
(Japanese)**
DOrLit-1974
EncWL-1981

Hototogisu Poets

Takdir Alisjahbana, Sutan 1908-
(Sumatran)
  DOrLit-1974
  EncWL-1981
  PengCOAL-1969
  PrEncyPP-1974

  New Writers' Circle/Pudjangga
  Baru

Tallet, José Zacarías 1893-
(Cuban)
  CaribWr-1979
  EncWL-1981
  OxSpan-1978
  PengAm-1971

  Afro-Cubanism

Talvik, Heiti 1904-1947 (Estonian)
  ClDMEuL-1980
  EncWL-1981
  GdMWL-1985
  PrEncyPP-1974

  Soothsayers Movement/
  Arbujad

Tamási, Áron 1897-1966
(Hungarian)
  CasWL-1973
  ClDMEuL-1980
  EncWL-1981
  GdMWL-1985
  PengEur-1969

  Populist Movement

Tambal, Hamza 1893-1960
(Sudanese)
  EncWL-1981

  Romantic Poets

Tammuz, Binyamin 1919-
(Ukrainian-born Israeli)
  CasWL-1973
  ClDMEuL-1980
  GdMWL-1985

  Metarealism

Tanase, Virgil 1940-   **(Romanian)**
  EncWL-1981

  Oneiric Movement

Taneda Santoka 1882-1940
(Japanese)
  EncWL-1981

  New Tendency School

Tanguy, Yves 1900-1955 (French-
born American)
  EncWL-1981

  Surrealism

Tarbell, Ida M(inerva) 1857-1944
(American)
  BenReEncy-1987
  OxAm-1983

  Muckrakers

Tarn, Adam 1902-1972 (Polish)
  EncWL-1981
  McGWD-1984

  Theater of the Absurd

Tarnawsky, Yuriy 1934-
(Ukrainian)
  EncWL-1981

  New York Group

Tate, Allen 1899-1979 (American)
BenReEncy-1987
CamGLE-1988
CasWL-1973
EncWL-1981
GdMWL-1985
LongCTCL-1975
OxAm-1983
OxEng-1985
PengAm-1971
PrEncyPP-1974

The Fugitives/Agrarians
New Criticism

**Tatlin, Vladimir 1885-1953
(Russian)**
HarDMT-1988

Constructivism

Tauns, Linards 1922-1963 (Latvian)
EncWL-1981
GdMWL-1985
PengEur-1969

New York Group

Taut, Bruno 1880-1938 (German)
HarDMT-1988

Expressionism

**Tayama Katai (pseud. of Tayama
Rokuya) 1872-1930 (Japanese)**
CasWL-1973
DOrLit-1974
EncWL-1981
GdMWL-1985
PengCOAL-1969

I-Novel/Watakushi shosetsu
Naturalism/Shizenshugi

**Taylor, Bayard 1825-1878
(American)**
CamGLE-1988
CasWL-1973
OxAm-1983
PengAm-1971

Genteel Tradition

**Tchelichev, Pavel 1898-1957
(Russian-born American)**
BenReEncy-1987

Surrealism

Teige, Karel 1900-1951 (Czech)
EncWL-1981
GdMWL-1985

Nine Powers Group/Devêtsil
Poeticism

**Teirlinck, Herman 1879-1967
(Belgian)**
CasWL-1973
ClDMEuL-1980
EncWL-1981
GdMWL-1985
PengEur-1969

Van nu en straks Group

**Teixeira-Gomes, Manuel 1860-1941
(Portuguese)**
ClDMEuL-1980

Portuguese Renascence
Movement

**Teliha, Olena 1907-1942
(Ukrainian)**
ClDMEuL-1980
EncWL-1981

Visnyk

Tendryakov, Vladimir Fyorodovich 1923-1984 (Russian)
BenReEncy-1987
ClDMEuL-1980
EncWL-1981
PengEur-1969

Village Prose

Tennant, Emma 1937- (English)
CamGLE-1988
OxEng-1985

Magic Realism

Tepeneag, Dumitru 1936- (Romanian)
EncWL-1981

Oneiric Movement

Tersánszky, Jeno J. 1888-1969 (Hungarian)
ClDMEuL-1980
PengEur-1969

Nyugat Group

Tetmajer, Kazimierz Przerwa 1865-1940 (Polish)
CasWL-1973
ClDMEuL-1980
EncWL-1981
GdMWL-1985
PengEur-1969
PrEncyPP-1974

Young Poland/Mloda Polska

Thach Lam 1909-1943 (Vietnamese)
DOrLit-1974
EncWL-1981

Ngày nay Group

Theer, Otakar 1880-1917 (Romanian-born Czech)
CasWL-1973
ClDMEuL-1980

Symbolism

The-Lu 1907- (Vietnamese)
DOrLit-1974
EncWL-1981

Ngày nay Group
Self-Reliant Group

Theotakas, Yorghos 1905-1966 (Greek)
EncWL-1981
GdMWL-1985
McGWD-1984
PengEur-1969

Generation of 1930

Thérive, André 1891-1967 (French)
BenReEncy-1987
ClDMEuL-1980
EncWL-1981
GdMWL-1985

Populisme

Thoby-Marcelin, Philippe 1904-1975 (Haitian)
CasWL-1973
EncWL-1981

Revue Indigène Group

Thomas, Dylan 1914-1953 (Welsh)
BenReEncy-1987
CamGLE-1988
CasWL-1973
CEnMWL-1963
EncWL-1981
GdMWL-1985

LongCTCL-1975
McGWD-1984
OxEng-1985
PengEng-1971
RCom-1973

Modernism
New Apocalypse
Surrealism

**Thomas, Edward 1878-1917
(English)**
BenReEncy-1987
CamGLE-1988
CasWL-1973
CEnMWL-1963
EncWL-1981
GdMWL-1985
LongCTCL-1975
OxEng-1985
PengEng-1971
PrEncyPP-1974

Georgian Literature

**Thoursie, Ragnar 1919-
(Swedish)**
ClDMEuL-1980
EncWL-1981
GdMWL-1985
PrEncyPP-1974

Poets of the Forties/
Fyrtiotalisterna

**Thurman, Wallace 1902-1934
(American)**
CamGLE-1988
OxAm-1983

Harlem Renaissance

**Thurzó, Lajos 1915-1950
(Hungarian-speaking
Yugoslavian)**
EncWL-1981

Hid Group

**Thwaite, Anthony 1930-
(English)**
OxEng-1985

New Lines Poets

**Tiempo, César 1906-   (Ukrainian-
born Argentine)**
OxSpan-1978

Boedo Group

T'ien Han 1898-1968 (Chinese)
CasWL-1973
DOrLit-1974
EncWL-1981
GdMWL-1985
PengCOAL-1969

Creation Society
South China Society

**Tikhonov, Nikolay Semënovich
1896-   (Russian)**
CasWL-1973
CEnMWL-1963
ClDMEuL-1980
GdMWL-1985
PengEur-1969

Serapion Brotherhood

**Tillich, Paul 1886-1965 (German-
born American)**
BenReEncy-1987
LongCTCL-1975
OxAm-1983

OxGer-1986

Existentialism

**Tilvytis, Teofilis 1904-1969
(Lithuanian)**
EncWL-1981
PrEncyPP-1974

Four Winds Movement/Keturi
Vejai
Socialist Realism

Tobino, Mario 1910-　　(Italian)
ClDMEuL-1980
EncWL-1981

Neorealism

Todd, Ruthven 1914-　　(English)
EncWL-1981
LongCTCL-1975

Surrealism

**Todorov, Petko 1879-1916
(Bulgarian)**
CasWL-1973
ClDMEuL-1980
EncWL-1981
GdMWL-1985
PengEur-1969

Misul Group

**Todorov, Tzvetan 1939-
(Bulgarian)**
BenReEncy-1987
CamGLE-1988
EncWL-1981
OxEng-1985
PrEncyPP-1974

Structuralism
Tel Quel Group

Tokombaev, Aalï n.d. (Kirgiz)
EncWL-1981

Socialist Realism

**Tokuda Shusei 1891-1943
(Japanese)**
CasWL-1973
DOrLit-1974
EncWL-1981

Naturalism/Shizenshugi

**Toledo, Enrique Juárez n.d.
(Guatemalan)**
OxSpan-1978

Grupo Acento

**Tolkien, J(ohn) R(onald) R(euel)
1892-1973 (South African-born
English)**
BenReEncy-1987
CamGLE-1988
CasWL-1973
CEnMWL-1963
EncWL-1981
LongCTCL-1975
OxEng-1985
PengEng-1971

The Inklings

Toller, Ernst 1893-1939 (German)
BenReEncy-1987
CamGLE-1988
CasWL-1973
CEnMWL-1963
ClDMEuL-1980
EncWL-1981
GdMWL-1985
LongCTCL-1975
McGWD-1984
OxAmThe-1984
OxEng-1985

OxGer-1986
OxThe-1983
PengEur-1969

Expressionism

Tolstoy, Alexey Nikolayevich 1882-1945 (Russian)
BenReEncy-1987
CasWL-1973
ClDMEuL-1980
EncWL-1981
GdMWL-1985
LongCTCL-1975
McGWD-1984
OxThe-1983
PengEur-1969

Socialist Realism

Tolstoy, Lev Nikolayevich 1828-1910 (Russian)
BenReEncy-1987
CamGLE-1988
CasWL-1973
ClDMEuL-1980
EncWL-1981
GdMWL-1985
LongCTCL-1975
McGWD-1984
OxEng-1985
OxThe-1983
PengEur-1969
RCom-1973

Moscow Art Theater
Naturalism
Realism

Tomashevsky, Boris Viktorovich 1890-1957 (Russian)
CasWL-1973
EncWL-1981

PrEncyPP-1974

Russian Formalism

Tonegaru, Constant 1919-1952 (Romanian)
EncWL-1981

Bucharest Group

Toomer, Jean 1894-1967 (American)
BenReEncy-1987
CamGLE-1988
EncWL-1981
OxAm-1983
PengAm-1971
PrEncyPP-1974

Harlem Renaissance

Topîrceanu, George 1886-1937 (Romanian)
ClDMEuL-1980
EncWL-1981

Poporanism

Torga, Miguel (pseud. of Adolfo Correia da Rocha) 1907- (Portuguese)
CasWL-1973
ClDMEuL-1980
EncWL-1981
GdMWL-1985
McGWD-1984
PengEur-1969
PrEncyPP-1974

Presencistas Group

Török, Gyula n.d. (Hungarian)
ClDMEuL-1980

Nyugat Group

Torralva Navarro, Fernándo 1885-1913 (Cuban)
CaribWr-1979

Cenáculo Group

Torre, Guillermo de 1900- (Spanish-born Argentine)
CasWL-1973
ClDMEuL-1980
EncWL-1981
GdMWL-1985
OxSpan-1978
PrEncyPP-1974

Ultraism/Ultraismo

Torres, Alberto 1865-1917 (Brazilian)
EncWL-1981

Modernism
Verde-Amarelismo

Torres Bodet, Jaime 1902-1974 (Mexican)
CasWL-1973
EncWL-1981
OxSpan-1978
PengAm-1971

Contemporaries/
Contemporáneos

Tóth, Árpád 1886-1928 (Hungarian)
CasWL-1973
ClDMEuL-1980
EncWL-1981
GdMWL-1985
PengEur-1969

Nyugat Group

Toulet, Paul Jean 1867-1920 (French)
CasWL-1973
ClDMEuL-1980
OxFr-1959
PengEur-1969

Fantaisistes Group

Tournier, Luc (pseud. of Christiaan J.H. Engels) 1907- (Dutch-born Curaçaon)
CaribWr-1979

Porch Group/De Stoep

Tozzi, Federigo 1883-1920 (Italian)
BenReEncy-1987
CasWL-1973
ClDMEuL-1980
EncWL-1981
GdMWL-1985

Neorealism
Solaria Group

Trakl, Georg 1887-1914 (Austrian)
BenReEncy-1987
CasWL-1973
CEnMWL-1963
ClDMEuL-1980
EncWL-1981
GdMWL-1985
OxGer-1986
PengEur-1969
PrEncyPP-1974

Expressionism

Trausti, Jón (pseud. of Gudmundur Magnússon) 1873-1918 (Icelandic)
CasWL-1973
ClDMEuL-1980

EncWL-1981

Realism

Traversi, Derek A. 1912-
(English)
  CamGLE-1988
  EncWL-1981
  OxEng-1985

  Scrutiny

Trayanov, Teodor 1882-1945
(Bulgarian)
  CasWL-1973
  ClDMEuL-1980
  EncWL-1981
  PrEncyPP-1974

  Symbolism

Treece, Henry 1912-1966 (English)
  BenReEncy-1987
  LongCTCL-1975
  OxEng-1985
  PengEng-1971

  New Apocalypse

Trefossa (pseud. of Henri Frans de
  Ziel) 1916-   (Surinamese)
  CaribWr-1979
  EncWL-1981

  Our Own Things Group/Wie
    Eegie Sanie

Tretyakov, Sergey Mikhailovich
1892-1939 (Russian)
  CasWL-1973
  OxThe-1983

  LEF

Trigo, Felipe 1864-1916 (Spanish)
  CasWL-1973
  ClDMEuL-1980
  GdMWL-1985
  OxSpan-1978

  Naturalism

Tripathi, Suryakant 1896-1961
(Indian)
  DOrLit-1974
  EncWL-1981

  Realism/Pragati-vada
  Romanticism/Chhaya-vada

Trocchi, Alexander 1925-1984
(Scottish-born English)
  OxEng-1985

  Underground Poetry

Truffaut, François 1932-1984
(French)
  BenReEncy-1987
  EncWL-1981

  New Wave/Nouvelle Vague

Trus, R. n.d. (Byelorussian)
  PrEncyPP-1974

  Socialist Realism

Trzebinski, Andrzej 1922-1943
(Polish)
  EncWL-1981
  McGWD-1984

  Condemned Generation Poets

Ts'ai Yüan-p'ei n.d. (Chinese)
  DOrLit-1974

May Fourth Movement/Wu-
ssu yün-tung

**Tschichold, Jan 1902(?)-1974
(German-born Swiss)**
HarDMT-1988

New Objectivity/Neue
Sachlichkeit

Tsirekidse, C. n.d. (Georgian)
PrEncyPP-1974

Blue Horns Group/Tsispheri
q'antesbi

**Tucholsky, Kurt 1890-1935
(German)**
CasWL-1973
EncWL-1981
OxGer-1986
PengEur-1969

New Objectivity/Neue
Sachlichkeit

Tuéni, Nadia 1935-   (Lebanese)
EncWL-1981

Surrealism

**Tuglas, Friedebert 1886-1971
(Estonian)**
CasWL-1973
ClDMEuL-1980
EncWL-1981
GdMWL-1985

Young Estonia Group

Tuktash, Ilya 1907-   (Chuvash)
EncWL-1981

Socialist Realism

**Tú Mo (pseud. of Ho-trong-Hieu)
1900-1976 (Vietnamese)**
DOrLit-1974
EncWL-1981

Ngày nay Group

**Turgenev, Ivan Sergeyevich 1818-
1883 (Russian)**
BenReEncy-1987
CasWL-1973
EncWL-1981
McGWD-1984
OxEng-1985
OxThe-1983
PengEur-1969
RCom-1973

Realism

**Turner, Walter James Redfern 1889-
1946 (Australian-born English)**
GdMWL-1985
OxEng-1985
PrEncyPP-1974

Georgian Literature

**Turtiainen, Arvo 1904-1980
(Finnish)**
ClDMEuL-1980
EncWL-1981
PrEncyPP-1974

Kiila Group

**Turusbekov, Joomart 1910-1943
(Kirgiz)**
EncWL-1981

Socialist Realism

**Turyansky, Osyp 1890-1933
(Ukrainian)**
ClDMEuL-1980

Young Muse Group/Moloda
Muza

Tuwim, Julian 1894-1953 (Polish)
CasWL-1973
ClDMEuL-1980
EncWL-1981
GdMWL-1985
PengEur-1969
PrEncyPP-1974

Skamander Group

**Twain, Mark (pseud. of Samuel
Langhorne Clemens) 1835-1910
(American)**
BenReEncy-1987
CamGLE-1988
CasWL-1973
EncWL-1981
GdMWL-1985
McGWD-1984
OxAm-1983
OxEng-1985
PengAm-1971
RCom-1973

Local Color School
Realism

**Tychyna, Pavlo 1891-1967
(Ukrainian)**
ClDMEuL-1980
EncWL-1981
GdMWL-1985
PengEur-1969

Symbolism

**Tynan, Kenneth 1927-1980
(English)**
BenReEncy-1987
CamGLE-1988
LongCTCL-1975
OxAmThe-1984
OxEng-1985
OxThe-1983
PengEng-1971

Kitchen Sink Drama

**Tynyanov, Yury Nikolayevich 1894-
1943 (Russian)**
BenReEncy-1987
CasWL-1973
ClDMEuL-1980
EncWL-1981
PrEncyPP-1974

Russian Formalism

**Tzara, Tristan (pseud. of Samuel
Rosenstock) 1896-1963
(Romanian-born French)**
BenReEncy-1987
CasWL-1973
ClDMEuL-1980
EncWL-1981
GdMWL-1985
OxEng-1985
OxFr-1959
PengEur-1969
PrEncyPP-1974

Dadaism
Surrealism

U

Udaltsova, Nadezhda 1885-1961
(Russian)
HarDMT-1988

Cubo-Futurism

Ujevic, Augustin 1891-1955
(Croatian-speaking Yugoslavian)
CasWL-1973
ClDMEuL-1980
EncWL-1981
GdMWL-1985
PengEur-1969

Expressionism

Unamuno y Jugo, Miguel de 1864-
1936 (Spanish)
BenReEncy-1987
CasWL-1973
CEnMWL-1963
ClDMEuL-1980
EncWL-1981
GdMWL-1985
LongCTCL-1975
McGWD-1984
OxEng-1985
OxSpan-1978
OxThe-1983
PengEur-1969
RCom-1973

Existentialism
Generation of 1898/Generación
del 1898
Modernismo

Under, Marie 1883-1980 (Estonian)
CasWL-1973
ClDMEuL-1980
EncWL-1981
GdMWL-1985
PrEncyPP-1974

Siuru Group

Ungaretti, Giuseppe 1888-1970
(Egyptian-born Italian)
BenReEncy-1987
CasWL-1973
CEnMWL-1963
ClDMEuL-1980
EncWL-1981
GdMWL-1985
OxEng-1985
PengEur-1969
PrEncyPP-1974

Hermeticism/Poesia Ermetica

Unilowski, Zbigniew 1909-1937
(Polish)
ClDMEuL-1980

Quadriga

Unruh, Fritz von 1885-1970
(German)
BenReEncy-1987
CasWL-1973
ClDMEuL-1980
GdMWL-1985
McGWD-1984

OxGer-1986
OxThe-1983
PengEur-1969

Expressionism

Upward, Allen 1863-1926 (English)
OxEng-1985

Imagism

**Urbina, Luis Gonzaga 1868-1934
(Mexican)**
OxSpan-1978
PrEncyPP-1974

Modernismo

**Uslar Pietri, Arturo 1905-
(Venezuelan)**

BenReEncy-1987
CasWL-1973
EncWL-1981
OxSpan-1978
PengAm-1971

Magic Realism

Usman Awang 1928-   (Malaysian)
DOrLit-1974
EncWL-1981

Generation of the 1950s/Asas
'50

Uyar, Turgut 1926-   (Turkish)
EncWL-1981
PrEncyPP-1974

Abstract Movement

V

Vaara, Elina 1903-   (Finnish)
ClDMEuL-1980
PengEur-1969

Flame Bearers Group/
   Tulenkantajat

Vacas, Humberto n.d. (Ecuadorian)
OxSpan-1978

Grupo Elan

Vaché, Jacques 1895-1919 (French)
BenReEncy-1987
ClDMEuL-1980
GdMWL-1985

Dadaism

**Václavek, Bedrich 1897-1943
(Czechoslovakian)**
EncWL-1981

Marxist Criticism

Vadim, Roger 1928- (French)
HarDMT-1988

New Wave/Nouvelle Vague

**Vaginov, Konstantin
   Konstantinovich 1899-1934
   (Russian)**
ClDMEuL-1980

EncWL-1981

OBEIRIU

Vailland, Roger 1907-1965 (French)
BenReEncy-1987
CasWL-1973
ClDMEuL-1980
EncWL-1981
GdMWL-1985
PengEur-1969

Great Game Group/*Le Grand
   Jeu*

Vala, Katri 1901-1944 (Finnish)
ClDMEuL-1980
EncWL-1981
GdMWL-1985
PengEur-1969
PrEncyPP-1974

Flame Bearers Group/
   Tulenkantajat

**Valencia, Guillermo 1873-1943
   (Colombian)**
CasWL-1973
EncWL-1981
OxSpan-1978
PengAm-1971
PrEncyPP-1974

Modernismo

Valera y Alcalá Galíano, Juan 1824-1905 (Spanish)
BenReEncy-1987
ClDMEuL-1980
EncWL-1981
OxSpan-1978
PengEur-1969

Realism

Valéry, Paul 1871-1945 (French)
BenReEncy-1987
CasWL-1973
CEnMWL-1963
ClDMEuL-1980
EncWL-1981
GdMWL-1985
LongCTCL-1975
OxEng-1985
OxFr-1959
PengEur-1969
PrEncyPP-1974
RCom-1973

Nouvelle Revue Française
Group
Symbolism

Valle, Juvencio n.d. (Mexican)
PrEncyPP-1974

Creationism/Creacionismo

Valle, Rosamel del n.d. (Mexican)
PrEncyPP-1974

Creationism/Creacionismo

Valle-Inclán, Ramón 1866-1936 (Spanish)
BenReEncy-1987
CasWL-1973
CEnMWL-1963
ClDMEuL-1980
EncWL-1981

GdMWL-1985
McGWD-1984
OxSpan-1978
OxThe-1983
PengEur-1969

Generation of 1898/Generación del 1898
Modernismo
Novecentismo

Vallejo, César 1892-1938 (Peruvian)
BenReEncy-1987
CasWL-1973
CEnMWL-1963
EncWL-1981
GdMWL-1985
OxSpan-1978
PengAm-1971
PrEncyPP-1974

Surrealism
Ultraism/Ultraismo

Valteri, Mika n.d. (Finnish)
EncWL-1981

Flame Bearers Group/Tulenkantajat

Van der Goes, Frank n.d. (Dutch)
ClDMEuL-1980

Movement of the Eighties/Beweging van Tachtig

Van der Hoeven, Jan n.d. (Belgian)
ClDMEuL-1980

Fifties Poets/Vijftigers

Van Heerden, Ernst 1916- (South African)
CasWL-1973

PrEncyPP-1974

The Dertigers

Van Itallie, Jean-Claude 1936-
(Belgian-born American)
EncWL-1981
OxThe-1983

Theater of the Absurd

Van Moerkerken, P.H. n.d. (Dutch)
ClDMEuL-1980

De Beweging

Van Nuland, Wim (pseud. of Father
Michael Mohlmann) 1920-
(Curaçaon)
CaribWr-1979

Porch Group/De Stoep

Vancura, Vladislav 1891-1942
(Czech)
CasWL-1973
ClDMEuL-1980
EncWL-1981
GdMWL-1985
McGWD-1984
PengEur-1969

Poeticism

Vargas Llosa, Mario 1936-
(Peruvian)
BenReEncy-1987
CamGLE-1988
CasWL-1973
EncWL-1981
GdMWL-1985
OxSpan-1978
PengAm-1971

Magic Realism

Varma, Mahadevi 1907-   (Indian)
DOrLit-1974

Romanticism/Chhaya-vada

Varma, Nirmal n.d. (Indian)
DOrLit-1974

New Short Story Movement/
Nayi Kahani

Varma, Ramkumar 1905-   (Indian)
DOrLit-1974
EncWL-1981

Romanticism/Chhaya-vada

Varoujan, Daniel (pseud. of Daniel
Cheboukiarian) 1884-1915
(Armenian)
DOrLit-1974
EncWL-1981

Mehian Group

Vas, István 1910-   (Hungarian)
ClDMEuL-1980
EncWL-1981
PengEur-1969

Nyugat Group

Vasconcelos, José 1882-1959
(Mexican)
BenReEncy-1987
CasWL-1973
EncWL-1981
GdMWL-1985
OxSpan-1978
PengAm-1971

Atheneum of Youth

**Vasconcelos, Mário Cesariny de
1923-   (Portuguese)**
ClDMEuL-1980
EncWL-1981

Surrealism

**Vasilev, Vladimir 1883-1963
(Bulgarian)**
CasWL-1973
ClDMEuL-1980
EncWL-1981

Golden Horn Movement/
Zlatorog

**Vasylchenko, Stepan 1878-1932
(Ukrainian)**
EncWL-1981

Modernism

Vauthier, Jean 1910-   (Belgian)
ClDMEuL-1980
OxThe-1983
PengEur-1969

Theater of Cruelty/Théâtre de
la Cruauté

**Vázquez Montalbán, Manuel 1939-
(Spanish)**
EncWL-1981

Novísmos Group

Vela, Arqueles n.d. (Mexican)
OxSpan-1978

Estridentismo

Veliev, Ali 1901-   (Azerbaijani)
EncWL-1981

Socialist Realism

**Venclova, Antanas 1906-
(Lithuanian)**
EncWL-1981

Third Front Movement/Trecias
Frontas

**Venegas Filardo, Pascual 1911-
(Venezuelan)**
EncWL-1981

Viernes Group

Vennberg, Karl 1910-   (Swedish)
CasWL-1973
ClDMEuL-1980
EncWL-1981
GdMWL-1985
PengEur-1969
PrEncyPP-1974

Poets of the Forties/
Fyrtiotalisterna

Verástegui, Enrique n.d. (Peruvian)
OxSpan-1978

Estos 13/Hora Cero

Veres, Péter n.d. (Hungarian)
ClDMEuL-1980

Populist Movement

**Veresayev, Vikenty Vikentyevich
1867-1945 (Russian)**
ClDMEuL-1980
GdMWL-1985

Znanie Group

Verga, Giovanni 1840-1922 (Italian)
BenReEncy-1987
CasWL-1973
ClDMEuL-1980

EncWL-1981
GdMWL-1985
LongCTCL-1975
McGWD-1984
OxEng-1985
OxThe-1983
PengEur-1969
RCom-1973

Realism
Verismo

Verhaeren, Émile Adolphe Gustave 1855-1916 (Belgian)
BenReEncy-1987
CasWL-1973
ClDMEuL-1980
EncWL-1981
GdMWL-1985
LongCTCL-1975
McGWD-1984
OxFr-1959
PengEur-1969
PrEncyPP-1974

Symbolism

Verhesen, Fernand 1913- (Belgian)
ClDMEuL-1980
EncWL-1981

Journal de Poètes

Verlaine, Paul 1844-1896 (French)
BenReEncy-1987
CamGLE-1988
CasWL-1973
ClDMEuL-1980
EncWL-1981
OxEng-1985
OxFr-1959
PengEur-1969
PrEncyPP-1974

RCom-1973

Symbolism

Vermeylen, August 1872-1945 (Belgian)
BenReEncy-1987
ClDMEuL-1980
EncWL-1981

Van nu en straks Group

Verwey, Albert 1865-1937 (Dutch)
CasWL-1973
ClDMEuL-1980
EncWL-1981
GdMWL-1985
PengEur-1969
PrEncyPP-1974

De Beweging
Movement of the Eighties/
 Beweging van Tachtig

Vesaas, Tarjei 1897-1970 (Norwegian)
CasWL-1973
ClDMEuL-1980
EncWL-1981
GdMWL-1985
McGWD-1984
PengEur-1969

Symbolic Modernism

Vestdijk, Simon 1898-1971 (Dutch)
CasWL-1973
ClDMEuL-1980
EncWL-1981
GdMWL-1985
PengEur-1969
PrEncyPP-1974

Forum Group

Vian, Boris 1920-1959 (French)
BenReEncy-1987
CasWL-1973
ClDMEuL-1980
EncWL-1981
GdMWL-1985
OxEng-1985
OxThe-1983
PengEur-1969

Theater of the Absurd

**Viana, Javier de 1868-1926
(Uruguayan)**
CasWL-1973
EncWL-1981
GdMWL-1985
OxSpan-1978
PengAm-1971

Gaucho Literature
Generation of 1900

Vicaire, Gabriel 1848-1900 (French)
HarDMT-1988

Symbolism

**Vicioso, Abelardo 1929-
(Dominican Republican)**
CaribWr-1979

Promotion of 1948

Vidal, Jules n.d. (French)
OxThe-1983

Théâtre Libre

**Vidric, Vladimir 1875-1909
(Croatian)**
CasWL-1973
ClDMEuL-1980
EncWL-1981
GdMWL-1985

PengEur-1969
PrEncyPP-1974

Moderna

Viebig, Clara 1860-1952 (German)
ClDMEuL-1980
OxGer-1986

Heimatkunst
Naturalism

**Viegelsberg, Hugo (pseud. of
Ignotus Osvát) 1869-1950
(Hungarian)**
EncWL-1981

Nyugat Group

**Vieira, Afonso Lopes 1878-1946
(Portuguese)**
EncWL-1981
PrEncyPP-1974

Portuguese Renascence
Movement

**Viélé-Griffin, Francis 1864-1937
(American-born French)**
CasWL-1973
ClDMEuL-1980
EncWL-1981
GdMWL-1985
OxFr-1959
PengEur-1969
PrEncyPP-1974

Symbolism

Viganó, Renata 1900-1976 (Italian)
EncWL-1981

Neorealism

Vilar, Jean 1912-1971 (French)
ClDMEuL-1980
EncWL-1981
OxThe-1983

Theater of Cruelty/Théâtre de
la Cruauté

Vildrac, Charles 1882-1971 (French)
BenReEncy-1987
CasWL-1973
ClDMEuL-1980
EncWL-1981
GdMWL-1985
McGWD-1984
OxFr-1959
OxThe-1983

Abbaye Group/Groupe de
l'Abbaye
Unanimism/Unanisme

**Vilhjálmsson, Thor 1925-
(Icelandic)**
ClDMEuL-1980
EncWL-1981
GdMWL-1985

Modernism

Viljanen, Lauri 1900- (Finnish)
ClDMEuL-1980
GdMWL-1985
PengEur-1969

Flame Bearers Group/
Tulenkantajat

**Villaespesa, Francisco 1877-1936
(Spanish)**
CasWL-1973
ClDMEuL-1980
EncWL-1981
GdMWL-1985
McGWD-1984

OxSpan-1978
PengEur-1969

Modernismo

**Villaurrutia, Xavier 1903-1950
(Mexican)**
CasWL-1973
EncWL-1981
GdMWL-1985
McGWD-1984
OxSpan-1978
PengAm-1971

Contemporaries/
Contemporáneos

**Villiers de L'Isle-Adam, Philippe-
Auguste-Mathias 1838-1889
(French)**
BenReEncy-1987
CamGLE-1988
CasWL-1973
EncWL-1981
OxEng-1985
OxFr-1959
PengEur-1969

Symbolism

**Vinhranovsky, Mykola 1936-
(Ukrainian)**
ClDMEuL-1980
EncWL-1981

Generation of the 1960s/
Shestydesyatnyky

**Visconti, Luchino 1906-1976
(Italian)**
BenReEncy-1987
EncWL-1981
McGWD-1984
OxEng-1985

OxThe-1983

Neorealism

**Visnapuu, Henrik 1890-1951
(Estonian)**
   CasWL-1973
   ClDMEuL-1980
   EncWL-1981
   GdMWL-1985
   PrEncyPP-1974

Siuru Group

Vitier, Cintio 1921-   (Cuban)
   CaribWr-1979
   EncWL-1981
   OxSpan-1978

Orígenes Group

Vitrac, Roger 1899-1952 (French)
   BenReEncy-1987
   CasWL-1973
   ClDMEuL-1980
   EncWL-1981
   GdMWL-1985
   LongCTCL-1975
   McGWD-1984
   OxThe-1983
   PengEur-1969

Theater of the Absurd

Vittorini, Elio 1908-1966 (Italian)
   BenReEncy-1987
   CasWL-1973
   CEnMWL-1963
   ClDMEuL-1980
   EncWL-1981
   GdMWL-1985
   OxEng-1985
   PengEur-1969

Neorealism

Solaria Group

**Vlahuta, Alexandru 1858-1919
(Romanian)**
   CasWL-1973
   ClDMEuL-1980

Samanatorism

**Vlysko, Olexa 1908-1934
(Ukrainian)**
   EncWL-1981

Neoromanticism

**Vodnik, Anton 1901-1965 (Slovene-
speaking Yugoslavian)**
   EncWL-1981

Expressionism

**Vodnik, Branko 1879-1926
(Croatian-speaking Yugoslavian)**
   ClDMEuL-1980

Moderna

**Vogler, Elkhanon 1907-1969
(Yiddish-speaking Lithuanian)**
   EncWL-1981

Young Vilna

**Vogt, Nils Collett 1864-1937
(Norwegian)**
   ClDMEuL-1980
   EncWL-1981

Neoromanticism

**Voiculescu, Vasile 1884-1964
(Romanian)**
   CasWL-1973

EncWL-1981

Gîndirea

Voight-Diederichs, Helene 1875-1961 (German)
OxGer-1986

Heimatkunst

Vojnovic, Ivo 1857-1929 (Croatian-speaking Yugoslavian)
ClDMEuL-1980
EncWL-1981
GdMWL-1985
PengEur-1969

Moderna

Vold, Jan Erik 1939-   (Norwegian)
ClDMEuL-1980
EncWL-1981

Concrete Poetry
Profil Group

Vollmoeller, Karl 1878-1948 (German)
OxGer-1986

Neoromanticism/Neuromantik

Voloshin, Maximillian Alexandrovich 1877-1932 (Russian)
CasWL-1973
ClDMEuL-1980
EncWL-1981
GdMWL-1985
PengEur-1969

Symbolism

Volpe, Galvano della 1895-1968 (Italian)
EncWL-1981

Marxist Criticism

Volponi, Paolo 1924-   (Italian)
ClDMEuL-1980
EncWL-1981
GdMWL-1985

Literature and Industry
Officina Group

Volynsky, Akim L'Vovich (pseud. of A.L. Flekser) 1863-1926 (Russian)
CasWL-1973

Symbolism

Vör, Jón úr n.d. (Icelandic)
ClDMEuL-1980

Form Revolution

Voronsky, Alexander Konstantinovich 1884-1943 (Russian)
CasWL-1973
ClDMEuL-1980
EncWL-1981
PengEur-1969

Pass/Pereval

Vorony, Mykola 1871-1942 (Ukrainian)
ClDMEuL-1980
EncWL-1981

Ukrainian Home Group

Votruba, Frantisek 1880-1953 (Czech)
ClDMEuL-1980

Modernism

Vrees, Paul de 1909-   (Belgian)
ClDMEuL-1980
EncWL-1981

Concrete Poetry
Fifties Poets/Vijftigers

Vrettakos, Nikiforos 1911- (Greek)
ClDMEuL-1980
EncWL-1981

Generation of 1930

Vries, Abraham H. de 1937- (South African)
EncWL-1981

The Sestigers

Vuco, Aleksandar 1897-   (Serbian)
ClDMEuL-1980
EncWL-1981

Surrealism

Vurghun, Samed 1906-1956 (Azerbaijani)
DOrLit-1974
EncWL-1981

Socialist Realism

Vvedensky, Alexandr 1904-1941 (Russian)
ClDMEuL-1980
EncWL-1981

OBEIRIU

W

Waddington, Miriam 1917-
(Canadian)
   CamGLE-1988
   OxCan-1983

   First Statement Group

Wadsworth, Edward 1889-1949
(English)
   CamGLE-1988
   OxEng-1985

   Vorticism

Wägner, Elin 1882-1949 (Swedish)
   BenReEncy-1987
   ClDMEuL-1980
   EncWL-1981
   GdMWL-1985
   PengEur-1969

   Tiotalister

Wahl, Jean 1888-1974 (French)
   DCLT-1979

   Existentialism

Wain, John 1925-   (English)
   BenReEncy-1987
   CamGLE-1988
   CasWL-1973
   EncWL-1981
   GdMWL-1985
   LongCTCL-1975
   OxEng-1985

   PengEng-1971

   Angry Young Men
   The Movement
   New Lines Poets

Walden, Herwarth 1878-1941
(German)
   EncWL-1981
   OxGer-1986
   PengEur-1969
   PrEncyPP-1974

   Expressionism
   Storm Circle/*Der Sturm*

Wallraff, Günter 1942-   (German)
   OxGer-1986

   Group 61/Gruppe 61

Walrond, Eric 1898-1966 (Guyanan-
born American)
   CamGLE-1988
   CaribWr-1979

   Harlem Renaissance

Walschap, Gerard 1898-
(Flemish-speaking Belgian)
   CasWL-1973
   ClDMEuL-1980
   EncWL-1981
   GdMWL-1985
   PengEur-1969

New Objectivity/Neue
  Sachlichkeit

Walser, Martin 1927-   (German)
  BenReEncy-1987
  CasWL-1973
  ClDMEuL-1980
  EncWL-1981
  GdMWL-1985
  OxGer-1986
  PengEur-1969

Epic Theater/Episches Theater
Group 47/Gruppe 47

Waltari, Mika 1908-1979 (Finnish)
  CasWL-1973
  ClÐMEuL-1980
  EncWL-1981
  GdMWL-1985
  PengEur-1969

Flame Bearers Group/
  Tulenkantajat

**Warren, Austin 1899-1986
(American)**
  EncWL-1981

New Criticism

**Warren, Robert Penn 1905-1989
(American)**
  BenReEncy-1987
  CamGLE-1988
  CasWL-1973
  EncWL-1981
  GdMWL-1985
  LongCTCL-1975
  OxAm-1983
  OxEng-1985
  PengAm-1971
  PrEncyPP-1974
  RCom-1973

The Fugitives/Agrarians
New Criticism

**Wassermann, Jakob 1873-1934
(German)**
  BenReEncy-1987
  CasWL-1973
  ClDMEuL-1980
  EncWL-1981
  GdMWL-1985
  OxGer-1986
  PengEur-1969

Neoromanticism/Neuromantik

**Wat, Aleksander (pseud. of
  Aleksander Chwat) 1900-1967
  (Polish)**
  ClDMEuL-1980
  EncWL-1981
  GdMWL-1985

Futurism

Watanabe, José n.d. (Peruvian)
  OxSpan-1978

Estos 13/Hora Cero

Watkins, Vernon 1906-1967 (Welsh)
  BenReEncy-1987
  CamGLE-1988
  CasWL-1973
  EncWL-1981
  GdMWL-1985
  LongCTCL-1975
  OxEng-1985

New Apocalypse

Watts, Alan 1915-1973 (English)
  OxAm-1983

Beat Generation

Waugh, Evelyn 1903-1966 (English)
BenReEncy-1987
CamGLE-1988
CasWL-1973
CEnMWL-1963
EncWL-1981
GdMWL-1985
LongCTCL-1975
OxEng-1985
PengEng-1971

Georgian Literature
Modernism

Wazyk, Adam 1905-1982 (Polish)
CasWL-1973
CEnMWL-1963
ClDMEuL-1980
EncWL-1981
GdMWL-1985
PrEncyPP-1974

Cracow Avant-Garde

**Wedekind, Frank 1864-1918
(German)**
BenReEncy-1987
CasWL-1973
ClDMEuL-1980
EncWL-1981
GdMWL-1985
LongCTCL-1975
McGWD-1984
OxEng-1985
OxGer-1986
OxThe-1983
PengEur-1969
PrEncyPP-1974

Expressionism

Wegener, Paul 1874-1948 (German)
EncWL-1981

Expressionism

**Weigel, Helene 1900-1971
(Austrian)**
EncWL-1981
McGWD-1984
OxGer-1986

Berlin Ensemble/Berliner
Ensemble

**Weill, Kurt 1900-1950 (German-
born American)**
BenReEncy-1987
CamGLE-1988
EncWL-1981
McGWD-1984
OxAmThe-1984
OxEng-1985
OxGer-1986

Group Theater
New Objectivity/Neue
Sachlichkeit

**Weinberg, Bernard 1909-1973
(American)**
PengAm-1971
PrEncyPP-1974

Chicago Critics

Weiner, Richard 1884-1937 (Czech)
ClDMEuL-1980

Expressionism

Weiss, Peter 1916-1982 (German)
BenReEncy-1987
CasWL-1973
ClDMEuL-1980
EncWL-1981
GdMWL-1985
McGWD-1984
OxGer-1986
OxThe-1983
PengEur-1969

Epic Theater/Episches Theater
Theater of Cruelty/Théâtre de
  la Cruauté
Theater of Fact

Wekwerth, Manfred 1929-
(German)
  OxThe-1983

  Berlin Ensemble/Berliner
    Ensemble

Wellek, René 1903-   (Austrian-
born American)
  EncWL-1981

  New Criticism

Wellershoff, Dieter 1925-
(German)
  ClDMEuL-1980
  EncWL-1981
  GdMWL-1985
  OxGer-1986

  Cologne School of New
    Realism/Kölner Schule des
    neuen Realismus

Wells, H(erbert) G(eorge) 1866-1946
(English)
  BenReEncy-1987
  CamGLE-1988
  CasWL-1973
  CEnMWL-1963
  EncWL-1981
  GdMWL-1985
  LongCTCL-1975
  McGWD-1984
  OxEng-1985
  PengEng-1971
  RCom-1973

  Edwardian Literature
  Georgian Literature

  Modernism
  Realism

Wen I-to 1889-1946 (Chinese)
  CasWL-1973
  CEnMWL-1963
  DOrLit-1974
  EncWL-1981
  GdMWL-1985
  PengCOAL-1969

  Ascent Group/Hsin-yüeh she
  Crescent Society

Weöres, Sándor 1913-
(Hungarian)
  CasWL-1973
  ClDMEuL-1980
  EncWL-1981
  GdMWL-1985
  PengEur-1969

  Nyugat Group

Werfel, Franz 1890-1945 (Austrian)
  BenReEncy-1987
  CamGLE-1988
  CasWL-1973
  ClDMEuL-1980
  EncWL-1981
  GdMWL-1985
  LongCTCL-1975
  McGWD-1984
  OxGer-1986
  OxThe-1983
  PengEur-1969
  PrEncyPP-1974

  Expressionism
  Theater Guild

Wesker, Arnold 1932-   (English)
  BenReEncy-1987
  CamGLE-1988
  CasWL-1973

EncWL-1981
GdMWL-1985
LongCTCL-1975
McGWD-1984
OxEng-1985
OxThe-1983
PengEng-1971

Angry Young Men
Kitchen Sink Drama

Westley, Helen 1879-1942 (American)
OxAmThe-1984

Theater Guild
Washington Square Players

Wevergergh, Julien n.d. (Belgian)
ClDMEuL-1980

Komma Group

Weyrauch, Wolfgang 1907-1980 (German)
ClDMEuL-1980
EncWL-1981
OxGer-1986

Group 47/Gruppe 47

Whalen, Philip 1923- (American)
EncWL-1981
OxAm-1983
PengAm-1971

Beat Generation

Wharton, Edith 1862-1937 (American)
BenReEncy-1987
CamGLE-1988
CasWL-1973
EncWL-1981
GdMWL-1985

LongCTCL-1975
McGWD-1984
OxAm-1983
OxEng-1985
PengAm-1971

Realism

White, Walter 1893-1955 (American)
BenReEncy-1987
CamGLE-1988

Harlem Renaissance

Wied, Gustav Johannes 1858-1914 (Danish)
BenReEncy-1987
CasWL-1973
ClDMEuL-1980
EncWL-1981
GdMWL-1985
McGWD-1984
OxThe-1983
PengEur-1969

Naturalism

Wiene, Robert 1881-1938 (German)
EncWL-1981
OxEng-1985
OxGer-1986

Expressionism

Wiener, Oswald 1935- (Austrian)
ClDMEuL-1980
EncWL-1981
McGWD-1984
OxGer-1986

Vienna Group/Wiener Gruppe

Wieners, John 1934- (American)
OxAm-1983

407

PengAm-1971

Black Mountain Poets

Wierzynski, Kazimierz 1894-1969 (Polish)
CasWL-1973
ClDMEuL-1980
EncWL-1981
GdMWL-1985
PengEur-1969
PrEncyPP-1974

Skamander Group

Wijaya Mala 1923-   (Malaysian)
EncWL-1981

Generation of the 1950s/Asas '50

Wilde, Oscar 1854(?)-1900 (Irish)
BenReEncy-1987
CamGLE-1988
CasWL-1973
EncWL-1981
LongCTCL-1975
McGWD-1984
OxAmThe-1984
OxEng-1985
OxFr-1959
OxThe-1983
PengEng-1971
RCom-1973

Symbolism

Wildenvey, Herman Theodore 1885-1959 (Norwegian)
BenReEncy-1987
CasWL-1973
ClDMEuL-1980
EncWL-1981
GdMWL-1985

PengEur-1969

Generation of 1905

Wilder, Thornton 1897-1975 (American)
BenReEncy-1987
CamGLE-1988
CasWL-1973
CEnMWL-1963
EncWL-1981
GdMWL-1985
LongCTCL-1975
McGWD-1984
OxAm-1983
OxAmThe-1984
OxEng-1985
OxThe-1983
PengAm-1971
PrEncyPP-1974
RCom-1973

Expressionism

Williams, Charles 1886-1945 (English)
BenReEncy-1987
CamGLE-1988
CasWL-1973
EncWL-1981
GdMWL-1985
LongCTCL-1975
OxEng-1985
PengEng-1971

The Inklings

Williams, Emmett 1925- (American)
PrEncyPP-1974

Concrete Poetry

Williams, Heathcote 1941-
(English)
OxEng-1985

Underground Poetry

Williams, Jonathan 1929-
(American)
EncWL-1981
PengAm-1971

Black Mountain Poets

Williams, William Carlos 1883-1963
(American)
BenReEncy-1987
CamGLE-1988
CasWL-1973
CEnMWL-1963
EncWL-1981
GdMWL-1985
LongCTCL-1975
OxAm-1983
OxEng-1985
PengAm-1971
PrEncyPP-1974

Imagism
Objectivism
Poetry

Wilson, Colin 1931-   (English)
BenReEncy-1987
CamGLE-1988
CasWL-1973
LongCTCL-1975
OxEng-1985

Angry Young Men

Wilson, Edmund 1895-1972
(American)
BenReEncy-1987
CamGLE-1988
CasWL-1973

EncWL-1981
GdMWL-1985
LongCTCL-1975
OxAm-1983
OxAmThe-1984
OxEng-1985
PengAm-1971

Provincetown Players

Wimsatt, W(illiam) K(urtz), Jr. 1907-
1975 (American)
CasWL-1973
EncWL-1981
PengAm-1971

New Criticism

Winters, (Arthur) Yvor 1900-1968
(American)
BenReEncy-1987
CamGLE-1988
EncWL-1981
GdMWL-1985
LongCTCL-1975
OxAm-1983
OxEng-1985
PengAm-1971
PrEncyPP-1974

New Criticism
Poetry

Wispeleare, Paul de 1928-
(Belgian)
ClDMEuL-1980
EncWL-1981

Komma Group

Wit, Henrik de n.d. (Dutch)
CaribWr-1979

Porch Group/De Stoep

Witkiewicz, Stanislaw 1851-1915 (Polish)
ClDMEuL-1980

Naturalism

Witkiewicz, Stanislaw Ignacy 1885-1939 (Polish)
CasWL-1973
ClDMEuL-1980
EncWL-1981
GdMWL-1985
OxThe-1983
PengEur-1969

Young Poland/Mloda Polska

Wittlin, Józef 1896-1976 (Polish)
ClDMEuL-1980
EncWL-1981
GdMWL-1985
PengEur-1969
PrEncyPP-1974

Skamander Group
Zdroj Group

Wivel, Ole 1921-   (Danish)
CasWL-1973
ClDMEuL-1980
EncWL-1981
PrEncyPP-1974

Heretica Poets

Woestijne, Karel van de 1878-1929 (Belgian)
CasWL-1973
ClDMEuL-1980
EncWL-1981
GdMWL-1985
PengEur-1969

Van nu en straks Group

Wohmann, Gabriele 1932- (German)
ClDMEuL-1980
EncWL-1981
OxGer-1986

Group 47/Gruppe 47
New Sensibility Movement

Wolf, Christa 1929-   (German)
CasWL-1973
ClDMEuL-1980
EncWL-1981
GdMWL-1985
OxGer-1986

Bitterfeld Movement/Bitterfeld Weg

Wolfe, Thomas 1900-1938 (American)
BenReEncy-1987
CamGLE-1988
CasWL-1973
CEnMWL-1963
EncWL-1981
GdMWL-1985
LongCTCL-1975
OxAm-1983
OxAmThe-1984
OxEng-1985

Carolina Playmakers

Wolff, Th. 1868-1916 (German)
OxGer-1986

Freie Bühne

Wolker, Jirí 1900-1924 (Czech)
CasWL-1973
ClDMEuL-1980
EncWL-1981
GdMWL-1985
PengEur-1969

PrEncyPP-1974

Nine Powers Group/Devêtsil
Proletarian Literature

Woolf, Leonard 1880-1969 (English)
CamGLE-1988
EncWL-1981
LongCTCL-1975
OxEng-1985
PengEng-1971

Bloomsbury Group

Woolf, Virginia 1882-1941 (English)
BenReEncy-1987
CamGLE-1988
CasWL-1973
CEnMWL-1963
EncWL-1981
GdMWL-1985
LongCTCL-1975
OxEng-1985
PengEng-1971
RCom-1973

Bloomsbury Group
Georgian Literature
Modernism

**Worringer, Wilhelm 1881-1965
(German)**
EncWL-1981
PrEncyPP-1974

Expressionism

**Wright, Austin McGiffert 1922-
(American)**

PrEncyPP-1974

Chicago Critics

**Wright, Richard 1908-1960
(American)**
BenReEncy-1987
CamGLE-1988
CasWL-1973
EncWL-1981
GdMWL-1985
LongCTCL-1975
OxAm-1983
OxEng-1985
PengAm-1971

Proletarian Literature

**Wylie, Elinor Hoyt 1885-1928
(American)**
BenReEncy-1987
CasWL-1973
EncWL-1981
LongCTCL-1975
OxAm-1983
OxEng-1985
PengAm-1971

Imagism

**Wyspianski, Stanislaw 1869-1907
(Polish)**
CasWL-1973
ClDMEuL-1980
EncWL-1981
GdMWL-1985
McGWD-1984
OxThe-1983
PengEur-1969
PrEncyPP-1974

Young Poland/Mloda Polska

X

Xisto, Pedro n.d. (Brazilian)
HarDMT-1988

Concrete Poetry

Xuân Diêu 1917-   (Vietnamese)
DOrLit-1974
EncWL-1981

Self-Reliant Group

Y

Yadav, Rajendra 1929- (Indian)
DOrLit-1974

New Short Story Movement/
Nayi Kahani

**Yamaguchi Seishi 1901-
(Japanese)**
DOrLit-1974

Hototogisu Poets

**Yanovsky, Yuriy 1902-1954
(Ukrainian)**
ClDMEuL-1980
EncWL-1981
GdMWL-1985

Free Academy of Proletarian
Literature/VAPLITE
Modernism

**Yasenov, Khristo 1889-1925
(Bulgarian)**
EncWL-1981

Symbolism

**Yashin, Alexandr (pseud. of
Alexandr Yakovlevich Popov)
1913-1968 (Russian)**
BenReEncy-1987
ClDMEuL-1980
EncWL-1981

Village Prose

Yashpal 1904- (Indian)
DOrLit-1974
EncWL-1981

Realism/Pragati-vada

**Yatskiv, Mykhaylo 1873-1961
(Ukrainian)**
ClDMEuL-1980

Young Muse Group/Moloda
Muza

**Yavorov, Peyò (pseud. of Peyo
Tolev Kracholov) 1878-1914
(Bulgarian)**
CasWL-1973
ClDMEuL-1980
EncWL-1981
GdMWL-1985
PengEur-1969

Misul Group

**Yeats, William Butler 1865-1939
(Irish)**
BenReEncy-1987
CamGLE-1988
CasWL-1973
CEnMWL-1963
EncWL-1981
GdMWL-1985
LongCTCL-1975
McGWD-1984
OxAmThe-1984
OxEng-1985

OxThe-1983
PengEng-1971
PrEncyPP-1974
RCom-1973

Abbey Theater
Edwardian Literature
Georgian Literature
Irish Literary Theater
Irish Renaissance
Modernism
Symbolism

Yefremon, Oleg Nikolayevich 1927-
(Russian)
OxThe-1983

Moscow Art Theater

Yeh Shêng-T'ao 1894-   (Chinese)
CasWL-1973
DOrLit-1974

Literary Research Association

Yehoshua, Avraham B. 1936-
(Israeli)
CasWL-1973
ClDMEuL-1980
EncWL-1981
GdMWL-1985

Metarealism

Yi Sang (pseud. of Kim Hae-
gyong) 1910-1937 (Korean)
DOrLit-1974
EncWL-1981

Naturalism

Yohansen, Mayk 1895-1937
(Ukrainian)
ClDMEuL-1980
EncWL-1981

Free Academy of Proletarian
Literature/VAPLITE

Yokomitsu Riichi 1898-1947
(Japanese)
BenReEncy-1987
CasWL-1973
DOrLit-1974
EncWL-1981
GdMWL-1985
PengCOAL-1969

New Sensationalist School

Yom Sang-sop 1897-1963 (Korean)
DOrLit-1974
EncWL-1981

Naturalism

Young, Andrew 1885-1971
(Scottish)
CamGLE-1988
CEnMWL-1963
GdMWL-1985
LongCTCL-1975
OxEng-1985
PengEng-1971

Georgian Literature

Young, Douglas Cuthbert 1913-1973
(Scottish)
CasWL-1973
EncWL-1981
PengEng-1971

Scottish Renaissance

Yovkov, Yordan 1880-1937
(Bulgarian)
CasWL-1973
ClDMEuL-1980
EncWL-1981
GdMWL-1985

PengEur-1969

Golden Horn Movement/
  Zlatorog

Yu Ch'i-jin 1905-   (Korean)
  EncWL-1981

Theatrical Arts Research Society/
  Kuk yesel yon'guhoe

Yü Kuang-chung 1928-   (Chinese)
  EncWL-1981

Blue Stars Society

**Yü Ta-Fu (pseud. of Yü Wên) 1896-
1945 (Chinese)**
  CasWL-1973

Creation Society

**Yungman, Moyshe 1922-1983
(Yiddish-speaking Israeli)**
  EncWL-1981

Young Israel

**Yunque, Álvaro (pseud. of Arístides
Gandolfi Herrero) 1889-(?)
(Argentine)**
  OxSpan-1978

Boedo Group

**Yurdakul, Mehmet Emin 1869-1944
(Turkish)**
  ClDMEuL-1980
  DOrLit-1974
  EncWL-1981

National Literature Movement/
  Millî Edebiyat

Z

Zabolotsky, Nikolay Alekseyevich 1903-1958 (Russian)
BenReEncy-1987
ClDMEuL-1980
EncWL-1981
GdMWL-1985
PengEur-1969

OBEIRIU

Zacchi, Ferdinand 1884-1966 (German)
OxGer-1986

Heimatkunst

Zagajewski, Adam 1945- (Polish)
ClDMEuL-1980

Teraz Group

Zagórski, Jerzy 1907- (Polish)
ClDMEuL-1980
EncWL-1981
McGWD-1984

Cracow Avant-Garde
Zagary Group

Zaheer, Sajjad 1905-1973 (Pakistani)
EncWL-1981

Progressive Writers' Movement

Zahn, Ernst 1867-1952 (Swiss)
EncWL-1981
OxGer-1986

Heimatkunst

Zahul, Dmytro 1890-1938 (Ukrainian)
EncWL-1981

Symbolism

Zalygin, Sergey Pavlovich 1913- (Russian)
ClDMEuL-1980
EncWL-1981

Village Prose

Zamacois, Eduardo 1873-1971 (Cuban-born Spanish)
CaribWr-1979
ClDMEuL-1980
GdMWL-1985
OxSpan-1978

Naturalism

Zamyatin, Evgeny Ivanovich 1884-1937 (Russian)
BenReEncy-1987
CasWL-1973
CEnMWL-1963
ClDMEuL-1980
EncWL-1981
GdMWL-1985

McGWD-1984
OxEng-1985
PengEur-1969

Russian Formalism
Serapion Brotherhood
Zavety (Behests) School

Zanzotto, Andrea 1921-   (Italian)
ClDMEuL-1980
EncWL-1981
GdMWL-1985

Hermeticism/Poesia Ermetica

**Zapolska, Gabriela 1860-1921
(Polish)**
CasWL-1973
ClDMEuL-1980
EncWL-1981
GdMWL-1985
PengEur-1969

Naturalism

**Zaretski, Michás 1901-1941
(Byelorussian)**
EncWL-1981

Uzvyssa Group

**Zarian, Gosdan 1885-1969
(Armenian)**
EncWL-1981

Mehian Group

Zarins, Guntis 1926-1965 (Latvian)
EncWL-1981
GdMWL-1985

Modernism

Záry, Stefan 1918-   (Czech)
ClDMEuL-1980

Nadrealisti Movement

**Zavala Muñiz, Justino 1897-
(Uruguayan)**
EncWL-1981
McGWD-1984
OxSpan-1978

Gaucho Literature
Generation of 1900

Zavattini, Cesare 1902-   (Italian)
CasWL-1973
EncWL-1981

Neorealism

**Zawodzinsik, Karol Wiktor 1880-
1949 (Polish)**
ClDMEuL-1980

Skamander Group

Zayas, Antonio n.d. (Spanish)
ClDMEuL-1980

Modernism

**Zaytsev, Boris Konstantinovich
1881-1972 (Russian)**
CasWL-1973
ClDMEuL-1980
EncWL-1981

Znanie Group

Zeberins, Modris 1923-   (Latvian)
EncWL-1981

Modernism

417

Zech, Paul 1881-1946 (German)
  ClDMEuL-1980
  OxGer-1986
  PengEur-1969

Expressionism

**Zegadlowicz, Emil 1888-1941
(Polish)**
  CasWL-1973
  ClDMEuL-1980

  Czartak Group
  Zdroj Group

**Zelinski, Korneliy L. 1896-
(Russian)**
  CasWL-1973
  PrEncyPP-1974

Constructivism

**Zelinski, Tadeusz 1874-1941
(Polish)**
  CasWL-1973
  ClDMEuL-1980

Young Poland/Mloda Polska

Zena, Remigio 1850-1917 (Italian)
  ClDMEuL-1980

Verismo

**Zeno Gandia, Manuel 1855-1930
(Puerto Rican)**
  CaribWr-1979
  OxSpan-1978

Naturalism

Zeromski, Stefan 1864-1925 (Polish)
  ClDMEuL-1980
  EncWL-1981
  GdMWL-1985

  PengEur-1969

Young Poland/Mloda Polska

**Zerov, Mykola 1890-1941
(Ukrainian)**
  ClDMEuL-1980
  EncWL-1981
  GdMWL-1985

Neoclassic Group

**Zhdanov, Andrei A. 1896-1948
(Russian)**
  EncWL-1981
  OxEng-1985

Socialist Realism

**Zhirmunsky, Viktor 1891-1971
(Russian)**
  CasWL-1973
  EncWL-1981

Russian Formalism

**Zodji (pseud. of U Thein Han)
1907-   (Burmese)**
  DOrLit-1974
  EncWL-1981

Testing of the Age/Khitsam

Zola, Émile 1840-1902 (French)
  BenReEncy-1987
  CamGLE-1988
  CasWL-1973
  ClDMEuL-1980
  EncWL-1981
  GdMWL-1985
  McGWD-1984
  OxAmThe-1984
  OxEng-1985
  OxFr-1959
  OxThe-1983

PengEur-1969
PrEncyPP-1974
RCom-1973

Freie Bühne
Naturalism
Realism

**Zoshchenko, Mikhail Mikhailovich
1895-1958 (Russian)**
BenReEncy-1987
CasWL-1973
CEnMWL-1963
ClDMEuL-1980
EncWL-1981
GdMWL-1985
PengEur-1969

Serapion Brotherhood

**Zuckmayer, Carl 1896-1977
(German)**
BenReEncy-1987
CasWL-1973
ClDMEuL-1980
EncWL-1981
GdMWL-1985
McGWD-1984
OxGer-1986
OxThe-1983
PengEur-1969

Deutsches Theater
Expressionism
New Objectivity/Neue
Sachlichkeit

**Zukofsky, Louis 1904-1978
(American)**
BenReEncy-1987
CamGLE-1988
EncWL-1981
GdMWL-1985
OxAm-1983
PengAm-1971

PrEncyPP-1974

Objectivism

**Zupancic, Oton 1878-1949 (Slovene-
speaking Yugoslavian)**
CasWL-1973
ClDMEuL-1980
EncWL-1981
GdMWL-1985
McGWD-1984

Moderna

Zvonak, A. n.d. (Byelorussian)
PrEncyPP-1974

Socialist Realism

Zweig, Arnold 1887-1968 (German)
BenReEncy-1987
CasWL-1973
ClDMEuL-1980
EncWL-1981
GdMWL-1985
LongCTCL-1975
OxGer-1986
PengEur-1969

New Objectivity/Neue
Sachlichkeit

Zweig, Stefan 1881-1942 (Austrian)
BenReEncy-1987
CasWL-1973
CEnMWL-1963
ClDMEuL-1980
EncWL-1981
GdMWL-1985
LongCTCL-1975
OxGer-1986
OxThe-1983
PengEur-1969

Young Vienna Group/Jungwien